VOICES OF SUMMER

VOICES OF SUMMER
RANKING BASEBALL'S 101 ALL-TIME BEST ANNOUNCERS

CURT SMITH

CARROLL & GRAF PUBLISHERS
NEW YORK

VOICES OF SUMMER
RANKING BASEBALL'S 101 ALL-TIME BEST ANNOUNCERS

Carroll & Graf Publishers
An Imprint of Avalon Publishing Group Inc.
245 West 17th Street
11th Floor
New York, NY 10011

AVALON
publishing group incorporated

First Carroll & Graf edition 2005

Library of Congress Cataloging-in-Publication Data is available.

ISBN: 0-7867-1446-8

9 8 7 6 5 4 3 2 1

Interior design by Maria Elias

Printed in the United States of America
Distributed by Publishers Group West

TO SARAH

CONTENTS

"The boys of summer come and go. The voices of summer stay with you for a lifetime."
—*Jayson Stark*

"You're the only link between the public and the game. You want to talk about a fat lady in a yellow hat sitting in the stands, or about the players, the sky, the weather, you're a wild bird. You're free."
—*Curt Gowdy*

1

"Are you sitting comfortably?" British broadcaster Julia Long often asked her audience. "Then I'll begin." Radio baseball began August 5, 1921, over America's first station, KDKA, from Forbes Field in Pittsburgh. From distant sites—Fenway Park, Yankee Stadium, the Polo Grounds—the medium ferried a cargo of big-league prose.

In 1925, only ten percent of Americans owned a radio. Sixty-three percent did by 1933. On August 26, 1939, Ebbets Field housed the first televised game. "Millions come to the park each year," said Ernie Harwell. "Others can't or don't." Voices became their eyes and ears.

We hear them everywhere: the porch, the car, even the Internet. "All sports do play-by-play," mused Red Barber. "Only baseball's shows your soul." Bob Costas suggests baseball even on the Olympics. "It's what I'd done, who I was."

Some announcers etch a team: the Pirates' Bob Prince, or the Cardinals' Jack Buck. Others recall yearning for a sense of time standing still: Barber, Mel Allen. Some spin almost existential pleasure: Harry Caray's "Holy cow!"

All show eloquence in varied tone and form. Dizzy Dean said, "Pod-nuh, you ain't just a-woofin' "—"pod-nuh" being anyone who loved the game.

In the early 1950s, New Yorkers debated Willie, Mickey, and the Duke—also, the Yankees' Allen, Dodgers' Barber, and Giants' Russ Hodges. Later the Bay Area compared Lon Simmons and Monte Moore. Sixties TV matched CBS's Dean and NBC's Bob Wolff. Critics liked Wolff. Viewers liked Ol' Diz's mix of Ma Kettle, Billy Sunday, and Tennessee Ernie Ford.

Buy a drink, start a fight. Who was better: Yanks' Phil Rizzuto, or Mets' Lindsey Nelson? Presently, same town/choice: John Sterling, or Gary Cohen? Who is more of a hoot to hear, ESPN's Jon Miller or Fox's Joe Buck? "Before we talk," said Plato, "let us define our terms."

A schoolboy compares players, parks, and managers. *Voices of Summer* ranks baseball's best-ever 101 mikemen from the more than a thousand calling it. Judging can be dicey, like throwing darts in the fog. Criteria help. The ten areas below are scored on a 1–10 point scale. Perfect score: 10 times 10, or 100 points.

Each Voice's total decides his rank from 1 (Vin Scully) to 101 (Harold Arlin). Each's essay airs high- and lowlights, turning points, and play-by-play—ultimately, a life and work. For the complete ranking, see page 392. This book does not claim infallibility. It does try to be fair.

"On the field often not a heck of a lot is happening," said Chuck Thompson. Announcers try more or less to compensate. In the end, many seem as family as your Uncle Fred. The criteria:

LONGEVITY: Harwell played the bigs for 55 years; Gordon McLendon, three. *CONTINUITY*: Scully *is* the post-1949 Dodgers. The Astros are Milo Hamilton's eighth team. *NETWORK*: Al Helfer did Mutual Radio's 1950s regular/post-season. Byrum Saam never called a Series in 38 years. *KUDOS*: Which Voices won a Peabody Award; nearly retired *The Sporting News* "Announcer of the Year"; and almost *became* National Sportscaster of the Year? (For those of you keeping score, Red, Joe Garagiola, and Curt Gowdy; Allen and Caray; Costas, respectively.)

LANGUAGE: Ralph Kiner said, "The Mets got their leadoff hitter on only once this inning." Bob Murphy bred "The happy recap"; Hamilton, "Holy Toledo!"; Marty Brennaman, "This one belongs to the Reds!" *POPULARITY*: In Pittsburgh, Prince was Mr. Baseball. The Northwest deems Dave Niehaus more exciting than the game. *PERSONA*: Joe Angel speaks in English and Spanish. Earl Gillespie became the "Fish Net Man." Nelson's 350 jackets made him broadcasting's Beau Brummel. One hangs in Cooperstown.

VOICE: Van Patrick's pipes could fill the Mormon Tabernacle. Miller mimes Scully in English, Spanish, and Japanese. *KNOWLEDGE*: Jack Buck said, "Baseball fans know their sport better than fans in other sports." Which announcers blur baseball and boccie ball? *MISCELLANY*: Garagiola wrote a best-selling book. Bud Blattner was world table tennis champion at 16. Thompson grew up in a boarding house that rented to Connie Mack.

Below, an example. Seeing the Red Sox win the 2004 World Series, this Voice would have picked the Cubs in '05.

VINCE LLOYD

LONGEVITY:	10	34 years.
CONTINUITY:	10	Chicago N.L. 1950 and 1954–86; Chicago A.L. 1957–64.
NETWORK:	1	Berthed pre-SuperStation WGN.
KUDOS:	5	First Voice to interview U.S. president at baseball game.
LANGUAGE:	8	Earthy.
POPULARITY:	10	Appreciated more by fans than front office.
PERSONA:	10	Holy Mackerel! Cubs' silver lining in tarnished years.
VOICE:	10	Roughhewn.
KNOWLEDGE:	9	No showboat.
MISCELLANY:	8	A.k.a. "The Voice For All Seasons." Long-time Voice of Big Ten football. Born Vince Lloyd Skaff.
TOTAL:	81	**(49th place among 101 announcers).** *Scores based on 1–10 point scale.*

Which team has the most announcers? (The Yankees, with 21. Other leaders: Giants 16, White Sox 15, Braves, Cubs, and Red Sox 13, Dodgers 11, and A's and Cardinals 10.) Which has none? (None.) Does ex-Cubs Voice Ronald Reagan crack the list? (He got detoured.) What of those who nearly made it? (They are saluted: John MacLean, Nat Allbright, Jack Quinlan, Charley Steiner.)

Some Voices have an identical point total: Longevity, continuity, network coverage, and kudos break the tie. Since they change, ratings even five years from now may, too. Let today's reader screech, curse, or stomp over any pick. From a rhubarb, baseball never wanders far away.

"Here lies the summit," Edmund Burke once described a colleague. "He may live long. He may do much. But he can never exceed what he does this day." Game Six, 1952 World Series: Allen and Barber, on NBC TV, climb a summit of syntax and vocabulary, an elegance of phrase and mood.

Mel terms John Mize "a sentimental hero, in any case." Rizzuto and Pee Wee Reese show "shortstopping by two great exponents of the art." "We acquainted you yesterday," Allen reminds a listener. Cameramen, atop the roof, silhouette "the uneven fringe of shadow." Mel glowingly introduces Red, who dubs him "the pot calling the kettle black."

Big Jawn (Mize) becomes "the storybook fella." A "trickle ball [reaches] the right side." The Yanks are "down a game and down a run." The see-saw day is "enough to give you the high spirits." It evoked your first visit to the park—fielder crouched, batter cocked, and pitcher draped against the stands—above all, surety that there was no place on earth that you would rather be.

As Scully says, "Pull up a chair." Recall play-by-play wafting from a friend, or passerby. Hail the enduring word. "The sky overhead is a very beautiful robin-egg blue," Barber said in 1936, "with very few angels in the form of clouds in it." Remember: "Football and basketball carry the announcer," notes Hank Greenwald. "The announcer carries baseball."

Only God has a monopoly on truth. Likening Voices, we make do with fact, instinct, and an almost Tinker Bell kind of faith.

2

Harold Arlin

Bob Elson

Graham McNamee

Arch McDonald

Tom Manning

HAROLD ARLIN

Lindsey Nelson termed televised baseball picture plus caption. "Ah, radio," he said, "there's a different beast." The announcer becomes actor, writer, producer, even cameraman. Shakespeare said, "The past is prologue." Retrieve a time before what comic Fred Allen dubbed TV's "collection of passport photos."

1904: Theodore Roosevelt graces a station of radio pioneer Guglielmo Marconi. 1909: Explorer Robert Peary messages, "I have found the Pole." 1912: The S.S. *Olympic* telegraphs a wireless operator: "S.S. *Titanic* ran into iceberg. Sinking fast." For three days and nights David Sarnoff reports "updates to reporters and friends." In 1926, he founds the National Broadcasting Company.

In 1920, the first licensed station, Westinghouse Company–owned KDKA, debuted in Pittsburgh. Its star: a LaHarp, Illinoisan who at five moved to Carthage, Missouri, graduated from the University of Kansas, and, joining Westinghouse, spied a station on the factory roof. "What's that?" Harold Arlin said. "I go up, audition for an announcing job, and get it."

KDKA began broadcasting on Election Night. Arlin soon did college football, Davis Cup tennis, and baseball scores. A Quebec housewife wrote: "Tell your announcer that I have four boys who listen to him every night. His pronunciation is so perfect that even though they speak French, they can still understand him."

Baseball seemed as obvious. In August 1921, Harold bought a Forbes Field seat, put a scorecard on a wooden plank, and used a telephone as microphone. The Pirates were first to use a tarpaulin (1906); put padding on the outfield wall (1933); host an evening All-Star Game (1944); wear knit uniforms (1970); berth a night Series game (1971); and have a 7-for-7 player (Rennie Stennett, 1975).

The most vital first: KDKA, and Arlin, siring baseball on the air.

What did he sound like that summer afternoon? Few live to say. Western Pennsylvania had a few hundred radio sets. Did anyone hear, or care? "Sometimes the transmitter wouldn't work. Often the crowd noise drowned us out. We didn't know whether we'd talk into a vacuum." Known: game score (Pirates 8, Phillies 5) and time (one hour, 57 minutes). Unknown: the sequel. "No one had an inking if we'd do baseball again."

Arlin did, through 1924. "Not enough time," he mused, repairing to the studio to interview, among others, Will Rogers, Lillian Gish, and David Lloyd George. One day Babe Ruth appeared. "I even wrote his speech. I introduce him and this garrulous guy—he can't say a word."

"Babe Ruth froze?" a reporter said.

"Mute. I grab the speech and now *I'm* Ruth. I read it and Babe tries to compose himself, smoking and leaning against the wall. We pulled it off. I sign off and Babe Ruth hasn't made a sound." Hundreds of letters praised his gloss and voice. The problem was time.

"By day, I was a foreman," said Arlin. "At night, I'd do KDKA." In 1925, he took a Westinghouse personnel job in Mansfield, Ohio. Stunned, a writer said: "Thousands of radio fans will regret loss of dear friend." About one million Americans now owned a receiver. "Don't much like TV," Harold said later. "It leaves nothing to the imagination." *His* medium, on the other hand, left all.

Arlin became Mansfield school board president, watched grandson Steve pitch in the 1970s big leagues, and died March 15, 1986, at 90, in Bakersfield, California. "Hard to imagine how far the wireless has come." Harder: baseball bereft of radio.

HAROLD ARLIN

LONGEVITY:	1	Four years.
CONTINUITY:	8	Pittsburgh N.L. 1921–24.
NETWORK:	10	KDKA rivaled today's ABC, CBS, and NBC. World Series 1921 bulletins (Westinghouse).
KUDOS:	5	Hall of Fame hails "the man who started play-by-play."
LANGUAGE:	4	"No one told me I had to talk between pitches."
POPULARITY:	10	A.k.a. "The Voice of America."
PERSONA:	10	Pleasance and pioneer.
VOICE:	4	Loud. Breaking the modulation meter, once knocked KDKA off-air. "After that we put on-air lights at each transmitter and the studio."
KNOWLEDGE:	5	Few then to compare him with.
MISCELLANY:	3	On his "Day," Bucs let Arlin broadcast in 1966.
TOTAL:	60	(101st place). *Scores based on 1–10 point scale.*

GRAHAM MCNAMEE

Early-twenties America worshiped the celebrity of the self-made man. F. Scott Fitzgerald wrote *This Side of Paradise.* Macy's Department Store hyped posh top coats from $28.25 to $57.50. The *New York Herald Tribune* told New York's baseball cognoscenti, "May we suggest the following items to contribute to your enjoyment of the National Game: Italian briar pipes; Three Castle cigarettes, packed in airtight tins of fifty each; or

Tampa blunts." Like radio, America-in-bloom was a view crossing age or class.

In 1921, Westinghouse, feeding WJZ Newark and WBZ Springfield, Massachusetts, aired its first World Series. Columnist Grantland Rice announced from field level. Arlin and Tommy Cowan gave half-inning bulletins. "Cowan sat atop . . . a building in a tiny shack," observed the *Newark Call*. "At the other end of a telephone was a man in the Polo Grounds, telling Cowan what happened [Giants' victory, 5 games to 3]."

On October 4, 1922, radio "for the first time carried the opening game . . . to great crowds [5 million] throughout the eastern part of the country," said *The New York Times*. Rice and W. O. "Bill" McGeehan did balls and strikes. "In place of the scorecards and megaphones of the past, amplifiers connected to radio instruments . . . made listeners feel as if they were in the grandstand." Huzzahs for Ruth "could be heard throughout the land."

Five miles from the Polo Grounds, a piano player pictured himself replacing Rice. Ultimately, more people heard his voice than any other broadcaster's of the first half-century.

Graham McNamee was born July 10, 1888, grew up in the Pacific Northwest, clerked for the Rock Island Railroad, and at 22 moved to New York with his mother. The divorcee insisted that her son take voice lessons. In 1921, he began as a professional, said *The New York Sun,* "with a justness, care, and style."

In May 1923, Graham entered the A.T.&T. Building on lunch break from jury duty, won a WEAF audition, and soon called the Johnny Wilson–Harry Greb middleweight fight. That October, the tenor became Series color man. ["Stations from Washington to Massachusetts]," said the *Times,* "will radiate the contests simultaneously with WEAF . . . connected with special land wires to microphones." At first McNamee said little. In Game Four, his born-for-wireless voice bumped McGeehan's play-by-play.

The Series ended Monday. By Saturday, WEAF got 1,700 letters: "With so few radios," said Jack Brickhouse, "it's like a million now." The natural called foreign visits, coronations, and at least ten sports, including boxing, football, and marbles. 1923: Calvin Coolidge addresses Congress. 1924: Democrats nominate John W. Davis on the 103rd ballot. 1927: Lindbergh returns from Paris. Graham did each. "How do you do, ladies and gentlemen of the radio audience?" he began, closing "This is Graham McNamee speaking. Good night, all"—radio's first leading name.

"During the year, few clubs used radio," Jack Buck recalled. "The emphasis was on the network Series, where McNamee stood alone." In 1925, more than

50,000 wrote after rain pelted Forbes Field, Graham's coat covered the mike, and Heywood Broun said, "He made me feel the temperature and the tension." Next year the first network started: NBC's "Red" (music/comedy) and "Blue" (public affairs). McNamee did the next nine Series—often more bodacious than the game.

"You must make each of your listeners," he said, "though miles away from the spot, feel that he or she too is there with you in the press stand, watching the pop bottle thrown in the air; Gloria Swanson arriving in her new ermine coat; McGraw in his dugout, apparently motionless, but giving signals all the time." In 1927, Graham was there for the Yankees' sweep of Pittsburgh; 1929, Hack Wilson's .471 average; 1933, Mel Ott's homer off Fred Schulte's glove.

"The Series *was* sport," Buck recalled, "and McNamee was the Series." The headliner knew it. So did writers of the day.

"I will freely admit," Graham said, "to being an entertainer first and broadcaster second." On January 1, 1927, he broadcast NBC's first Rose Bowl, etching Pasadena's greenery. That fall, Ring Lardner typed: "I don't know which game to write about, the one I saw or heard Graham McNamee announce." Once a reporter pierced the air: "McNamee, will you pipe down?" Bile flowed from envy—and inchoate fear. "Radio threatened papers," said Buck. "Why read if you could hear?"

In 1934, Graham motored to Detroit. "In just about 15 minutes, the World Series will be opened by the umpire who will howl 'play ball.' " "Wild-eyed rabid fans" jammed the stands. "All hint of rain has been dispelled." Next year, Commissioner Kenesaw Mountain Landis rained on his parade. "He chose Series Voices," said Red Barber, "and thought Graham inflated." Baseball's Pinza missed his first Classic since 1922. He never called another big-league a.k.a. bigs game.

For a decade, Graham's name, apart from voice, etched *gravitas*. "If an event was big," said Mel Allen, "McNamee was there." In April 1942, he graced "Elsa Maxwell's Story Line": "This is Graham McNamee, saying, 'Good night, all, and good-bye.' " Next day he entered the hospital, dying May 9, at 53, of a streptococcus infection.

Broun observed: "McNamee justified the whole activity of radio broadcasting. A thing may be a marvelous invention and still dull as dish water." Only personality could make water ripple. "He has been able to take a new medium of expression and through it transit himself—to give it vividly a sense of movement and of feeling. Of such is the kingdom of art."

Long live the king.

GRAHAM MCNAMEE

LONGEVITY:	5	13 years.
CONTINUITY:	9	Westinghouse 1923–25 and NBC 1926–35.
NETWORK:	10	World Series 1923–25 (Westinghouse) and 1926–34 (NBC). All-Star Game 1933–35 (NBC).
KUDOS:	9	National Sportscasters and Sportswriters Association (NSSA) Hall of Fame 1964. American Sportscasters Association (ASA) Graham McNamee Award and Hall of Fame 1984.
LANGUAGE:	10	Estimated he used more than ten times the number of words of an unabridged dictionary—e.g., trademark "Whee!"
POPULARITY:	10	Thirties variety shows including Ed Wynn's, Rudy Vallee's, and "Behind the Mike on NBC."
PERSONA:	10	Mr. Radio.
VOICE:	10	Riveting.
KNOWLEDGE:	3	In 1926, introduced N.L. President John Heydler as John Tener, who resigned as league head in 1918.
MISCELLANY:	9	Twelve straight Series trail only Allen.
TOTAL:	85	**(33rd place).**

HAL TOTTEN

The first daily play-by-play man grew up at a time when baseball meant pen, not mike. "In the 1910s," he said, "the game was for writers. They blanketed the sport."

Special editions hailed "our national game." Newspaper windows blared a daily inning-by-inning score. Bylines read Rice, the courser of the press box; Damon Runyon, Salieri of the short story; and Lardner, *le pere grand* of Alibi Ike.

Born in Newark, Hal Totten moved to Ithaca, New York, then to Chicago at 11, and Northwestern University in 1919. "I knew I wanted to work in baseball." He did not know it would involve his tongue, not his hand.

In college, Hal was a Chicago *Journal* and *Daily News* stringer and football writer. "I got seven cents an [column] inch and $13 a week in summer." Strapped, he joined the *Journal* full-time, took night courses at Northwestern, and earned a 1924 degree.

Joining the *News,* Totten called the first game (that April 23) of the first station (WMAQ) to air an entire home schedule (Cubs 12, Cardinals 1). Originally Cubs owner Philip Wrigley wanted an ex-jock. "When Solly Hofman bombed, I volunteered lickety-split," said Hal. "It was a great way to see games free." In 1926, he added the White Sox. Exclusivity, schmivity: outlets eyed listeners, not rights.

"Forget sponsors. Nobody paid for the privilege of carrying games." By 1929, five stations aired the Sox and Cubs. Johnny O'Hara bucked WJKS; Quin Ryan and Bob Elson, WGN; Pat Flanagan and Truman Bradley, WBBM. "Wrigley made Chicago radio baseball's Mecca. 'The more outlets, the better. That way we'll own the city.' "Actually, Wrigley already did.

He lowered the field, built a scoreboard, and double-decked the grandstand —ergo, Friendly Confines. Even friendlier were four flags from 1929 to 1938. Antipodal were the Pale Hose: said Totten, "a synonym for their fans. They didn't expect notice, and didn't get it." In 1934, Hal took them (Cubs, too) to NBC's "Blue Network" WCFL.

"It was a stronger station. I could do things like road trips" and hiring a No. 2. "Before, I'd done it by myself—no relief or sponsor." Also soloing: Boston's Fred Hoey, Cleveland's Tom Manning, Cincinnati's Barber, and St. Louis's France Laux.

Network coverage was different. For a time, it became Totten's winnowing force for good.

Baseball can mean odd plays, blown calls, and beguiling memory. Hal aired *Daily News* 1926–27 World Series coverage—also, with Ted Husing, the 1928–29 infant Columbia Broadcasting System's. Later he joined NBC. A listener heard "foot on the slab," "funny little hop," and "pretty husky fellow": not "flashy like McNamee," said Elson, "just baseball like it was." In 1926, it was Grover Cleveland Alexander fanning Tony Lazzeri; 1928, Lou Gehrig hitting .625; 1929, the A's scoring 10 runs in an inning. Totten called 12 Series, tying McNamee and Elson.

In 1933, another Classic began at Comiskey Park. Before the All-Star Game, Hal interviewed its apotheosis. "We're ducking pre-game fouls, and Babe's getting the raspberry from Sox fans, who hated his Yanks." Ruth homered, made a diving catch, and led a 4–2 A.L. victory. Less lucky: the greatest Voice who then existed in the Republic.

"I knew Chicago, yet NBC put Graham on play-by-play and me commentary," said Hal. Soon it told him to take over. "McNamee announced the change and graciously said it should have been this way from the start." Totten shook his head: stringing for college seemed a lifetime away.

"Graham, Ruth, Dizzy Dean," he mused. "I'm calling 'em, knowing each. If those weren't big names, whose were?" Gradually, his daybook included basketball, boxing, golf, hockey, polo, table tennis, and wrestling; air, auto, and horse racing; and NFL Bears and college football. Missing: baseball. Cause: Mutual Radio's Series and All-Star exclusivity starting in 1939 ("it wanted new voices"); the Federal Communications Commission, making NBC sell a network ("Blue" became ABC); and WCFL, kicking the Cubs and Hose to WIND and WJJD, respectively.

"Radio's funny. You love a sport, and then it's gone." The ex-copy boy rejoined the *News*, did Mutual's 1945–50 "Game of the Day," then bought a Keokuk, Iowa, station. In 1951, adding a Three-I League team, he attended a supposedly one-day meeting. "Turns out it was two, so I went out to buy a new shirt." Returning, Hal did a double-take: League owners had made him head. In 1962, he dissolved the 77-year-old Southern Association.

"Television killed the minors, the majors carrying games and the

---

HAL TOTTEN

LONGEVITY:	9	27 years.
CONTINUITY:	9	Chicago N.L. 1924–44; Chicago A.L. 1926–44; Mutual "Game of the Day" 1945–50.
NETWORK:	10	World Series 1926–27 (*Chicago Daily News*), 1928–29 (CBS), 1931–33 and 1935 (NBC), and 1936–39 (Universal Newsreel). All-Star Game 1933 and 1936 (NBC). "Game" 1945–50 (Mutual).
KUDOS:	4	Southern Association's last head.
LANGUAGE:	6	Sign-off, "G'bye now."
POPULARITY:	7	Regular fellow.
PERSONA:	9	"Voice of Baseball in Chicago."
VOICE:	6	High, gentle.
KNOWLEDGE:	10	Real goods.
MISCELLANY:	7	In 1927, did second Dempsey–Tunney fight at Soldier Field. "My son John was born in the morning, I aired a doubleheader in the afternoon, and covered the fight that night."
TOTAL:	77	(68th place).

medium in general." Totten entered advertising, retired to Florida, and found baseball still a writer's game. "Cover to cover, I still can't get enough." Hal read until his death.

PAT FLANAGAN

Bing Crosby played Father Flanagan in the Oscar-winning 1945 film *Boys Town*. From 1929 to 1943, another Flanagan (Charles Carroll) made of baseball a religion. "It's one of those unique gifts," he said of his nickname, "Pat." Others included gray hair, brown eyes, and a made-for-TV face, none of which swayed radio. A breezy voice, can-do knack, and blueprint of a mind did.

Flanagan arrived in Chicago in late 1928. The Cubs and Sox aired their entire home schedule. Away games were ignored, which got Pat to puzzling. "Stations didn't do the road because line charges were expensive." But how could you cover baseball without *being* at the park?

Answer: wireless telegraphy, like Western Union's Simplex machine, "[giving] play-by-play," wrote *The Sporting News,* "within three seconds of the time it occurs." An operator sent Morse Code to the station. B1L meant ball one, low; S2C, strike two, called. Eureka! A Voice could catch play he never saw.

One day, Pat used Simplex for a game from Cincinnati. "If you want these out-of-town games regularly, write and tell us," he said, signing off. Next day 9,000 listeners did. "Harold Arlin invented baseball on radio," said Brickhouse. "Pat invented re-creations," buoying baseball for the next thirty years.

Virginia is the Mother of Presidents. Iowa fathered or schooled nine of the *Voices of Summer*. Twist and shake: Born in Clinton in 1893, Flanagan graduated from Grinnell College, fought in World War I, practiced chiropractic at Palmer School in Davenport, and sang songs, led exercise, and taught philosophy on its station.

"Some first year!" Pat later said. The 1929 Cubs won the pennant. CBS's Flanagan dueled McNamee on the Series. In the opener, A's manager Connie Mack started Howard Ehmke, 35, "who hadn't pitched much. Connie loved surprise." The retread K'd a Series-record 13. Then, up 2 games to 1, Chicago led Game Four, 8–0. "In the seventh, the A's suddenly score ten runs." During that inning, Mule Haas flied to center. Hack Wilson thought it a can of corn.

"He's over, getting under it," Pat began. "Wait, it looks like Hack's lost it [in the sun]! He has . . . the ball falls! [Joe] Boley scores, and Max Bishop!

And here comes Haas. An inside-the-park homer!" The inning whipsawed the Classic: Philly, 10–8.

In 1930, Hack knocked in a still-record 191 runs. Two years later, Charlie Grimm became the first skipper hired after mid-season to win a pennant. Even odder: Chicago, *expecting* an every-third-year N.L. flag—"an itch," chirped Flanagan, "like clockwork." The Cubs' clock stopped after 1929–32–35–38.

The 1921–35 White Sox flunked the first division. Pat tried not to notice, speaking 30,000 words in a typical nine-inning game. A listener patented a "word-meter": Flanagan averaged 240 words per minute; 200 meant "stalling speed." In 1933–34, he called his first midsummer and last Fall Classic, respectively. Next year the Wrigleys lost their fifth straight Series. "Maybe we should skip October," said Grimm.

By 1935, four Des Moines outlets called the Cubs. "Most did some games live from Chicago," said WHO's Ronald Reagan. "Thanks to Flanagan, I could do them from hundreds of miles away." Once the wire stopped. Reagan considered returning to the station. "Then I thought, no, if we put music on people'll turn to another station doing it in person." What to do? Make a big *to*-do.

"Fouls don't make the box score, so for seven minutes I had Billy Jurges set a record." Pitcher Dizzy Dean used the resin bag, mopped his brow, tied a shoe. Rain neared. A fight began. "None of this happened, but at home it seemed real." Finally the wire revived. "Jurges popped out on the first ball pitched."

In 1937, Reagan left for Hollywood. A year later, Pat salved his last three-year itch. On September 28, Chicago trailed Pittsburgh by a half-game. Inning nine began 5-all. "It's dusk, Wrigley had no lights. The ump said game's over if no one scores this inning." The Bucs and first two Cubs went meekly. Gabby Hartnett faced Mace Brown. "This is it," said Flanagan. "The Cubs have to score. A long drive to deep left-center! Lloyd Waner going back! Gone! Gone! Cubs win!" They clinched the pennant October 1.

The City of Big Shoulders then shouldered another blow. "We've played 'em twice [also 1932] now," Pat said of the Yankees' sweep. "Win a Series? I'd settle for a game."

In 1943, braving cancer, he would have settled for good health. Flanagan retired to the Cubs' longtime training site, Catalina Island, off Los Angeles. "I love it. I've been coming here for years."

He died in 1963, at 70, a decade after Pittsburgh became the last team to mint live road coverage. "Pat wouldn't like radio now," said Brickhouse at the time. "He'd miss re-creations." The world outliving baseball's Father Flanagan was not a world he knew.

PAT FLANAGAN

LONGEVITY:	5	15 years.
CONTINUITY:	10	Chicago A.L. and N.L. 1929–43.
NETWORK:	3	World Series 1929, 1932, and 1934 (CBS). All-Star Game 1933 (CBS).
KUDOS:	2	Won a Silver Star in World War I.
LANGUAGE:	7	Gabby.
POPULARITY:	9	Re-creations, said a writer, blared "supernatural insight."
PERSONA:	8	Kit Carson.
VOICE:	9	Urgent.
KNOWLEDGE:	9	Knew product.
MISCELLANY:	3	"I tried to make studio play-by-play real," Pat said. One fan called WBBM asking where he sat at the park.
TOTAL:	65	(98th place).

JOHNNY O'HARA

The Midwest, circa 1920s. The White Sox' steel and concrete home wraps double-decked to each dugout. A single tier reaches each pole. Brick studs Comiskey Park's exterior. The feel is blue-collar, working-class, Irish and Eastern European.

Eight miles away, gales off Lake Michigan lead pitchers to schizophrenia. "For the first time," said Bill Veeck, Jr., son of the then-Cubs head, "Wrigley's shell resembled today's." In St. Louis, Sportsman's Park straddles Grand Avenue and Dodier Street: to the lower Midwest, Lourdes.

Each spring, the Cardinals train in Florida. In 1927, the Cubs begin training on Catalina Island. "Ultimately," said Veeck, "Johnny O'Hara would call all four St. Louis [Browns, too] and Chicago teams—only guy to do so."

For now, Chicago's new Voice seemed grateful for another place to go.

Born in Brooklyn, O'Hara graduated from New York University, got a government wireless license, boarded frigates and passenger liners, and for

seven years toured the globe. At bed in Singapore, the extra-first grade operator dreamt of Shibe Park, Fenway Park, and Crosley Field.

In 1923, Johnny, then 19, became a WOK Chicago radio engineer.
Bored, the adventurer hopped a hull and took sail again. "I'd copy presses. It
killed me to read the scores." He returned home, built a portable station, and
entered vaudeville, telling yarns from the seven seas.

One night, the regular M.C. had a bender. O'Hara subbed, wowed
WDT's station manager, and was hired as announcer. In 1927, he joined
WCFL, the Voice of Labor in Chicago. "I wanted the working or idle listener
—anyone you could find!"

Daily he did the Cubs, White Sox, and a 5 P.M. hot stove show. "Al
Capone gets paid by the bullet," Johnny told an audience. "How come I can't
get paid by the word?"

O'Hara aired an All-Star Game, did three World Series, and in 1936, rode the
Chicago and Alton train to KWK St. Louis. "Chicago likes his style," wrote
The Sporting News. "St. Louis just had more money." Later he taught radio
code to Army Air Corps instructors. Many toured Guadalcanal, Remagen,
and Monte Cassino. Johnny envied them. Nothing could ease his lust.

In 1943, ex-pitcher Dizzy Dean joined the vagabond. Next year, the
Redbirds won a third straight flag. Improbably, the A.L. Browns took their
first. O'Hara was not considered for Mutual's all-St. Louis Series. Worse, Diz

JOHNNY O'HARA

LONGEVITY:	5	14 years.
CONTINUITY:	7	Chicago A.L. and N.L. 1927–33; St. Louis N.L. 1943–46; St. Louis A.L. 1944–49.
NETWORK:	4	All-Star Game 1933 (CBS). World Series 1936 (CBS), 1937 (Mutual), and 1938 (NBC).
KUDOS:	4	*The Sporting News* 1943 "Announcer of the Year."
LANGUAGE:	7	Untethered to any wharf.
POPULARITY:	9	"Knows baseball from A to Z," a 1943 KWK ad read. "St. Louis's most popular announcer."
PERSONA:	8	Pulled up baseball's jib.
VOICE:	5	Cheery.
KNOWLEDGE:	8	Studied game on three continents.
MISCELLANY:	4	In 1933, did first college football All-Star Game (CBS).
TOTAL:	61	(100th place).

became a then-220-pound gorilla. "Try confronting *that!*" historian Bob Broeg said. "Gradually Cardinals broadcasts became Diz and company."

In 1947, O'Hara exclusively joined the Browns. Having written a book, *Experiences of a Wireless Operator at Sea,* he put out to sea in 1949. "Retiring, Johnny became a radio operator on Merchant Marine vessels," said Broeg. The Happy Wanderer entered his final port June 3, 1963.

BOB ELSON

"You have to know when to hold 'em," sings Kenny Rogers, "know when to fold 'em." Bob Elson, a gin rummy whiz, had pigeons in every town. *Chicago Tribune* columnist Jerome Holtzman asked about lessons. "That is like asking Jascha Heifetz to teach you to play the fiddle," Bob snapped. "I give lessons, but they will cost." On 1929–71 baseball, he was confident of his cards.

Elson patented "*He's* out!*", shilled like an artisan, and hatched the on-field interview. In 1943, The Old Commander—U.S. Great Lakes Naval Training Center, 1942–45—was given leave for the Series. "Franklin Roosevelt asked that he announce," Jack Brickhouse said. "Only time that a president pulled rank to get a uniformed baseball guy home."

Raised in Peoria, Bob's protege deemed him "the most imitated, creative announcer who ever lived"—a god. In 1960, hearing him for the first time, I thought TOC ungodly dull. "You should have heard him when I did!" boomed Jack, a "pup out of Elson like [later] Earl Gillespie, Gene Elston, Bert Wilson, and Milo Hamilton."

I couldn't, through accident of birth. When I did, Elson wasn't Elson. He should have folded before the dealer closed.

In 1914, Bob, nine, sang in Chicago's famed Paulist Chorister Choir. "I was like O'Hara. They toured the world." He entered Loyola, transferred to Northwestern, and studied medicine. In 1928, visiting pool whiz Willie Hoppe, TOC stayed at St. Louis's Chase Hotel. Its top floor housed KWK. Touring the station, Bob found 40 men in line. "You're the last today [for an audition]," a woman misinterpreted. What the heck, Elson figured, his career taking a carom shot.

Bob read a script, became a finalist, and was picked by listeners. Next day WGN brass read about his coup. "'You're from Chicago?' they called me. 'What are you doing down there?' " Debuting, he quickly tired of organ music, hooked the Cubs and Hose, and became the bigs' pre-war network prism and progenitor. "I was close to Kenesaw Landis when he was making assignments. He'd bellow, 'Don't mention any movie stars attending the World Series even if they slide into second base.' "

Bob's first Series was 1930. 1932: Babe Ruth did/did not prophesy a homer. "He really did point." 1935: Mutual's first Classic used Elson, Barber, and Chicago's Quin Ryan. 1937: "Yankees 1, Giants 0 . . . And there's a long one! It's going toward the stands! . . . Joe DiMaggio has hit a home run over the roof!" 1939: Ending multiple coverage, the Gillette Company gave exclusivity to Red and TOC. "The parallel was McNamee in the twenties," said Hamilton. "Bob on an event meant it mattered."

Like Totten, O'Hara, and Flanagan, Elson did the first All-Star Game. In 1941, Ted Williams's ninth-inning belt won Detroit's, 7–5: "Ted told me later his mother did a backward somersault when she heard me call the homer." Two years later baseball released its first Series film. Bob narrated them through 1948. "There was an excitement to him," Brickhouse said. "His voice cut through the air."

Jack reddened. "If Bob had lived in New York, he'd have been the first inducted into the Hall of Fame [receiving its Ford C. Frick Award]." He was third, in 1979. Brickhouse asked for a recount, even then.

"You're like shit," Ralph Houk once told Howard Cosell. "You're everywhere." So was Elson. He read ads, hyped bands, and interviewed actors, singers, and politicos from the Chicago Theatre, Pump Room (Ambassador East Hotel), and "Twentieth Century Limited" (LaSalle Street Station). Bob's worst guest was DiMag: "the world's greatest introvert, who married the world's greatest extrovert, [another guest] Marilyn Monroe." In 1930, TOC quizzed Connie Mack. "First interview on the field. Judge Landis said it was okay to run a wire from the booth. At first players were antsy. Before long they got the swing." Everywhere.

"Either place was great," Elson described his day job. Comiskey swung to an old-timey feel. "Luke Appling catches cleats on a coffee pot in the ground from when it was a [truck garden and garbage] dump." Bob Michel was 1981–95 U.S. House Minority Leader. "I remember him from Wrigley Field. I'd be painting screens in my folks' Peoria yard. Great marriage of guy and team."

In 1946, he returned from World War II to find WIND's Bert Wilson blowing for the Cubs. Rowing to WJJD, The Commander tried to bail out the Sox. Don Wells grew up in Pontiac, Illinois, throwing a ball against a corn crib. "I heard Bob, now [1953] I join him. No one had such energy." One day he, Brickhouse, and 18 others paid a stripper $40 to crash Elson's 15-minute show. "I'm reading sports, and she takes everything off except her shoes."

By 1959, the Hose could finally take on the Yanks. New York had waved nine flags since 1949. The South Side was pennantless in forty years. Cy Younger Early Wynn went 22–10. Nellie Fox hit an MVP .306. Luis Aparicio presaged Garciaparra, Rodriguez, and Vizquel—the first great Latin short-stop. "We beat you, 2 to 1," Bob said. "No Murderers' Row"—instead, pitching, defense, and speed.

Chicago clinched September 22 over Cleveland. On the final out, Mayor Richard Daley ordered city air raid sirens to blast. "Prophetic," mused Elson, later. Their wail preceded his.

From 1947 to 1965, Gillette, the Commissioner, and NBC TV chose Series mikemen. "They'd pick one guy from each team," said Bill Veeck. "Both called half of each game." The Yanks' Mel Allen had done the Classic since 1946. "With the Sox in, it couldn't be him," said the Peacocks' Lindsey Nelson. "The problem was that Tom Gallery didn't think Elson was in Allen's league."

Improbably, TOC and NBC's 1952–63 sports head had grown up on the same block. "They'd rubbed each other wrong as kids," said Nelson. "I remember Tom shouting, 'That bastard will not do our Series!' " Lindsey set to thinking. " 'You know,' I said, 'Jack Brickhouse does Sox TV. You could always pick him.' "

The NBC audience topped 120 million. Shunted to WCFL, "I reached 10 people," Elson said, still bitter, in 1975. "Not doing it was the biggest hurt of my career." The Sox and he began a slow list leeward. Fewer peopled the ancient park, under a cloudless sky, with the moon over 35th and Shields.

"Try broadcasting," Bob mused, "with a lousy team and interest." The age made it worse. "I've made it a point never to criticize a player, never second-guess a manager." The Commander hated the mid-to-late sixties muck of "Do your own thing," "Don't trust anyone over 30," and self-congratulatory "Tell it like it is."

Milo Hamilton grew up in Iowa. "Bob didn't feel you tuned in to hear him. The game was the thing." Now Elson's 1961–65 colleague saw the public ebbing. "People began calling him a square." Once TOC asked how a Depression giant could become a Woodstock gnat.

Bob was more relaxed with family, in watering holes, and at the gin rummy table. Univac even tried to match him against a machine. Daily he read box scores, taxied to the park, and phoned his broker. Shilling was as chronic.

"Ball two," Bob said, "and we had a ball at Mama's restaurant." Nelson laughed. "Elson *had* to be on the take. His plugs weren't even sponsors."

In 1969, Richard Nixon hailed baseball's centennial at the White House. "Oh, I know Bob," he said, halting an aide's introduction. "I even knew him back when the White Sox had a good team." Axed in late 1970, TOC visited troops in Viet Nam. "One of the great experiences of my life." Less grand: 1971 Oakland. "I didn't agree," said A's owner Charlie Finley, "but people said he talked too much about old-timers like Landis and Connie Mack."

Elson returned to Chicago, did commentary, and began a memoir. "If I wrote a thousand pages, I still wouldn't be able to thank all the people who helped me." In 1976, "a failing heart," wrote David Condon, "forced him to lighten his load."

Bob died March 10, 1981, at 76. Said Irv Kupcinet: "No one doubts that he has already found a gin rummy pigeon among the angels." Hold 'em, fold 'em. For the first time, the dealmaker owned all The Old Commander's cards.

BOB ELSON

LONGEVITY:	10	39 years.
CONTINUITY:	10	Chicago N.L. 1929–41; Chicago A.L. 1929–41 and 1946–70; Oakland A.L. 1971.
NETWORK:	10	World Series 1930–41 and 1943 (Mutual). All-Star Game 1933–34 (CBS) and 1935–1942 (Mutual).
KUDOS:	9	Cooperstown's Ford C. Frick Award 1979. *TSN* 1940–41 "Announcer of the Year."
LANGUAGE:	5	Report, not rage.
POPULARITY:	10	Microphone put in Hall, 1971.
PERSONA:	9	Bridged networks' McNamee and Allen.
VOICE:	8	Cultivated.
KNOWLEDGE:	9	Exception: golf. Sam Snead used "green tees on the fairway and yellow tees in the trap."
MISCELLANY:	10	"[His] Pump show was so popular," wrote *Chicago* Magazine, "that drivers would avoid going out on West Wacker Drive because they lost reception." Only Allen topped 23 Midsummer/Fall Classics in 14 (1930–43) years.
TOTAL:	90	(16th place).

FRANCE LAUX

"Swarming up from the Texas wheat fields, the Georgia cotton lands, the West Virginia coal mines, the Oklahoma cow ranges, [they] redramatized for the public that old traditional story about the talent of common men," drama critic Lloyd Lewis wrote of the thirties Cardinals. They wed spunk, zest, and a grand sobriquet.

The Gas House Gang mimed Willard Mullin's sketch of clubs, not bats, on players' shoulders fleeing the bare gas tank part of town. Their Voice turned the century. Born: Guthrie, Oklahoma, 1897; degree, Oklahoma City College; service, U.S. Army Air; after World War I, insurance and real estate broker and football referee.

The 1927 World Series opened October 5. By noon KVOO Tulsa station head Fred Yates was in a world of trouble. "I didn't have a guy to re-create," he said. France Laux lived in nearby Bristow. "Someone said his name. I get in my car and find him" driving down a street.

"Can you broadcast baseball?" he shouted, pointing France's car to the shoulder.

"Never done it. Why?"

"Get in. We're going to the studio."

Arriving minutes before the game, Laux did Bucs-Yanks, added college football, and in 1929 got a KMOX St. Louis 30-day trial. Through 1942, he aired the Browns, baseball's Anna, a salaried governess, and Redbirds, the Royal Palace of Siam. "Forget a booth," France said. "At Sportsman's I sat in boxes near the field."

The Gas Housers baited umpires, dropped water bags from windows, and filled lobbies with workmen's tools. Their Mississippi Mudcats band played "Rock Island Line" and "The Wreck of the Old '97" on fiddles, harmonicas, washboards, and guitars. Said Frank Frisch: "I am possibly the only manager that carried an orchestra. We traveled with more instruments than we did shirts or anything else," winning flags in 1930, 1931, and 1934.

For nearly a decade Pepper Martin manned their minor-league assembly factory. In 1931, promoted, he got a Series record-tying 12 hits. "Wild, he had a lot of company," *Globe Democrat* writer Bob Burnes said. Joe Medwick had a stevedore's body. Leo Durocher earned the signet Lip. Dizzy Dean treated discipline like cyanide. By contrast, France sought, if not anonymity, a certain distance and reserve.

"Laux spoke in a flat, metallic way," said Bob Broeg, with a soft tone and clipped precision. He worked alone, even on a doubleheader. Few found fault in an Okie whose propriety, not newly formed, was neither bogus nor offensive.

KMOX helped. "It went everywhere," said Burnes. "Score there, the network noticed." CBS gave Laux the 1933 All-Star Game and Series. Carl Hubbell K'd five straight A.L.ers in 1934. "You can imagine the thrill when I said, 'Hubbell has struck out Ruth,' " said France, "'also, he puts over a third strike on Gehrig and down the line.' "

That October, saturnine in success, Laux, Flanagan, and Ted Husing called the "first sponsored Series [Ford gave CBS and NBC each $500,000]," said France. Will Rogers, making more than both, snatched the mike in Detroit.

"You don't happen to know Judge Laux out in Oklahoma, do you?" Will said.

Laux replied, "Just slightly. He's only my dad."

Two years later Tony Lazzeri hit a Series slam. "He jogs in and stabs the plate for the fourth run on that hit!" cried France. "This has been quite an inning for the Yanks!" Game Six began quite a skein. "A ground ball to Gehrig. Scoops it up! Touches the bag for the third out—and the 1936 World Series is over!"—first of four Yanks titles in a row.

Next season Laux became first *TSN* staff-picked "Announcer of the Year" for "outstanding service to radio and baseball . . . and being chosen oftener than any other announcer to report World Series and All-Star Games." His *adieu* was 1941. "And there goes a drive going out to right field! Looks like it's going to be a home run . . . for [Pittsburgh's] Arky Vaughan!" Williams gave the A.L. a 7–5 stunner. Gillette then dropped France like a loaf of stale bread.

"It decided who got assignments," said Broeg. "Competition killed him. France wasn't hip enough nationally." He drifted back to St. Louis, which soon found him lacking, too.

In 1945, Harry Caray and Gabby Street began on WEW and WTMV East St. Louis. Dean keyed St. Louis' WIL. "They called the Browns and Cardinals," said Broeg, "and were flashier than France." In 1947, Caray won Redbirds exclusivity. France bought a bowling house, became American Bowling Congress secretary, and called the Browns (regularly, through 1948; weekends, 1953).

"Baseball people knew who Laux was," said Jack Buck, joining Caray in 1954. "If others did, it was through bowling or like, 'Gee, he was a pioneer,' " less skin and bones than catchphrase or caricature. Many forgot he had called a strike.

In 1976, wife Pearl died after 47 years of marriage. Laux moved to a nursing home, dying two years later. "I just lived too long," he told a friend.

FRANCE LAUX

LONGEVITY:	7	21 years.
CONTINUITY:	8	St. Louis N.L. 1929–42 and 1945; St. Louis A.L. 1929–42 and 1948–53.
NETWORK:	7	All-Star Game 1933–38 (CBS), 1939–41 (Mutual), and 1948 (independent TV). World Series 1933–38 (CBS).
KUDOS:	5	St. Louis Radio Hall of Fame 2002. *TSN* 1937 "Announcer of the Year."
LANGUAGE:	6	Descriptive; e.g., Joe Medwick's "bulging biceps."
POPULARITY:	7	Depended on year and opposition.
PERSONA:	8	Modest, honest, and good enough for thirties radio.
VOICE:	6	Homely.
KNOWLEDGE:	9	Played/managed semipro baseball.
MISCELLANY:	5	First to introduce singing cowboy Gene Autry, then telegraph operator in Chelsea, Oklahoma, on radio.
TOTAL:	68	**(94th place).**

FRED HOEY

Fancy two strangers from Providence, Rhode Island, and Penobscot, Maine, stranded on a South Sea isle. They clash in age, race, and faith. Their tie is the Red Sox. Boston won five of baseball's first 15 Series—but none for 86 years after the Twenty-sixth Division entered France. Its moniker was the Yankee. Who says the military lacks wit?

In New England, Sox 'r' us. Fenway Park's odd angles, high and low fences, and drop-dead closeness are, in turn, the Sox. Fred Hoey was 27 when it opened in 1912. In 1925, he joined WNAC Boston's six-state 22-station Yankee (later, Colonial) Network.

By then, Red Sox aped Dead Sox: second division, 1919–33. "No wonder they gave me a Day in '31 [and gold, a pipe, and $3,000 certificate of deposit]," blurted Hoey, exiting in 1938. "Fred also did the Braves, but it's the Sox who registered," mused once-Voice Ken Coleman. "In each case, he was the first—and the first, you don't forget."

Raised in Saxonville, near Framingham, a Boston suburb, Hoey, 12, saw his first game in 1897 (Temple Cup Series: Beaneaters vs. Baltimore). Later he played amateur and semipro baseball, ushered at the Red Sox' Huntington

Avenue Grounds, and wrote schoolboy and big-league sports. "I never met or heard him," said Ned Martin, joining the Sox in 1961. "But I feel I knew him, because people still swear *by* him."

Hoey was repetitive—"He throws to first and gets his man!"—and abided early radio. Most games were daytime. At six, the Yankee Network broke for news. "Ninth inning, tied, no matter," said Coleman. "The carriage became a pumpkin." Fred could vend—mostly Kentucky Club pipe tobacco and Mobil's Flying Red Horse—and stir Euripidean concern. He could not whip the sauce.

In 1933, Hoey reached the booth before Game One of the Series with evident fumbling and breath. His prose was incoherent: CBS yanked Fred off the air. Explanation: a "bad cold." Sober, he returned a conqueror. "In Boston, where people knew about his drinking, all was forgiven," Ken said. "Letters flooded the papers. 'How dare you hurt our Fred?' "

The 1925–31 cellar Sox hurt yearly. In 1934, Hoey met new owner Thomas Yawkey, who began reworking Fenway. "The park was run down," said Soxaphile A. Bartlett Giamatti. "Restoring it, Yawkey saw himself as owning the team, but to many *became* the team." The '37ers finished fifth. That fall, Yankee head John Shepard, III, axed our Fred. "Booze again," mused Ned. Pickets swamped WNAC. Even President Roosevelt asked that he be rehired.

Reinstated, "Fred thought he owned New England," mused forties Voice Leo Egan. In 1938, Jimmie Foxx's team-record 50 homers did. Next spring, Bobby Doerr told a rookie, "Wait till you see Foxx hit."

FRED HOEY

LONGEVITY:	5	14 years.
CONTINUITY:	9	Boston A.L. and N.L. 1925–38.
NETWORK:	1	World Series 1933 (NBC). All-Star Game 1936 (Mutual).
KUDOS:	3	New England's "Mr. Hockey" as coach, manager, player, and referee.
LANGUAGE:	4	Austere.
POPULARITY:	10	"His mail," said *TSN*, "keeps the postman loaded down."
PERSONA:	8	To Ken Coleman, "The man who did the games."
VOICE:	4	Gruff.
KNOWLEDGE:	10	Covered 1909–46 baseball for half of Boston's daily papers.
MISCELLANY:	8	Malapropisms endeared. Once Jimmie Foxx homered. Said Fred: "Homer hits a Foxx."
TOTAL:	62	(99th place).

Replied Ted Williams: "Wait till Foxx sees *me* hit." Soon Fred saw neither.

That October, Hoey demanded a raise. Again Shepard canned him. Once more a goodly portion of the public stormed Fenway. Replacing the Red Horse and Kentucky Club, General Mills and Socony Oil yawned.

"They wanted their own announcer," said Coleman. "Plus, radio was changing. Fred paused a lot. Sponsors wanted somebody glib." Hoey died November 17, 1949, at 64, in a gas-filled room, of accidental asphyxiation, his body found by a delivery boy.

"He was generally credited with building up baseball broadcasting to the lofty spot it holds," read the *Boston Daily Globe*. Joe Castiglione does today's Sox radio. "Whenever you hear me, remember where it began."

TY TYSON

"Detroit has [always] been one of the great baseball towns in the country," Joe Falls wrote. By twos and threes, fans headed for Tiger Stadium like Charlemagne nearing Spain. Steep-rowed seats enclosed the park. Popgun lines flanked a yawning center field. Right's overhang turned pop flies into homers. Like tableaus, announcers reemerge.

Ernie Harwell was a paladin. George Kell mimed a favorite uncle. Van Patrick roared louder than a Packard coupe. Tigers radio began April 19, 1927, on WWJ: "Good afternoon, boys and girls, this is [Edwin] Ty Tyson speaking to you from [then] Navin Field."

Detroit won, 8–5, vs. Cleveland. Ultimately, Ty won the Four Seasons Wonderland of Lions and Tigers and (by train) even Bears.

Tyson attended Penn State, was a World War I 103 Trench Mortar Battery doughboy, and joined WWJ as weatherman, news reporter, and "all sorts of things, including introducing of bands." One thing was baseball. "By the late 1920s," wrote the *Detroit Free Press*'s Bob Latshaw, "there wasn't an afternoon the Tigers played that anyone could escape Tyson. It was possible for a youngster to leave school, walk a half-mile, and never miss a pitch."

An hour from Detroit, the choir met in Billy Williams's garage, turned on the Capehart radio, and began chewing snuff. "Richfield Springs was a four-corners settlement," said future *Saturday Evening Post* editor Maynard Good Stoddard. It had two dozen houses, a general store, gas pumps, and hope. Puptown and Henpeck lay one and seven miles away. Baseball was their world.

"Radio was new," said Maynard. "Ty helped bring it alive." Leon Goslin—"Goose"—flapped his arms while chasing pops. Hank Greenberg became "Hancus Pancus"; Jo Jo White, "The Tiger Man." Charlie Gehringer was a strong, silent type. Roomie Chief Hosgett asked for salt. No answer. Finally: "What'd I say wrong?" Charlie: "You could have pointed." Richfield Springs pointed to the former high school, semi-pro, and college pitcher.

A 1933 radio annual read: "[Tyson's] technique is deliberate and sure, flavored with a dry humor which has made him a favorite with listeners and players." A year later Babe Ruth went deep at Navin, howling "I want that ball back!" of dinger 700. Lennie Bieleski swapped it for a better seat, $20, and an autographed ball. Stoddard can still replay Ty's "It's going, it's going, and it's a home run!"

The Tigers' last flag had been a quarter-century gone. In 1934, they finally made it back to the Series. Landis dubbed Tyson "[too] partisan" for CBS or NBC. Michigan's response: a petition of 600,000 names. Yielding, the Commissioner let him man WWJ. "It showed how popular Ty was locally," said Harwell. "He was the first. They had no one to compare him with. He enjoyed himself quietly"—1935, even more.

Gehringer K'd just 16 times in 610 ups. MVP Greenberg had 170 RBI. Detroit again won the flag. Doing NBC, Ty bumped into Landis before Game One. "The Series is for people who work and love baseball," the Judge glowered. "*That—only* that—is why you're here." Losing the 1908, 1909, and 1934 Series, the "Tiges," in Harwell's term, took a 3–2 game lead. "We go back home," Goslin said. "Will it happen again?"

Detroit's ninth began 3-all. Singling, Mickey Cochrane took second on an out. Goose faced the Cubs' Larry French: "If they pitch this over the plate," he told umpire Ernie Quigley, "you can take that monkey suit off." They, and he, did. "Plenty of racket out here," Tyson bayed. "A drive up the middle! And the winning run will score!"

Even Grantland Rice was relieved: "The leaning tower can now crumble and find its level with the Pisan plain. After waiting for forty-eight years, the Detroit Tigers at last are champions of the world."

WWJ (nee 8MK) aired Series "summaries" as early as 1920. Until 1934, it deemed baseball sponsors *declasse*. Henceforth a game began, "This is brought to you by Mobil Oil." Ending, it again noted Mobil. "That was it, two men-tions," laughed Ty, less cheery about a competitor.

That spring four-time batting champion Harry Heilmann cracked the Michigan Radio Network. "It was unique," mused Harwell. Tyson talked to greater Detroit. Heilmann's flagship WXYZ fed outstate Michigan. "Same game, every day," said Stoddard. "The networks kept battling," finally fusing in 1942. The next laugh was Harry's. "He knew the new owners, had a bigger name," said Ty, dispatched.

In 1947–48, respectively, Tyson became Detroit's first TV Voice—and Tigers, last American League team with lights. "The [June 15, 1948] game didn't start till 9:30 at night because we didn't think lights would work till then." By 1951, cancer had attacked Heilmann: to *Sports Illustrated,* "God, the Creator, the Controller, Communicator of the only universe of importance—Tigerland." Retrieving radio, Ty wowed Henpeck and Pup-town over WJBK.

Life deserves a postscript. Tyson's dotted 1965, three years before his death. Harwell invited him to Father's Day at Tiger Stadium. Ty addressed the crowd, did an inning, and warmed his "boys and girls" grown old. "The reaction was overwhelming," said Ernie. "One of the most popular broadcasts we ever had."

Listening, Maynard Good Stoddard thought Ty never sounded better.

TY TYSON

LONGEVITY:	7	20 years.
CONTINUITY:	9	Detroit A.L. 1927–42, 1947–48, and 1951–52.
NETWORK:	2	World Series 1935–36 (NBC).
KUDOS:	3	Detroit Sports Broadcasters Association gives yearly award in his honor.
LANGUAGE:	6	Slow.
POPULARITY:	10	"He made it generational," said Harwell. "A grandfather brought his son, who brought his, who brought his."
PERSONA:	8	"The Tyrone Tradition," born in Tyrone, Pennsylvania.
VOICE:	4	Dry.
KNOWLEDGE:	9	Didn't miss much. "A young man in a pair of brown plush pants" caught one foul.
MISCELLANY:	7	Aired earliest surviving regular-season recorded game: Tigers–Yanks, September 20, 1934.
TOTAL:	65	**(97th place).**

TOM MANNING

Some fact more or less forms us. John Kerry's was Viet Nam; Mario Cuomo, the immigrant experience; Adlai Stevenson, language-made-literate. Tom Manning's was a mania to risk, talk, *do.* "It's like he had an extra gland," someone said of Lyndon Johnson. Tom's brass evoked John Connally: "I like to win big or lose big, but what's the sense of losing small?"

He was born in Cleveland September 11, 1899, for its Spiders a sad-sack year: 20–134, still-record 24-game losing streak, and N.L.'s worst-ever percentage (.134). It promptly dropped them like a wrong note in *South Pacific.* "Guess that first year," Tom laughed later, "showed my life would be extreme."

Excess showed in high school. Bowling, Manning had a 198 average. He played golf, baseball, hoops, football, and handball. Thrice Tom won the National Amateur Baseball Federation title as player, coach, or skipper. "I was making up for lost time—or '99."

Manning was also a teenage corner newsboy. In 1918, the *Cleveland Press* held a convention. "A big event was a yelling contest. I had a high falsetto with unlimited carrying power and I won." That fall he attended a boxing match whose public address Voice was missing. "There's the kid who won the yelling contest," cried a bystander, spotting Tom. "He can do announcing," and did.

By 1922, he stood behind home plate at League Park, pointed a four-foot-long megaphone, and howled batteries to the crowd. In 1928, Manning began reading radio scores for $3 daily. Said 1948–67 Indians Voice Jimmy Dudley: "What had been newsprint, Tom brought alive." His debut almost died: Deeming the mike a megaphone, Manning blew the transmitter. Through 1931 he called the Tribe on WTAM. A new flagship then tapped Jack Graney: "Cleveland's loss," said Dudley, "becoming NBC's gain."

In 1929, joining McNamee, Tom called his first of 10 straight Series. 1931: Martin hit .500 vs. Philly. 1936: Lou Gehrig dinged twice in Game Two. "There it goes, a long smash deep into center field! Way up! Going, going, going! A home run!" In 1930, another Bomber, Mark Koenig, was dealt to Detroit. Buying him, the 1932 Cubs withheld a full Classic share. In Game Three, Ruth eyed their dugout. Mates cried "cheapskates." The Cubs tossed liniment, and one fan a lemon. Charlie Root forged a 2–1 count. Raising two fingers, did Babe point to center? We wonder, even now.

"Never," Root barbed. "If he had, next time up I'd have stuck it in his rear." Manning disagreed. "Now [he] is pointing out at center field and he's yelling at the Cubs that the next pitch is going into center field! Here's the pitch. It's going! Babe Ruth connects and here it goes! The ball is going, going, going—high into the center-field stands, into the scoreboard! And it's a home run! It's gone! Whoopee! Listen to that crowd!"

In 1933, Manning aired the first All-Star Game. Franklin Roosevelt flung 1937's opening pitch with an unorthodox, overhanded lob. Stephen Spender's "I Think Continually of Those" ends: "Born of the son they travelled a short while towards the sun." By now Tom had travelled a long while toward the top.

He called each 1933–37 Presidential opener, adding boxing, football, golf, hockey, track and field, air crashes, floods, and national conventions, announcing from a plane, tugboat, and submarine. One runaway All-American Soap Box Derby racer hit his booth, cracked two ribs, and put Tom in a hospital. Manning drove a trotting horse in a grand circuit meeting, carting a 30-pound transmitter. In 1938, *The Sporting News* touted "his uncanny ability to shoot from the hip at a microphone." Yet the hypothetical intrudes.

In 1939, Gillette, dumping NBC for Mutual, traded one redhead, Manning, for another, Barber. Tom drifted to Cleveland TV: sports, live, at 6 and 11. Today we rarely liken him to longer-running Voices—France Laux or Ty Tyson. Would we, had he aired the post-'31 Indians?

TOM MANNING

LONGEVITY:	5	13 years.
CONTINUITY:	8	Cleveland A.L. 1928–31 and 1956–57; NBC 1929–38.
NETWORK:	10	World Series 1929–38 (NBC). All-Star Game 1933–34 and 1936–40 (NBC) and 1935 (Mutual).
KUDOS:	3	*TSN* 1938 "Announcer of the Year."
LANGUAGE:	6	Staccato.
POPULARITY:	10	Upon death, City Council named him one "of the ten most important men" in Cleveland history.
PERSONA:	9	The Megaphone Man.
VOICE:	8	Beguiling.
KNOWLEDGE:	10	"His hearers, many novice fans," said a writer, "thoroughly understood his broadcasts."
MISCELLANY:	4	Color him red—hair, air, and nickname.
TOTAL:	73	(84th place).

In 1956, Cleveland held his day. "I've wondered for 30 years how Tom Manning kept so active," said Bob Hope, a native. "His winter invasions of the West Coast consistently led to the big question, 'Who does his hair?' "That year he reclaimed Tribe radio. "I needed a partner," said Dudley, "but Tom was losing his hearing, and the jet travel, night games, were too much."

Manning died, at 69, September 3, 1969, the ex-newsboy who preached the fast-lane life. He no longer needed that extra gland.

JACK GRANEY

Recall Dizzy Dean's "sludding into third." Joe Garagiola, doing play-by-play in the bullpen. Bob Uecker, signing with the Braves for $3,000. "That bothered my dad because he didn't have that kind of dough. But he eventually scraped it up." Jack Graney commenced the athlete-become-announcer.

"I'd hear McNamee and Manning on day network stuff," Jack Buck said of the 1930s, "but what I loved was lying in bed at night." Graney described Hal Trosky and Earl Averill and Bob Feller. To a young Clevelander, it fused Bali Hai, Timbuktu, and the Czar's Winter Palace.

"I didn't want to be a policeman or fireman," Buck mused. "Jack made me want a living calling ball." He enjoyed being odd man out: a Canadian in America's game; player-turned-mikeman; rough voice in a velvet craft. "I didn't dislike being in the minority," said Graney. Fact is, he liked breaking the mold.

Jack played in 1908 and 1910–22, averaged .250 in 1,402 games, and was first to bat vs. Babe Ruth (1914) and wear a uniform number (1916). Later the outfielder became "the best play-by-play man the Indians ever had . . . short on ego and long on talent," wrote *Plain Dealer* columnist Bob Dolgan. Today radio no longer deems jocks unfit.

Born June 10, 1886, in St. Thomas, Ontario, John Gladstone Graney tried hockey, preferred baseball, and turned to pitching. One nickname was "Glad." The other augured wildness: "Three and Two Jack."

One day N.L. umpire Bob Emslie saw Graney K several batters. Jack was drafted, gladhanded Cubs farm spots at Rochester, Erie, and Wilkes-Barre, and joined Cleveland at 1908 spring training. Quickly he yearned for a night train out of Georgia.

Nap Lajoie entered the cage as Graney began to throw: "so wild," said the

Tribe player/manager, "each batter stood over the plate for five minutes before he got in the vicinity." Pining to impress, Jack threw "the fastest ball I had ever pitched. I thought it would strike him out." Instead, it *knocked* him out. That evening the lefty found Nap with an ice bag on his head.

"Anyone as wild as you belongs in the Wild West," he said. "You're going to [Pacific Coast League] Portland." In 1910, Graney returned to Cleveland. New League Park tied the A.L.'s smallest size (21,000), nearest fence (290 feet), and farthest turf (505). Gentling, Lajoie gave Jack a bull terrier he named Larry. "Not everyone liked me," Glad said, "but they all liked him."

At night, Larry relieved himself, "found his way to the stairs or elevator, and came to the right room." Often he crossed Lake Erie to Ontario. Put on shore, the Tribe mascot got on a trolley, rode to St. Thomas, and raced to the Graney home. In 1913, visiting the White House, Jack left him with a doorman. "Where's Larry?" said Woodrow Wilson. "I've got to meet that remarkable dog."

Six times Wilson's first pitch opened the season. "Three and Two Jack" now meant a discerning eye: "I was told to take two strikes for the team and one for me," averaging more than 100 walks a year. In 1919, Tris Speaker became player/manager. A year later the Indians won their first World Series. They got there *en famille*.

The '20 Tribe hit .303. Speaker rapped a record 11 straight hits. In August, New York's Carl Mays beaned Ray Chapman at the Polo Grounds. The ball broke the Cleveland shortstop's neck, fractured his skull, and rebounded to Mays on the fly. In the clubhouse, Jack tried to revive his roommate. "Give him a pencil, something to hold on to." Dropping it, Ray died 12 hours later: baseball's first fatality from a thrown or batted ball.

Bill Wambsganss played second base. A scout was asked, "What's he got?" Response: "The funniest damn name I ever heard"—German for a kind of overcoat. In the Series, a writer told Wambsganss, hitting .154, to "Stay with it. This [Game Five] could be your day." Brooklyn's Pete Kilduff and Otto Miller led off the fifth inning safely. Clarence Mitchell lined to Wambsganss, who touched second, tagged Miller, and effected the first Classic triple play.

Next year, Graney hit a career-high .299. In 1922, he retired, later managed a Western League team, and, buying a Ford agency, left baseball "to make some money." At the time there was a lot to make.

By 1929, the average of common prices on the New York Stock Exchange had leapt 123 percent since 1926. On October 29, 16,410,030 shares were traded: thousands of speculators threw holdings in the pit. Depression knocked "the legs out from under me," Graney said. For a while, he sold used cars. For escape, he bought a radio.

In 1931, 32 million homes owned a wireless. "It was cheap," mused Buck, "filled the hours, the one medium Depression hadn't crushed." That fall, the Indians joined WHK, whose Ellis Vander Pyle flopped. General manager Billy Evans's square peg fit Graney's round hole. "I was broke, and he needed an announcer," said Glad. "Before my first game, I was so nervous I almost changed my mind and ran out of the booth."

At League, the Tribe ran out of room. In 1932, vast Municipal Stadium became a holiday/weekend home. Jack liked the old. Girders cloaked the right-field wall. Hitting one, a ball stayed in play. "Away I'd re-recreate," often waking in a lather. Had he botched a name, put a man on the wrong base, reversed two Indians scoring? "I'd get letters: 'It's Trosky, then Averill, not the other way around!' "Telegraphy favored him. "Having played, I knew each park."

In 1934, CBS gave Glad the Series. "Too partial," huffed Landis. "He played in the American League." Graney wrote a letter: "I am now a sports-caster, and should be regarded as such."

Next season, he became the first ex-jock to cover the Series and All-Star Game. "I just follow the ball, leave knocks to others." What Jack didn't leave was Cleveland.

On August 23, 1936, Bob Feller, 16, fanned 15 Browns in his first big-league start. He won 266 games, led the A.L. seven times in Ks, and had a record 12 one-hitters. Glad saw each. Feller opened 1940 at Chicago. "Grannie Mack is on the ground with one knee, scrapes it up with his glove hand, flips it over to Trosky at first," Graney said. "A close decision—and he's out! Bob Feller has his first no-hit game! Boy, listen to that crowd!"

In 1941, Joe DiMaggio's single began a 56-game hit streak. On July 17, baseball's then-largest night crowd, 67,648, packed Municipal. In the eighth, DiMag lashed Jim Bagby's 1–1 pitch. "On the ground to shortstop! Boudreau has it. Throw to second, on to first! Double play! The streak may be over!" Players soon streaked to war. "Look out, Bud [forties partner Richmond]!" Jack said, striking the desk to denote a foul. "Whew! That was a close one." The hitter took a pitch. "Strike through the center." Next: "A hot smash! It's a h-i-g-h throw!"

Graney's was "a high voice, but distinctive," said Buck, in bobbed rhythm with his game. The Indians hadn't won since Verdun. Said Glad: "I'm tired of having the patience of Job."

"Remember," Bob Baucher wrote of post-World War II. "There was almost no television or air conditioning, so people sat on porches and cooled off listening to the game." Buying the Tribe, Bill Veeck closed League in 1946—too peewee for what he had in mind. The '48ers won the Series. Jack wrongly thought that "with our club I'd see more." Luke Easter's dingers became "bazooka shots." A pitcher threw a "sad iron" fastball. New flagship WERE tripled the Indians network.

"It's time," Glad said, retiring in 1953. The Tribe honored him at the Stadium: Feller and Speaker spoke. He did TV, moved with wife Pauline near their daughter in Missouri, and knocked baseball on the air. "They don't give a complete description. Tell about the ball as it takes a roll through the infield!" Years earlier Buck had fallen asleep to Graney. Glad now heard him daily over KMOX.

In 1977, the Graneys feted their 61st anniversary. "I guarantee there are no perils with Pauline," Jack quipped, "or it wouldn't have lasted that long." Glad, 91, lasted till the next April. "Three and Two" had run out the string: full count, full life.

JACK GRANEY

LONGEVITY:	7	21 years.
CONTINUITY:	9	Cleveland A.L. 1932–44 and 1946–53.
NETWORK:	2	All-Star Game 1935 and World Series 1935 (CBS).
KUDOS:	4	Day, given by Indians, 1953. Canadian Baseball Hall of Fame 1984.
LANGUAGE:	9	Crisp.
POPULARITY:	10	No Tribesman topped him.
PERSONA:	10	Pathfinder.
VOICE:	5	Raspy, vital.
KNOWLEDGE:	10	Jock who grasped the game.
MISCELLANY:	6	Held lit, but unsmoked, cigarette in booth. "It'd burn my hands, but I couldn't puff and talk." Re-created in auto showroom, clients gawking behind glass.
TOTAL:	72	(87th place).

ARCH MCDONALD

For a long time, the re-creation was a rite like gloves left between innings on the field. A stick on hollow wood simulated bat vs. ball. The soundtrack included background murmur. Infielder: "Come on, babe, bear down." Manager: "Don't give in!" Fan: "You couldn't hit my *house!*" Not much was real. Reality: It didn't matter to "the Rembrandt of Re-Creations."

Arch McDonald did them in a People's drug store three blocks from the White House. Said the *Washington Star*'s Morris Siegel: "He'd draw more people than the Senators at Griffith Stadium." Recalling the ex-butcher, crop hand, fight referee, oil rigger, patent medicine man, peanut vendor, refrigerator salesman, and soda jerk, it is easy to see why.

On March 4, 1933, Franklin Roosevelt took the oath of office. A banking crisis veiled his inauguration. Contagion roiled 16 million unemployed. A year earlier, Arch became the first *TSN* "Announcer of the Year." "At [Class-A] Chattanooga!" gaped *Washington Post* writer Shirley Povich. "He wins a fan vote over *big*-league guys." The Arkansan had struggled to make a living. "All owners have a players' scouting system," he allowed. "Thank God [Senators'] Clark Griffith had one for announcers, too."

In 1934, Arch trudged to Washington, second division for 20 of the next 23 years. Presently it heard "right down Broadway" (strike) and "ducks on the pond" (runners) and "There she goes, Mrs. Murphy" (Nats home run). Upon a save, key hit, or "our boys'" 6–4–3, Washington, brace thyself: McDonald would sing a hillbilly ballad, "They Cut Down the Old Pine Tree."

In 1937, Arch began daily exhibition coverage. In 1939, small-town and -timey, he entered, despite its bombast, a phantasmagoric place. "Feel you will go over as big in New York City as you did in Washington," wrote umpire Bill McGowan. He didn't: "Yanks fans thought him country," said Siegel. After a year McDonald sailed home. D.C. still loved him. The Nats still swam in catatonia and disarray. Some people impress you most on first meeting. Arch grew, like the bourbon he inhaled.

In 1942, *TSN* again honored him. "McDonald can emit a banshee wail when a player hits into a bases-loaded double play," it read. "And he can whoop it up like a holy roller when Washington runs are crossing the plate." The Old Pine Tree broadcast in pre–air conditioning undies. In 1946, Arch ran for Congress, losing to Republican Glen Beall in suburban Montgomery County.

"Politics, broadcasting, it's entertainment!" McDonald howled. Proof: his cave of re-created peals.

Roy Campanella said famously, "You have to be a man to be a big leaguer, but you have to have a lot of little boy in you, too." There was a lot—260 pounds—of McDonald. Much was little boy. Arch filled the G Street drug store's second floor. "He's beside a window with crowd noise and taped bells going off," said Povich. "He'd broadcast, and outside groupies'd roar."

Ultimately, he moved to the basement studio. "Dad was in a glass booth, with bleachers around," said son Arch Jr. "The Senators were always in the cellar—but all the seats [350] were gone." Western Union brought nuts and bolts. On each safety, pop struck a gong. "Clint Courtney singles, and Dad hit it once. Roy Sievers parks one, four times it's crashed."

McDonald made each game a carnival, day a Mardi Gras, and fan a king (Bill Veeck). The Senators left D.C. in 1960. Four years earlier, they left Arch. "It was a sponsor change," Siegel explained. "He never saw another game." On October 16, 1960, the football Redskins entrained for Yankee Stadium. Returning, The Old Pine Tree, 59, died of a heart attack while playing hearts.

Many Washingtonians would like to re-create his life.

ARCH McDONALD

LONGEVITY:	8	23 years.
CONTINUITY:	9	Washington A.L. 1934–38 and 1940–56; New York A.L. 1939.
NETWORK:	2	All-Star Game 1937 (CBS). In 1939, manned CBS's Hall of Fame opening.
KUDOS:	7	Cooperstown 1999. *TSN* 1932 and 1942 "Announcer of the Year," chosen by fans and staff, respectively.
LANGUAGE:	7	Florid.
POPULARITY:	10	Southern man, then-Southern town.
PERSONA:	10	Knew pitchers, peers, and presidents.
VOICE:	7	Antebellum.
KNOWLEDGE:	7	Baseball was Barnum's prop.
MISCELLANY:	6	Named Joe DiMaggio "The Yankee Clipper." Did 1940s and '50s Redskins and college football.
TOTAL:	73	(85th place).

3

Red Barber

Byrum Saam

Ernie Harwell

Jack Brickhouse

Bob Wolff

RED BARBER

By the 1930s, baseball twitched with angst. Who would pay if you could hear for free? Landis ordered a moratorium on more radio coverage. Next, he told teams to charge a broadcast fee. By 1938, all but three teams aired their home schedule. "Can you believe it?" Bob Elson smiled. "The only exception was New York"'s expiring five-year ban. That year, the National League named the Reds' president to save Brooklyn from insolvency. Larry MacPhail said his new club would use the wireless.

In 1939, the Dodgers' first Voice followed MacPhail from Cincinnati. "MacPhail believed in [radio's] promotional power . . . he became sold on it," said Walter Lanier ("Red") Barber, who sold the game. From any seat at Ebbets Field, you heard players jabber, saw faces harden, felt tension creep. Said Bob Costas: "Barber was the voice of that experience." You could walk down the street, a hundred windows open, and hear every play.

Vin Scully thought Red a palatine. "A cabbie'd say, 'That Barber, he's too fair.' " To Costas, he detailed the borough's joys, worries, and confessions of the heart. "Red's appeal soared because people sensitive about the image as dees and dems—'I'll meet ya at Toydy-toyd and Second Avenue'—were pleased that this erudite man represented them."

MacPhail grasped how "radio [made a game] played by two teams . . . a contest involving personalities who had families, troubles, blue or brown eyes," said Barber. Frank Sinatra sang, "There used to be a ballpark." In Brooklyn, there used to be a broadcaster constitutionally unable to say a prejudicial word.

Born, Columbus, Mississippi, in 1908, the distant relative of writer Sidney Lanier moved at 10 to Sanford, Florida. In 1929, he hitchhiked to the University at Gainesville. A part-time job was cleaning a teacher's boarding house. One day the professor asked Red to read his paper on WRUF campus radio. Barber had wanted to teach English. "By the time I finished the paper, I wanted to drop out of school."

Red became the station's $50 a week Voice and director. When school ended, "I'd look for broadcast jobs." In 1933, the Reds went belly-up. A bank hired MacPhail, who sold tycoon Powel Crosley a majority chunk. Halving his salary, Crosley hired Barber for then-500,000-watt WLW. "I want a chance," Red told his dad. Said MacPhail: "He didn't know how to score a game. On the other hand, it was like nothing they'd heard."

Since 1930, WFBE Cincinnati's Harry Hartman had chanted *socko* and *bammo* and *belto* and *whammo*. He weighed 320 pounds, sat behind the plate, and broadcast in his underwear. Red would have sooner stripped. "Doing re-creations, some guys had crowd noise, pretending they were at the game." Not Barber, placing the mike by the telegraph. "No con. You heard the dot-dash," said Scully—also a man who treated custom like a dangling participle.

On May 24, 1935, Red aired baseball's night inaugural. That fall bred his, and Mutual's, first World Series. Landis collared him before Game One. "Suppose a player . . . spits in my face. Report each step he makes. Report how much spit hits me. Report my reaction. Don't worry about the Com-missioner. That will be my job. Yours is to report the event." Barber did: Detroit's first world title.

Next year, Cincy hosted the first Ladies' Night. In June 1938, anything worth doing was worth doing twice. Johnny Vander Meer no-hit Boston, 3–0. Four days later a) Ebbets Field debuted at night and b) Vandy cobbled a second straight no-no. "Baseball here seems a different planet," Red mused. On ours, the Third Reich crossed the Polish border September 1, 1939, starting World War II.

Five days earlier, baseball crossed a line upon which it would never double back.

"The players were clearly distinguishable," wrote *The Sporting News*'s Harold Parrott of the bigs' TV baptism, "but it was not possible to pick out the ball." By contrast, you could pick up Red, in Ebbets' second deck, on the third-base side, hawking Ivory Soap, Mobil Gas, and General Mills. "Yes-suh," he drawled of Wheaties, "that's a Breakfast of Champions."

Making history, Barber was flying blind. "No monitor, only two [W2XVS] cameras. One was by me, the other behind the plate, and I had to guess from which light was on where it pointed." Few had to guess about Brooklyn's niche. Until 1898, the borough was an independent city. Incor-porated into New York, it still felt like a Nation-State. "Manhattan had sky-scrapers, wealth, and fame. The only way Brooklyn could strike back was with their club. The fans were personal, like the park."

Most of the 32,111 seats had a good view—if you weren't behind a post. Housewife Hilda Chester waved a cowbell in the bleachers. Behind first, Jake the Butcher roared "Late again!" of a pickoff. The Dodger Sym-Phony was a vaguely musical group. "Their specialty," said Steve Jacobson, "was piping a visiting strikeout victim back to his bench with a tune 'The Army Duff.'

[Because] the last beat was timed for the moment the player's butt touched," he might tardily sit down. "The Sym-Phony still had that last beat ready." Anything, Red said, could happen here—yes-suh, and did.

In 1919, ex-Bum Casey Stengel returned, doffed his cap, and had a sparrow fly away. In 1930, Brooklyn got three on base. Punch line: "Yeah, which base?" (Third.) In 1940, the Bums taunted plate umpire George Magerkurth. A parole violator attacked him on the final out. "Before I know it," marveled George, "he's beating me to a pulp."

The archetype fan screams, "Kill the ump!" Fearing the con might, colleague Bill Stewart helped police haul him to the jug. N.L. head Ford Frick then fined and suspended skipper Leo Durocher for "inciting a riot." Just another day in Flatbush USA.

Barber did "College Football Roundup," the Army-Navy Game, Rose, Orange, and Sugar Bowls, NFL title game, five All-Star Games, and 13 Series. "Because of him," wrote David Halberstam, "and radio's importance then, we remember the messenger as distinctly as the message." Red's favorite year was the last of an uncertain peace. On April 13, 1941, Brooklyn honored him with a Day. Next week, he read a script for the New York Philharmonic's "Symphony in D for the Dodgers," rejoicing that urban Brooklyn had spurned the farm.

Each regular arrived from another club. The Dodgers won a franchise-high 100 games, drew a record 1,214,910, and began their Subway Series. Behind, 2 games to 1, Brooklyn led, 4–3, with two out in the ninth. Reliever Hugh Casey worked Tommy Henrich to a 3–2 count. "Casey then threw the craziest curve I ever saw," said Barber. Larry Goetz boomed "Strike three!" Fooling catcher Mickey Owen, it settled near the screen. Henrich reached. DiMaggio singled. Charlie Keller hit a two-strike pitch off the right-field wall: 7–4, Yanks. You could hear a sigh.

"The condemned jumped out of the chair and electrocuted the warden," a writer said. A day later New York won its ninth title. The Cathedral of the Underdog played a tired and humbled dirge.

Across the river, Mel Allen gabbed slickly for the pinstripes. Red talked around a stove, a 3-minute egg timer telling him to give the score. "When the crowd shouted, so did you," Allen said. Barber cleaved. "Never raise your voice. When the crowd yells, shut up."

If a million people saw the Bums, wrote Robert Creamer, 10 million heard the Redhead. "A person could cover the length of the beach of Coney Island," added the *Daily News,* "and never lose his voice." The mound became a "pulpit." The pitcher "tied the hitter up—turned him every way but loose." Once Barber said: "You ought never talk past your audience, and surely never talk down."

Talk wed "catbird seat" and "tearin' up the pea patch" and "rhubarb on the field." A field was "the sun garden"; bat, "a dirty brown-looking stick, well-seasoned"; game, "as tight as a brand-new pair of shoes on a rainy day." Said Creamer: "The language he used . . . became part of everyone's speech." In 1944, the Yanks' and Giants' sponsor tried to part Barber from Brooklyn.

"My [$50,000] contract had a year left," said Red. "Gillette said, 'Break it, we'll pay legal costs.' " Livid, he stayed. In 1945, Branch Rickey, Walter O'Malley, and John Smith bought half of the Ebbets estate. Anything can happen: Rickey broke baseball's color line. Barber eyeballed his soul: "I'd been one of the first he told: I was the Voice, and from the South." At first he thought of quitting. Later Jackie Robinson hailed his healing. "If there are any thanks involved," Red said, "I thank him."

Jackie debuted April 15, 1947. "I was there," said Larry King, living in Bensonhurst. "He just seemed to glide." Barber never said, or had to, that Robinson was the bigs' first black. "Every word I said, or didn't, was carefully weighed." Brooklyn won his second flag. Allen joined Red on the Series. The Yanks took a 2–0 lead. The Bums then won a 9–8 parody. Next day New York led, 2–1, after 8 2/3 innings.

Rarer: Starter Floyd ("Bill") Bevens had ceded 10 walks and no hits.

Form demands ignoring an at-work no-hitter. "What I did or didn't say wouldn't influence what happened on the field," said Allen of Mutual. "But players on the bench think you jinx it by talking. It's part of the romance— one of the great things that separates baseball from other sports, like the seventh-inning stretch or the lack of a clock."

Game Four was timeless. Mel called the first four and a half innings: "I respected the tradition." Barber, a "reporter, not a dealer in superstition," did not. Instantly he leaked Brooklyn's line score: one run, two errors, no hits. Allen gasped, Red recalled, like he was trying to swallow chinaberry seeds. "Before Red, most Voices were hacks," said Ernie Harwell. "He rejected that for perfection." Bevens had lost perfection. A no-hitter would suffice.

Ninth inning. Two out. Al Gionfriddo steals second base. Pete Reiser works Bevens to a 3–1 count. Manager Bucky Harris walks the potential winning run. "The pitch [to pinch-hitter Cookie Lavagetto]," said Red. "Swung on, there's a drive hit out toward the right-field corner! Henrich is going back! He can't get it! It's off the wall for a base hit! Here comes the tying run and here comes the winning run!"—on Brooklyn's only hit: Series, tied. Then: "Well, I'll be a suck-egg mule!"

Game Five fizzled: New York, 2–1. Next day fused a record Series crowd (74,065), longest regulation game (3:19), and ooh-ah denouement. Dodgers, 8–5, in the sixth: two out, two on, and DiMag at bat. "Leans in. He has one for three today, six hits so far in the Series. Outfield deep, around toward left, the infield overshifted," Barber said. Then: "Swung on. Belted. It's a long one! Deep into left-center! Back goes Gionfriddo! Back, back, back, back, back, back! He makes a one-handed catch against the bullpen! Oh, Doctor!"

DiMaggio kicked dirt near second, a rare show of fury. Game Seven: Stripes, 5–2. "Great year, sad end," said Brooklyn's Pee Wee Reese. He was playing the Redhead's song.

In 1946, the then-CBS Sports director created "College Football Roundup." Two years later Barber nearly died of a hemorrhaged ulcer. That fall, still weak, he was phoned by A. Craig Smith, the Gillette ad czar who asked Red to jilt Brooklyn in 1944.

"Smith took it personally, tried to end my Series. Saving me was only how the Commissioner began naming Voices." In 1948, television sets waxed from 165,000 to 3 million. "The world's changing," Craig said, "and you're the only guy who can make it [Gillette TV] go." Barber balked, then caved. "I said OK. Every hour I worried I'd hemorrhage again and cough up blood."

The postlogue hemorrhaged Brooklyn. 1949: "Going way back, back, that's the ball game, a home run for Tommy Henrich!" Red said in the Series opener. "Look at him grin! Big as a slice of watermelon." The Yanks took the third chapter of their serialized novel. 1950–51: Flatbush lost a last-day flag. 1952: Red telecast his second Classic. Going home, the Bums held a 3–2 game edge. They got the Bum's rush: 3–2 and 4–2. In Game Seven, Duke Snider found Bedford Avenue. "Boom. Look out. Look out." Noise crested. Finally: "You needn't look any more."

The '53ers went 105–49, scored a near-league record 955 runs, and led it in eight other categories. Since 1939, Gillette had run the Series. "It was growing an empire, but announcers only got a demeaning $200 a game," said Barber, then 45. Most took it. In September, Red tried to up it, demanding "the right to negotiate my fee." Gillette told him to jump off the Tallahatchie Bridge. Naively, he phoned a man who deemed him a pain in the patootie.

O'Malley had owned the Brooks since 1950. One night, at Toots Shor's, he and Yankees owner Dan Topping got thoroughly gassed. "I hate the son of a bitch," Walter said of Barber. Topping then trashed Mel. "Tell you what," O'Malley urged. "I'll trade you the son of a bitch." Dan flushed. "I'll give you Allen." Sober, next day they reneged.

O'Malley was less likely than A. Craig Smith to back Red's right to negotiate. "That is *your* problem," he sniffed. "I'll nominate Scully to take your [Series] place." Barber wrote: "I said to myself, 'Walter, the Dodgers are now *your* problem.' " Resigning, he was replaced by the son Red never had.

"I have to be careful about Vin Scully," Barber said. "He's my boy." The protege replied: "He became like a father to me in every way."

Scully joined Red in 1950. "Near the end of the season, Boston, it's dark," he said. The Dodgers needed to win. "To Brooklyn, he made that tempest a symbol of time running out." Rain neared. Brooklyn took the lead. "If the Dodgers could retire the side in the fifth, keeping their edge, the game was official." The first two men made out. Rain pelted Braves Field. "Red described raindrops as Pee Wee took a grounder and threw to first. I'll never forget how, by that gentle power of his voice, he made the game come alive."

In late 1953, Brooklyn's weatherman became Allen's aide. A month later, surgery caused permanent deafness in one ear. "New league," he said, "I don't know the players, my head's like a sea." Manager Casey Stengel could be hard on young players. By contrast, one old gentleman might save another. "He knew without my mentioning it that something was wrong. He'd brief me, take all the time in the world." Photos show him standing next to Red's good ear.

NBC's Tom Gallery thought the lay preacher "a sanctimonious, Psalm-singing son of a bitch." Prim and distant, Red hated flaws and fools: "So different," said Harwell, "from his relaxed, Arthur Godfrey on-air image." Increasingly, that core turned public in the Bronx. "In Brooklyn, Red may have been the best ever," said Costas, "but later he turned dry, somewhat bitter, almost interior, nowhere as good as Mel."

Possibly, he simply missed being boss.

In 1964, the Yanks won a pennant on the next-to-last day. Shockingly, Mel was fired. "Red was not considered to do the Series [Phil Rizzuto was]," said a friend. "Not family." The Stripes' became dysfunctional. On September 22, 1966, the day Michael Burke became president, 413 pocked the last-placers' 65,010-seat park. Barber thought it "the perfect place for Burke to start, nowhere to go but up."

Red asked the WPIX TV director to pan the stands. No shot. He asked again. No go. "I later found out [Yanks media head] Perry Smith was in the control room. He told them not to show the seats." *Report,* Barber knew from teletype. "I don't know what the paid attendance is today, but whatever it is, it is the smallest crowd in the history of Yankee Stadium, and this crowd is the story, not the game."

Next week, asked to breakfast, he expected a new pact. Burke skipped sugar: "There is no reason to be talking pleasantries. We have decided not to renew you." Axed, Red was freed. "I'd become a servant to the microphone. On my own, I'd have gone back for who knows how long." The next quarter-century became a valentine: seven books, dozens of radio/TV events, and feathers in the cap for excellence.

In 1978, with Allen, this mix of "old courtliness and the flintiness of the utterly independent man," wrote Halberstam, became the first Voice to enter Cooperstown. In 1981, Red began each-Friday commentary on National Public Radio's "Morning Edition." Depending on date and mood, he traced cats, cooking, squirrels eating birdseed, or crape myrtle blooming in his Tallahassee yard.

Once Barber segued from 1984 Vice-Presidential candidate Geraldine Ferraro to Mary, Queen of Scots, to caddies at the British Open. Time of discourse: three minutes. No egg timer needed.

"Red's notion was that education continues no matter what your age," said NPR host Bob Edwards. "A man who remembered when cars and airplanes were new inventions found some new marvel each day." The real marvel died October 10, 1992, jarring the show's 3.5 million listeners. "Fridays will never be the same."

In a eulogy, Steve Kelly said that "some people are meant to be immortal. Their voices and their visions are meant to continue from generation to generation"—bringing letters to language; and shading, sport. Owning himself, Red could not be bought.

"Do a little plowing," Barber quoted cousin Eula of Boston, Georgia, "because if you stop, you're gone." We had him for 84 years. He never did.

RED BARBER

LONGEVITY:	10	33 years.
CONTINUITY:	8	Cincinnati N.L. 1934–38; Brooklyn N.L. 1939–53; New York A.L. 1954–66.
NETWORK:	10	World Series 1935, 1939–42, 1947, 1949, and 1951 (Mutual), 1936–38 (NBC Radio), 1948 and 1952 (NBC TV). All-Star Game 1938 (NBC) and 1939–41 and 1943 (Mutual). National Public Radio 1981–92.
KUDOS:	10	Cooperstown 1978. NSSA Hall of Fame 1973. ASA 1984, Radio, National Association of Broadcasters, Florida, and two other Halls. *TSN* 1939 "Announcer of the Year." George Polk Award 1979. George Foster Peabody Award 1990.
LANGUAGE:	10	"All I did was speak correctly and try not to get my tenses fouled up." Linked "walkin' in tall cotton," Carlyle, and Thoreau.
POPULARITY:	10	Brooklyn Chamber of Commerce Citizen of Year. Borough chairman, record-breaking 1944 Red Cross War Fund drive.
PERSONA:	10	Apotheosized Flatbush more than Baseball Bill Bendix.
VOICE:	10	Lilting, elegant.
KNOWLEDGE:	10	Stickler for preparation.
MISCELLANY:	7	Son of a teacher and locomotive engineer.
TOTAL:	95	(fifth place). *Scores based on 1–10 point scale.*

ROSEY ROWSWELL

Ask a seven-year-old about baseball. He likes the soul-crushing poke—the homer. Announcers like it, too. Mel Allen cried, "Going, going . . . gone!" Harry Caray closed a million bars. "It might be . . . It could be . . . It is!" Harry Kalas yelps, "It's outta here!" Aunt Minnie dwarfed them all.

One day in 1938, the Pirates' play-by-play man unveiled his calling card. A drive neared the scoreboard. Out of the blue Albert K. ("Rosey") Rowswell yapped, "Get upstairs, Aunt Minnie, and raise the window. Here she [baseball] comes!" An aide dropped a pane of glass. To listeners it meant the window.

"Too bad," Rosey sobbed. "She tripped over a garden hose. Aunt Minnie never made it." She never did, but was never heard to grouse.

Rowswell was a humorist, poet, and banquet speaker—"a 112-pound toothpick [a.k.a. 'Hercules' or 'Muscles']. Gentle, sensitive," said Bob Prince—

who wrote "Should You Go First" after musing with wife Gyp what each would do *sans* other. It ended: "I'll want to know each step you take / That I may walk the same / For some day down that lonely road / You'll hear me call your name."

From 1909 to 1929, Rosey was secretary of Pittsburgh's Third Presbyterian Church. Baseball as religion: he prayed at the Pirates' hull, and Boston, New York, and Philadelphia. In 1936, the Bucs made him Voice—to Prince, "the logical choice. There were big-league clubs, but to Rosey only one big-league hub."

Most play-by-play is local: a scout sets the style. At Fenway, Curt Gowdy tracked Fred Hoey's: keep it simple. Rowswell rooted for the home team: Not winning was a shame. "America's [self-styled] most partial baseball broadcaster" set an alarm clock for Pennsylvania, east Ohio, and West Virginia: housewives began dinner when Rosey signed off.

Once 5,000 women listeners stormed WWSW to see him re-create. "Even schoolkids knew his sayings," said skipper Billy Meyer. The Pirates were "Picaroonies." Like Barber, his bases were "FOB: [Full of Bucs/Brooklyns]." A "doozie marooney" (extra-baser) might clear the sacks, a "dipsy doodle" (K) fan the side. "Oh, my aching back," he said, losing. Winning was yummier. "I'll be home soon," he told Gyp. "Put on the lamb chops now."

In 1939, Aunt Minnie commenced at Forbes, in an Austin car, at a KDKA TV exhibit. "Later people claimed that they were her," said Prince. "Actually, Rosey invented her" to mask Bucs stench. Silver linings: Lloyd Waner's .316 average, brother Paul's third batting title, and Rip Sewell's blooper, or "Eephus," pitch. Ralph Kiner hit 294 homers, leading the N.L. each year from 1946 to 1952. After his last at-bat, half the crowd would leave.

One afternoon a Bucs part-owner shared the mike. "I'd like to see Ralph improve a little on his showing so far this afternoon," Bing Crosby said. "Against Rush he couldn't do much. . . . Maybe he can do a little better! [vs. Doyle Lade]. And he did! . . ." Rosey, interrupting: "There goes a long one—open the—it may go in there! Aunt Minnie! [shouting] Boy, it goes clear out over the scoreboard." Der Bingle, barely audible: "Oh, what a blast . . ." Rosey: "Over into Schenley Park, a long homer for Ralph Kiner—his first of the 1948 season!" Crosby: "Oh, did he . . ." Rowswell: "Let's hope that it's the first of 61!"

Bing seemed obtuse. "Sounds great," laughed Prince, "but you haven't had the mike for 10 seconds." Rowswell was as daft. "My Lord," Bob said, "do you know who you just stole the mike from?" Years later Bob shook his head. "When you upstage Bing Crosby, you've really pulled the cork."

Another part-owner midwifed Prince's 1948 hiring. "Tom Johnson insisted," said broadcaster Ted Patterson. "Rosey said, 'I'm afraid of him, he's brash,'" busting the rookie to reading ads. Finally Bob cornered him. "What do you have against me?"

"You're nothing but a fresh punk."

"Look, I'm not after your job. All I want to do is succeed you when you retire."

In time, Prince loved the Rosey Ramble. "We'd be losing, and Rowswell'd start talking poetry and crazy sayings." An inning might star a recipe, the weather, and local zoo. "It's not just play-by-play that matters," Rosey said. "What counts is what's said between pitches." *Any* pitch might hatch Aunt Minnie.

For a while aides dropped glass. Too messy, felt Bob. "So up comes a dumbwaiter's tray with bells, nuts, and bolts—*anything* for noise." Prince dropped the tray on command. "On radio, it resembled an earthquake. All the time you're hearing, 'Poor Aunt Minnie. She didn't make it.' " Meanwhile, Bob, on all fours, retrieved material "in case the *next* guy hit one."

In 1954, the Picaroonies added weekend road TV to WWSW Radio's 20-station network. Rowswell died of a heart attack February 6, 1955.

A plaque in the Bucs' press box hails the "Pittsburgh Pirates' first announcer." Memory ties the dipsy doodle, doozie marooney, and putting lamb chops on the stove.

Open the window, Aunt Minnie, and don't forget that garden hose.

ROSEY ROWSWELL

LONGEVITY:	7	19 years.
CONTINUITY:	10	Pittsburgh N.L. 1936–54.
NETWORK:	1	World Series 1938 (NBC).
KUDOS:	2	Gold watch, given by 1925 champion Bucs.
LANGUAGE:	9	Ripley's "Believe It Or Not" hailed speaking 400 words a minute.
POPULARITY:	10	Dedicated many hits to shut-ins.
PERSONA:	10	Aunt Minnie's puppeteer.
VOICE:	4	Crackling.
KNOWLEDGE:	10	"Knew ball," said Billy Meyer, "better than our players."
MISCELLANY:	7	Dead air could mean Rosey walking around his chair to bring team luck.
TOTAL:	70	(91st place).

JIM BRITT

Chemistry fuses molecules. Jim Britt fused nouns and verbs and terms. "No broadcaster better used the language," said Ken Coleman. Many thought Britt savvy. Some felt him snooty, panning the average Joe.

"There are 27,000 *persons* here today," Jim observed.

"Jim, you always say *persons*," said Coleman. "Is there a reason you don't say *people* or *fans*?"

"Yes, Ken, *people* is correct," Britt stiffened. "And *fans* are correct. But *persons* is *more* correct."

English is said to be mistaught in public school. Britt taught much about the vagaries of public life.

By 1921, the 11-year-old son of a Burroughs Adding Machine Co. CEO had lived in San Francisco, Erie, Baltimore, and Denver. In 1935, the high school debating, public speaking, and dramatics teacher graduated in prelaw from the University of Detroit. Dad made computers and calculators. Britt now calculated what to do. He got married and earned a USC law degree, but never took the bar.

"Why not?" a writer said.

"Because I'm an idiot." Actually, he preferred mike to bench.

Britt's radio career began in South Bend, Indiana. In 1937, Russ Hodges, working in nearby Gary, told of a job at WBEN Buffalo. Soon Jim did the Triple-A Bisons. Roger Baker was their swell. "They'd recreate the same game," said partner Leo Egan. "Roger stayed a half-inning behind in case the wire broke. Not Jim." The man in a hurry finished 20 minutes ahead.

Egan joined the Yankee Network, which dumped Frank Frisch in late 1939. "I'd helped get Frank's job. Now I help pick his successor." Arriving, Britt confronted its daily "Superman" show. "Didn't matter who was up at 5:15," he said. "It pre-empted us. We came back at 5:30." Usually, Jim signed off: "Remember, if you can't take part in a sport, be one anyway, will you?" In 1942, he joined the Navy. "If you can't take part in the war, buy bonds anyway, will you?"

Britt attacked enemy-held Nauru Island, hit another U.S. plane, and barely remade his Pacific base. "Our mission had only eight survivors." Baseball seemed a lark. In 1946, he returned to Boston's new flagship, WHDH. Said Coleman: "After having guys fill in from 1942 to '45, you were glad to have him back."

The forties Sox and Braves shunned live away coverage. "Tom Hussey did most of our re-creations," said Egan, "no crowd noise, just 'Ball one, ball two.'" Hussey was a warm glass of milk. Britt's martini mixed twist and taste. Their post-war clubs left New England with a hangover.

The 1946 Braves made the first division for the first time since 1934. Drawing 1,455,439, more than they had or would, the '48ers won a first-since-'14 pennant. Cleveland won the six-game Classic. "Take away Game Five [Boston, 11–5]," said skipper Billy Southworth, "and we scored six runs all Series." In a doubleheader, Ted Williams often had that many RBI.

In 1946, No. 9 whacked Fenway's longest-ever blast off the hat of a construction engineer. "The sun was right in our eyes," said Joseph Boucher. "They said it bounced a dozen rows higher, but after it hit my head, I wasn't interested." The Red Sox waved their first flag since the Wilson Administration. "A year ago I'm at war," Britt said. "Now I'm doing the World Series [for Mutual, with Arch McDonald]."

In Game Seven, St. Louis' Enos Slaughter got an eighth-inning single. With two out, Harry Walker hit to left-center. Leon Culberson relayed to shortstop Johnny Pesky, who—at this point, views cleave—was/was not shocked to see Enos running and did/did not hesitate before throwing toward the plate.

"It can't be!" cried Jim. "He's coming home! The throw . . . He scores [the winning 4–3 run]!" For Boston, the play began a half-century of Murphy's Law (if anything can go wrong, it will) dwarfing the Law of Averages (life is fair; things even out).

In 1948, the Sox lost a playoff. A year later they blew the last day to New York. "With our team, we should have won three Series in four [1946–49] years," said Britt—to the *Globe*'s Ray Fitzgerald, "the biggest name in Boston radio at a time when Boston meant the game."

Power made him prickly. A Northeasterly blew a blast back toward the infield. "Jim yells, 'That ball is gone!' " said Egan. "But no—it's an out."

Another hitter went long. "Britt yells, 'It's gone!' Same thing: The wind blows it back."

Later the Sox again buzzed the fence. "'It's smashed,' he said, 'and I don't care what *anybody* says, it's gone!' " Leo shook his head. "*Another* out, and now Jim's berserk."

Once a hitter cleared Braves Field's right-field inner wall. "It's way outta here!" Britt said. "It's gone *under* the fence!" Egan began laughing. Off-air Jim asked why.

"You said, 'Under the fence,' " said Leo.

"I did not, did not."

Thirty years later Egan reworked the dialogue. "Like a little kid, Jim wouldn't admit he made a mistake." His real "mistake" was not preserving what he had.

In 1950, leaving WHDH, Boston's N.L. team returned to the Yankee Network: Torn, Britt must choose. "He picked the Braves," said Coleman, "which was a terrible misjudgment about the relative popularity of the teams."

Increasingly, the Braves of Boston since 1876 "played to the grounds help," said new Sox Voice Curt Gowdy. In April 1953, they left for Milwaukee. "Jim's two teams were gone," mused Ken. Down, he soon was out.

Britt did 1954–57 Indians TV. Bobby Avila was the All-Star second baseman. Local dialect preferred Ah-VEE-la. Jim liked AH-vee-la. One night sponsor Ian Dowie, like *row* or *dough,* asked him to convert. Britt smiled: "All right with me, Mr. Dewey."

Retrieving WHDH, Jim hosted bowling and "Dateline Boston," was axed, and moved to Detroit, St. Petersburg, and Sarasota. "The Sox' 'what if'

JIM BRITT

LONGEVITY:	5	14 years.
CONTINUITY:	7	Boston A.L. 1940–42 and 1946–50; Boston N.L. 1940–42 and 1946–52; Cleveland A.L. 1954–57.
NETWORK:	6	World Series 1946, 1948, and 1950 (Mutual), 1949 and 1951 (NBC TV), and 1950 (CBS TV). All-Star Game 1942 and 1946 (Mutual) and 1951 (NBC TV).
KUDOS:	3	Great Heart Award, cancer charity Jimmy Fund. Brotherhood Award, Massachusetts Committee of Catholics, Protestants, and Jews.
LANGUAGE:	10	Grammarian's delight.
POPULARITY:	9	Fit Athens of America.
PERSONA:	8	*Roget's.*
VOICE:	10	Silken.
KNOWLEDGE:	9	Knew game, not himself.
MISCELLANY:	8	Aired NFL, Notre Dame, and Rose and Sugar Bowl and Blue–Gray Game two, seven, and four times, respectively.
TOTAL:	75	(78th place).

haunted him," said Egan. He braved divorce, unemployment, and arrests for drunkenness.

Britt died, at 70, December 28, 1980, in Monterey, California. "In truth," wrote Fitzgerald, "life had turned its back on him a long time ago."

BYRUM SAAM

To Dixie, the Lost Cause means the recent unpleasantness; Baby Boomers, long-playing record; Britt's Red Sox, Twentieth Century. To Byrum Fred Saam, it topped even a Burma Road of malapropisms.

- "Hello, Byrum Saam," his first game began, "this is everybody speaking."
- "[Outfielder Bob] Johnson is going back. He hits his head against the wall. He reaches down, picks it up, and throws in to second base."
- In 1959, Mel Allen introduced him on NBC's Series: "And here's the amiable, affable, able Byrum Saam." Distracted, By misheard him. "Right you are, Mel," he replied.

"He'd say the wrong thing," said colleague Richie Ashburn, "so innocent, then wonder why people laughed." Less jolly: calling more baseball defeats than anyone. "Here we are," he would say, "rolling into the eighth inning." Making Cooperstown, By deserved a Purple Heart.

Saam's 1938–54 Athletics and 1939–49 and 1951–75 Phillies finished 3,239–4,395. "Simple," he allowed. "You focus on things beyond the field." A brawl could roil the stands. Shibe Park hosted the first A.L. night game. Its roof press box made some tie rope around a waist. "It wasn't easy. You're getting killed and everybody's at the shore" getting a cheesesteak, beer, and burn.

The Ft. Worth native attended high school with Ben Hogan, played hoops with Sammy Baugh at Texas Christian University, and did football P.A. "One day I'm running on the sidelines when a local radio owner hears me. He figures, 'This kid's better than anyone I've got.' " By rolled into the Southwest Conference, aired on CBS's "Football Roundup."

Ted Husing recommended him to 50,000-watt outlet WCCO Minneapolis, which requested a baseball audition, putting Saam in a bind. "I'd never done baseball," he said, re-creating the 1935 Series. Getting it, By transferred to the University of Minnesota, began the Triple-A Millers, and did Temple football by 1937. Next year began the bigs.

WCAU listeners soon felt a bond. "Would you talk a little louder?" wrote one woman. "My radio battery is getting weak." Shibe Park's turf was large; feel, cozy; boo-birds, of brass. "What can I say?" By reasoned. "Vulgar fans beat no fans." In 1941, they ogled Jim Britt's part-Gibraltar and part-child.

On September 27, Boston played at 21st Street and Lehigh Avenue—or would have, without rain. No one had hit .400 since 1930. Williams, 23, was batting .3995—.400 in the record book. Manager Joe Cronin vainly urged him to skip the last-day doubleheader. The Kid went 6-for-8: One double broke the loud-speaker horn. "Baseball history! No backing in!" cried Saam of .406. John Wayne was never more compelling on film.

In 1950, Philadelphia's N.W. Ayer & Son ad agency ended the road re-creation: for the first time, each team did its entire schedule live. Kicker: no station could handle inventory. The A's stayed at then-flagship WIBG, the Phils choosing WPEN. "[By] had to weigh a close relationship with the kindest man who ever lived," picking A's manager, owner and patriarch Connie Mack.

Lost Cause: Saam placed last. By contrast, the 1950 Nationals won their first flag in 35 years. "It must have bothered him," said Ashburn. "You do the Phillies so long, then leave the year they win." In late 1954, the A's moved to Kansas City. A year later Saam rejoined the Phils.

"I hated Mr. Mack leaving," he said, "but I'd missed the Phillies." Together they approached their Gallipoli—1964.

Nineteen sixty-four. The phrase stands alone, needs no explanation, so affixed to Philadelphia that even non-Quakers grasp the spoken tone reserved for a drunken spouse or wayward child.

For 73 straight days the team gripped first place. Rookie Richie Allen hit 29 dingers. Chris Short went 18–11. Jim Bunning (19–8) no-hit the Mets on Father's Day. "He gets it! He gets it! A perfect game!" Saam said on WFIL. On September 20, Philly led by 6 1/2 games, then aped a horse who, lacking food and water, nears the finish line in shock and fear.

The Phillies started Short and Bunning eight of their last 12 games. Ten straight losses wrote *finis*. The Reds and Cardinals led by a game on closing day. "We beat Cincy, the Cards lose to the Mets, and it's a three-way playoff," said Saam. "They win, and get the pennant." Phils romp, 10–0. Didn't matter. St. Louis: 11–5.

"It's a good thing I got to do a network Series on my own," By joked. "After a while I knew I'd never get there with the Phils."

"Through it all, the great thing about Saam was that even as opposing hitters were playing ping pong off the outfield fence," said the *Philadelphia Inquirer*'s Frank Dolson, "he would still leave with you with a smile on your face."

Egg followed 1964. In 1969, By visited expansion Montreal. "You know, 85 percent of the people up here speak French. But they're nice people, anyway." One night he broadcast from San Francisco. "And now for all you guys scoring in bed." Ashburn laughed a quarter-century later. "Imagine *that* stir! How could you not love the guy?"

In 1971, Saam moved to Veterans Stadium. A flaw was *faux* grass. "It's hard for anyone to pick up the baseball on artificial turf," said partner Harry Kalas. "That was especially true when By got eye trouble." One batter went deep. "There's a ground ball to short," Saam began, "and it's gone!"

By 1975, he faced that vision thing. "I should have had cataract surgery, but I was leaving, so let it slide." By retired that October. Next year's irony renewed 1950's: Phils win! Richie had his pal call the N.L. East clincher. "Thirty-eight years and no winner. Damn right he deserved a title."

In 1990, Saam rolled into another: a Hall of Fame reception evoked his

BYRUM SAAM

LONGEVITY:	10	38 years.
CONTINUITY:	10	Philadelphia A.L. 1938–54; Philadelphia N.L. 1939–49 and 1951–75.
NETWORK:	2	World Series 1959 and 1965 (NBC Radio).
KUDOS:	8	Cooperstown 1990. Philadelphia Hall of Fame Broadcast Pioneers 1993.
LANGUAGE:	8	Sober, yet surreal. "He'd crack us up between innings," said Kalas. "But he'd been raised to be serious on the air."
POPULARITY:	10	Hear the latest?
PERSONA:	10	Mrs. Malaprop's spouse a.k.a. "The Man of a Zillion Words."
VOICE:	10	"He never projected pessimism," said the 1954 book *The Mackmen*.
KNOWLEDGE:	10	Nearly 8,000 games rubbed off.
MISCELLANY:	8	Did 13 no-nos. Nineteen teams placed last. Called football Eagles, University of Pennsylvania, Blue–Gray Game, and Cotton and Sugar Bowl.
TOTAL:	86	(30th place).

quirky, falling-off-the-turnip-truck charm. Each napkin read, "Right you are, Mel!" At that moment the Lost Cause seemed triumphant, after all.

BERT WILSON

From Sheffield Avenue, the top deck opens, putting geography in relief. Charters import pilgrims from the far outposts of Wrigleyville. Ivy cloaks the brick outfield wall. Bleachers rise to form a deep V. The scoreboard boasts line scores, lineups, and yardarm flags of N.L. cities and standings, falling or rising daily.

Afterward a banner flies a white "W" (on blue backdrop) or blue "L" (against white). "I Don't Care *Who* Wins As Long As It's the Cubs!" caroled Bert Bertram Puckett. He already knew the score.

From 1944 to 1955, Wilson held a pencil ("I keep it in my hand all game. Not to write with, just to know it's there") and quaffed beer ("I'd see him," said Jack Brickhouse, "and by the third he's crocked") and broadcast alone. ("I'd say, 'Get help!' " mused Saam. "But he kept doing ads, play-by-play, color. Maybe he had more stamina than the rest of us.") Maybe he liked to talk.

Born in Ohio, Bert moved to Cedar Rapids, played the trumpet, and entered the University of Iowa. "I'd sing and broadcast on its station [WSUI]." At 20, he junked engineering for commercial radio. No local outlet had baseball. Wilson convinced WMT. A release read: "[He] sat on a housetop across from the center-field fence bringing listeners play-by-play."

By 1943, he did hockey, hoops, roller derby, Iowa football, Indianapolis 500, and Double-A baseball. Pat Flanagan needed an aide. An ex-sponsor suggested Bert audition. "Despite laryngitis," WIND gusted, "he managed to talk his way in. Retiring, Pat yielded the [city's] number one sportscasting job." Soon Chicago brayed "I Don't Care *Who* Wins. . . ." Wilson, of course, did.

To Brickhouse, he "was a souped-up Elson." The Midwest Cheering School of Milo Hamilton, Jack Quinlan, Harry Caray, and Vince Lloyd, among others, began with IDCW2ALAITC. His first-yearers began 1–13. Bert "almost went back to my trumpet." Instead, in 1945, MVP Phil Cavarretta hit a league-high .355, Andy Pafko had 110 RBI, and the Cubs won a pennant.

"At the team victory party," James Enright wrote, "[manager] Charlie Grimm had a pair of shears. Everybody who had a necktie on contributed. He had a quilt made." Soon its fabric, like Grimm's Fairy Tale, tore.

"It was just a tease," a writer dubbed the World Series vs. Detroit. "You knew we'd lose Game Seven." The 598–786 Cubs lost for the next decade. Bert vowed: "We'll light a candle, not curse the dark." His eternal flame wafted from the Kansas City Monarchs. Ernie Banks homered for the first time September 20, 1953.

The Cubs' future two-time MVP/Good Humor Man hit 290 of his 512 homers at Wrigley. "He's the real McCoy," Wilson said in 1954. Most were illusory.

"I've had a good chance to see all the promising young rookies who'll be fighting for a job this summer, and believe me, they look great," Bert claimed, dreamily, one day next March.

"The Cubs' infield generally is recognized as one of the best in the big leagues already, and there are several outfielders who look like real major leaguers. Pitching is a cinch to be much better, and the catching department was given a big boost when Harry Chiti [who would hit .231], a fellow built like Gabby Hartnett [and played like Gabby Hayes], came back from the service. Yes, it looks like a very interesting season for the Chicago Cubs this year."

This "one of the best . . . real major leaguers . . . very interesting" team finished 72–81. It also finished what business manager Jim Gallagher termed "the biggest Cubs fan I've ever known." At Wrigley Field, hearts break every year.

BERT WILSON

LONGEVITY:	4	12 years.
CONTINUITY:	10	Chicago N.L. 1944–55.
NETWORK:	1	1950s Mutual.
KUDOS:	3	Local, not national.
LANGUAGE:	7	Didactic. "There's no such things as a neutral Cubs fan. If you like the Cubs, I make sense. If you don't, you won't tune in anyway."
POPULARITY:	10	Climbed up Cubs' down staircase.
PERSONA:	10	Pre-Banks Mr. Cub.
VOICE:	8	Tuneful.
KNOWLEDGE:	10	"He was always around the park," said Brickhouse. "You could bury him at Wrigley Field."
MISCELLANY:	6	Ham radio operator. In traffic jam, once honked SOS on car horn to driver a block away.
TOTAL:	69	(93rd place).

Bert Wilson's heart stopped beating November 5, 1955. IDCW2ALAITC was 44 years old.

WAITE HOYT

In 1960, Bob Costas, 8, moved from Long Island to Los Angeles. The car radio became a trip-tik. Bob Prince meant western Pennsylvania; Earl Gillespie, the upper Midwest; Harry Caray, Cardinal Nation. By Nevada, Costas heard Vin Scully. "We can hear the Dodgers," dad said. "We're almost there."

In Cincinnati, Bob found why Mark Twain vowed to come for the apocalypse because the city lagged 20 years behind the time. "Given that," said Ohioan and Hall of Fame librarian Lee Allen, "you marvel how it looked ahead."

Firsts include professional team (1869 Red Stockings); charter member of first N.L. and American Association year (1876 and '82, respectively); dual nine-inning no-hitter (1917, Fred Toney and Jim Vaughn); park leased to the Negro League ('20s Cuban Stars); and night game (1935).

Another precedent stirred Costas. Unlike any announcer before or since, Waite Hoyt's tense was past.

The ordinary mikeman says, "Ground ball to the shortstop, who fields it and throws to first." Whatever else he was, the Reds' 1942–65 Voice was not ordinary: "The shortstop fielded it, threw to first, and the runner beat the throw." Why: "*accuracy!*" he rasped. "As I speak to you, what happened a moment ago is gone."

Hoyt grew up in Brooklyn, pitched for Erasmus Hall High School, and in 1913 failed a Dodgers tryout. Next year pop drove to the *Giants* Manhattan office. "I couldn't sign a contract," said Waite, 15, "but dad did to make it legal."

Will Wedge coined the term "aristocrat of baseball." Hoyt first seemed a commoner, making seven stops in the minor leagues. In 1918, the lefty finally pitched an inning in the bigs. Later he studded a Lynn, Massachusetts, semipro team, was signed by A.L. Boston, and joined A.L. New York in 1921.

"The secret to success as a pitcher is getting a job with the Yankees," Hoyt said. The minstrel's son also composed, danced and sang at the Palace Theater. The road was more extempore. Once Waite trailed roommate Joe Dugan to a church. "Hi, pal," said Hoyt, surprising him. What gave?

"I've tried everything else," said Dugan, lighting a candle. "I thought maybe with this I'll get some help with my hitting."

"Then light one for me!" Hoyt said. "I'm pitching today."

Dugan did. Waite was shelled. "What happened?" he asked. Joe looked down. "Some bloody Protestant sneaked in and blew the candle out."

Hoyt bounced to Detroit, A.L. Philadelphia, Brooklyn, the Polo Grounds, Pittsburgh, and again Flatbush, where in the dialect of its borough a paper screamed "Hert Hoite!" of an injury. In 1938, retiring, he signed with Brown and Williamson Tobacco Company. "They put me on [WMCA New York] 'Grandstand and Bandstand.' I'd developed a name, and they thought I could help sales."

The 1939 Yankees began daily coverage. Sponsor Wheaties KO'd an audition. "They didn't think ex-ballplayers had enough vocabulary to do a decent job." Umpire George Moriarty knew better. "You're out of your element," Waite told him, disputing a call. "You should be a traffic cop so you could stand in the middle of the street with a badge on your chest and insult people with impunity." *Element? Impunity?* From a *jock?* On the *field?*

Red Barber prized anyone who never split an infinitive. In 1940, he named Waite Dodgers pre/post-game host/analyst. "He'd never done baseball, but I thought he would take to it [color] naturally." Hoyt did, wanting more. By late 1941, WLW and WSAI Cincinnati aired the Reds. His agency, William Morris, called WKRC. "They wanted baseball, too," he said, "and were looking for play-by-play."

John Gunther noted Cincinnati's "stately and also sleepy quality." Waite was a night owl. The Rhineland closed after dark. "I didn't know if I'd like it," he confessed, "but found a happiness that I'd never known"—except that one is the loneliest number. From 1946 to 1951, Hoyt announced by himself. "I did everything, even Burger Beer ads," cadging plots and tales and Yankees past and Reds present.

"He had a million stories," said general manager Gabe Paul. "Cobb and Speaker and Ruth—Hoyt ran with Babe before he stopped drinking." One cited Ruth's 1948 death, of cancer. Hoyt and Dugan helped carry his coffin from St. Patrick's. "Lord," moaned Joe, sweltering, "I'd give my right arm for a beer."

Murmured Waite: "So would the Babe."

Hoyt would have given his left arm for a team. "Allen and Barber were *good* news broadcasters." He smiled, vaguely. "I was a *bad* news broadcaster." Reds president Warren Giles once called him on the carpet. "Why can't you be enthusiastic? Look at Bert Wilson. Why don't you cheer like him?"

Hoyt flushed. "Why *shouldn't* Wilson cheer? The Cubs've got stars. Last year ['45] won the pennant. But us! Your top hitter's a lousy .267! Your best pitcher's won eight games! What is there to cheer?" Not much, as it occurred.

The fault was not Crosley Field's, leading the league in smallest size (27,603) and turf (387 feet, center) and most brown-bagging visitors. Liking the snug feel, Waite loathed the rooftop booth. "It was open. When it rained, you got flooded," lightning striking before the team.

The 1944–55 Reds missed the first division. Good news flared belatedly: the '56ers hit a record-tying 221 homers. By 1960, the club was "[again] a shabby bunch," said Hoyt. Next year it broke 5–10, won nine straight, and neared a first flag since 1940. In August, Cincy visited Los Angeles. "[Don] Drysdale [thrice] knocked Frank Robinson, then hit him and got tossed." A sweep retook first—for good.

Robby became MVP. Vada Pinson hit .343. The Reds clinched a tie September 26. "We fly back," said manager Fred Hutchinson, "drive downtown, and thousands line the road." Carolers packed Fountain Square. Loudspeakers blared Dodgers-Bucs play-by-play. At 11:26 P.M., L.A. was eliminated, uncorking joy in Lynchburg and Loudonville and Springdale and Sardinia.

Shakespeare said, "The past is prologue." The Series was ugly postlude. Whitey Ford opened, 2–0. The Reds' Joey Jay countered, 6–2. Games Four–Five sent Cincy packing, 7–0 and 13–5. Hoyt manned NBC Radio. The secret to success *still* involved the Yanks. "They called us ragamuffins," Waite said. "Not much talent, but heart. The problem is that even heart gets old."

The '61 Reds were "a conglomeration of castoffs who banded together for one last stand," said an official. Waite's ended by cutting a 1965 record, "Waite Hoyt's Stories in the Rain." The team held a Day September 5. A year later Wiederman became Reds beer sponsor. Hoyt, 66, joined Burger's publicity staff. "I'm still telling stories, just now to groups, not on the air."

The past tense still went deep. "There was the pitch! Snider belted it to left field! Bell went back and couldn't get it!" On August 25, 1984, the present went down swinging. Waite died, of heart trouble. He was 85 years old.

WAITE HOYT

LONGEVITY:	9	26 years.
CONTINUITY:	10	Brooklyn N.L. 1940–41; Cincinnati N.L. 1942–65.
NETWORK:	1	World Series 1961 (NBC Radio).
KUDOS:	7	Cooperstown 1969, inducted as 237–182 pitcher.
LANGUAGE:	7	The way we were.
POPULARITY:	10	Strangers asked for rain delay yarns.
PERSONA:	10	Cranky, but beloved.
VOICE:	6	Bristling.
KNOWLEDGE:	10	Aired "inside baseball" quarter-century before term—and N.L.'s first radio/TV simulcast (1952).
MISCELLANY:	8	Part-time thirties mortician. "I'm knocking 'em dead on Sixth Avenue [stage] while my partner is laying 'em out in Westchester."
TOTAL:	78	(62nd place).

RUSS HODGES

Almost everyone knows where they were when the Japanese attacked Pearl Harbor, Franklin Roosevelt died, Harry Truman upset Tom Dewey, and Bobby Thomson swung. Russ Hodges did.

"It made him," said colleague Jim Woods. "Say Russ, you think that day." Like December 7, 1941, Thomson's October 3, 1951, homer froze in amber. "The most famous sports moment of all time," added ESPN's Jon Miller. "Hodges made it last."

On August 11, Russ's New York Giants trailed Brooklyn by 13 1/2 games. Retrieve the wonderwork of The Shot Heard 'Round the World.

"Making the homer so dramatic was their rivalry," Hodges said a decade later. The teams played 22 games yearly. Radio/TV coursed through the city. The '51 Jints finished 37-7. On September 28, they tied the Dodgers at 94–58. Both won twice to force a best-of-three series. "Great battle, a city throbbing," mused Russ. "A world focused on the playoff."

It began in Flatbush: Giants, 3–1. Next day changed place and score: Bums, 10–0. A schoolboy knows Game Three's script. At 3:58 P.M., behind 4–2, Thomson hit a ninth-inning, two-on, one-out pitch. "Branca throws.

There's a long drive!" Hodges bayed on WMCA Radio. "It's going to be, I believe! The Giants win the pennant! The Giants win the pennant! The Giants win the pennant! The Giants win the pennant! Bobby Thomson hits into the lower deck of the left-field stands! The Giants win the pennant! And they're going crazy! They are going crazy! Oh-oh!"

Confetti flew. Brooklyn staggered to its clubhouse. Eddie Stanky wrestled Giants skipper Leo Durocher to the ground. "I don't believe it! I don't believe it! I do not believe it!" said Russ, noise thick enough to chew. "Bobby Thomson hit a line drive into the lower deck of the left-field stands, and the whole place is going crazy! The Giants—[owner] Horace Stoneham is now a winner—the Giants won it by a score of 5 to 4, and they're picking Bobby Thomson up and carrying him off the field!"

Few events were then recorded. Even fewer laymen had machines. Brooklyn restaurant waiter Laurence Goldberg taped the ninth. "Ahead, he thought he'd enjoy Russ cry," said colleague Harwell. "Later he sent Russ the tape." Chesterfield cigarettes released a record on "the most exciting moment in baseball history"—then/now, more honest than revisionism.

Some wrote that Russ screamed for 15 minutes before telling what happened. "For two minutes," said one, "he stood on his chair to chant 'The Giants win the pennant!' " Red Barber dubbed Hodges "unprofessional," to which Lon Simmons cried nuts. "He was dramatic, but gave the essentials," said his 1958–70 sidekick. "Score, meaning, who won." Russ lived off the shot for his final 20 years.

In 1978, Red and Mel Allen became the first Voices to enter Cooperstown. Hodges joined them in 1980, a pleasant but bromidic pick. "I know darned well I don't have a good radio voice," he said. On the other hand, "I know sports well."

A voting member ascribed Russ's choice to "the committee's New York tilt." That, likability, and the Miracle of Coogan's Bluff.

TV rules our cosmos. Radio ruled 1951's. "I happened to be doing TV for Thomson's shot," said Harwell. "What do I get? Anonymity! Russ gets immortality!" For a time he would have settled for a job.

Ironically, Russ's father, a Southern Railroad telegrapher, seemed to get a new one each year. "When he got promoted I'd move as a kid up the line." In 1928, at the University of Kentucky, Hodges broke an ankle playing football, became a spotter, and said a "few words on air. I was terrible, but got the bug bad." Graduating, he entered the University of

Cincinnati, passed the bar, but never practiced. "In those days, lawyers were jumping out of windows."

In 1932, the bug-bitten barrister cracked radio in Covington, Kentucky, then at WFBE Cincinnati. Barber's 1934 arrival put him on the street. Unfazed, Russ did Chicago baseball, boxing, and Big Ten football, then trekked to Class-B Charlotte. "Plus, I re-created all sorts of big-league games. For three years I didn't see a park."

Once Landis summoned him for contradicting an umpire. "I was so terrified," Hodges said, "I couldn't move from my chair." In 1942, he moved to Washington. "No flag, but finally I did games in person." That year, leaving the Army, the Yankees' Allen began listening to tapes.

Even a volcano needs a rest. "I called Arch [McDonald], who said Russ'd be a great assistant," said Mel. Soon they went drinking at Shor's. "We hit it off—marvelous chemistry. Before long Russ and I could almost read each other's mind."

They read through 1948. That offseason Hodges crossed the Harlem River. "While Barber gave his listeners corn-fed philosophy and humor," wrote Wells Twombly, "and Allen told you more about baseball than you cared to know, Hodges of the Giants told it the way it was."

The Polo Grounds fused pigeon stoops, bullpen shacks, and an oblong shape: 279 feet to left; 257 feet, right; center, ghostly 483. On May 25, 1951, Willie Mays reported from Triple-A Minneapolis. The rookie went hitless his first 12 ups. "What's wrong, son?" said Durocher, who heard him crying.

"Mister Leo, I can't play here," Mays, 20, moaned.

"I brought you here to do one thing—play center field. And as long as that uniform says 'New York Giants' and I'm the manager, you will be in center field every day." Next day he cleared the roof.

Brooklyn-born comic Phil Foster dubbed Thomson's homer "D-Day—Dat Day." The Giants lost the Series: Russ and Allen keyed NBC TV's 64-outlet network, including an affiliate in Matamoros, Mexico. Mays joined the Army, returning to rob Cleveland, over the shoulder, in the 1954 Classic opener. Dusty Rhodes pinch-homered to win Games One–Two. Each sired "Bye-bye baby!"—Russ's riposte to "How about that!"

Giants sweep: having called Rhodes "useless," Leo changed his mind. By 1957, Stoneham changed his about staying in New York. Page 1 of the New York *World-Telegram* mourned: "It's Official: Giants to Frisco." On September 29, the Giants lost to Pittsburgh, 9–1. For Hodges, moving day had truly come.

That year he hired Woods, recently fired by the Yankees. "Russ saved me. No one will ever know the guys that he gave money or advice." Jim pined to join him in California. Instead, Simmons—"I was local. Horace wanted that"— needled "The Fabulous Fat Man, more fabulous than fat." Columnist Charles McCabe mocked "their Madison Avenue style." Most liked the streamer of art, rib, and scheme.

"How ya doing, everybody?" Russ began each broadcast. Better than his duds.

"Ross/Akins asked him to take the labels out of his clothes," Lon laughed. "Said he was ruining their image."

The '59ers almost won the flag. Hodges and Allen called the first 1961 All-Star Game. We had been this way before: 1962 Bums–Jints playoff. L.A. led the decider, 4–2. "All that effort—for what?" Mays mused. A last-inning flurry: Giants, 6–4. Chemistry/memory: Russ and Mel shared a last Fall Classic.

Game Seven: New York, 1–0, ninth inning, two on and out. The Yanks' Ralph Terry had ceded Bill Mazeroski's 1960 Series-ending dinger. "[Now] my heart was in my throat," almost swallowing a 1–1 pitch. Willie McCovey lined to Bobby Richardson. The Giants reached their next Series in 1989. Hodges never called another network game.

The real Russ was an epicure of hooch. "If we win the game, we'll drink because we're happy," he told a colleague. "If we lose, we'll drink because we're sad. The only way we won't drink is if we tie." Curfew extended an extra-inning game. "We're just gonna break a rule." Mays broke the mold: 3,283 hits, .302 average, 11 Gold Gloves, 24 All-Star Games, and 660 homers. Hodges called the first 630. "He was like my older brother," said Willie. "I trusted him about everything."

In 1963, Russ released a memoir, *My Giants*. Mays became a two-time MVP (other, 1954) in 1965. That August 17 San Francisco's Juan Marichal hit vs. Sandy Koufax. Catcher John Roseboro "threw the ball back too close to my ear," said Marichal, clubbing him with the bat. "An amazing fight by base-ball standards," Hodges jibed. "Almost worthy of Coogan's Bluff."

In New York, Horace telecast the entire home schedule. He limited Frisco's—"No home coverage to protect attendance"—to nine games from Dodger Stadium. It worked till the A's invaded Oakland, divided the Bay. Russ retired in late 1970. "He'd had enough traveling," said Simmons. Be careful for what you ask.

"Russ agreed to do Giants P.R. and baseball for me when I was busy with the 49ers, but it wasn't the same." The chain smoker died April 19, 1971, at 61, of a heart attack—"really, a *broken* heart." Mays, weeping, was a pallbearer.

October 3, 1951. "Hartung down the line at third base, not taking any chances. Lockman with not too big of a lead at second, but he'll be running like the wind if Thomson hits one." Fate threw. Thomson hit one. "The Giants win the pennant!"

RUSS HODGES

LONGEVITY:	10	33 years.
CONTINUITY:	6	Cincinnati N.L. 1933; Chicago A.L. and N.L. 1935–37; Washington A.L. 1942–45; New York A.L. 1946–48; New York N.L. 1949–57; San Francisco N.L. 1958–70.
NETWORK:	7	N.L. playoff 1951 (CBS TV). World Series 1951, 1954, and 1962 (NBC TV). All-Star Game second 1959 and first 1961 (NBC TV).
KUDOS:	7	Cooperstown 1980. NSSA Hall of Fame 1975. *TSN* 1950 "Announcer of the Year."
LANGUAGE:	7	Spartan.
POPULARITY:	9	Affection, not adoration.
PERSONA:	9	Big brother.
VOICE:	7	Sonorant.
KNOWLEDGE:	10	Point-by-point.
MISCELLANY:	9	In 1949, one side of face paralyzed by Bell's Palsy. Reviving, did NBC football, Kentucky Derby, and Wednesday "Fight of the Week" and other bouts, including Cassius Clay's rematch with Sonny Liston.
TOTAL:	81	(51st place).

GORDON MCLENDON

For a time baseball's radio world yoked only big-league cities. By mid-century, 14 of 16 teams added a network for distant burgs and farms. Dayton heard the Reds. Champaign liked the Cubs. Like Sherman, the Senators seized the Shenandoah Valley. The problem was geography. America's baseball clock read 12 to 3.

"Every team was in the Northeast and Midwest quadrant," mused Lindsey Nelson. Coverage began in Maine, ended in Missouri, and ceased near Washington, D.C. By contrast, those west of the Mississippi and south of

Virginia got only the network All-Star Game and Series. "They were thirsting for coverage." A solution began brewing in The Old Scotchman's head.

The Scotchman was Gordon McLendon: born, Paris, Texas, 1921; county newspaper editor at 14; Yale '42, major, Oriental Languages. He called baseball and basketball, working with classmate and future actor James Whitmore. "A great voice," said Gordon, whose own rose and fell like a roller coaster.

In World War II, McLendon interpreted Japanese. Home, he began interpreting a map. "I knew from Armed Forces Radio how troops loved baseball. I also knew that people outside the Northeast wanted baseball"—and that the Federal Communications Commission wanted new outlets in the South, Southwest, and West.

Gordon did, too. "My dad had bought me a station in Oak Cliff [Texas, near Dallas]," he explained. In 1949, KLIF formed the Liberty Broadcasting System. In 1949, "Game of the Day" became its core. Each outlet sold ads, paid line charges, and gave him $10 a game. In return, baseball's first regular-season series marked for many a pivot in their lives.

"He had a minimum of cash and maximum of ingenuity," said Nelson. The upshot, quoting Liberty's station break: "America's second-largest network" —a stunning 458 affiliates by 1951.

"If we wanted to do a game from Detroit, interview a guy in Cleveland, Gordon'd say okay," aide Jerry Doggett chuckled. His sole cost was salary—and $27.50 for Western Union. "Most games were re-created," mused another Voice, Bud Blattner. "Without leaving the studio, McLendon *made* $4,000 each game."

To seem live, he mixed two general and two loud crowd turntables in studio. Another fillip: local color. "We tape accents at, say, Fenway Park, then use them for the Sox," said Gordon. He found that the men's room sired a grand P.A. echo chamber. Each day an employee in the john simulated the effect.

Once Nelson re-created a game from Griffith Stadium. Entering a booth, he said in studio, "is the President of the Liberty Broadcasting System, Gordon McLendon."

"Ah, yes, Washington [not saying he was there]. At this time of year the cherry blossoms are beautiful." Even the moniker was a ruse. Barely 30, The Old Scotchman was so vivid—"casual pop flies had the flow of history behind them, double plays resembled the stark clashes of old armies, and home runs deserved an acknowledgement on earthen urns," Willie Morris wrote in *North Toward Home*—that games in person seemed dull.

A team's "hope is as black as the inside of a cat." The first inning became "the hello half of the home frame." Habit was vital: two games daily, two more each holiday, 300 a year. To protect local coverage, outlets were blacked out within 75 miles of a major league city. Unharmed: 90 of America's then-140 million people. Said Nelson: "Gordon and his network became better known than more famous announcers and far more solid companies."

In 1949–50, three of four flags settled the final day. A patron could be forgiven for preferring Nevada to New York City. "In a big league city you just heard your team," said Blattner. "The sticks got the entire majors." Next year LBS did the last month of the Giants–Dodgers joust. McLendon then aired the playoff. In every sense, you inhaled The Scotchman live.

"From the bay of Tokyo, to the tip of Land's End, *this* is the day," he began at the Polo Grounds. Thomson's blast bred "The Giants win the pennant!" Silence. Crowd noise. Finally, "Well, I'll be the son of a mule."

Bob Costas was born March 22, 1952. "On tape, he's roaring from the first pitch—no letup. All the stops are out. The end of the world, Armageddon"—apt, since McLendon's lay around the bend.

In 1952, Gordon, doubling his per-game fee, added non-baseball program-ming. Unintended consequences were lost affiliates and higher costs. Worse, new Commissioner Ford Frick mugged "Game"'s lifeblood. "He barred Gordon from parks," Nelson said, "got Western Union to stop re-creations. Six clubs even refused to let games be covered."

LBS sued baseball for $12 million for "illegally hindering and restruc-turing . . . commerce." The Scotchman shrugged unconcern. "They have admitted all that we have charged them with." The bigs' reply: "Our agree-ments [were not] made behind the barn." In 1952, a judge KO'd McLendon's bid for a temporary injunction. "Game" died that May, its fall even faster than its rise.

Gordon denounced "the brazenry, ruthlessness, and illegality of those who are corrupting our fine national game." He forged the "top 40" musical format, began the first all-news station, yet "loved 'Game,' " said Bud, "more than anything he ever did." Another lieutenant raised his glass. "I'll be in some obscure place," Lindsey glowed in 1988, "and out of the blue people of middle age will say, 'I used to listen to you every afternoon.' "

Imitation spells flattery: Mutual's 1950–60 daily "Game," CBS TV's

1955–64 "Game of the Week," ESPN's 1990– "Sunday Night Baseball." John Kennedy said we recall people for one thing: Sally Rand, baring all; Ike, World War II; Bill Gates, the computer. Peoria knew little of McLendon's stratagem. It loved him as daily priest.

"By two o'clock almost every radio in town was tuned to the Old Scotchman," Morris wrote of Yazoo City, Mississippi. "His rhetoric dominated the place. It hovered in the branches of the trees, bounced off the hills, and came out of the darkened stores; the merchants and the old men cocking their ears to him, and even from the big cars that sped by, their tires making lapping sounds in the softened highway, you could hear his voice, being carried . . . in the delta."

Baseball is a beer-drinking sport. Even now, The Scotchman pours.

GORDON MCLENDON

LONGEVITY:	1	Four years.
CONTINUITY:	8	Liberty "Game of the Day" 1949–52.
NETWORK:	4	"Game" 1949–52 (Liberty).
KUDOS:	4	*TSN* 1951 "Announcer of the Year."
LANGUAGE:	9	Classical, with vast vocabulary.
POPULARITY:	10	What's not to like?
PERSONA:	10	To provinces, Father Christmas.
VOICE:	10	Bass, full, and rich.
KNOWLEDGE:	10	Could discuss GNP or RBI. Died in 1986 worth an estimated $200 million.
MISCELLANY:	8	Before the fall: Non-sports Voices included William L. Shirer, Westbrook Pegler, Joseph C. Harsch, and Mickey Rooney.
TOTAL:	74	(83rd place).

AL HELFER

John Wayne, entering a room. Norma Jean Baker, raising her skirt. Errol Flynn, breathing.

Presence.

Al Helfer braved World Wars I and II, did Mutual's 1950–54 "Game," became "Mr. Radio Baseball," and called New York's pre-1958 bigs trinity. "He drank triples without any apparent effect, and sometimes wore a cashmere cardigan that cost the lives of a herd of goats," wrote Ron Bergman. Al explained why few found him neutral: "I don't mess around."

Helfer was born 30 miles southwest of Pittsburgh to a 5-foot-9 dad and 5-3 mom. Go figure: The 6-foot-4, 275-pounder—"They never knew why I was so big"—played basketball and football at Washington and Jefferson. Entering radio, he re-created the Bucs, then joined Barber in Cincinnati. "Five bucks a week, and I was worth every cent!"

One day Helfer called a bicycle race. "And here comes DiBaggio," he roared, "like a bat out of hell!" Temper followed him to NBC New York. In 1939, Al dedicated a hotel. Thrice the open failed. "Are we going on this goddamned network?" he flared. Quick thinking saved the day. Using a pseudonym, Helfer said he was still in Cincinnati. "What about that phony name guy? He was fired from New York."

That spring, Red phoned. "Let's get together again and give 'em hell." Next year, the Yankees and Giants tried to muscle in. "'Leave Barber,' they said. 'Come here.' " Instead, in 1942 Al began 3 1/2 years in the Navy. His 1943 signal launched the Allied invasion of Sicily. Radio's "Cavalcade of America" starred Alfred Drake as Lt. Commander Helfer.

Returning, Al spurned Brooklyn—"Connie Desmond was Number 2, and I didn't want him hurt"—for the Yanks, Jints, and wife Ramona. Friends debated the greater test.

Ramona had her own band, played piano with Paul Whiteman's Orchestra, and performed at Buckingham Palace. "A 4-foot knockout," said Mutual's Al Wester, "who assuredly handled Al." In 1946, Larry MacPhail bought the Stripes, approached Barber, and was vetoed. He hired Allen, who dumped Helfer for Hodges. In 1949, the now-Giants' Russ hired Al! "Wherever you looked, we were playing musical chairs."

That year, Liberty bred "Game of the Day." Older (1935) and larger (nearly 700 outlets), Mutual took it personally. "We had more to lose and offer," said sports head Paul Jonas. Would a daily series dilute All-Star/Series coverage? "Game" might cost $4 million. Could Jonas make it up? "If we did baseball, we wanted to do it right." Ultimately, that meant *live*.

Mutual's "Game" began April 18, 1950. "Everything *as* it happened, from *where* it happened," said Wester. Jonas weighed 100 pounds. As Voice, he chose someone who could lift him with one hand. Once he and Helfer entered a hotel lobby. "My God," someone cried, "here comes Jonas and the whale!"

Each day but Sunday, Al would board a plane, once or twice daily, for

Boston, Brooklyn, Chicago, Detroit, or St. Louis. "Different game, different city," he said, repairing late Saturday to Helfer's home outside New York. "The Ghost of Hartsdale" got fresh laundry "and left before the door swung shut. My daughter was growing up. I loved, but didn't know, her."

Mutual loved "Game"'s success. "A guy in Oklahoma had devoured baseball in the paper," said Jonas. "Now he's hearing Helfer each day"—also sidekicks Art Gleeson, Gene Kirby, Bud Blattner, leaving Liberty, and a man who despised, and was despised by, Al.

Helfer and Dizzy Dean called the other "bastard," argued between innings, and refused to share a plane. "Huge weight and ego. Between 'em they were 600 pounds," laughed Wester. "In a small booth, like Milwaukee, the tubs'd almost come to blows."

Once Diz sang "The Wabash Cannonball." Al nearly took a punch: "Want to be a damn comedian? Visit Las Vegas." For five straight years, he visited the World Series over Mutual, Canadian Broadcasting Corporation, Mexican and South American affiliates, and Armed Forces Radio—as many as 1,490 outlets. In 1952, a record 65 percent of U.S. homes heard at least one game.

By 1954, Helfer had traveled "four million miles: I counted it"—for Mutual. "Finally, the doctor told me to resign." He joined the 1956–57 Dodgers—"Great pipes, but hard to work with," said Jerry Doggett—and Houston's 1962 Colt .45s. "Alien turf," said partner Gene Elston. "He didn't take." A last outpost of work berthed 1968–69's Oakland A's.

Once he forgot the first name in a post-game interview after Cesar Tovar played each position. Another night Reggie Jackson homered with Ted Kubiak on third base. "And Kubiak will score easily on the play," Helfer said, intently—no longer Mr. Radio Baseball, but still able to stir a fuss.

Al died May 16, 1975, still swaggering like a sailor. His eulogy sung a grace note. In 1952, Bucky Braham in North Carolina began sending letters. "The young boy wanted to be a baseball player," said Helfer. Ultimately, letters stopped. A 1953 telegram said that Bucky, with polio, was not expected to live. Asked to "say a few words on the air to cheer him," Al did.

Next day a telegram read: "We don't know what you did, but you have done something medical science couldn't." Bucky had been paralyzed. "[Now] the boy will live." His dad, a doctor, signed. Al last heard from Braham in college. "He was playing baseball. You can't ask the Good Lord for more than that."

Helfer never asked God for presence. It came, like manna, from above.

AL HELFER

LONGEVITY:	6	17 years.
CONTINUITY:	2	Cincinnati N.L. 1935–36; Brooklyn N.L. 1939–41 and 1956–57; New York A.L. 1945; New York N.L. 1945 and 1949; Mutual "Game of the Day" 1950–54; Houston N.L. 1962; Oakland A.L. 1968–69.
NETWORK:	10	All-Star Game 1939 and 1950–54 (Mutual) and 1955–58 (NBC TV). "Game" 1950–54 (Mutual). World Series 1950–54 (Mutual) and 1957 (NBC TV).
KUDOS:	5	With Barber, first play-by-play cooperative.
LANGUAGE:	10	Bald.
POPULARITY:	9	Unafraid.
PERSONA:	9	Endearing lout.
VOICE:	10	Thunderclap.
KNOWLEDGE:	8	Could play/call game: at 18, chose radio over pact tendered by Connie Mack.
MISCELLANY:	8	Did 1940s and '50s Rose Bowl and Army–Navy Games.
TOTAL:	77	(69th place).

VAN PATRICK

Two centuries ago the ability to wield a sword and ride a horse implied leadership. "My," a writer said, "how impressive the General looks upon a steed." Public, proud, and portly, Van Patrick impressed with oratory, working a room like a pol. A friend compared him to a bobbed cork: you could not keep Van down.

Growing up, he got by on six hours of sleep. At TCU, Patrick lettered in four sports, then worked the Southern Association and Three-I, Texas, and International Leagues. By 1947, Bill Veeck thought him ready to help fill the Indians' 78,000-seat redoubt.

"First time every game was at Municipal Stadium, and also on radio," said Van. In April, Jackie Robinson cracked baseball's color line. "One afternoon when [our] team trots on the field, a Negro will be out there with them," said Veeck. "I want to sign him quickly so that there won't be much pressure."

On July 5, he bought Larry Doby from the Negro League Newark Eagles. Pinch-hitting at Comiskey Park, Doby became the A.L.'s first black. "You just didn't think of race," said WGAR Radio's Patrick, not noting it. Like television, equality was heard of, but rarely seen.

In 1948, Pittsburgh lacked a TV station. The Red Sox and Braves lacked broadcast equipment. Cleveland was as far behind the curve. Read the April 21 TSN: "No television plans made by club at present time." Van seethed. "Talk about your ridiculous situations. I come here, allegedly to do TV, and can't get on the air."

With Barber, he telecast NBC's World Series. Pro: Cleveland won. Con: Less than 10 million saw. Impatient, Patrick joined Tigers TV in 1949. Goebel Brewery sponsored exclusivity. In turn, Van drank as much, worked as hard, and invested better than any other Voice of his time.

On the eve of the 1951 All-Star Game, feting Detroit's 250th birthday, Harry Heilmann died of cancer. Patrick moved to radio, his Tigers never reaching third. Aides were less static: Ty Tyson, Dizzy Trout, and Mel Ott. "I was in awe of him," said George Kell, arriving in 1959.

That year Stroh Brewery succeeded Goebel. The new sponsor deemed Van a gasbag. "They didn't want him, and he thought, 'Hell, I own four radio stations, have a chateau in Dearborn,' " said Wester. "He did Lions and Michigan football, just thought it was time to move on"—to Mutual, as sports head and baseball Voice. Van never imagined moving "Game of the Day."

In 1960, Patrick visited Forbes Field, Busch Stadium, and Candlestick Park. Hannibal and Savannah felt he never sounded better. The bigs then bellied to 18, then 20, teams. "Suddenly, 'Game' stations were switching to the new expansion teams," said Al.

The series died in 1961, running out of country. Van then ran even faster than before.

At Mutual, he called basketball, golf, the Olympics, Monte Carlo Grand Prix, and Notre Dame and "Monday Night Football," seldom looking back to baseball, or the Tigers to him. "He was flamboyant, intimidating to follow," said Ernie Harwell, replacing Van in 1960. Next year he caught a break: Detroit nearly won the pennant.

In 1973, Patrick contracted cancer. He died September 29, 1974, at 58, of surgery, on Game Weekend, at South Bend, Indiana. "It was an awful *way* to die, but the right *place* to die," Wester said of "this beautiful hulk of a man."

Van Patrick was buried four days after being scheduled to air Irish–Purdue. It is hard to imagine his voice, broken or even bent.

VAN PATRICK

LONGEVITY:	4	12 years.
CONTINUITY:	7	Cleveland A.L. 1947–48; Detroit A.L. 1949 and 1952–59; Mutual "Game of the Day" 1960.
NETWORK:	2	World Series 1948 (NBC TV). "Game of the Day" 1960 (Mutual).
KUDOS:	5	Majority non-baseball.
LANGUAGE:	8	Plain-spoken.
POPULARITY:	9	Tame Tigers failed a million only once.
PERSONA:	10	A.k.a. self-styled "The Ole Announcer" was, said George Kell, "too big for Detroit."
VOICE:	10	A symphony.
KNOWLEDGE:	9	Jumbo.
MISCELLANY:	5	At TCU, baseball catcher, football lineman, hoops guard, and track shotputter.
TOTAL:	69	(92nd place).

BOB WOLFF

On April 12, 1945, Harry Truman ended a dry day presiding over the Senate by inviting Speaker of the House Sam Rayburn for a drink. At 5:12 P.M., the White House switchboard ordered the vice president across town. Arriving, he found that FDR was dead of a cerebral hemorrhage. Was there anything Truman could do for her? he asked Eleanor Roosevelt. "Is there anything we can do for *you*?" she said. "For you are the one in trouble now."

The 1947–60 Voice of the Senators found that trouble could condense the language. "I never had to say who was winning or losing," said Bob Wolff. "I just gave the score."

Yearly his team vetoed the first division. To distract, Bob interviewed scouts, players, and concessionaires: "fans in the stands." In 1957, the Nats won the first game of a doubleheader. Wolff then told his guest, "Let's play a game. Don't say your name until we're finished talking."

Bob asked about the opener. "Well, of course," said the visitor, "being a Washington fan, I thought it was great."

They spoke for seven minutes. Climax: "Are you originally from Washington, sir?" Wolff said.

"No, I'm a Californian."

"What sort of work do you do, sir?"

"I work for the government," said the guest, 44.

"Oh, for the government?"

"Yes, yes, I work for the government."

"What sort of work do you do, sir?" Bob probed.

"Well, I'm the vice-president," said Richard Milhous Nixon.

Bob Wolff kept the Senators from cloning the Atlantis of the American League.

"Everything good in my life has been through a great break," said the native New Yorker. In 1938, at Duke on a baseball scholarship, Bob broke an ankle sliding into second base. The freshman began hosting radio's variety "Your Duke Parade." Pleased, he grew confused. "I've never see an arm or leg outlast a voice," coach Jack Coombs said. "If you want the big leagues, start talking." Hurt, Phi Beta Kappa '42 was helped. "Another break—best advice I ever got."

A naval commission led to Harvard Business school, Seabees in Camp Perry, Virginia, and Solomon Islands. "Its [supply officer] procedures were a mess, alien to what I'd learned at Harvard." Aghast, Wolff wrote a manual revising the system. Shortly the Navy Department asked him to create Supply Corps books and films. "I could have been in the South Pacific. Instead, I'm transferred to Washington."

In 1946, WINX Radio named Bob sports director. Next year, 26, he became the DuMont Network's WTTG TV pancaked, perspiring Voice. "Those lights! So hot, so huge! You'd lose 20 pounds in an hour." Few saw him sweat: TV interest paled vs. radio's. The only other commercial station was WABD New York.

"How'd I get the job?" said Wolff. No one *wanted* it. Papers shunned daily coverage. "Stores put sets in the window to spur sales. People had little faith in TV's future."

His soon lacked sleep in a 24/7 life.

By 1949, Bob called boxing, Maryland and Washington Capitols hoops, college and pro football, and Nats radio/TV. "I'd do the first and last three innings on TV, and the other three on radio. With [colleague Arch] McDonald, it was reversed." Ironically, the senior feared the junior partner. "Arch was bigger locally," said reporter Morris Siegel, "but Bob outworked him." Industry bred envy. Who could keep up?

Each day Wolff did taped/live pre/post-game radio/TV. "Four programs, a nightly TV and radio show, syndicated baseball column, and the game!" Eight times, the Nats placed next-to-last or last. One 1954 game drew 460. A year earlier Mickey Mantle hit the first "tape measure" blast, off Griffith Stadium's 60-foot-high left-field National Bohemian scoreboard, into Perry L. Cool's yard at 434 Oakdale Street: 391 feet to the wall; another 69, outer wall; and 105, across Fifth Street (565 total).

National Bo painted an "X" where the ball struck the board. "Not liking it," said Wolff, "[President] Clark Griffith painted it over." Victim Chuck Stobbs later flung baseball's longest wild pitch, bouncing to a concession stand. In 1956, Mick almost hit the first ball out of Yankee Stadium—"still rising when it hit the copper frieze. I called all these record plays"—vs. Washington.

Few Senators failed more grandly than 1956–59 infielder Herbie Plews. One day hits and errors ricocheted off his chest, legs, arm, and head. "If we took Herb out it might cost his confidence," said Bob. "If he stayed in, it might cost the game." He stayed. "If there'd been a crowd, it would have roared."

The next batter bounced to Plews, who bobbled, snatched the ball, and nipped his man. Washington still trailed in the ninth inning. Herbie lashed a two-out triple. Nats win. Players sob. "Herbie Plews! Tell me there weren't giants in the land."

"I wasn't like Allen. He had a team. All I had were stories." Once, D.C. began the ninth seven runs behind. On a whim, Bob midwifed fantasy. "Our camera has a magic ray. If we focus on a fielder, the ray will so mesmerize him that the ball will go through, by, or over him. This demands a concentrated thought process. If even one of you isn't thinking 'hit,' our rays can malfunction."

The camera eyed the rival shortstop. The first Senator singled. The next shot fixed the third baseman: a ball escaped his glove. One by one, Nats reached—"each after the camera predicted where the baseball'd go"—bringing Washington within a run. Bases full; two out; Mickey Vernon lined toward right. Leaping, the first baseman snagged the game.

Dazed, Bob hailed his audience. "They'd almost wrought a miracle until perhaps one had to leave the TV," ending the spell. He went to break, trying to cast one. "Remember," Wolff later said, "When the sponsor writes your name, What he wants to hear, It's not who won or lost the game, But how you sold the beer."

By 1953, Bob was baseball's sole ambidextrous beer-pourer: "amphibious," to Yogi Berra. In Florida, he poured smartly. Opening Day overflowed the glass. Mystery left a post-game huddle. "This is *hot* beer!" said aide Joe DiMona. "In spring training beer was refrigerated." Cigars were another sponsor. "Don't do it like Mel," said DiMona. "He puts it in the front of his mouth. Put the cigar on the side."

Bob put it in the ashtray. "Stop!" the producer said.

"What happened?"

"Cigarettes, put in the ashtray. Cigars, put in your mouth." The Nats hoped merely to keep from putting out to sea.

Wolff felt a gentle protectiveness for their owner and padrone. Daily Griffith watched TV's "The Lone Ranger." "He grew up in the West, was a small-town kid. The show brought back memories." Clark died in 1955. Son Calvin became president. Having made the bigs, Wolff despaired of making them big.

Then another break occurred.

In 1956, Gillette was baseball's sole network sponsor. "I'd say, 'How about [Mutual] network work?' They'd say, 'If your name gets big enough, we'll put you on.' I'd say, 'Put me on tonight, and my name will be big enough tomorrow.' " In 1956, D.C. hosted the All-Star Game. "I wore Gillette out. Plus, I knew the park," airing the only game where Musial, Mays, Mantle, *and* Williams homered.

That March, Bob asked Ted on his pre-game show. "'Don't bother me,' Williams said, then recoiled when we met." Grudgingly he agreed if hitting .340 by late summer. On August 7, Ted blew a fly, was jeered, spit at Fenway, entered the dugout, came out and spit again. Tom Yawkey fined him $5,000. "The incident made headlines everywhere," said Wolff. Radio/TV raged.

Next stop: Washington. Bob cornered Williams, batting .357. "Ted, I understand if you don't want to keep our agreement. But if you do, I have to ask about the spitting." No. 9 appeared, hating it. "He grimaced, expressed remorse, and said he was there because of our 'friendship.' " Having already interviewed Mantle—"with Ted, sport's most famous athlete"—Wolff took their tapes to New York.

Syndicated series were rarer then than later. Bob sold Colgate Palmolive a pilot. "From that came programs I did for the Yankees, Red Sox, and A's—a different one per club." By September, finally-a-name aired eight shows daily.

Gillette gave up, giving him the 53rd World Series.

On October 8, 1956, before 64,519, the Yanks and Dodgers played Game Five at The Stadium. New York led, 2–0. Dale Mitchell hit in Brooklyn's ninth. "I'll guarantee that nobody—but nobody—has left this ball park," cried Wolff on Mutual. "And if somebody did manage to leave early—man, he's missing the greatest! Two strikes and a ball! . . . Mitchell waiting, stands deep, feet close together. Larsen is ready, gets the sign. Two strikes, ball one. Here comes the pitch. Strike three! A no-hitter! A perfect game for Don Larsen!"

One break begets another. "[Next day] Robinson waits. Here comes the pitch—and there goes a line drive to left field! Slaughter's after it, he leaps! It's over his head against the wall! Here comes Gilliam scoring! Brooklyn wins [its last Series game]! Jackie Robinson is being pummeled!" Others: 1958 and 1961 Series, Rose, Gator, and Sugar Bowls, Colts, Browns, and Redskins, and 1958's Greatest Game Ever Played—"The Colts win! [NFL overtime title game, 23-17] Ameche scores!" Unlike the Nats, play-by-play sufficed.

Bob headed the local Knothole Gang, petitioned hangers, coat hooks, and bottle openers, and sold his scorebook at Griffith Stadium. Jerry Lewis, Bill Dana, and Jonathan Winters headed celebrities in the booth. "They appeared in the middle innings. I was too busy setting the stage earlier and capping it later"—but not for "The Singing Senators."

Ask players now to start a *gratis* glee club. "Their answer couldn't go in a book." Albie Pearson, Jim Lemon, and Roy Sievers, among others, sang melody. Howie Devron played accordion. Wolff stringed ukelele. "The Senators" played NBC's "Today Show" in 1959. That year, Harmon Killebrew's 42 dingers led the league. Power and shyness shaped a Garbo of the game.

One day Wolff coined a plan. "I'll bring you to a father and son game and insert you as Mr. Smith. After you hit the ball 10 miles, I'll say on the P.A., 'That's Harmon Killebrew.' "

Anonymous *sans* uniform, he thrice missed or grounded out. "The catcher tipped the bat. Let's try again," Bob said. No. 3 barely tapped the next pitch. Wolff: "Harmon Killebrew is the batter but doesn't want to lose your softball. Just to show his power, he'll fungo it and we'll bring it back."

Pop-up. "Let's get back to the game," he told the crowd. "It's getting late."

Returning to D.C., Bob consoled his rider. "Don't worry. You'll be a Hall of Famer in hardball. Skip the softer stuff."

After the 1960 season, Griffith tried to elude the sheriff by moving the team to Minneapolis-St. Paul. "Even with Killebrew we weren't drawing," Wolff said. "Calvin wanted me to go with him." He did, but missed the East. Expansion Mets G.M. George Weiss phoned in late 1961. The *Daily News* pealed: "Wolff Coming." Problem: no station/sponsor. Time passed. The renamed Minnesota Twins pressed Bob to decide. "I went to Weiss, and he was sorry but just couldn't make a commitment"—another break, unseen.

Like dominoes, Weiss signed WABC Radio, WOR TV, and Lindsey Nelson, airing NBC baseball since 1957. "He got what might have been my Mets job," Wolff said. "Then NBC comes to me with Lindsey's job!" becoming with analyst Joe Garagiola "Major League Baseball"'s 1962–64 alternative to CBS's Dizzy Dean.

"We were bigger in cities, but Dean was monumental elsewhere," said Bob. Perfect and fractured English clashed each Saturday and Sunday afternoon. Wolff did NBC's 1962–65 Series pre-game show and 1962 Giants–L.A. playoff, Game Two a record four hours and 18 minutes. "Each half-hour the network said, 'This program will not be seen tonight because of baseball.' Another 30 minutes later, they'd chop another."

In 1965, ABC bought regular-season exclusivity. After several games Bob was approached by Madison Square Garden, a P.A. boss since 1954. "They floated a new cable network, the chance to launch something big." He began by hyping "the wonderful aroma" of Robert Burns Imperial. The sponsor especially loved Wolff waving a cigar under his nose.

"Terrific," he said. "One suggestion. Next time you praise the wonderful aroma"—pause—"take the cigar out of the glass tubing first."

Bob did as many as 250 MSG events a year, including the Stanley Cup, NBA final, and Westminster Kennel Club Dog Show. Donning coaching garb, he gave dogs in a locker room a "pup talk." Missing was Wolff's favorite-since-childhood game. "I love baseball, but travel kills you." His valedictory still lives.

Joining News 12-Long Island, Bob became America's longest-running TV sportscaster. In 1995, entering Cooperstown, he strummed "Take Me Out To the Ballgame" on "The Singing Senators'" ukelele. Six years later my wife and I adopted two young children in Ukraine. We saw a *bandura* for sale—Ukrainian for the instrument. Buying it, I played baseball's *Marseille*.

That year Wolff gave the Hall of Fame his 1950s TV series. In 2002, retrieving them, he sold the MSG Network "Bob Wolff's Scrapbook." The program evoked baseball's then-hold on the American sensibility. "Darned if it didn't become a hit," he said.

The final break was *ours*.

BOB WOLFF

LONGEVITY:	7	19 years.
CONTINUITY:	8	Washington A.L. 1947–60; Minnesota A.L. 1961; "Major League Baseball" 1962–64 (NBC TV); "Game of the Week" 1965 (ABC TV).
NETWORK:	10	All-Star Game 1956 (Mutual). World Series 1956 (Mutual), 1958 and 1961 (NBC Radio). "Major League Baseball" 1962–64, N.L. playoff 1962, and World Series pre-game show 1962–65 (NBC TV).
KUDOS:	10	Cooperstown 1995. NSSA six-time New York State Sportscaster of the Year and Hall of Fame 2003. Emmy award 1989–90. Cable ACE award 1983. Boys and Girls Clubs of America "Legends of Sport" 1992.
LANGUAGE:	10	Precise.
POPULARITY:	9	"The Hall is merely a throw-in," mused the New York Post.
PERSONA:	10	Gentleman with a mike.
VOICE:	10	Elegant.
KNOWLEDGE:	10	For many years taught journalism at Pace and St. John's University.
MISCELLANY:	5	Past Commissioner, Atlantic Collegiate Baseball League.
TOTAL:	89	(23rd place).

JIMMY DUDLEY

Point. In 1948, Cleveland averaged 33,598 per date, drew a bigs record 2,620,627, and won its first World Series since 1920. "For someone my age [39]," said rookie Jimmy Dudley, "it was Utopia." Counterpoint. The 1960–67 Tribe never drew a million people, placed as high as third, or breathed past June.

"The longer I stayed, the worse they played," Dudley said. In 1997, he made the Hall. Raised in Lansing, Ohio, Phil Niekro was not surprised. "We had Wynn, Feller, and Garcia. But Jimmy was as big a hero as I had."

The hero died February 12, 1999, of Alzheimer's disease compounded by a stroke. To many, he still meant "Wait Till Next Year [again]."

Born in Alexandria, Virginia, three miles from the White House, Jimmy moved to Charlottesville as a boy. At the University of Virginia, he played baseball, football, and hoops, majored in chemistry, and was hired by DuPont. Trying radio, Dudley joined WOL Washington. "I was opposite Arthur Godfrey. Marconi had more listeners." Waterbury, Syracuse, and

Pittsburgh followed, then Chicago, as Hal Totten's gopher. "He banned play-by-play. Like Ted Husing, he said, 'First thing you know, you take my job.' "

In World War II, Jimmy took an Army Air Force plane to India for operations intelligence. "What do you do, sell 'em or repair 'em?'" a GI mocked his vow to re-enter radio. In 1946, WJW Cleveland hired Dudley for football and hockey. Next season, he called a sandlot exhibition at Municipal Stadium.

Point. "I thought, 'This might be as close to the bigs as I get.' " Counterpoint: A Carling Brewing sponsor was listening. "That's who I want to do our games, the guy I just heard on the radio." Bill Veeck obliged. "'Get the fans interested!' he'd roar," said Dudley. Belly dancers roamed the stands. Each woman visitor got a Hawaiian orchid. Joe Early wrote that he, the average fan, deserved a night. Veeck gave him a car and boat.

"Bill stuck S&H green stamps under certain seats, signaled, and had everybody close theirs to see if they won. Manhattan never heard such noise." Municipal was loud enough: in 1948, an American League day, night, and twinbill record 71,181, 78,392, and 82,781, respectively, filled the lakefront bowl.

To Dudley, each game seemed supernal. Later he rued not quitting while ahead.

"Greatest season ever," the rookie called player/manager Lou Boudreau's .355, 155 RBI, and MVP. Gene Bearden and Bob Lemon each won 20 games. Satchel Paige, 42, had girls around the league. One vamped Boston's South End platform. "Hey, baby," Satch said, "when you walk you shake that thing just like a caboose." She smiled. "Big boy, you ain't seen nothing. You ought to see me when I got a passenger."

On October 4, the Tigers and White Sox networks carried Jimmy's feed of the Red Sox–Indians playoff. Ironically, he had dogged Ted Williams all year like a bone. Bald since his twenties, Dudley finally roused the spunk to seek an interview. "Jesus, you skinhead," Ted roared, "I thought you'd never ask." Each wondered why Boston pitched journeyman Denny Galehouse. "They figured it didn't matter," guessed Jimmy. "Going into Fenway was like throwing the Christians to the lions!"

Instead, Tribe, 8–3: Birdie Tebbetts made the final out. "Keltner moves in, knocks it down, finds the handle. Here's the throw to Robinson and . . . the ball game is over!" said Dudley. "Yes, the Cleveland Indians win their first American League pennant in 28 years. And man, oh, man, how I'd like to be down on Euclid Avenue right now!" The Christians had a better pitcher. Next week a downtown parade hailed the Series.

In 1954, Dudley called Mutual's All-Star Game from Municipal: A.L., 11–9. On September 12, 84,587 jammed the oval. Early Wynn, Bob Feller, Mike Garcia, and Lemon forged an Arthurian Big Four. The Indians went a league-record 111–43. Their Classic was less Camelot than charade. "We own the world, then get swept by the Giants," said Jimmy, softly. "In many ways, the franchise was never quite the same."

Dudley ended a game by saying "So long and lots of luck, ya heah?" Each began: "Hello, Baseball Fans Everywhere." In between, he oozed "The string is out [3–2 count]," "stay-alive fouls," and "come on down to the old ball orchard." The post-game guest came on for an electric razor. "I'm just glad it's not a straight razor," said one, Jimmy Dykes. "Watching some of our players play can drive you to cut your throat."

Five times the 1951–56 Tribe finished second to New York. Casey Stengel knocked skipper Al Lopez for using only three starting pitchers one September: "I knew it couldn't be done but somehow, it don't always work." A friend of Dudley's put Al's picture in her kitchen. "Lopez, you do as I tell you, or I'll use this on your head," she said, bashing his photo with a rolling pin.

Point: 1956 attendance fell to 722,256. Counterpoint: the second place '59ers so matched strength with Chicago that more than three decades later an Ohioan might say, "There was our last hurrah, if only we had known it." The Indians next won a pennant in 1995.

Oil and water. France and Britain. Jimmy Dudley and Bob Neal. In 1957, Neal left TV for radio. Jimmy was soft, quick, and fairly sang even ads: "Garfield-1, 2-3, 2-3," of an aluminum siding firm. Neal was loud, brash, and could not brook being Number two. They never talked on the air, or off.

Point: Neal blocked Dudley's view of a game by raising a briefcase lid on the countertop. Counterpoint: Jimmy cracked peanuts into a mike as Bob did play-by-play. Point: Talk host Pete Franklin once sat between the egotists. Counterpoint: speaking to him, they ignored each other. "Their chill," he said, "could cause pneumonia."

Dudley lit what there was of sixties Tribe warmth. "He was a man with a smile in his voice and a warm handshake for strangers," wrote Terry Pluto. "No broadcaster ate more bad chicken, swilled more cups of bitter coffee, and made more speeches to Rotary Clubs." He tethered Erie and Ashtabula and Meadville and Oil City. Detroit's Joe Falls thought Jimmy "a baseball broadcaster broadcasting a baseball game—not a soap salesman."

Point: Dudley was named 1967 NSSA Sportscaster of the Year. Counterpoint: In January 1968, he was bounced. "We were not dissatisfied," a WERE lackey said. "It's just a changing world." Not at liberty for long, he became Seattle's 1969 expansion Voice. Each lasted a year. In 1970, the renamed Brewers moved to Milwaukee. Jimmy spent the next few years on the phone. "Jobs came up with the White Sox, Blue Jays, Pirates, Mariners," said a friend. "They all went to an ex-player or younger guy."

The 1947–92 Tribe trained in Tucson, Arizona. In 1976, the man pen pals titled "Baseball Fans Everywhere, Cleveland, Ohio" called its P.C.L. Toros. Next season Seattle rejoined the bigs. *TSN* wrote, falsely: "Rumor has it that Dudley will be returning." At 89, Dudley returned to the ground from a Tucson convalescent home.

Once, a blind boy in Ontario wrote letters in Braille transcribed by his father. He ended, "God bless you, Jimmy, and remember you are my eyes." Cleveland's baseball prosopopeia doubtless watches from above.

JIMMY DUDLEY

LONGEVITY:	7	21 years.
CONTINUITY:	10	Cleveland A.L. 1948–67; Seattle A.L. 1969.
NETWORK:	1	All-Star Game 1954 (Mutual).
KUDOS:	7	Cooperstown 1997. NSSA 1967 Sportscaster of the Year.
LANGUAGE:	10	Rapid. "Over to second, one away . . . back to first, a double play!"
POPULARITY:	10	Poetic.
PERSONA:	9	Storyteller.
VOICE:	10	"You could hear the molasses," wrote Hal Lebowitz.
KNOWLEDGE:	10	Knew football, too: Cleveland, Baltimore, and Ohio State.
MISCELLANY:	9	In 1949, married actress who played Laura Lane in radio's "Captain Midnight."
TOTAL:	83	(41st place).

JACK BRICKHOUSE

On July 31, 1983, John Beasley Brickhouse gave a talk devoid of dogma. In a moment rich with feeling, he evoked a restless boy, unaware of himself, yet aware of a larger world. "I stand on what I consider the hallowed ground of Cooperstown. I feel at this moment like a man who is sixty feet, six inches tall."

On Induction Eve, Jack and Joe DiMaggio began talking in the Otesaga Hotel. A man interrupted for the Clipper's autograph. Said Joe D.: "I'm sure you'd also like the autograph of another Hall of Famer, Jack Brickhouse."

Stunned, Brickhouse recalled Wrigley Field and Comiskey Park and rain delays and hot afternoons. For five decades, his calling card, "Back, back, back! That's it! Hey-Hey!" upon a homer, roused each side of the Second City.

A reporter mused that even if Jack didn't make Cooperstown, his suitcase would. "Fortunately for me," said Brickhouse, "we arrived together."

Wrigley opened the year of Hey-Hey!'s 1916 birth in Peoria. The White Sox' post-'19 quiet desperation made Jack a Cubbies fan. He played basketball, was a newspaper boy, and "tried to cover a lack of sports knowledge with slang." At 18, Brickhouse finished fifth in a WMBD broadcast contest, but "got a job as a $17-a-week spare announcer and switchboard operator." Off-duty, he tuned to the master of the day.

"Elson got us identifying with baseball." Jack did news, called the Three-I League, and got a 1940 telegram: "Expect call from WGN as a staff announcer and sports assistant. Remember, if asked, you know all about baseball. Best of luck, Bob Elson." Hired, he introduced Les Brown's band, became Kay Kyser's Voice, and "had to fight the urge to imitate Bob." In 1942, Brickhouse replaced the Navy-bound Commander, inheriting the Sox and Cubs.

"I didn't like that sophisticated approach of New York," he said, dripping hope and vim. "People call me gee-whiz! I've never seen a mirror that doesn't smile back if you smile first." Unforeseen: WGN, axing baseball after 1943. "Mutual was the parent, and day games killed profitable kiddie shows." By 1944 Jack's WJJD darned the Sox. Next year WIND's Cubs won a pennant.

"On the last weekend Bert Wilson's berserk, and I'm doing the Sox by ticker tape." In 1946, Elson rejoined them, booting him to the Polo Grounds. A year later Brickhouse returned not to Midwest ticker tape but a protean rectangular tube.

"Anyone who could see beyond their nose knew that television would be important," he said. More than one in ten U.S. TV sets spiked Chicago. In 1948, WGN Channel 9 turned pioneer: each home game, *live,* from its two big-league teams.

"It worked because the Cubs and White Sox weren't home at the same time. You aired the Sox at Comiskey, or Cubs at Wrigley Field." Daytime forged the edge. "Wrigley didn't have lights, so kids came home from school, had a sandwich, and turned the TV on. You win Chicago by winning kids."

At first, carpers feared less interest. Instead, it ballooned. "Maybe you'd draw a thousand less because the game was on," said Brickhouse, televising more baseball than anyone—more than 5,000 games. "But long-term continuity made lifetime fans."

Ultimately, baseball looked at television and saw that it was good—especially the large man with the large voice who was seemingly, like Elson, everywhere.

"I'd do a day game, studio, wrestling three nights a week," Brickhouse said. Firsts included TV's daily Voice (140–180 games yearly); WGN mikeman (boxing, Chicago Stadium); center field camera (1951). "A guy at a schoolboy game saw the scoreboard and thought, 'A camera there'd show the hitter and pitcher.' " All envied Hey-Hey!'s energy: "If you worked 80 hours a week, you were dogging it."

Jack aired fires, barn dances, "Marriage License Renewals" with couples at City Hall, one-on-one with seven U.S. presidents, 1945 and 1969 Inaugurals, 1944, 1960, 1964, and 1968 political conventions, Churchill's funeral, Berlin Wall's rise, and audience with Cubs manager Leo Durocher and Pope Paul VI—alas, a writer said, not simultaneously. "He and I go back a long way," Ronald Reagan said. "That personality, that voice, that charisma." Pause. "Have you thought about going into politics?"

In 1950, Brickhouse did CBS's Series; 1952, perked Mutual's 700 outlets; 1954, beamed NBC's Tribe–Giants opener: eighth inning, 2-all. "There's a long drive way back in center field. Way back, back! It is . . . oh, what a catch by Mays! . . . Willie Mays just brought this crowd to its feet with a catch which must have been an optical illusion to a lot of people! Boy! . . . Notice where that 483-foot mark is in center field?" he asked Russ Hodges. "The ball itself . . . had to go about 460, didn't it?" It did, the fifties becoming his Holy See.

"Name it, I did it"—golf, boxing, wrestling, hoops, and Notre Dame, College All-Star, Orange, Rose, and Sugar Bowl, 1947 Cardinals and 1953–76 Bears football—too busy, Jack said, to be tired. "I feel sorry for folks stuck in a job because of security. Especially in baseball, I loved where I worked." Comiskey greased pitching, had an ardor for the underdog, and hated the Cubs and don't you forget it. Wrigley was tended, painted white, and lacked a bad seat in the house.

"Walking through the crowds into that great small old stadium, and there they were in the flesh," wrote poet Donald Hall. "I can see them now in their baggy old pants, the players that I had heard about, of whom I'd seen photographs, but there they were, really walking around, live people, and the absolute enchantment, the enthrallment, the tension of starting the game, 'Play ball.' "

Brickhouse was asked if the wait was worth it. "The Cubs fan is born so that he can suffer," Jack said. He did, again and again.

Hey-Hey!'s 1947–66 Cubs matured not knowing the first division. Once Lou Novikoff—"The Mad Russian"—hit to right-center field. A runner rounded third base, held up, and regressed. Head down, Novikoff passed second and slid into third.

"Where the hell ya going?" said coach Charlie Grimm.

Rising, Lou said, "Back to second if I can make it."

Novikoff called the outfield's ivy poison; others thought him wall-shy. Dying is easy. Cubs comedy was hard. In 1959, umpire Vic Delmore called Bobby Anderson's pitch to Stan Musial ball four. It rolled to the screen, was retrieved by the batboy, and given to P.A. Voice Pat Pieper. "Looked good to me," said third baseman Alvin Dark, throwing to shortstop Ernie Banks. In the genes: the Cubs forgot to call time out.

Born to suffer: Delmore and catcher Sammy Taylor never saw the heist. Vic gave another ball to Sammy, who threw to Anderson, who, seeing Musial near second, threw into right-center field. "I figure it's the only ball," said Stan, "so I get up and Ernie tags me." Delmore ruled him out. Later Brickhouse asked why Vic put a second ball in play. "I've been lying in my room looking at the ceiling, asking myself the same question and I don't know."

Postscript: May 6, 1960. "I want you to make a trade," said Philip Wrigley. "[Cubs radio analyst Lou] Boudreau for [then-manager] Grimm."

"Boudreau for Grimm?" Jack said.

"Yes," Wrigley said. "Charlie's worrying himself sick over the team, out walking the streets when he should be resting. If the Cubs don't kill him his sore feet will."

Grimm moved to radio. Lou replaced him on the field. "A manager for a broadcaster," said Brickhouse. Only with the Cubs.

Frank Sinatra sang "My Kind of Town" about a North Siders' town, at heart. TV, the Friendly Confines, and slapstick: How could the White Sox compete? The '59ers had a thought: their first pennant in forty years. Jack and Vin

Scully did the Series. The Hose won the 11–0 opener; Los Angeles, Games Two-Four. Postponing the inevitable, the Sox won, 1–0, then lost, 9–3. "It was a great year," mused Brickhouse. Chicago left 43 runners: key hits would have made it greater. He foresaw a blur of flags. "Fox, Aparicio, I couldn't wait." Instead, the Hose refound the fringe.

In 1968, dumping WGN for Chicago's first UHF (ultra-high frequency) outlet (WFLD), Sox owner Arthur Allyn began each-game coverage. "Until now," said Jack, "neither team had televised away with the other at home." Livid, Wrigley telecast the Cubs' entire schedule, blaring "[Brickhouse's] boyish enthusiasm that nothing could shake," said producer Jack Rosenberg. "Didn't matter whether the team was in first or last."

We knew where the Cubs usually were. Another Chicago team was luckier.

In 1924, Jack, eight, heard Illinois's Red Grange score four touchdowns vs. Michigan. A listener called WGN to urge Quin Ryan's firing: "He obviously doesn't know a touchdown from a first down. No man can score that often in that short a time [less than 12 minutes]." By contrast, the Bears accented defense— the "Monsters of the Midway." In 1965, owner George Halas—to Brickhouse, "the kindest and cheapest man I ever knew"—signed Dick Butkus to a $200,000 pact. "George," Jack told him, "knowing you that's $1,000 a year for 200 years."

Yearly Brickhouse plucked pro football's War of the Roses. One Sunday a brigade of Packers drunks woke him at 2 A.M. "Fellas, how 'bout toning it down? I have to work today."

A boozer recognized him. "Hey, ain't you Brickhouse?"

"I am."

"Brickhouse is a *jackass,*" he yelled. "*Hey-hey!*"

Doors opened. The hotel hall filled. Soon Jack was singing the team theme song, "Bear Down, Chicago Bears." Analyst and columnist Irv Kupcinet had officiated the NFL. No one was better wired. Brickhouse "never forgot the day Harry Truman, Bob Hope, and middleweight champ Carmen Basilio walked into the booth looking for Kup."

Once Chicago led, 10–3, near halftime. "It's comforting that even if something catastrophic happens the worst the Bears can be at halftime against these powerful Vikings is a 10–10 tie," said Jack. A Minnesota touchdown and field goal then bookended a Bears fumble.

"Thirteen–ten, Vikings," Brickhouse recalled. "Me and my big mouth. Sort of like saying, ' '69 is the Cubbies' year.' "

On April 8, 1969, Willie Smith's Opening Day eleventh-inning euphoria-began-working-overtime pinch-homer beat Philadelphia. Billy Williams's 895 straight games played set an N.L. record. The bigs' best infield tied Banks (106 RBI), Ron Santo (123), Glenn Beckert (.291), and Don Kessinger (.273). Ken Holtzman no-hit Atlanta August 19. Plenty of nothin': no hits or Ks.

Rarely had the Confines seemed friendlier. Santo began clicking heels upon each victory. Towel-waving reliever Dick Selma conducted the Bleacher Bums. The Cubs held a 9 1/2 game mid-August lead. Who guessed that the benign-as-Benji Mets would go 38–11 while Chicago set in shock?

The Cubs finished eight games behind. Depressed, Jack did not despair. Banks faced Pat Jarvis May 12, 1970. "He swings and a drive—a liner, left field! It is—there it is! Mr. Banks has just hit his five hundredth career homer! He is getting a standing ovation! . . . Doffs his cap as he steps on home plate! . . . Waves to the fans as he jogs into that dugout! They are standing here at Wrigley Field and giving Ernie an ovation!"

Mr. Cub retired a year later. Brickhouse narrated a best-selling album, "Great Moments in Cubs Baseball." In 1981, the Tribune Company bought the club subsidiary WGN had treated as mom 'n' pop. "Baseball now got corporate," Jack said, "not personal, like, say, vaudeville."

Hey-Hey! died August 6, 1998, at 82, of a stroke after brain surgery, having penned a tombstone: "Here lies the guy who could do the best soft-shoe anywhere for 'Tea for Two.' "

In *Winesburg, Ohio,* Sherwood Anderson wrote "how at the same instant, and if the people of the town are his people, one loves life so intensely that tears come into the eyes." Brickhouse did his final game September 27, 1981. Afterward, a large crowd huddled on a concourse under the front-office level. "That got to me," Jack mused. "I was holding out pretty good till then." Asked to describe himself, he said, "He can ad-lib; a reporter at heart; he can read copy, do a commercial. You can put him on a parade, a disaster"—again, those Cubs.

A team program read: "If you're from the Midwest, given the words 'Hey-Hey,' who comes to mind? Unless you have spent the last thirty-plus years in an Arctic snow drift, the answer is elementary." In 1983, Jack got an advanced degree. "The trains, the planes, the cabs, the buses," he said at Cooperstown, "they have carried me millions of miles through the years to get me where I most wanted to be—the ballpark."

Hey, look me over. Hey-Hey! likely is.

JACK BRICKHOUSE

LONGEVITY:	10	40 years.
CONTINUITY:	10	Chicago A.L. 1942–45 and 1947–67; Chicago N.L. 1942–43 and 1947–81; New York N.L. 1946.
NETWORK:	9	World Series 1950 (CBS TV), 1952 (Mutual), and 1954 and 1959 (NBC TV). All-Star Game 1950 (CBS TV), 1951–53 (NBC TV), and 1962 (WGN).
KUDOS:	10	Cooperstown 1983. NSSA Hall of Fame 1983. ASA Hall 1985. Seven other Halls, including Cubs and pro wrestling. Five-time Illinois Sportscaster of the Year. First satellite telecast, 1962.
LANGUAGE:	7	Hopeful.
POPULARITY:	10	"The voice of Chicago in our youth," said Mayor Richard M. Daley.
PERSONA:	10	Chicago's big shoulders.
VOICE:	10	Infectious.
KNOWLEDGE:	9	"I am a professional, secondarily a sports, announcer." Wrote yearly sports summary for Encyclopedia Britannica Yearbook.
MISCELLANY:	8	In 1990, Chicago renamed block of North Michigan Avenue "Jack Brickhouse Way." Perhaps next: statue outside Wrigley Field beside Harry Caray's.
TOTAL:	93	(eighth place).

ERNIE HARWELL

We come to praise a famous man—but how?

"He could have been mayor of Detroit, if not governor," Joe Falls wrote of the 1960–91 and 1993–2002 Tiger. Alas, politics can hail swarmy men.

"The most modest man I've met," said Brickhouse. Still, Churchill noted, modest men often have much to be modest about.

W. Earnest Harwell didn't: first Voice to be dealt for a player; air coast-to-coast TV; be baptized in the Jordan River.

Pitchers throw low and outside. Ernie pitched low maintenance, sitting at the organ to compose a song. "Eisenhower has, and retains, a magic that is peculiarly his," wrote Theodore H. White. "He makes people happy." Ditto the magnolia baritone.

"The batter," he said, "stood there like the house by the side of the road." Harwell's harbored essayist, lyricist, magazine writer, author, family man, and a founder of the Baseball Chapel Program.

How to praise baseball's 1948–2002 lay preacher? Call him beloved.

In a pinch, we fall back on memory. Born: January 25, 1918, Washington, Georgia. First job: *Gone with the Wind* author Margaret Mitchell's paperboy. Early Everest: at eight, staged a Max Schmeling–Young Stribling boxing puppet show. "I did play-by-play, like Graham McNamee did in real fights," said Ernie, "and since Stribling was a Georgian I'd have him knock Schmeling out."

Each day the towhead stuttered baseball at Doc Green's drugstore. Special speech—"expression"—lessons helped. In 1923, the Southern Association Crackers built Ponce de Leon Park. Hooked, Harwell sold popcorn and became visiting batboy, never paying for another game. "Anything to get in free and to follow my Crackers," invisible in *The Sporting News*.

At 16, Ernie sold editor Edgar G. Brands on becoming Atlanta correspondent. First piece: "Saddened Crackers Tumble." At 18, Harwell won *Scholastic Magazine*'s "best [U.S.] high-school column" award. Emory University bred a post (newspaper editor), wife (Lulu Tankersley, high school beauty queen), and post-degree gig (WSB Radio sports director).

In World War II, Ernie interviewed Eleanor Roosevelt, covered the Japanese surrender of Wake Island, and wrote for the Marines magazine *Leatherneck*. Postwar, he did the Crackers and visited GI hospitals. The Harwells celebrated a pennant with three-year-old son Bill. "The Lord's going to bring us a baby," Lulu told him. That week outfielder Lloyd Gearhart rang their doorbell. "Mama," cried Bill, answering, "the Lord is here and he doesn't have our baby."

By 1947, General Mills babied 115 teams, more than General Foods, Kellogg's, or Atlantic Refining. "A Wheaties scout'd hit the road," said Ernie. "With luck, it'd promote you." One night he hit Atlanta. Harwell re-created each play, ad, and break of a 21-inning game. After midnight, he fell into the lobby. Surely, the man had hung on every word. "Then I saw him. For hours he'd been asleep."

W. Earnest narrated for his dad, an invalid. "Every time a ball's pitched, your mouth and brain have to describe it without frills." Crackers skipper Kiki Cuyler put a radio in the dugout. "Ernie was that good," said owner Earl Mann. In 1948, Branch Rickey asked to release him when Red Barber's ulcer hemorrhaged. "I won't stand in his way," Mann said. "But first I want Cliff Dapper," Brooklyn's Triple-A catcher.

At 30, Harwell swelled New York's colony of Barber, from Mississippi's clay and talcum; Russ Hodges, rural Kentucky; and Mel Allen, near Birmingham.

"I'm asked why so many guys were Southern. I say we were too lazy to work! Actually, it's where we grew up."

The South fused oral density and a lulling, siren past. "On the porch you'd hear about the local banker and beauty parlor operator and who married whom." Their rhythm became radio baseball's, mythy and sweetly rural.

The listener could picture, among other things, bags, positions, batter, and pitcher. A Dodger might hit to left-center field. "Mentally, you saw it all at once—base runners, fielder chasing, shortstop with the relay, catcher bracing." Even a vanilla Voice made TV football bearable: "It's better packaged for the screen." Radio baseball was better packaged for the mind.

Radio was a sonata, falling on the ear. TV was still life, deadened by statistic. Barber played the Met: "first to study players, take you behind the scene." In 1950, Harwell left him for Hodges, pounding piano at a roadhouse. "Wouldn't talk as much, no gimmicks, but authenticity."

Red was better; Russ, better to work *with.* Once Barber called the first quarter of a football game. "Now for the second quarter," he said, "here is Russ Hughes."

"Thank you, Red Baker," said Hodges. Like Queen Victoria, Barber was not amused.

Baseball as story-telling: three from the 1950s.

- Coogan's remote booth lacked a toilet. Urinating in paper cups, Russ and Ernie placed them in a corner. One visitor accidentally kicked a cup, leaking liquid into lower boxes. "Hey!" usher Barney O'Toole said. "We're getting complaints. People said to quit spilling beer." The beer, Harwell winked, was used. "We'll be careful, but don't tell the folks what hit 'em."
- "I was a mild and lazy guy long before Steve Martin became a wild and crazy guy." Leo Durocher mistook Ernie for a patsy, slapped his newspaper, and began wrestling. "If you took the bullying, you became his stooge. Leo fought so often he didn't recall it." Harwell did—the sole brawl of his career.
- In 1954, the transplanted Orioles hired him. The new kid on the block finished 54–100. "With a bad club, you need the unusual," Ernie said, finding it in 1957. Behind, 4–3, Dick Williams hit at 10:19 P.M. Local law forced a 10:20 curfew. "All [Chicago's Paul]

LaPalme has to do is eat the ball, game ends." He threw a game-tying homer.

The O's won the replay. Harwell won Baltimore. *News American* columnist John Steadman wrote: "He could talk, and write," gracing *Colliers, Look,* and *The Saturday Evening Post.* In 1955, Ernie composed a poem. Ultimately, "A Game for All America" was translated into six languages, became its greatest essay, and has aged even less than him.

"It's America, this baseball. A re-issued newsreel of boyhood dreams. Dreams lost somewhere between boy and man," he wrote. "In baseball, democracy shines its clearest. Here the only race that matters is the race to the bag." Baseball was "a ballet without music. Drama without words. A carnival without kewpie dolls." It was "Chagrin in being picked off base. . . . Humor, holding its sides when an errant puppy eludes two groundskeepers and the fastest outfielder. And Pathos, dragging itself off the field after being knocked from the box."

Nicknames were baseball. "Names like Zeke and Pie and Kiki and Home Run and Cracker and Dizzy and Daffy." It told "the story of David and Goliath, of Samson, Cinderella, Paul Bunyan, Homer's Iliad, and the Count of Monte Cristo." Baseball was "cigar smoke, roasted peanuts, *The Sporting News,* winter trades, 'Down in front,' and the Seventh-Inning Stretch. Sore arms, broken bats, a no-hitter, and the strains of the Star-Spangled Banner.

"This is a game for America, this baseball!" he ended. "A game for boys and for men."

In 1960, the literalist replaced Van Patrick on TV/radio. "Van was so popular. I went with a chilly feeling." Warming: a hearth with almost every seat on the field. "Tiger Stadium was like Ebbets, only bigger, but fans were like the Giants'—a history lacking in Brooklyn. This was really the best park of all."

The '60 Tigers were 71–83. Next year, their menagerie moved uptown. Norm Cash hit .361. Rocky Colavito had 45 homers. Frank Lary went 23–9. Detroit crashed New York 1 1/2 games behind for a September 1–3 series. "The first night, the Lions had a preseason game. Baseball interest was so high they postponed it so people could watch TV."

Detroit lost thrice. For a long time afterward, Harwell eclipsed his club. He wrote books, shot a hole-in-one, invented a bottle-can opener, spoke at a Billy Graham crusade, had a race horse named after him, and sang a duet with Pearl Bailey. In *One Flew Over the Cuckoo's Nest,* Jack Nicholson, a schizophrenic, strains to hear NBC Radio's 1963 World Series. "Yep, me," said Ernie. "Wish I got a residual [from that and five other films]." The mild and lazy guy ditched football and Tigers video. "The season overlap killed football, and George Kell began TV."

In 1967, rioting in Detroit killed 38. Certain constants soothed. A park was "the ballyard." The Red Sox were the "Bostons." An outfielder "tried to climb the wall and buy a ticket." Motown lost a last-day flag. Its owner then penned a note: "John Fetzer has just died. This is his ghost speaking."

You can't buy class. Like Fetzer, Harwell never had to rent it.

Entering 1968, Detroit was unsure if it would burn or win a first pennant since 1945. Would smoke again shroud Tiger Stadium? No one knew. "A strange thing [then] happened," Falls said. "The ball club . . . started winning games. . . . As the streets began to heat up, people began staying in at night to listen to Ernie Harwell on radio. . . . And when the team was at home . . . there was . . . a place to go. A place where a guy could let off steam." Outside Michigan, The Year of the Pitcher blew the whistle on interest. "No one could hit the ball," said Ernie. "There wasn't much fun." Antipodean, Detroit broke its all-time gate—2,031,847.

"People ask my favorite image of all the years I did ball," Harwell often said: Al Kaline, in the right-field corner, throwing to second base. No. 6 wed 3,007 hits, 10 Gold Gloves, and 18 All-Star teams. In 1968, he buoyed Willie Horton (36 dingers), Mickey Lolich (17–9), and MVP/Cy Young Denny McLain (31–6)—"the biggest player we ever had in his impact on the public."

September 14: ninth inning vs. Oakland. Horton hit "a drive to left— that'll be the ball game!" Ernie said. "Here comes Stanley in to score . . . and the Tigers win, 5 to 4! Denny McLain is one of the first out of the dugout . . . as the Tigers come from behind and McLain has his 30th victory of the 1968 season!" Next week "[another] big crowd [was] ready to break loose." Don Wert "swings—a line shot, base hit, right field, the Tigers win it! [flag, 2–1, vs. New York] . . . Kaline has scored. The fans are streaming on the field. . . . Let's listen to the bedlam here at Tiger Stadium!"

On October 2, 1963, Harwell called Sandy Koufax's Classic-high 15 Ks. Five years later to the day he began another Series. "Gibson has tied the record. . . . Trying for number 16 right now against Cash. . . . Swing and a miss! He did it!" St. Louis took a 3–1 game lead. In Game Five, Ernie suggested blind folk-singer Jose Feliciano for the Anthem. He crashed NBC's switchboard. "This was Viet Nam—people saw him, thought hippies with the guitar and dark glasses." The Cardinals scored three first-inning runs. Jose should have sung a coda.

Detroit forced Game Seven. Scoreless inning shadowed inning. Cash and Horton singled in the seventh. Jim Northrup lined to center. "Here comes Flood," said Harwell. "He's digging hard. He almost fell down! It's over his head for a hit!" Tigers: 4–1. Patient: baseball. Placebo: Detroit.

"'Sixty-eight," Ernie said as in a rosary. "People obsessed, wondering when we'd win again [1972 A.L. East]." In the clubhouse, the Baptist shunned profanity. On the air, the teetotaler touted Stroh. On the road, he visited friends.

"You can read books listening to Ernie, or go smelt fishing listening to him, or pick mushrooms in the woods with him in your ear," William Taaffe wrote. In 1973, Henry Aaron passed homer 700. Harwell wrote "Move Over Babe, Here Comes Henry"—55th of his more than 70 songs. "I'm drawn to words [for Sammy Fain, Johnny Mercer, and B. J. Thomas, among others]. I get an expression and work on rides from one city to another."

In 1976, a tyro expressed himself as no one had: "for one year," said Ernie, "even bigger than McLain." On June 28, Mark Fidrych acknowledged the first network TV sports curtain call. "They're not going to stop clapping until the Bird comes from the dugout," said ABC's Warner Wolf. "Mark Fidrych is born tonight on coast-to-coast television." "The Bird," after the "Sesame Street" TV character, jammed stadia, addressed the ball, and manicured the mound.

Infielders Lou Whitaker and Alan Trammell became a more enduring institution. Another could be heard saying, "That ball nabbed by a guy from Alma, Michigan." Each day a different town snagged a foul. "Hey, Ernie, let a guy from Hope [Holland, or Sarnia] grab one!" pled a bystander. As a boy I recall thinking that he had a lot of friends.

Detroit did in 1984: only the fourth team to lead the league or division each day. It swept the L.C.S., took a 3–1 game Series edge, and led next day, 5–4. Manager Sparky Anderson tried a ploy. "Five bucks you don't hit one out," he yelled from the dugout. Steamed, Kirk Gibson signaled, doubling the bet. "He swings, and there's a long drive to right!" said Harwell. "And it is a home run for Gibson! . . . The Tigers lead it, 8 to 4!"

By now Michigan would no more miss Ernie—"Mr. Kaline"; "lovely Lulu"; "two for the price of one!"; "a big Tiger hello"; "lonnng gone" of a dinger; "he played every hop perfectly except the last"—than burn the U.S. flag. In 1990, ex-football coach Bo Schembechler became Tigers president:

too arrogant to grasp his baseball ignorance, and too ignorant to grasp his arrogance.

On December 19, Harwell said he would not return—"I'm fired"—after 1991. The *Free Press* screamed: "A Gentleman Wronged." A chant filled Joe Louis Arena: "We Want Ernie!" T-shirts blared, "Say It Ain't So, Bo!" A Detroit TV poll showed Harwell 9,352, Schembechler 265. Dishonor among thieves: Bo and WJR Radio swapped blame. Their Grinch stealing Christmas was mean, coarse, and dumb.

The '91ers closed at Baltimore. Our hero was feted in the Oval Office and on Capitol Hill. "Someone said I was lucky. They pointed out usually you have to die before people say nice things about you." Tony Hanley, 13, wrote from Belding, Michigan: "If you need anything, a job, or money, or you need a place to stay, or even a new organ, just call."

Next year Harwell called CBS Radio's "Game of the Week." Finer: ire at his firing greased the franchise's sale. Mr. Tiger was rehired. Axed, Schembechler finally got the Importance of Being Ernie. "Mel and the Yankees, Brooklyn and Barber, so many Voices canned," said Bob Costas. "Baseball is clueless about how the announcer helps their team."

Pro: Detroit's booth rivaled pinball. "On a fall night, few people, outfielders would hear you," said Harwell. Con: Tiger Stadium aged, closing September 27, 1999, its flag lowered and passed among 65 ex-Tigers in a chronological line from the flagpole to the plate for transfer to Comerica Park. Ernie said good-bye over the P.A. microphone, voice breaking, lights dimming. "Farewell, old friend. We will remember."

His last broadcast year was 2002. Harwell opened the American Stock Exchange. The Tigers unveiled a statue on Ernie Harwell Day. "The only other day I remember was when the sheriff of Fulton County in Georgia gave me a day to get out of town." Croquet was then the hipster sport, then the NFL, then NBA. Baseball would survive: "an individual sport like Gary Cooper in *High Noon*. A distinctly American sport"—and life.

In 1981, he invoked "a tongue-tied kid from Georgia, growing up to be an announcer and praising the Lord for showing him the way to Cooperstown." You thought of *Ernie,* as in Harwell; *Tiger,* as in baseball; *class,* as in friend.

He still made people happy.

ERNIE HARWELL

LONGEVITY: *10*   55 years.

CONTINUITY: *8*   Brooklyn N.L. 1948–49; New York N.L. 1950–53; Baltimore A.L. 1954–59; Detroit 1960–91 and 1993–2002; California A.L. 1992; CBS Radio "Game of the Week" 1992–97; ABC/NBC TV The Baseball Network 1994–95.

NETWORK: *9*   N.L. playoff 1951 (CBS TV). All-Star Game 1958 and second 1961 and World Series 1963 and 1968 (NBC Radio). L.C.S. 1969 (Robert Wold Radio) and 1976–83, 1985–86, and 1988–89 (CBS Radio). "Game" 1992–97 (CBS Radio). TBN 1994–95 (ABC/NBC TV).

KUDOS: *10*   Cooperstown 1981. NSSA Hall of Fame 1989. Seven other Halls, including ASA 1991, Georgia, Michigan, and Radio. Guinness World Records: "most durable baseball announcer." *SI* Voice, all-time dream team.

LANGUAGE: *10*   Anecdotal.

POPULARITY: *10*   Forty-one percent of 2004 Michigan Harris poll named him favorite Voice—two years after retiring.

PERSONA: *10*   Kin.

VOICE: *10*   Hypnotic.

KNOWLEDGE: *10*   Expert by age 10.

MISCELLANY: *10*   Donated 4,000 books, hundreds of photos, and 75,000 clippings to Detroit Public Library. Missed two games: Cooperstown and brother's funeral.

TOTAL: *97*   (third place).

4

Mel Allen

Dizzy Dean

Vin Scully

Jack Buck

Harry Caray

MEL ALLEN

Walt Whitman wrote, "I hear America singing, the varied caroles I hear." Mel Allen sang through eleven U.S. presidents, nine commissioners, and four major wars. In 1939, he became Voice of the Yankees. He was fired in 1964 after 18 flags, 12 world titles, and nearly 4,000 games. Allen left the air, knew private hell, then forged TV's brilliant "This Week In Baseball." He had all, lost all, and, incredibly, came back.

At peak, Mel was sport's five-star mouthpiece—to *Variety* magazine, "one of the 25 most recognizable voices in the world." It was deep, full, and Southern, mixing Billy Graham and James Earl Jones. In Omaha, Allen once hailed a cab. "Sheraton, please," he said, simply. The cabbie's head jerked like a swivel. "The voice was astonishing," said 1953–56 Yankees colleague Jim Woods. Ibid, debate *about* The Voice.

Depending on your view, Mel was a saladin, random chatterer, or surpassing personality of the big city in the flesh. Red Barber thought him prejudiced. The Mets' Lindsey Nelson was antipodal: "The best of all time to broadcast the game." All conceded Mel's drop-dead lure.

Damn Yankees sang, "You've Gotta Have Heart." Born on Valentine's Day, Mel fused "Dear Heart," "Heart of Gold," and "Heartbreak Hotel."

"Give me a child until he is seven," vowed Saint Francis of Assisi, "and you may have him afterward." Melvin Israel was born in 1913 to Julius and Anna, Russian emigrants who owned a clothing store in Johns, Alabama, 25 miles from Birmingham. (In 1940, he dropped Israel and adopted his dad's middle name. "The Yanks' idea," Mel said, wryly. "They told me it was more generic.")

The child walked at nine months, spoke sentences at one year, read box scores at five. "I'd go to our outside john," he said, "and devour a Montgomery Ward catalogue." Allen graduated from grammar school at 11; high school, 15; the University of Alabama, 23. New York had the adult afterward. In 1936, he went there for a week's vacation. The trip lasted 60 years.

On a lark, Mel auditioned as a $45-a-week CBS Radio announcer. He understudied Bob Trout and Ted Husing, interrupted Kate Smith to report the *Hindenburg* crash, and introduced Perry Como on "The Pick and Pat Minstrels Show." Work at warp-speed: Kentucky Derby, International Polo Games, and Vanderbilt Cup auto race. "The weather is awful and I'm in a plane when the race is called off." Filling time, he ad-libbed for an hour.

"Allen [went] up there a raw kid from the turntable department," wrote Ron Powers. "He came back down a star." Often the ex-Piedmont League bat boy drove from CBS to the Polo Grounds and Yankee Stadium, watched players isolated in his attention, and broadcast *sotto voce*. "I sat and thought, 'I'd give anything to broadcast in a place like this.' " God answered through soft soap, not hard sell.

In 1939, the Stripes and Jints debuted on radio. Arch McDonald had formerly done the Senators. One day an aide began an Ivory Soap ad by saying "ovary." He laughed, repeated it, and was fired, replaced by Mel. Soon Arch beat a path back to Washington. Within a year, so far, so fast, too fast, he often said, for his own good, Allen had traded baseball's fringe for core—the Voice of the Yankees, at 26.

Mel knew what he had—"more history to call," said Nelson, "than any sportscaster ever." Its stage was The Stadium's vast power alleys, pee-wee lines, and triple tiers. The stars were idols: Phil Rizzuto (to Mel, "Scooter") and Allie Reynolds ("SuperChief") and Lou Gehrig ("Iron Horse," a quiet man, a hero). Said Bob Costas: "Not just baseball players, but personalities of the time."

On July 4, 1939, the Bronx housed baseball's Gettysburg Address. Said Gehrig: "I consider myself the luckiest man on the face of the earth." Next spring, dying of amyotrophic lateral sclerosis, he visited the dugout, shuffled to the bench, sat down, and patted Allen's knee. "I never got a chance to listen to your games before because I was playing every day. But I want you to know they're the only thing that keeps me going." As Gehrig left, Mel sobbed.

At that moment Allen seemed a Yankee to his pinstriped underwear. Their sunny-dark star wore none. By 1947, racked by cancer, Babe Ruth could barely talk. The trademark camel-hair coat and matching cap draped a shell. Mel introduced him on his Day. "Babe, do you want to try and say something?" he bayed above the crowd.

Ruth croaked, "I must."

Babe returned to the dugout. Mel returned to selling more cigars, cases of beer, safety razors, and fans on baseball than any broadcaster who ever lived.

Allen's first World Series was 1938. Before the 1942 opener, he thought, "as I always did, about one solitary fan—Ralph Edwards [from 'This Is Your Life'] taught me this—who I imagined sitting a few feet away. In my mind, he was my audience. I was talking to him."

That morning Mel had read *Time* magazine. "In U.S. drug stores, lunch wagons, barbershops, parlors, and pool halls over 25 million radio listeners will cock their ears next week to listen to three men [Allen, Barber, and Bill Corum] that broadcast the World Series." Recalling the story, the "solitary fan" seemed a horde.

"I bumbled along for a while before I got my wits," laughed The Voice, ultimately yoking the Rose Bowl, JackPot Bowling, heavyweight fights, "Mel Allen Sports Spot," record 24 All-Star Games, Little League World Series, and Fox newsreels: "This is your Movietone reporter." The real Series dwarfed them. Allen became its post-World War II badge.

"Ask any kid," said Joe Garagiola, growing up in East St. Louis. "It wasn't October till I heard that voice." Retrieve 1947–48–49 Mutual Radio: respectively, Bill Bevens's near–no-no, Phil Masi's near-pickoff, and Tommy Henrich's Game One-winning blast. A record 26 of 39 million homes with radio heard "Old Reliable" homer. By 1952, one of two NBC TV sets watched the Brooks and Stripes.

Mel jeweled Game Seven: "It's fairly cool today—it's topcoat weather, but you can be assured that as far as those men on the diamond are concerned it's mighty hot." A camera fixed the dugout: "Tension everywhere. Moving around. Slapping hands." The Bums later filled the sacks. "It's a high pop-up! Who's going to get it? Here comes Billy Martin digging hard—and he makes the catch at the last second! How about that!" or this: Yanks, 4–2.

"Freeze that moment," said Nelson in his melodic lilt. "There was no Super Bowl or overlapping seasons. Nothing approached the Series." Before 1966, local-team Voices called it. "The Yanks were in almost every year. Mel did those, and others"—22 overall, including 1946–63's record 18 straight. "How about that!" turned national idiom. "Hello there, everybody, this is Mel Allen!" bound stardom of name and game.

Bill Glavin, a teacher, grew up in Albany. "Each year, the nuns arranged for the Series to be piped into class over the loudspeaker. You'd hear it from people you never knew—'The Duke [Snider] parked one' or 'Damn Yankees!'" He shook his head. "Games were daytime. You spent all morning talking about it, heard or saw it, then argued for hours afterward."

A popular Broadway song of the time was "Happy Talk." Allen ensured that baseball's was.

Bill Millsaps, ultimately a Richmond columnist, was the son of a Tennessee schoolmaster. On October 8, 1956, dad appeared at the boy's classroom and led him to the hallway.

"Come with me," said the father.

Bill panicked. What had he done? Walking past several secretaries, they finally neared dad's office.

"What is it? What's wrong?"

"Close the door, Billy, and turn on Mel Allen. You won't believe what Don Larsen is doing to the Dodgers."

The Yankees and Dodgers played six times between 1947 and 1956. Wrote Stan Isaacs: "Their meetings were almost like adventure chapters in a serialized novel." The 1958 Series matched Milwaukee and New York. A wire arrived in Game Two: "Allen, you Yankee-lover, shut up." By contrast, Tom Gallery felt that "something in his presence brought a drama to the moment."

Mel called Casey Stengel's ten Yanks Series. "Ask a question and he'd talk about every club he played with and fans who gave him dinner before he'd answer the question which now you'd forgot. Oh, yeah, 'How did you like playing under John McGraw?' " Pause. Casey was a minor-league player, manager, and president. "He didn't like it, and finally figured out what to do." He quit as a player, fired himself as manager, then resigned.

What a couplet: the Perfessor spinning, and Allen speaking. "White Owl Wallops" and "Ballantine Blasts" were "going, going, gone." A full count prompted "three and two. What'll he do?" Yankees-haters charged praise-by-association—Bert Wilson: "It's easy to broadcast when you win"—panning Mel about two teenagers in the bleachers.

"That's interesting," he said. "He's kissing her on the strikes, and she's kissing him on the balls."

Phil Rizzuto shook his head. "Mel," said Allen's 1957–64 partner, "this is just not your day."

Each day he vied with another Dixied tongue.

"Even now, when you talk announcers," said Vin Scully, "you start with Mel and Red." They shared eight World Series—baseball at mid-century. Often likened, they differed, too.

Barber was white wine, crepes suzette, and bluegrass music. Allen was hot dogs, beer, and the U.S. Marine Band. Like Millay, Barber was a poet. Like Sinatra, Allen was a balladeer. Detached, Red reported. Involved, Mel roared. Barber chatted on the small of his chair. Allen frayed its edge, filibustering for hours. "To care, to root," Red sniffed, "these are not the rights of the professional." The Voice cleaved: "Of course, I wanted the Yankees." Inevitably, you favored one or the other.

In 1953, Mel aired the first tape-measure homer (Mantle's). Another first: CBS TV's 1957 prime-time "Person to Person" profiled a sportscaster. In 1961, Roger Maris lined record-tying homer 60: "There it is! There it is! If it stays fair, there it is! . . . They are pushing him from the dugout! This is most unusual!" Audio of the 1960 Series shows him rising, receding, and cresting, a boom box holding sway. "There's a long drive into deep left field! Look out now!" he cried of Bill Mazeroski's decisive dinger. The warning soon applied aptly to himself.

One night Allen froze on a local newscast. At The Stadium he began to struggle on the air. In 1963, Mantle homered in Game Four of the Series. "The [Dodger Stadium] crowd roared. I started to roar, too. Then suddenly I lost my voice"—a gasping, wheezing sound. Gallery yanked Mel from the booth. Outsiders ascribed causes to his silence: sinus, laryngitis, or shock. Dick Young wrote that Allen couldn't accept L.A.'s sweep. "His voice refused to believe it, and therefore he could not repeat it."

Jerry Coleman, a Yankees announcer, recalled a game earlier that year. "In a rain delay, Mel got to talking. He wouldn't stop. It was wild. Something was happening. You just didn't know what."

In 1964, the Stripes played their first Series *sans* Allen since 1943. On December 17—with no reason, not even a release—they fired their apotheosis. "He gave them his life," gaped Barber, "and they broke his heart."

They still had, years later. "The Yankees never held a press conference," Mel began, flushing color. "They left people to believe what they wanted. [NBC and Movietone also ditched him in 1964.] The lies were horrible—that I was gay or a lush or beat people or had a breakdown." Lacking explanation, "Allen became a victim of rumors," *Sports Illustrated* wrote. "He was supposed to be a drunkard, a drug user. Neither rumor was true, but he couldn't fight them. It was as if he had leprosy."

Researching books in the 1980s, Nelson and I supposed by mail. One doctor hinted at mini-strokes. Another recalled Mel's physician, Max Jacobson a.k.a. "Dr. FeelGood," giving President Kennedy a strange blur of vitamins, horse placenta, and amphetamines. Broadcaster Bud Blattner said: "Mel was always going—Yankees, commercials, Movietone. He'd take a pill to get going, a pill to wind down." Did they dull speech, or mind? "Who can say?" Lindsey said. Allen tried.

"Ballantine was our chief sponsor, and they made a bad mistake," he said. "Most breweries built regional affiliates to cut shipping. Ballantine *enlarged* its

[Newark] base. Transportation soared. They cut the budget, and mine was the head that rolled." He smiled. "If we'd only had time to talk, I'd have taken a cut, done"—softly—"*anything* to stay."

Replacing him, Garagiola got a telegram. "Mel said he hoped I'd stay on the job as long as him. I said—here he is, heart breaking—'I didn't know there were still guys like you around.'" Vanishing, Allen—childless, unmarried—began a decade of curiosa: banquets, random Braves radio and Indians TV, and voiceovers, including Ballantine's.

For years, an unknown admirer had sent one red rose each day. Mel's garden was now bare.

July 1968: Minnesota hosts Cleveland. Allen, interrupting Harry Jones, says, "This is the land of 10,000 lakes. They have these picturesque names." Reciting them, he paddles to Lake Superior, site of Henry Wadsworth Longfellow's poem, "The Song of Hiawatha."

Does Harry know the poem? Wearily, Jones mutters that he does.

"Let's see now, how does it go?" asks The Voice, repeating its first 37 lines.

Jones glared. Coleman later laughed. "Who else could make Longfellow and baseball twins?" Nodding, I relived that good-bye song. For a long time Mel seemed deader than Marley's Ghost. Baffled, the public felt a gentle protectiveness. "I mean, actors leave, they're forgotten," Allen said in 1975. "Folks are still writing the Yankees, asking where Mel is." John Sterling joined the Stripes in 1989: "You could be here till 2525," he said, "and Mel will always be the Voice of the Yankees."

F. Scott Fitzgerald wrote that "In America, there are no second acts." Bereaved, but not bitter, Allen pined for his first. Then, in 1977, "This Week In Baseball" began on syndicated (later, NBC) TV—ultimately, sport's highest-rated serial. One Saturday a sometime fan entered the living room. My mother could not have heard his crisp-voweled vent since 1964. "I can't believe it. Is *that* Mel Allen?"

At that moment it seemed he had never been away.

"TWIB" made Mel a Grand Old Man of Broadcasting. "Everywhere I go," said creator Joe Reichler, "players tell me, 'Jesus, wait till Mel gets ahold of *that* play.'" Tug McGraw claimed "the world's best Mel imitation." Young touted "The Comeback Kid." *SI* called "[him] back where he belongs, an old campaigner, a keeper of tradition. For years he was a forgotten man, but it has all come back to him in abundance. The taste must be sweet."

Allen added Yanks mid-eighties cable. "He gets him!" The Voice cried in 1983. "A no-hitter, a no-hitter, a no-hitter by Dave Righetti! How about that!" Next year he did a rap tune voice-over: "Man alive! What a drive! A grand-slam homer! That ain't no jive!" One "TWIB" feature explored Alaskan baseball: "Penguins admitted free," Mel ad-libbed as eyeballs rolled. "Our show," said executive producer Geoff Belinfante, "introduced him to a whole new generation."

In 1984, Alabama's Farrah Law School named a chair. Class of '36 recalled how joining the Stripes—"the Voice of the Yankees," he said, almost to himself—once seemed as remote as men on the moon. "'Today we are afraid of simple words like goodness and mercy and kindness,' " Mel quoted Chinese writer Lin Yutang. "'We don't believe in the good old words any more because we don't believe in the good old values any more.' "

Listening, you swore that a florist decorated his voice.

MEL ALLEN

LONGEVITY:	10	46 years.
CONTINUITY:	9	New York A.L. 1939–43, 1946–64, and 1982–85; New York N.L. 1939–43; Milwaukee N.L. 1965; Cleveland A.L. 1968; "This Week In Baseball" 1977–96.
NETWORK:	10	World Series 1938 (CBS), 1940–42, 1946–50, and 1954 (Mutual), 1951–53, 1955–58, and 1960–63 (NBC TV), and 1959 (NBC Radio). All-Star Game 1938–40 and 1943 (CBS), 1941–42 and 1946–51 (Mutual), 1952–both 1959, second 1960, first 1961, and second 1962 (NBC TV). "TWIB" 1977–96.
KUDOS:	10	Cooperstown 1978. Ten-time *TSN* "Announcer of the Year." NSSA 1952–53 and 1955 Sportscaster of the Year and Hall of Fame 1972. ASA Hall 1985.
LANGUAGE:	10	Relied on mood, not script. "How about that!" changed vernacular.
POPULARITY:	10	Became game's marquee team and series.
PERSONA:	10	The Voice of baseball.
VOICE:	10	Best there ever was.
KNOWLEDGE:	10	Who better knew the infield fly?
MISCELLANY:	10	1949–63 Rose Bowl (NBC TV). Movietone 1938–63. Called ABC, CBS, NBC, and Mutual. At one time or another, did Westminster Kennel Club Dog Show, Notre Dame football, and WOR New York's "Mel Allen's Popsicle Clubhouse." Forged sport's first college or pro TV replay: July 17, 1959.
TOTAL:	99	(second place). *Scores based on 1–10 point scale.*

Allen died, at 83, 12 years later. The Stadium flag flew at half-mast. Robert Merrill sang the National Anthem at Stamford, Connecticut's, Temple Beth-El. "TWIB" honored "Mel Allen: 1913–1996." Through 2002 his talking mannequin—"Hello there, everybody!"—began and closed each show.

Such a life deserved a coda, and got it, when in 1990 SUNY at Geneseo in upstate New York celebrated the first annual Mel Allen Scholarship. I had seen politicians laid siege to, but not like this: The Voice, flanked by teenagers and 70-somethings, falling back on his career.

Allen later dubbed the night "among the most emotional of my life." Most still thought him better than being at the park. Even Yankees-haters no longer hoped for laryngitis. All prized the comeback—America with him, with him because it loved him.

Once Mel said, in his not immodest way, "I always thought I had the kind of a voice that was not unpleasant."

How about *that*!

VIN SCULLY

I recall, like yesterday, October 26, 1991. Since morning I had worked on a speech at the White House. At 10:15 P.M., I left, found my car, and tuned to an already classic Fall Classic.

Three of the first five World Series games were decided by a run. In Game Six, a Twins runner reached second base. At this point, Allen blurts "How about that!"; Harry Caray, "Holy cow!"; Jerry Coleman, a malapropism. Instead, the Voice cited *Death of a Salesman*'s "tiny ship" (runner) seeking "safe harbor" (home).

Only Vin Scully could fuse baseball and Arthur Miller, joining the Dodgers before "Tokyo Rose" went to prison, William Faulkner won the Nobel Prize, and the last member of the Grand Army of the Republic died. Once he said, "It was so hot today the moon got sunburned." A master linguist still links baseball's sun, moon, and stars.

Explain the inexplicable. Phil Rizzuto was born in Flatbush. Vin was born a fly ball from the Bronx on November 29, 1927, to a silk salesman and an "Irish, red-haired, and like me, at times unemotional" mother. Their radio became a sudden magic place—"a monster that sat so high off the ground that I was able to crawl up under it—actually *under* it."

Each Saturday, he sat with saltines and milk and heard Ted Husing air football. "I shouldn't have cared about a game like Florida–Tennessee. But I got goose bumps hearing the roar of the crowd." The Giants fan loved Brooklyn's evangelist. "Red made me want to be a sportscaster. At 8, I wrote a composition on broadcasting for the nuns. My friends wanted to be a doctor, lawyer—not me." Radio was neither a belated nor acquired taste.

Growing up, Vin delivered milk and mail, pushed garment racks, and cleaned silver in the basement of the Pennsylvania Hotel. By 1949, he left Fordham Preparatory, joined the Navy, entered Fordham University, formed its FM station, sang in a barbershop quartet, played center field, got a degree, and sent 150 letters to stations along the seaboard.

"I got one response": WTOP Washington, making him a fill-in. One day, interviewed at CBS New York, Scully asked for Red. "He headed network sports and only had a second, but told me to leave my address." That fall, CBS needed a backup Voice for "College Football Roundup." Recalling Vin, Barber asked WTOP for references, phoned his home, and "got my mother, who took the message, but told me it was from Red Skelton."

Quit clowning. Vin broadcast on the roof of Fenway Park with a long cable cord, microphone, and 60-watt bulb for light. Next week Red called again. "The producer told me about your awful facilities. You'll have a booth on Saturday—Harvard–Yale."

In October 1949, Ernie Harwell crossed the East River to the Polo Grounds. On Opening Day 1950, Scully, replacing him, began radio/TV baseball's longest same-team skein. For the rookie, 22, still living with his parents, humility, not history, was in the air.

"One day I brought the lineup. Barber said, 'This man hit third yesterday. Why is he fifth today?' It was the last time I didn't know." Red taught to avoid hearing other Voices. "'Don't copy. You will water your own wine,' he'd say. Instead, bring to the booth an ingredient no one else could—me, and whatever qualities made me a human being." Soon the newcomer's intuitions were in tune.

"No other baseball team," wrote Leonard Koppett, "generated a richer collection of memories, more closely held by so many people," than Vin's Dodgers. Gil Hodges spelled respect. Billy Cox turned doubles into slumps. Roy Campanella made Flatbush an arcade. Surnames seemed superfluous: Oisk, Big Newk, and Preach, not Carl Erskine, Don Newcombe, and Preacher Roe. All were family, other sports something to take or leave.

Brooklyn cross-hatched victory and misery: six post-war pennants, but with a thing about losing a last-day flag or Series (1946–47, 1949–53, and 1956). "You know what I really don't understand?" Pee Wee Reese asked.

"What?" said Jackie Robinson.

"How after all these years playing baseball I haven't gone insane."

As we have seen, the Dodgers ditched Barber on the 1953 Classic. Heartsick, Vin asked his advice. "If there was anyone I'd want to take my place, it'd be you." Scully, 25, did. By 1955, having lost seven straight Series, the Borough of Churches sought absolution.

In Game Seven, Vin called the final out of the Dodgers' 2–0 deliverance.

"Ladies and gentlemen," Scully said on NBC, "the Brooklyn Dodgers are the champions of the world." All winter people asked how he remained so calm. "The hard truth is I was so emotionally overwhelmed that if I had said another word, I would have cried."

Even harder, Walter O'Malley already was thinking of moving to Los Angeles. Vin saw no cause to leave. He was happy, in his home town. The team had drawn a million people a record 13 straight years. How could you trade them for a place Fred Allen called "great, if you're an orange"?

Easily, it occurred, in October 1957.

"Historically, we shall be proven right," O'Malley said of the Dodgers' apostasy. Scully wondered. "Everything I cherished was in New York. It's like the wife whose husband is transferred. She may not want to go, but she goes."

The second-year Angelenos won a pennant playoff: "Big bouncer over the mound, over second base," said Scully. "Up with it is Mantilla, throws low and wild! Hodges scores! We go to Chicago!" A *New Yorker* cartoon showed a Brooklynite crying at Ebbets Field: "Somewhere the sun is shining, somewhere hearts are light." Vin telecast the Series. "Somewhere" meant L.A.'s weird temporary den.

"The problem," Vin mused, "is that the [Memorial] Coliseum was a football and track place—and football and baseball need different configurations." First-base stands almost touched the foul line. Third's seats lay somewhere off Marina del Rey. A visitor absorbed white shirts, coolie hats, 251-foot left-field line, and 93,000 capacity. In center field, you needed binoculars to spot home plate.

"Until '58, the closest big-league city was St. Louis," said *Los Angeles Times* columnist Jim Murray. "The Dodgers had a selling job." O'Malley had beamed each game from Ebbets Field. In L.A.—"We're not giving away our product"—he barred home TV. The move gave Vin, with his rhythm and tempo and bending vowels and similes and allusions—twilight's "little footsteps of sunshine"; "He catches the ball gingerly, like a baby chick falling from the tree"—vast leverage. Interest turned to radio, of which Scully was a wiz.

"Walter knew there were probably more radios in this area than anywhere in the world," Vin said, "and that for every guy listening, many would come to the park." To writer Rick Reilly, the Portable Vinnie made L.A. a transistor town. "Forget video. [His] musings drift up from every traffic jam and outdoor cafe."

Scully's voice was everywhere—Venice Beach, Whittier Market, in the stands, on the field. In 1960, he noted that it was umpire Frank Secory's birthday. "So I said over the radio, 'I'll count to three and everybody yell, "Happy birthday, Frank."'"

Scully: "One, two, three."

The Coliseum cast of thousands: "Happy birthday, Frank!"

The '62ers opened Dodger Stadium. The A.L. Angels became a tenant. One day Baltimore changes pitchers. Fans begin to cheer. Orioles Voice Chuck Thompson says, "These are great fans here, cheering Baltimore." Next day the O's change pitchers. Again, applause. "What's going on?" he said, finally seeing earplugs. "They're hearing *Vinnie,* cheering when something happened." Millions took Scully's offer to "pull up a chair."

Vin didn't *do* the Dodgers. Wrote Reilly: "Vinnie *is* the Dodgers." It is fair enough to ask why.

A hunch:

- Scully was a scout. "L.A.'d have loved anybody when the Dodgers came west," said Bob Prince. "It was his fortune to be first—to set the style." Bob later snubbed a San Diego Padres offer: "You've got desert to the east, Mexico to the south, ocean to the west, and Scully to the north."
- Knowledge. "He'd played baseball," said Murray. "Plus, it can lag and Vinnie distracts you. He'll move into a story about Duke Snider so smoothly you'd swear Duke was playing now."
- The Coliseum, so large that viewing resembled pantomime. "A lot of people couldn't see, so they brought radios to hear me talk," Vin said. "Then it became a habit even after we moved in '62."

- Being near, but not of, Hollywood. "Authenticity counts in the living room," said Pacific Palisades neighbor Ronald Reagan. Affable and courteous, he treated you like a guest.

Even then, Los Angeles sprawled *sans* focal point. "When you talk about [it], you're talking about the drifter. Californians aren't in contact with their neighbors," Theodore H. White wrote in *The Making of the President 1964*. "People are lost. They have no one to talk to. And the doorbell-ringer has an importance . . . they've reached out and touched." Vin became a doorbell-ringer, a friend you would want to know.

By the late sixties, he had missed only two games (birth of a child, and sister's marriage), become two- (ultimately, four-) time National Sportscaster of the Year, and called four (of a record 19) no-hitters, including Sandy Koufax's in 1965. "There are 29,000 people in the ballpark, and a million butterflies," he said. The mound had "become the loneliest place in the world."

Finally: "Swung on and missed! A perfect game! On the scoreboard in right field it is 9:46 P.M. in the City of the Angels, Los Angeles, California." Prose was telling: Vin's eyes were already on the clock.

"How much more time do I have for trying something new?" he said in 1969. "Could I have become a moderator? An actor? A singer?" Starting NBC's quiz show "It Takes Two," Scully's schedule approached rush hour in Riverside. "I'll read books, magazines, talk with experts. I'm afraid of going out and sounding like a horse's fanny, which is one reason why I prepare. Sir Laurence Olivier was asked what makes a great actor and he said, 'The humility to prepare and the confidence to bring it off.' Believe me, I'm loaded with the humility to prepare."

Could L.A. wave the flag? Vin asked on radio. (From 1967 to 1973, no.) Turn to "It Takes Two": Miss, how many feet of nylon thread in a pair of stockings? (There once was a girl from Nantucket . . . oops, wrong card.) Where *were* we, anyway? NBC? Dodger Stadium? "I'm glad I did it all," he laughed. "It's just that with the crazy scheduling, I'd hate to do it again."

"It Takes Two" died in 1971. CBS's 1973 "Vin Scully Show" lasted 13 weeks. More abiding was a gag. One day a car used in an old George Raft film drove on the set. Backstage crews, actors, and "Laugh-In"'s entire company watched. Vin "was to open the trunk to find the answer to a question on bootlegging," read *TV Guide*. Innocently, he did. "His jaw fell. Reclining within, unseen by the audience, was a delicious redhead, who had starred in *Playboy*. She leaned on an elbow, staring soulfully at Scully. She was as naked as a jaybird."

Fordham had not prepared Vin for ladies who had on not a stitch. "[He] was speechless. His first impulse was to remove his coat and cover the lady, but he realized this would stir suspicion among the audience. Nervously, he lifted the answer from the trunk and closed it. The plotters in the wings roared."

Two decades of play-by-play, and Vin was still transported. "I still get goose bumps when I hear a roar before the first pitch. Maybe it means I haven't grown." Sadness had. In 1972, wife Joan, 35, died of an accidental medical overdose. "I had three young kids. The road was awful. My best friend there was a book. Once I got to Atlanta and my oldest son, Mike [who died in a 1994 helicopter crash], said, 'Why don't you come home, Dad?' I said, 'I'll be there in only 12 days.' I felt like a louse."

Being Catholic, bleeding Irish, Vin said, "I was brought up thinking about death. Tomorrow is so uncertain." As a single parent, job one became staying home. "He spurned 'Monday Night Football' and NBC baseball," said *Times* writer Larry Stewart. In late 1973, Scully got engaged. Sandra Schaefer had two children. Soon they bore another. "Baseball'd been enough," he said. "Now we needed money"—i.e., CBS 1975 tennis, golf, and football pact. "I could still do the Dodgers. Network baseball was never a big deal [CBS didn't carry it]. I was happy as it was."

To many, baseball *sans* Vin equaled Bogart *sans* Bacall. "Only a Dodgers flag," said Murray, "put him on the Series." He did 1966's, then 1974's. "[NBC's] Curt Gowdy, Tony Kubek, and Monte Moore sounded like college radio rejects [vs.] Scully," wrote Henry Hecht. ABC shrugged in 1977. "In their first Series," the *New York Post*'s Phil Mushnick said, "they wanted their own [football's Keith Jackson and Howard Cosell]. Vin was offered a bit part," declining. Insult stung: baseball's Secretariat, dumped for two Mr. Eds.

In 1978–79, he did CBS Radio's All-Star Game and Series, respectively. *The New York Times* noted "fans turning off [ABC] TV's sound . . . and onto his commentary." Willie Stargell's homer won the Classic. "He's done it!" cried Scully. "Pops has hit it out!" Listening, you thought: Vin does that each night.

In 1982, he had a Night at Dodger Stadium, entered the Hall of Fame, and got a star on the Hollywood Walk of Fame. That fall NBC inked a $550 million major-league six-year pact. Return on investment demanded Scully. "I was doing fewer Dodger games [home radio/road TV]. It was easier to say yes [to an annual $2 million salary]." Pulling up a network chair seemed as comfy as Vin's childhood Emerson.

"He is baseball's best announcer [four L.C.S., 12 All-Star Games, and *nonpareil* 25 Series]," said NBC sports head Thomas Watson. "Why shouldn't he be ours?" Mused columnist Jack Craig: "Skeptics could wonder how well [Scully] will do on TV [vs. radio] on a network [vs. local] level." By mid-1983, it was hard to find a critic who admitted doubt. Weekly Vin made network baseball breathe, dance, *sing.*

"So Rice hits a long out, and Tony Armas hits one out long!" he said one Saturday. The 1984 Tigers began 35–5: "The first-place Bengals are clawing up a storm." A first baseman made an error: "[By contrast] Gil Hodges's big hands made his glove as handy as Michael Jackson's." It seemed inevitable: "Game," Scully's Everest. Or was that the '84 Series? "Perhaps no sports event," wrote *TSN,* "has been told as well."

Lance Parrish dinged Goose Gossage. "With the clocking of the [speed] gun, the Goose has been clocked." Tim Lollar was "trying to keep San Diego from disappearing without leaving an oil slick." Detroit's Mickey Lolich receded to a Bob Uecker seat. "*Sic transit gloria,*" said the Latinist of the ex-Series ikon. ("Thus goes the glory.") Vin even lip-read on-field dialogue. "Tom Lasorda is the easiest guy in baseball to read."

A sense of when to hush made Vin a breeze to hear. In 1974, Al Downing ceded Hank Aaron's 715th homer. Rising, Scully left the booth: "I didn't want the temptation to talk over noise." Finally, he returned: "And it is a great moment for all of us, and particularly for Henry Aaron." A decade later Kurt Bevacqua went Series yard. "For one minute, as the replay showed Bevacqua turning around in a circle and jumping for joy," said *The Washington Post,* "[Vin] didn't say a word."

Mookie Wilson's grounder ends 1986's Game Six. "It gets through Buckner! Here comes Knight! And the Mets win it!" cried Scully, shushing. Kirk Gibson hits a 1988 Capraesque homer. "A long fly ball to deep right field! She is gone! In the year of the implausible, the impossible has happened!" Vin fled the mike, deferring to the viewer. Such class is hard to find.

Scully liked the local/network tandem. At 61, he called 45 innings in 27 hours: four teams, in two cities, awarded a writer's Purple Lozenge. One game ended at 2:52 A.M. A worse end was CBS TV's, buying 1990–93 bigs exclusivity. It killed "Game," junked regular coverage, and threw their grandstand in the trash.

"It's a staple that's gone,"Vin said. "I feel for people who come to me and say how they miss it, and I hope me." Many turned to him on 1990–97 CBS Radio. In 1999, Kevin Costner's *For the Love of the Game* starred Scully's Irish tenor. Next year he gave Fordham's 155th commencement speech: "Don't let the winds blow away you or your faith in God." For an hour, Class of '49 tethered work, honor, and what writer Ellen Glasgow called "the infinite feeling for the spirit of the past, and the lingering poetry of time and place."

By now, Dick Enberg mused, Vin had become the anti–21st Century—"against the flow, deep and authentic, oblivious to fad." His "safe harbor" has

---

VIN SCULLY

LONGEVITY:	*10*	55 years.
CONTINUITY:	*10*	Brooklyn N.L. 1950–57; Los Angeles N.L. 1958– ; NBC TV "Game of the Week" 1983–89.
NETWORK:	*10*	"Game" 1983–89 (NBC TV). All-Star Game second 1959 and 1962, 1963, 1983, 1985, 1987, and 1989 (NBC TV) and 1990–91 and 1995–97 (CBS Radio). L.C.S. 1973 (Robert Wold Radio) and 1983, 1985, 1987, and 1989 (NBC TV). World Series 1953, 1955, 1956, 1959, 1963, 1965, 1966, 1974, 1984, 1986, and 1988 (NBC TV) and 1977–83, 1990–93, and 1995–97 (CBS Radio).
KUDOS:	*10*	"Most memorable [L.A. Dodgers] personality" 1976. Cooperstown 1982. Star, Hollywood Walk of Fame 1982. NSSA 1959, 1966, 1978, and 1982 Sportscaster of the Year and Hall of Fame 1991. ASA Sportscaster of the Year 1985 and Hall 1992. Named top 20th century sportscaster 2000. Ronald Reagan Media Award 1987. Twenty-five-time California Sportscaster of the Year. Sports Lifetime Achievement Emmy Award 1996. "Vin Scully Way" at Vero Beach training site. Press box at Dodger Stadiun named in honor.
LANGUAGE:	*10*	*Nonpareil.*
POPULARITY:	*10*	Owns Southern California.
PERSONA:	*10*	Baseball's Olivier.
VOICE:	*10*	"The Fordham Thrush," said Murray, "with the .400 larynx."
KNOWLEDGE:	*10*	*L.A. Times:* "Dodgers fans say they'd rather have Scully managing the club than Walter Alston."
MISCELLANY:	*10*	Dodgers radio/TV print ads place his name above team's.
TOTAL:	*100*	(first place).

berthed nearly 9,000 games: each ferrying the humility to prepare. The sixth-century Greek Heraclitus said, "A man's character is his fate." Baseball's fate has profited from an Artful Dodger's character.

CONNIE DESMOND

Connie Desmond was Eddie Fisher, losing Elizabeth Taylor; Bill Clinton, throwing greatness in the can; or ESPN founder Bill Rasmussen, selling before the getting was good. Put another way, he might have been Vin Scully.

In 1943, Desmond joined Barber at Ebbets Field. "I never thought of suc-ceeding him," he said. "Why would he leave?" The earth turned flat in late 1953: Red moved to Yankee Stadium. Connie took a knockout future—and flushed it down the flask.

"There are more old drunkards than old doctors," said Proverbs. Desmond became a drunkard as tomorrow seemed young. Sober, he might have become Walter O'Malley's Coronado. Instead, recall Churchill's "Ter-rible Ifs."

The Victorians called cloudless spells "Queen's Weather." A dreambox voice lit Desmond's. Holy Toledo! In 1932, he crashed radio on hometown WSPD. "I sang and did band remotes, but I really wanted baseball." He got it through a Wheaties Toledo Mud Hens ad.

By 1942, Connie called Triple-A Columbus. "'Help me do the Giants and Yankees,' Mel Allen said. I was shocked." Next season he moved to Brooklyn. In 1946, flagship WHN for the first time aired all games live. One day Carvel "Bama" Rowell broke the scoreboard clock. Dousing Walker, glass drove old Dixie down.

1947: Commissioner Happy Chandler suspended Leo Durocher for "conduct detrimental to baseball." 1948: Brooklyn began TV on WCBS Channel 2. 1949: Desmond added video. 1950: The Dodgers moved to WOR Channel 9. Even the P.A. announcer wrote an only-at-Ebbets plot. Tex Rickard wore a sweater, sat near the home dugout, and made English a second language. "A little boy has been found lost," he said. A pitcher left the game. Rickard explained: "He don't feel good." Another time coats draped a wall. "Will the people along the railing in left field please remove their clothes?"

Like Connie, he could not imagine a team removed from Brooklyn.

About this time, the Dodgers' new president began clothing baseball's largest re-created body. "Mr. O'Malley told me, 'Find a voice,' " said general manager Buzzie Bavasi, "for an idea I've got." The Voice had already re-created games in the South Atlantic League. The idea became the Brooklyn Dodgers Radio Network.

As a child, Nat Allbright broadcast to himself in the Class B Bi-State League. "The Dodgers were a natural," he chimed. "I'd been re-creating since seven!" More than 200 now call major-league radio and free/cable TV. A select group of 35–40 did the early 'fifties bigs. "Most had an aide, some two. They stayed forever."

The upshot was inertia. "The Yanks couldn't air games into Boston. A gentleman's agreement thrived for years." No gentleman, O'Malley would beam where he liked. "Much of the East wasn't served by baseball," said Bavasi. "Walter saw an opening," driving Allbright through.

They began with Bobby Thomson: "a tease for '52." By 1953, the Dodgers network had tied 117 outlets. A listener fancied Nat and Red cozying. In fact, Allbright never left D.C. "I'd say, 'There's Newcombe, perspiration dripping down his face.' You couldn't *tell* it was a re-creation."

For a while the network seemed as in-the-saddle as its team. Dodgers' ratings licked the *Pirates*' in McKeesport, near Pittsburgh. In Washington, they beat the Nats' over WINX, WEAM, and black WOOK. Owner Clark Griffith telegrammed Bavasi: "Get your games out of here." The G.M. waited two years to reply: "No one," he wrote, "tells me what to do with my broadcasts. Sincerely, E.J. Bavasi."

In 1956, O'Malley sold Ebbets Field. A year later he sold out Brooklyn. Allbright found Eden on Bedford Avenue. It vanished three thousand miles and a world away. "What killed us was the move west. Home games would end at 1:30 in the morning. The audience was gone," like the club.

"We began the day the Dodgers lost the pennant," Nat said of Thomson. Full circle: In 1962, they lost another last-day flag. That fall, the network pulled the plug. The Dodgers had long ago pulled Desmond's.

In 1955, the Brooks became the Stripes. "We dood it! We beat 'em! We beat them Yankees!" bannered Willard Mullin's Brooklyn Bum. "We spot 'em th' foist two games . . . an' we beat 'em! That [Johnny] Podres! Woil Champeens! Me!" Podres went deer hunting near his upstate New York home.

Belatedly, the impact reared. "Hey, Podres," he howled in the woods, "you beat the Yankees in the World Series! Where do you go from here?"

In Connie's case, the tank. Drinking in Ike's America was more kosher than in our politically lockstep time. Commuter trains rocked to gray flannel suits getting sloshed. Real men drank pals under the table. Desmond went a drink too far.

"He couldn't handle it," said Red. "Even when I was there, he'd stop showing up." In the film *My Favorite Year,* Peter O'Toole plays boozy actor Alan Swann. "With Swannie," an admirer says, "you forgive a lot, you know?" For a long time O'Malley forgave, too.

Desmond missed September 1955. Walter sacked him. Next year Connie begged a final chance. Reluctantly, the Bums agreed. "People thought O'Malley was hard. With me, he was more patient than I deserved." Reclimbing the wagon, Desmond fell off again.

To Brooklyn, reality soon meant exile. Connie's meant not doing another game. Harold Rosenthal covered the post-war Dodgers. "Without drinking, he might have replaced Barber." Instead, Desmond returned to Toledo, did the Mud Hens, and died in 1983, at 75.

"I had it, had it all," he said, quietly, perhaps not grasping his past, but no longer at its mercy.

CONNIE DESMOND

LONGEVITY:	5	15 years.
CONTINUITY:	8	New York A.L. 1942; Brooklyn N.L. 1943–56.
NETWORK:	1	Occasionally Mutual.
KUDOS:	3	Almost all before 1956.
LANGUAGE:	10	Stylish.
POPULARITY:	9	Diction and command.
PERSONA:	7	What might have been.
VOICE:	10	Intoxicating.
KNOWLEDGE:	7	Ten sober, four smashed.
MISCELLANY:	10	With Al Helfer, only Voice of the Apple's Dodgers, Giants, and Yankees. Did 15 Orange Bowls—also, locally, NFL Giants and NBA Knicks.
TOTAL:	70	(90th place).

GENE KELLY

In 1957, at Connie Mack Stadium, Gene Kelly heard of Joe McCarthy's death. He extolled the man who never played in the bigs, but played them like a bass. Some called Marse Joe pushbutton, he said. Others hailed the best manager of all time. "I couldn't write a better eulogy," Gene confessed. A producer then phoned to say that U.S. Senator Joe McCarthy had died.

"Of all people, I should be careful about names!" laughed the 1950–59 Phillies Voice. Meeting Kelly, strangers expected to hear "Singing In the Rain."

Raised in Philadelphia, Bob Brinker hosts the national radio financial show, "Money Talk." Think of mikemen as playing bass. Speaking, some seem to squeak. To Brinker, Gene showed his soul.

"Poetry in motion," he said. "He brought baseball play-by-play to its highest level." Kelly's seventh-inning stretch chanted "rub your noses, cross your fingers, tug on your caps, and knock on wood." It was no knock on lead Voice Byrum Saam to say that many preferred Gene.

"You gotta expect a strange life when you're born in Brooklyn [1919]," he laughed. On February 22, 1939, the Class of '41 journalism major debuted at Marshall College. "I was on the P.A. system [basketball, not baseball, which he played]. They needed a guy to fill in. I got $3 a game."

Kelly inked a minor-league pact, hurt his arm, and left Class C. Ahead: WGUA Washington, Pennsylvania; World War II; WXLW Indianapolis; and Mutual's 1946–49 Indy 500. Saam did the A's and Phils. Changing outlets, the no-world-title, last flag 1915, 1933–48 second-division 1950 Nationals tapped Gene.

Growing up in suburban Wayne, future Boston Voice Ned Martin liked the A's. "Yet there was no magic like '50—the Phils', and Gene's." Del Ennis's 126 RBI led the league. MVP Jim Konstanty relieved in 74 games. Robin Roberts went 20–11. A franchise high 1,217,035 saw an honest-to-God *pennant race*—the team vs. its history of gaffe and fear.

Philly led by 7 1/2 games on September 20. Pitcher Curt Simmons joined the National Guard. Roberts started thrice in the last five days. The final came at Brooklyn: win, or brook a playoff. Dick Sisler hit a three-run 10th-inning flag-clinching homer. The wireless knit Center City.

CBS TV aired the Series. Philly preferred Mutual's Kelly and Mel Allen. Skipper Eddie Sawyer started Konstanty in the opener: Yanks, 1–0. Next afternoon, Roberts lost, 2–1. The stage moved to Yankee Stadium, confusing the Whiz Kids, average age, 26. Pinstripes sweep. Gene was singing through his tears.

Coming home: Kelly covered the 1953 Yanks–Brooks convention. In Game Three, 35,270 jammed Ebbets Field. "The fans know that [Carl] Erskine has either equaled or bettered a record [Howard Ehmke's 1929 13 Ks]," he said on Mutual. "They want to see him beat it now. The Oh-two pitch to Mize from Erskine. He struck him out! Carl Erskine has set a new all-time World Series record! He has struck out 14 men. To a man, woman, and child— they're up on their feet out here in Flatbush!"

In Philadelphia, the Quakers began video. By 1955, Philly became a one-league town. "The Phils should have taken advantage." Instead, they hit bottom in 1958. Gene, Saam, and Claude Haring were "the anti-Phillies," said Brinker. "Mediocre on the field; great, above." Gene had mistaken McCarthy. He could not mistake the stench.

In late 1959, new flagship WFIL decided to cleanse Kelly. "I was given 30 days to find another job in Baltimore. I didn't get it [Bob Murphy did]." A decade later, another Phils Voice was sacked. "People ask, 'What do you think of what happened to Bill Campbell?' I feel like asking, 'What do you think of what happened to *me*?' "

GENE KELLY

LONGEVITY:	4	12 years.
CONTINUITY:	8	Philadelphia N.L. 1950–59; Cincinnati N.L. 1962–63.
NETWORK:	3	World Series 1950 and 1953 (Mutual). All-Star Game 1954 (Mutual).
KUDOS:	1	Marshall College prized alum.
LANGUAGE:	9	Lively.
POPULARITY:	10	Hard to tell By Saam was No. 1.
PERSONA:	8	Irish lilt/Eastern swank.
VOICE:	10	In 1970, the *Inquirer*'s Frank Dolson recalled "the old warmth, the old flair, the old corn . . . the machine-gun voice."
KNOWLEDGE:	10	Draped Big Ten and Ivy football, Philadelphia pro and Cincinnati college hoops, and American Hockey League.
MISCELLANY:	8	Probably tallest non–ex-jock announcer—6-foot-8.
TOTAL:	71	(89th place).

In 1962, Kelly drifted to Cincinnati. He missed the Seaboard. The Reds paroled Gene in late 1963. A stroke then reimprisoned him. "Recovery wasn't easy. I'd forget things, there were medical mistakes." A Philadelphia UHF station hired/fired him. He lasted three games on Notre Dame football.

"They got scared I was going to die." Kelly did, September 18, 1979, at 60. Joe McCarthy preceded him by a year. Neither funeral aired song and dance.

EARL GILLESPIE

On March 18, 1953, Milwaukee acquired the Braves of Boston since 1876. "It was a holiday when we heard they were coming," said Bud Selig, then 18.

In Boston, tickets dropped from windows into trucks on Gaffney Street. Brewtown fixed to kill its new team with love. A downtown parade led to the Schroeder Hotel. "People put up a Christmas tree!" said pitcher Ernie Johnson. "Since we'd missed Christmas, they said let's celebrate it now."

Through 1959 Milwaukee won two flags, barely missed two more, and mimed an All-Star team. Del Crandall caught. Henry Aaron, Bill Bruton, and Wes Covington outfielded. The infield tied Joe Adcock, Red Schoendienst, Johnny Logan, and Eddie Mathews. Burghers gave players rent-free cars. Tailgating invoked Wisconsin vs. Purdue.

"We'd go into Forbes Field—the Pirates were lousy—and there'd be 30,000," said Earl Gillespie. "Wrigley or Ebbets were jammed. Baseball's smallest town became its capital," leading the bigs in 1953–58 attendance. The Braves were the first franchise to change sites in half a century. Nirvana ensured it would not be the last.

Red Barber defined a borough. Mel Allen meant the Big Ballpark in the Bronx. Harry Caray packed the Church of Cardinals Baseball. "None came close to what we had," said Gillespie, whose river ran through Wisconsin, Michigan, and parts of Minnesota, Illinois, and Iowa. "The phenomenon was hard to verbalize." Harder to imagine: a *Chicagoan* embodying the Braves.

Earl played first base at Lane Tech, made Class D's Wisconsin State League, entered the Marine Air Corps, and bided a final year in D ball— "only guy who played four seasons in that class without advancing." Gillespie turned to real estate. Bored, he soon got out. In 1948, WJPG Green Bay hired his live-wire voice.

"Earl worked alone for hours in an empty studio," said station manager

John M. Walker, "screaming into a dead mike"—and winning an audition with the American Association Brewers. The 1951–52ers won the Little World Series and A.A. flag, respectively. Getting the bigs, sponsor Miller Brewery decided to double the fun.

"[Brewers flagship] WMEP and [50,000-watt] WTMJ wanted to head our network," said Gillespie. Miller let each, starting in an exhibition. Allen's booth sat next door. "I was so excited I could barely breathe. Local play-by-play was tops in broadcasting. There was a glamour, a prestige."

Milwaukee had a blue-collar cast. Earl blared an idealized self-image: "vervy," said Johnson, "a showman's flair." Lifting Caray's "Holy cow!" he got mail of China cows, lucky pennies, and a fishing net for fouls. One inning, nature called. "People think we sound alike," said Bert Wilson, tapping Earl's window. "Talk into my mike and yours till I get back. Nobody'll know the difference."

Gillespie did as he was asked. For a time, the Braves did, too.

On April 14, 1953, 34,359 trooped to the then-35,911-seat park at 46th Street off Blue Mound Road. "Some opener," Selig said. "Bruton's [game-winning 10th-inning] homer went off Enos Slaughter's glove." Milwaukee placed second. "For a while it got better," Earl smiled, "year after year."

1954: The Braves drew an N.L.-high 1,862,397. 1955: Gillespie did County Stadium's All-Star Game. 1956: Milwaukee lost a last-day pennant. 1957: "Rush for tickets," a writer said, "rivaled only by *My Fair Lady* [total, 2,215,404]." Warren Spahn went 21–11. Aaron led in homers (44) and RBI (132). He faced St. Louis September 23. "A swing and a drive back into center field!" cried Earl. "It's back at the fence . . . and is it gone or not? It's a home run! The Braves are the champions of the National League!"

Next: the Series, on NBC Radio. Ahead 2–1 in games, New York led, 5–4, in overtime. A hit batsman, Logan double, and Mathews homer countered: 7–5. Game Seven was breezier: Braves, 5–0, in the ninth. "Hank Aaron is pulled around in left-center field," said partner Bob Neal. "Burdette's [bases-loaded] pitch. Swung on, lined, grabbed by Mathews who steps on third—and the World Series is over and the Milwaukee Braves are the new world champions of baseball!"

The 1954–57ers topped 2 million each year. The bloom then began to wilt, though few knew so at the time. Next-season attendance fell to 1,971,101. Earl aired another Series. Milwaukee blew a 3–1 game lead. "I guess," said Casey Stengel, "this shows we could play in the National League."

No one had pitched a perfect or no-hit game for more than nine or eleven innings, respectively. On May 26, 1959, Pittsburgh's Harvey Haddix retired 36 straight Braves. Worse: a playoff loss to Los Angeles. "With wins the last day of '56 and '59," said Gillespie, "I'd have made four straight Series."

The aging 1960 Braves placed second. Next year, Spahn won his 300th game. (He still leads N.L. lefties in shutouts, wins, and innings.) "Earl teared up. Spahn was his favorite player," Johnson said. "Listening in Chicago, Gillespie's mom could tell when he pitched. The voice got more excited."

In 1963, Spahn became the oldest 20-game winner, tying Christy Mathewson. The Braves wiled 773,018. Milwaukee watched Chairman of the board Bill Bartholomay crave a future home in Georgia.

"It was obvious that's where they were going," said Earl. In October 1964, the Braves admitted that they would become the first team to move its franchise twice.

Resigning in late 1963, Gillespie joined Milwaukee's WITI CBS TV affiliate. "My wife had raised four kids on her own. When I got the chance to be sports director, get weekends off, I jumped."

On September 22, 1965, the Braves played their last game at County Stadium. Since 1957, the National League had shed Milwaukee, Brooklyn, and

EARL GILLESPIE

LONGEVITY:	4	11 years.
CONTINUITY:	10	Milwaukee N.L. 1953–63.
NETWORK:	3	All-Star Game 1955 (Mutual). World Series 1957–58 (NBC Radio).
KUDOS:	6	Eight-time Wisconsin Sportscaster of the Year. Wisconsin Athletic Hall of Fame 2001.
LANGUAGE:	8	Carnival barker's.
POPULARITY:	10	Of a piece with Braves'.
PERSONA:	9	Holy cow! a.k.a. The Lip.
VOICE:	10	Effervescent.
KNOWLEDGE:	10	As infielder, then announcer, worked and called run-down play.
MISCELLANY:	4	Did the Green Bay Packers, Marquette, and Wisconsin.
TOTAL:	74	(81st place).

New York. "Even when the Brewers came here five years later, a lot of us could never forgive baseball's cruelty."

Retiring in 1985, Earl moved to Florida. Golf was a blue-chip dividend. His VCR aired another. Each year in the fifties Miller made a highlight film. One showed Gillespie, in blue suit and bow tie, introducing "the story of, the glory of, the Milwaukee Braves."

Earl died December 12, 2003, at 81. A decade earlier, "Milwaukee's Pied Piper" formed a sad, slow smile. "We showed people around the city in boats, on bikes, at beer cafes. They all had radios on. They were listening to the games. Like Brooklyn and the Dodgers, Milwaukee *meant* the Braves."

To many, still does.

DIZZY DEAN

It is no trick to retrieve Jay Hanna (Jerome) Dean—gloom and mucus or revival hour, depending on your view. In 1953, he began the ABC "Game of the Week"—TV sport's first network series. Two years later it entered the swankier household of CBS. For a decade Ol' Diz sang "The Wabash Cannonball," read telegrams to "good ol' boys," and razed the language. Batters "swang." Pitchers "throwed" the ball with "spart." Runners returned to "their respectable bases."

We loved the 300 pounds, string tie, and Stetson—the whole rustic goods. "Pod-nuh," Dean called us—his dowry, our badge. "In the hinterlands and small towns, it was incredible," said CBS sports head Bill MacPhail. "Watching Dizzy Dean was an absolute religion." Each Saturday and Sunday afternoon Pleasantville closed down.

In 1953, the big-league righty entered Cooperstown. "The Good Lord was good to me," said Dean. "He gave me a strong body, a good right arm, and a weak mind." As a child I was unaware of Diz's pitching genius. I knew only how he made of baseball joy.

The son of a migratory cotton picker was born in an Arkansas shack—but when? (January 16, 1910)—citing an array of dates. "I was helping writers out. Them ain't lies—them's scoops." Schooling stopped in second grade. "And I wasn't so good in first, either." At sixteen, Dean crashed the Army for $21 a month. Next season, joining the Cardinals' Western League team, he bearded its president at 4 A.M. "So the old boy is out prowling by hisself, huh? Us stars and presidents must have our fun."

Diz won his first bigs game in 1930. "I think he'll be a great pitcher," said Redbirds manager Gabby Street, "but I'm afraid we'll never know from one minute to the next what he's going to say or do." From 1933 to 1936 he won at least 20 games each year. "Hold that success against the country's tone," wrote Bob Broeg. "In the thirties, states around St. Louis were reeling, and you wouldn't draw flies," the exception being Sunday.

St. Louis played a doubleheader. Gates opened at 9 A.M., outlanders filling Sportsman's Park. Among them: the Fellers of Van Meter, Iowa. "We'd muster a couple dollars, and sit in the bleachers," said son Bob, knowing that Dean would pitch, since the Cardinals stacked the schedule. "To us, Franklin Roosevelt was no bigger than Ol' Diz."

Baseball brims with single-season art. 1912, Joe Wood, 34–5; 1968, Bob Gibson, 1.12 ERA; 1999, Pedro Martinez, 23–4. Each was child's play vs. Dean's 30–7 in 1934. In March, he vowed that "Me 'n' [younger brother] Paul will win 45 games." They won 49. Jay strewed three hits to open a twinbill. Paul then no-hit Brooklyn. "Dawgonnit, if I knowed Paul was gonna throw a no-hitter, I'd 'a' throwed one, too."

The Swifties trailed New York by 7 1/2 games in August. Ending 20–5, they clinched the last day. A headline prefaced the World Series vs. Detroit: "Dean: 'Me 'n' Paul'll Win Four.' " In Game Four, Diz, pinch-running, was hit in the head by a throw. Papers plagiarized one another: "X-Rays of Dean's Head Show Nothing."

Diz won the 11–0 final. By 1937, he had a 121–65 record. "He threw so smoothly and efficiently," said Broeg, "that my guess is with luck he'd have pitched into the '50s." Instead, Dean's ran out at the All-Star Game.

Lou Gehrig homered. Earl Averill's drive then struck Diz's left toe.

"Your big toe is fractured," a doctor said.

"No, it ain't. It's broke."

The doctor applied a splint. Prematurely, Dean pitched, hurt his arm, and lost his fastball. The Cubs bought him in 1938. Said Broeg: "He had nothing left but his nothin' ball." It nearly pivoted the Series.

Diz led Game Two, 3–2: eighth inning, one on. Yanks shortstop Frank Crosetti homered. "You'd never 'a' done that if I'd had my fastball!" Dean screamed.

"Damned if you ain't right!" said Frank.

In 1941, Diz began Browns and Cardinals radio. "I feel like a prisoner walking to his death." The Ozark encyclopedist soon penned his own reality. Cleveland filled the bases. "That loads the bags full of Indians." A one-handed catch was "a la carte," fly "can of corn," quarrel "like argyin' with a stump. Maybe you city folks don't know what a stump is. It's somethin' a tree has been cut down off of." Don't fail to miss tomorrow's game, he brayed. Dialect never did.

"No one resembled him," said Mel Allen. "It was the language and accent"—twangy, deep, and full. A batter had an "unorsodock stance." Of Cubs pitcher Ed Hanyzewski, "I like to broke my jaw tryin' to pronounce that one. But I said it by just holdin' my nose and sneezing." One station offered a job spinning classical music. "You want me to play this sympathetic [symphonic] music and commertate on them Rooshian and French and Kraut composers? *Me* pronounce the composers' name?" Dean couldn't ennunce Boston's infield.

Galled, the St. Louis Board of Education tried to yank him off the air. They had to be his words, Diz said, because no one would take them. Few took the Browns: "Peanut vendors is in the stands," Jay laughed. "They is not doing so good because there's more of them than customers." Then, in 1944, they won the flag. NBC asked Dean to commertate the all–St. Louis Series.

"His diction is unfit for a national broadcaster," refused Judge Landis. Boiling—"How can that Commissar say I ain't eligible to talk?"—Diz missed the last Series where the teams shared a site. Behind, 2 games to 1, the Redbirds won. "We should have known better," said a Browns official. "It was too good to last."

Was Diz, 37, still good enough to pitch? The 1947 Americans threw him Opening Day. Dean singled, spaced three hits in four innings, and pulled a muscle. "Get him out of there before he *kills* himself!" said wife Pat. The again-Voice gave a lecture: "Radio Announcing I Have Did." The Soviets domineered Eastern Europe. "Got to get me a bunch of bats and balls and sneak me a couple of empires and learn them kids behind the Iron Curtain how to bat and play baseball." Joseph Stalin—"Joe Stallion"—could run concessions. "[That way] he'd get outta politics and get in a honest business."

Through 1948, Diz jazzed the tone-deaf Browns. "I slud along with them as long as I could, but I eventual made up my mind to quit." Joining the Yanks, he graced TV's "What's My Line."

"The guest could be Dizzy Dean," blindfolded panelist Arlene Francis said.

Dorothy Kilgallen: "Oh, no, this man is much too intelligent."

One day a rhubarb roiled the field. "That batter shakin' his head down there—he don't know what's goin' on. I don't know what he don't know, but I know he don't know." Critics howled. The Apple yawned. "He laid an egg," Allen said. "Too rural, it didn't work." In 1952, Diz rejoined what had: Falstaff Brewery's 20-station Browns network.

His partner was Rotarian. Dean was, yes, Falstaffian. Bud Blattner liked fact and strategy. Diz shunned biography. "People liked him giving everything but the score"—fishing, hunting, thanking Grandma's Biscuits for meal, said Bud—"but wanted me to restore sanity." Some Voices script a program. Diz *was* the program. "He created the audience before we said a word."

In 1952, they added Mutual. One "Game" was in Detroit. Dean's first inning was "polished, so unlike the usual chaos." At break he winked. "'That's enough a' that poop. Now Ol' Diz is gonna make money. I'm going to butcher this today,'" foreseeing what he would say, and when.

Dean could not predict crossing TV's Rubicon. Edgar Scherick did.

In early 1953, Scherick was a bit ABC TV aide—"a nothing network, fewer outlets than CBS or NBC." Upside: It needed paid programming—"anything for bills." Falstaff pined to go national. Edgar broached a Saturday "Game of the Week." ABC hesitated. Baseball was a regular-season *local* good. How would "Game" reach TV? Who would notice if it did?

"Football fans watch regardless of team," said Scherick. By contrast, Phils–Cubs needed a Voice *surpassing* team: "straight out of James Fenimore Cooper by way of Uncle Remus," wrote Ron Powers—Diz. In April, Edgar set out to sell teams rights: "'Game of the Week.' I expected a breeze." Instead, he hit a gale. Only the A's, Tribe, and White Sox signed. Worse, baseball barred "Game" within 50 miles of any bigs park. "'Protect local coverage!' They didn't care about national appeal."

ABC, which did, grasped that "most of America was still up for grabs." In many cities ABC was weak or nil. Unvexed, "Game" wooed an 11.4 1953 rating (one point: 1 percent of TV homes). Blacked-out cities had 32 percent of households. In the rest, 3 in 4 sets in use watched Diz. Had "Game" sunk, said MacPail, "maybe sports TV has a different future." Instead, by 1955 its road led to the Network of the Eye banked on floating clouds.

"CBS stakes were higher," said Blattner, leaving Mutual to rejoin Dean. "They wanted someone who'd known Diz, could bring him out": becoming, wrote Powers, "a mythologizing presence" not courtly like Barber, or eastern like Husing, or a blast furnace like The Voice. "The reaction was stunning," mused MacPhail. In Hollywood, Clark Gable golfed each Saturday. "Clark'd play nine holes," said Bud, "watch us in the saloon, then play nine more."

CBS added a Sunday "Game" in 1957. Outlets cheered in Phoenix, Little Rock, and Cedar Rapids. Dean cracked Gallup's most-admired list. CBS offered a prime-time series. Hillary Clinton said it takes a village to raise a child. A baseball generation's children were raised on Diz.

"America had never had TV network ball," said Blattner. "Now you're getting two games a week [four, counting NBC, by 1959]." Dean cleaned the Peacocks, notably in the Plains, West, and South.

"We would never have on our network a person as uncouth as him," a CBSer told a sponsor meeting.

"But . . . he's *on* our network . . . every weekend, on CBS," said MacPhail, watching, he later said, in "suspended terror. I had no control, just wondering what he'd say or do."

Once Dean eyed Eddie Lopat. "See if you can tell why he gets these batters out. If you can't, Ol' Diz'll tell ya." The junkman retired them. "Figured it out? *Testicle* fortitude." Bud blanched. "Well," Diz said, quickly, "I think ya know what I mean." MacPhail loathed, but forgave, him: "No manners, ran you over, but first to put comedy into a game."

Dean refused a Falstaff ad—because the date was Mother's Day. United Airlines backed "Game." Hating to fly, Diz said, "If you have to, pod-nuh, Eastern is much the best." In 1958, he made MacPhail's gray hair white. "I don't know how we come off callin' this the 'Game of the Week.' There's a much better game—Dodgers–Giants—*over on NBC*."

Batters had an edge: "The ball they're playing with isn't lively, it's hysterical." Umps ranked below English. "That was quite a game," he told one. "What a shame you didn't get to see it." Cincinnati's Ted Kluszewski, Bob Borkowski, and Fred Baczewski filled the sacks. "I was sweatin'," Diz said, "hopin' that nobody'd get a hit so I didn't have to pronounce them names."

The batter hit toward left-center.

"There's a long drive"—gulp—"and here's ['Game' producer] Gene Kirby to tell you all about it."

Dean was "the guy," said Bud, "that dropped off the truck and wandered barefoot into town, saying, 'Fellas, what's it all about?' " Reality was more complex. The boozer and eater ate and drank little. The public man loved humanity, but not people. "Hi, pod-nuh" became mask and sign. "He didn't know you from Adam, but you thought, 'My God, he remembered me 'cause he called me *pod-nuh.*' "

In 1960, as we will see, his partner became a retired Dodger shortstop.

"In Pee Wee they got a better player, but lesser announcer [than himself]," Blattner said. Dean called the first four innings. Reese asked what the pitcher threw. Diz: "I believe that's a baseball." At one time or another he sang "Precious Memories," ate a watermelon on play-by-play, and fell asleep. Pee Wee requested a closeup. "Pod-nuh," he said, nudging Diz, "am I keeping you awake?" The two ex-jocks coursed through Idlewild (now Kennedy) Airport. Suddenly Dean, in Western boots and Stetson, yelled, "Hey, Pee Wee."

"Yeah."

"How come you played here for 18 years and nobody knows you? Everybody knows Ol' Diz."

Reese laughed. "If I had that hat on, everybody'd know me, too." Later he ribbed the old pitcher in Dean's room. "Dizzy Dean, high hard fastball. I wish I'd had a chance to hit your shit." In pajamas, Diz started winding. "You might have hit it, pod-nuh, but you'd be on your ass."

By 1964, they worked at Yankee Stadium, Wrigley Field, St. Louis, Philadelphia, and Baltimore. New York got $550,000 of CBS's $895,000. (Six NBC clubs got $1.2 million.) "In '53, no one wanted us," said Scherick. "Now teams begged for 'Game' 's cash." That year the NFL began a $14.1 million revenue-sharing pact. Turning green, baseball ended the big-city blackout, got $6.5 million for 1965 exclusivity, and split the pot. "A mint," said MacPhail, "so they thought."

ABC began mere 28-game Saturday/holiday coverage. Ratings tanked: Tigers–Twins left, say, Boston cold. Meanwhile, CBS ended with a 21-game Stripes slate. In 1966, the Yanks joined NBC's package: 28 games vs. 1960's three-network 123. Soon Dean denoted an age so far removed that it was hard to recall it existed. It did: you do not reinvent youth at the time.

Mine broke Saturday with grass stain, grounder, and broken window. Pickup games preceded late-morning TV: Sky King, Roy Rogers, and Dale Evans. Next: lunch, Cliff Arquette as Charlie Weaver, Dennis James's TV newsreel, 'toons culled from forgotten files. "Game" began at 2. Sunday wed the morning paper, church, and short walk home. Watching, we were "pod-nuh"—still are, even now.

Dean did 1967–68 Braves TV, fished, hunted, and wondered at the pastime's mind. An Alabaman wrote to *The Sporting News:* "We simple people really miss Dizzy Dean. He added life to the game . . . hours of clean, wholesome fun. Baseball has always been for ordinary folks like me. Please bring Ol' Diz back." Astute and self-aware, Dean might have laughed—except that, enlarged in exile, he missed "Game," too.

One day he golfed with Reese. "Pod-nuh, lots of trees on the right." Next tee: "What'd you get on that hole?" after Pee Wee bogeyed. Next: "Sand traps on the left." A decade later Reese shook his head. "He'd loved the 'Game.' Still had the ego, but the forum wasn't there. We were just a couple country boys that said things about which people knew."

On May 21, 1973, NBC put Diz on a Monday "Game." Out of the closet came a sense of yesterday once more. "When they told me I could say hello to all the fans we used to have, I was so tickled I almost jumped for joy."

Where did Dean live? Curt Gowdy asked.

"Why, in Bond, Mississippi."

Where was Bond? Curt said.

"Oh, 'bout three miles from Wiggins."

Where was Wiggins?

DIZZY DEAN

LONGEVITY:	9	26 years.
CONTINUITY:	7	St. Louis N.L. 1941–46; St. Louis A.L. 1941–48; New York A.L. 1950–51; Mutual "Game of the Day" 1951–52; ABC TV "Game of the Week" 1953–54; CBS TV "Game of the Week" 1955–64; CBS TV "Yankee Baseball Game of the Week" 1965; Atlanta N.L. 1967–68.
NETWORK:	10	"Game" 1951–52 (Mutual). "Game" 1953–54 (ABC TV) and 1955–64 (CBS TV). "Yankee Baseball" 1965 (CBS TV).
KUDOS:	10	Cooperstown 1953, inducted as 150–83 pitcher. Five Halls of Fame include NSSA 1976. *TSN* 1944 "Announcer of the Year."
LANGUAGE:	10	Unforgettable.
POPULARITY:	10	Unrecoverable.
PERSONA:	10	Ol' Diz.
VOICE:	10	Homey, warm.
KNOWLEDGE:	7	As irrelevant as Sharon Stone's IQ.
MISCELLANY:	9	"*Syntax?* Are those jokers up in Washington putting a tax on that, too?"
TOTAL:	92	(ninth place).

"Oh, 'bout three miles from Bond."

Diz died at 63, on July 17, 1974, of a heart attack, the fox taken as a buf-foon who winds up taking the taker. His words, indeed.

BUD BLATTNER

The good die young. In Blattner's case, the young play well. Twice in the 1930s the teenaged St. Louisan became world's doubles table-tennis titleist. In 1938, Bud signed with the hometown Cards. "My dad started me playing games with a ball when I was three. I was playing [baseball] on a 15-year-old's level at nine." In World War II, he called service boxing and baseball on Guam. "I got thinking of radio. Looking back, good thing."

In 1942 and 1946–49, Blattner hit .247 with the Redbirds, Jints, and Phils. "I was already 26 after the war. My skills had gone. So I looked else-where," selling television shows and directing and calling sports. Beats included Golden Glove boxing, BAA Bombers, and the International Hockey League.

Before a game, he studied the road roster. "I'd use the players' last name, get familiar, then use the first." A hockey player was surnamed Dick. Bud added his first name before long. The producer howled. "I hadn't even thought of the combination. Harry Dick in the penalty box, and Harry Dick on the boards."

In 1950, Detroit's Pat Mullin's late-inning slam tied the Yanks on a Lib-erty twinbill. "I was exhausted, and Mullin was coming up [in the 10th]. Except for Pat I'd have been home." Blattner wrote, "The bastard," beside his name. Partner: "Now to the bastard, I mean batter."

That year Bud joined a new Browns mikeman from Washington. Man bombs. Brass rechecks his resume: Washington, *Pennsylvania*. "Guess it fore-told," said Blattner, "my brush with the English language ahead."

Bud began doing games alone. Browns seats were as empty. Commencing rescue, Bill Veeck liked to drink, seem a regular fellow, and tub-thump the team. In 1951, the new owner returned from a speech. "Wouldn't it be nice to get our leadoff man on in the first?" Bud, driving, nodded. Bill renewed the vision. "Getting a man on in the first would be some event."

Veeck signed new leadoff man Eddie Gaedel. "Bet I could hit any pitch," said the 3-foot-6, 62-pound midget. Bill snapped, "If you make one move with that bat at home plate it'll be your *last*." A huge-by-Browns-rule 20,299 graced an August twinbill. Veeck's A.L. semi-centenary salute vaunted jugglers, acrobats, aerial bombs, and Satchel Paige on drums. Before Game Two, Gaedel sprung from a papier-mache cake. "Bill set people up," said Bud. "They thought *that* was the celebration."

Suddenly the P.A. boomed: "Leading off, batting for Frank Saucier, No. 1/8, Eddie Gaedel." The ump called time. Browns skipper Zack Taylor produced a contract. Crouching, Gaedel took four straight balls. League head Will Harridge sent him packing. "Advise," wrote Veeck, "the minimum height of players."

A few days later Taylor rocked in a chair near his dugout. Fans voted by holding signs: "Bunt" or "Hit away." In late 1953, the Browns-turning-Orioles contacted Blattner. "They wanted me in Baltimore, but I liked living in St. Louis." Soon life meant a CBS suitcase. "I loved each bit of 'Game'—Falstaff, Diz, baseball royalty." The Kid, of course, was king.

"Williams was so volcanic, yet a softie." One 1957 "Game" aired from Boston. Friday, Diz and Blattner met Ted at the Kenmore Hotel. Bud had recently seen a 10-year-old leukemia patient's shrine—"a room of Ted memorabilia"—in a Midwest hospital. Daily he sat on the floor, holding a wooden bat. The nurses rolled a ball. "He'd swing and they'd say, 'Base hit by Ted!' "

Blattner asked if Williams could autograph a ball or cap. "No problem," Ted said. "Tell you what. I'll come to see the boy"—Ted flew a private plane—"but on two conditions": only his parents were to know; Bud must never tell. He finally did, in 1977. By then, Blattner had been estranged from "Game" since the year Hawaii became a state.

On September 27, 1959, Milwaukee and Los Angeles forced a best-of-three playoff. Falstaff asked tobacco company L&M to co-host. Diz had trashed cigarettes on the air. "Falstaff said, 'L&M won't take Dean. You [Bud] and George Kell do the games.' " At that point Diz vowed to quit "Game" if Blattner called the series.

Four decades later, nerve-ends still stung. "Dean couldn't stand that I'd do the games, not him," said Bud. His threat cowed Falstaff, pulling Blattner, who resigned. "Diz never grasped why I left. I couldn't have looked in the mirror if I hadn't."

In December, Bud finally shed his $75,000 contract. "I spent thousands of dollars in legal fees. I knew I could never again work with Diz." Pursed lips, set jaw. "When we saw each other in the future, he'd make out like nothing had happened. His only reaction was that I'd lost my mind."

That winter he resumed St. Louis Hawks basketball even as honor cost, "bluntly, the world's best baseball broadcast job." In Syracuse, a referee called a charging foul. "They [officials] are walking the wrong way," Bud said, coining a trademark. He never doubted that his way was right.

Blattner returned to 1960–61 Redbirds TV, began the "Buddy Fund" local charity, then moved to Dodger Stadium. "Talk about a challenge!" he termed the expansion Angels. The same-park Dodgers had tradition, skill, and cash.

Don't peak too soon: the '62ers almost won the flag. In 1965, the Halos drew 476 one game. Next season they moved to Anaheim Stadium, two miles from Disneyland. The 1967 All-Star Game gave America its first extended look. Bud and Curt Gowdy shared NBC TV: a record 30 K'd. "[Wife] Babs and our daughters missed me. It wasn't home." In 1969, he retrieved what was.

"It took two seconds to say yes," Blattner said of the rookie Royals. He wiled the banal and giant, self-assured and unself-confident, shy and strutting people of the Midwest. "People grew up on him—to millions, a professor,"

BUD BLATTNER

LONGEVITY:	9	26 years.
CONTINUITY:	6	St. Louis A.L. 1950–53; Liberty "Game of the Day" 1950–51; Mutual "Game of the Day" 1952 and 1954; ABC TV "Game of the Week" 1953–54; CBS TV "Game of the Week" 1955–59; St. Louis N.L. 1960–61; Los Angeles A.L. 1962–66; California A.L. 1967–68; Kansas City A.L. 1969–75.
NETWORK:	9	"Game" 1950–51 (Liberty) and 1952 and 1954 (Mutual). "Game" 1953–54 (ABC TV) and 1955–59 (CBS TV). All-Star Game 1964 and 1967 (NBC TV).
KUDOS:	4	Founder, "Buddy Fund" charity, underprivileged children. U.S. Table Tennis Association Hall of Fame 1979. Missouri Sports Hall of Fame.
LANGUAGE:	8	Casual.
POPULARITY:	9	Civil.
PERSONA:	10	Thy "pod-nuh"'s keeper.
VOICE:	9	Heartland.
KNOWLEDGE:	10	Grasped job, and Diz.
MISCELLANY:	7	"I was the straight man for the performance."
TOTAL:	81	(48th place).

said sidekick Denny Matthews. "I'd like to have a nickel for every fine point that he taught."

In 1975, the mentor, 65, was axed. "Denny was getting restless," said a friend. The Bucs offered Bob Prince's job. "I felt burned out. I didn't want somebody leaning over a bar saying, 'I can remember when he was good.' " Blattner retired to Lake Ozark, Missouri. "We're building a tennis complex [among the U.S. best]. It's maybe the most satisfying thing I've done."

In 1998, doctors diagnosed prostate cancer. Beating it, Bud won the Senior National Olympics tennis title. "To an extent, staying active may have saved my life." Absent were pity and hostility. "I don't have a dime, but live like a king." Listening, you recalled 1959: "Pod-nuh" was still a gentleman.

PEE WEE REESE

In 1937, an A.L. Boston scout discovered a 130-pound, marble-shooting, shortstop-playing cable telephone splicer in a church league game. Pee Wee Reese, 19, the son of a railroad detective, looked 12. In 1940, Brooklyn bought him from the Red Sox. "I was a country kid," he said, born near Louisville. "I get to the city, it's another planet"—a.k.a. Ebbets Field.

Presently an employee mistook the 5-foot-9, 140-pound Reese for the bat boy. Thereafter he became a borough's glove and glue. "Every year we were in it," said the Kentucky Colonel. "Lose a playoff [1946 and '51], win pennants [seven from 1941 to 1956]. Lose a Series [six] to the Yankees." No one hated losing more than Jack Roosevelt Robinson.

In 1946, Reese left the Navy. Next year, Robinson arrived in Flatbush. "I hadn't known many black people," said Pee Wee. "I just knew I had to play." Reese spurned a petition for Jackie's return to Triple-A Montreal. One crank threatened to shoot No. 42 if he played. Robinson sidled over in warmup. "Don't stand so damn close to me," said the Captain. Each laughed.

In 1955, both ran into luck. Games One through Six of the Series split. Brooklyn led, 2–0: sixth inning, Stripes on first and second. Yogi Berra hit to left field, Sandy Amoros bolting for the pole. "If he'd been a righty, the ball might have dropped," said Johnny Podres. Instead—the Sphinxes crumbled; the Sahara froze—Sandy caught the ball. Reese relayed to Gil Hodges: double play.

In the ninth, Elston Howard grounded out, Captain to Quiet Man. "Far into the night rang shouts of revelry in Flatbush," wrote the *Times*'s John

Drebinger. "Brooklyn at long last has won the World Series and now let someone suggest moving the Dodgers elsewhere." In two years, someone did.

"Just being there was amazing," said Reese, "like entering a bar and saying, 'Hi ya, Ben,' or 'How you doing, Joe?' " The faithful, "you joked with 'em on a first-name basis." Enduring is a Flatbush of the mind.

Later Pee Wee felt that Walter O'Malley always meant to leave. He did not think so at the time. "I bet a couple guys that we'd stay. They said, 'We're moving.' I said, 'What are you talking about?' Those people would have done anything to keep them. [1945–57 attendance topped each N.L. team's.]" He hesitated. "There'll never be another like Ebbets Field. No sir, no way."

Reese had 2,170 hits, led the league in runs and walks, and made the 1942 and 1946–1954 All-Star teams. In L.A., he became a coach. "I was like an old fire horse watching the rest of 'em gallop past." Roy Campanella could not even walk, having broken his neck in a car accident that left him paralyzed in both arms and legs.

On May 3, 1959, the bigs' largest-ever crowd, 93,103, cheered Campy, wheeled by Pee Wee from the tunnel. Lights paled at the Coliseum. Each person lit a candle. "It looked like fireflies," said the Dodgers' owner, who flamed for No. 1.

"Mr. O'Malley kept telling me, 'One day you'll manage this club.' " Reese replied: no day, or way.

The Captain doubted that he was tough enough to manage. By late 1959, CBS TV didn't doubt who Dizzy Dean's next partner should be. "Try it," jibed Buzzie Bavasi. "More than likely you'll screw it up. Even if you do, you've got a job with us." Reese yielded, having never called a pitch.

In early 1960, he bought a tape recorder, watched video, and worked with Gene Kirby. In March, the greenhorn called a game: "an exhibition, and I'm sweatin'!" Dean asked if he had a problem. "Boy, no kidding," Pee Wee said. "Here's all you do," roared Diz, belting "The Wabash Cannonball."

For a while, a peaceful easy feeling eluded Reese like a bad-hop ball. He breakfasted with Kirby. "Oh, by the way, Diz is on vacation this week. You're doing play-by-play."

Reese feigned calm. "You okay?" said Gene.

"Sure."

"So how come you're pouring coffee on your pancakes?"

Slowly, Dean steadied him; like the Colonel, Robinson. "I loved the big oaf. He protected me," eased angst. "'Pod-nuh, why don't I take this over?'

'Pod-nuh, here's all you need.' 'Podnuh, let me pick this up,' " after a commercial. "'You just lost some sales.' "

One week Diz left the booth in Philadelphia. "Pee Wee, I'm going out for a hamburger. Want one?"

"Yeah."

"Pickles, lettuce, or mustard?"

"Onions," Reese said. A narrow ladder reached the booth. The next camera shot showed Ol' Diz, impaled.

In 1966, NBC, replacing CBS, traded a circus for a seminar. "Curt Gowdy was its guy, and he didn't want Dean—too overpowering," said Pee Wee, becoming proxy. "Curt was nice, but worried about mistakes. Diz and I just laughed."

Convenience lasted through 1968. Next March, Reese was dumped. "I just wonder what went wrong. Did I talk too much? Didn't I talk enough?" He drifted to Cincinnati and Montreal. "Other teams wanted me later. Who needs the hassle?" Not the bowling alley, grocery store, and storm window business owner, also flacking for Hillerich and Bradsby Company. "What am I gonna do?" he laughed. "Wash my storm windows ever' afternoon?"

PEE WEE REESE

LONGEVITY:	4	12 years.
CONTINUITY:	6	CBS TV "Game of the Week" 1960–64; CBS TV "Yankee Baseball Game of the Week" 1965; NBC TV "Game of the Week" 1966–68; Cincinnati N.L. 1969–70; Montreal N.L. 1971.
NETWORK:	8	"Game" 1960–64 (CBS TV) and 1966–68 (NBC TV). "Yankee Game" 1965 (CBS TV). All-Star Game 1966–68 and World Series 1966–68 (NBC TV).
KUDOS:	8	Cooperstown 1984, inducted as player. Society of American Baseball Research (SABR) 1997 Hero of Baseball award.
LANGUAGE:	5	Simple.
POPULARITY:	10	Peepul's Choice.
PERSONA:	9	Modest, droll, and wise.
VOICE:	6	Comfortable.
KNOWLEDGE:	10	Street- and game-smart.
MISCELLANY:	7	Each Dodger had a clubhouse stool. In an armchair, Reese smoked a pipe. "Walking in," said Vin Scully, "you knew there's the man."
TOTAL:	73	(86th place).

In 1985, Pee Wee retired to Venice, Florida. A year earlier, he and Curt made Cooperstown. At card shows, locals queued to meet No. 1. Few mentioned Brooklyn USA. "To this day, folks come up and say, 'Baseball hasn't been the same since you two left.' "

Had he missed the series? "Nah, not the exposure, not really," he said, softly, before his death in 1999. "But those years were the greatest of my life. I sure miss Ol' Diz."

MERLE HARMON

Try working for Charles O. Finley; airing the Milwaukee-headed-to-Atlanta Braves; or replacing Dizzy Dean on network television. Merle Harmon did each, remaining nature's nobleman. For a time, life mirrored the Twilight Zone. "More like *Alice in Wonderland,*" he amended. The curiouser and curiouser is how Merle prevailed.

His window on mid-America opened in southern Illinois. Then: Graceland College, the Navy, University of Denver, and radio in Colorado. Harmon debuted on a 1949 Class C doubleheader. "It lasted eight hours, the temperature was 104, and I had a headache," duly noted on the air. A listener wrote: "Don't tell us your troubles. Broadcast the game."

Topeka's team bus carried 17 players. Often it stopped, had to be pushed to a gas station, and maxed at 40 miles an hour—downhill. One rider, pitcher Eddie Lubanski, bearded owner Joe Magoto: "I'm quitting baseball— my salary." Joe pulled a gun: "Pitch your next game." Lubanski packed, turned pro bowler, and snubbed meal money: $1 a day.

"The bucks went to the big club," Harmon said. "Other things kept your interest." One was Joplin's 1950 shortstop. "At 18, Mantle already hit balls out of sight." Doing 1952 basketball, Merle improved *his.* "No more bad passes," Kansas coach Phog Allen said. "You players gotta see things happen— skip movies—rest your eyes."

Allen mentioned Max Baer. Doctors told the boxer to visit California, lie on the sand, and look at the stars. "Instead, Max went there," Phog said, "laid the stars, and looked at the sand." Harmon never forget the vision.

In 1954, he did Kansas City's last Triple-A season. Next year the Athletics relocated. Harry Truman threw out the first ball on Opening Day. Harmon huzzahed illusion: A's 6, Tigers 2. "[Manager] Lou Boudreau, later an announcer, said, 'If your team is good, you can criticize. If it's lousy, show patience.' In Kansas City, I was the most patient man in the world."

The club never matched the '55ers' place (sixth) or gate (1,393,054). Nine skippers left. The A.L. lost K.C.'s 1960 All-Star Game, 5–3, despite a seven-Yanks roster. "[A's owner Arnold] Johnson gave 'em Art Ditmar, Ralph Terry, Roger Maris," said Harmon. "How it goaded us—'Yankees cousins.' " The A's once bashed New York for 27 hits. "*We* felt like the powerhouse. 'Course, the feeling didn't last long."

In December 1960, Chicago insurance broker Finley bought 52 percent of the team. Then Merle snubbed his "Poison Pen Day" for *Kansas City Star* sports editor Ernie Mehl. "Ernie got baseball here in '55—and Finley's trashing him!" said Harmon. Deeming him a traitor, Charlie sacked Merle in late 1961.

Nietzsche says, "That which doesn't kill you makes you stronger." What happened next made Harmon feel like Charles Atlas. "Out of the frying pan, into the fire."

By late 1963, baseball's ex-capital had become a lonely post, drawing 32 percent of 1957's attendance. Resigning, Earl Gillespie saw Milwaukee's writing on the wall. Could Merle, replacing him, retrieve its past? Attendance rose. Baseball yawned: only a temporary court order kept the Braves in town. "What a mess. They had to play '65 in a city which *knew* it was losing them." Mild and upright, Harmon became the loci of curse, slight, and hate.

"*Hot*? My seat *burned*! If I praised the Braves, people said, 'Don't root for traitors.' If I didn't, die-hards said, 'Don't mess up another club.' " Upping angst: an N.L. team record six players with 20 or more homers. "How could you *not* get excited?" Milwaukee vied till September, "baseball afraid we'd make the Series and County Stadium would be empty."

Curiouser: a) Wisconsin swore the Braves' 45-outlet network did games *gratis*. "A bank and three breweries paid, but wouldn't say so—guilt by association"; b) WSB Radio Atlanta aired 53 games, 26 from Milwaukee. "One city doing every game even though its team is leaving. Atlanta doing a team it doesn't even have"; c) The Voice, reemerged as ghost.

In 1955, Merle visited Yankee Stadium—"first time, I'm quaking." Entering the booth, he thought, "My God, it's him." Smiling, Mel Allen said, "Anything you need, let me know." Fired in 1964, he took the Atlanta job to avoid seeming yesterday's dessert. Said Harmon: "We'd have cookouts in my yard and Mel'd pour his heart out about the Yankees." Why?—he, like Milwaukee, asked.

In October 1965, the Braves marched toward Georgia. Merle's next mission: make Saukeville forget Dizzy Dean.

August 1961. Since 1955, CBS TV's "Game of the Week" had exteriorized baseball. One morning the phone rang at the A's hotel in New York.

"Merle Harmon?" a man said.

"Yes," he said, half-asleep.

"This is Chet . . . ," the voice said. "Would you be interested in doing a national sports show for ABC TV?" Harmon tensed. A player was plainly kidding him.

"Sure, if I can work it into my schedule. Talk to my agent."

"Who's your agent?" said the man, undeterred.

"He's tied up."

"We'd be glad to contact him, but can we see you? We're leaving for Chicago today to do the [football] All-Star Game."

Merle sat up. "Excuse me. Who *are* you?"

"Chet Simmons of ABC TV sports production. We want to talk to you about a show—today."

"I must sound like a moron."

"Boy, it must be fun to travel with a baseball team."

Next month, Merle Harmon began "Saturday Night Sports Final." ABC named him lead baseball Voice in 1965. CBS's "Game" entered only non-bigs cities—its rub, and beauty. "The heartland was its habitat," said Harmon. By contrast, the blackout of, say, St. Louis hurt.

ABC's "Game" aired Saturday, Memorial and Labor Day, and Fourth of July in every city. Like Brickhouse, Merle evoked just folks. Like Scully, he dashed cliche. Like Gowdy, he was "breezy, relaxed, and stylish," said *TV Guide*.

"We had a sense of the 'first ever,' " he said, "a prototype for baseball TV since"—truly national. The problem was habit: weekends meant Ol' Diz.

The 1965 CBS "Yankee Game of the Week" slayed Merle in Dallas and Des Moines. Worse, local TV split the big-city audience. "ABC'd show Cubs–Cards in New York, and the Mets'd kill us." Desperate, one Saturday the network tendered a great chatterbox of the time.

At D.C. Stadium, Vice-President Hubert Humphrey joined the booth. "So loquacious. I almost asked him to do play-by-play, but feared it would demean the office." The Nats' Bob Chance pinch-hits. Humphrey says, "Is he related to Dean Chance?" Bob was black, Dean white: Much of

America still hailed Jim Crow. "I don't think so," said Merle, retrieving the game.

Coverage ended Saturday, October 2. Harmon spent Friday phoning New York. Ahead by a game, Los Angeles hosted Milwaukee. If L.A. won, Merle flew to Cleveland—or via Chicago to Minnesota for the A.L. champion Twins. A Dodgers loss would revive the tailing Jints—and put him in San Francisco. Writer Jorge Luis Borges said, "I have known uncertainty." Harmon now bore the "most uncertain 24 hours of my life."

The last plane left at 12:15 A.M. Saturday. "I'll only know where I'm going when I find how the Dodgers do!" Naturally, they go overtime. At the airport, Merle tells the cabbie to "turn on the game!" L.A. wins. "Let's see, this means Cleveland. Take me to United, quick." Finding a seat, he checks the ticket. Panic. "*Cleveland*? I'm supposed to be in *San Francisco*!" Arriving, Harmon calls ABC's hotel. "Yes, Merle, this is your destination." Going home, he was tempted to take a train.

That month, NBC bought 1966–68's "Game." Merle had already aired the Jets and Steelers (local radio) and NCAA and AFL (ABC). He liked—more than respected—football. "You're fine if you prepare weekly like a player. Baseball—try finding something interesting as you say the pitcher throws the ball—especially if your team is out of the pennant race."

Harmon found Minnesota in 1967. Dean Chance went 20–14. Harmon Killebrew had 44 homers. The Twins drew 1,483,547, more than they had or would at Metropolitan Stadium, and lost a last-day flag. "If we'd beaten Boston, I'd have done the Series with [NBC's] Gowdy." He hurt, but shone. "I'll never forget the letter I got from a woman criticizing me for not rooting for the Twins."

Harmon aired them through 1969. On April 1, 1970, his old town bought the Seattle Pilots for $10.8 million. "Calvin Griffith [releasing him] knew what Milwaukee meant to me." County Stadium (re)opened April 7: Angels, 12–0. "I learned quickly that it'd be a long year"—too, how the Braves' rape stung. "The feeling was: 'We won't be hurt again.' "

In 1973, Milwaukee passed a million for the first time since the Kennedy administration. Slowly, the feeling warmed. 1975: 48,160 cheered Hank Aaron's return from Georgia. 1978: The Brewers grand-slammed a record thrice in the first three games. 1979: Milwaukee more than tripled the Braves' last-year gate.

"It took a while," said Harmon, "to get back a decent team, then fans to get excited." The '82ers won a pennant. Curiouser: He was 850 miles away.

In late 1979, inking a multi-year NBC TV pact, Merle ogled the 1980 Moscow Summer Olympics. "I'd have missed a dozen Brewers games." Flagship WTMJ demanded he do each. Harmon chose none. "[He] will make more money [NBC]," mused *The Milwaukee Journal,* "get more exposure, and do less traveling." Merle did "SportsWorld," backup "Game," and 1980 World Series. He did not, alas, call the Games. In December 1979, the Soviet Union invaded Afghanistan. America boycotted Moscow. NBC promptly pulled the plug.

"A great letdown," said Harmon. Another: being axed by NBC in 1982 for Bob Costas, 29. What goes/comes around. In 1966, Gowdy replaced him on "Game." Each joined the Rangers in 1982: Merle, play-by-play; Curt, planning and evaluation. Another cycle was Nolan Ryan's, K-ing 21 Hall of Famers, in four different decades. One batted August 22, 1989. "Three and two to [Rickey] Henderson!" said Harmon. "Ryan gives the okay. Strike three! He did it! He did it! Number 5,000 for Nolan Ryan! A record that will never be broken!"

MERLE HARMON

LONGEVITY:	10	32 years.
CONTINUITY:	6	Kansas City A.L. 1955–61; Milwaukee N.L. 1964–65; ABC TV "Game of the Week" 1965; Minnesota A.L. 1967–69; Milwaukee A.L. 1970–79; NBC TV "Game of the Week" 1980–81; Texas A.L. 1982–89.
NETWORK:	4	"Game" 1965 (ABC TV) and 1980–81 (NBC TV). World Series 1980 (NBC TV).
KUDOS:	6	NAIA Outstanding Alumnus Award 1959. Graceland College Service Award 1978. ASA Graham McNamee Award 1993. Texas Baseball Hall of Fame 1996.
LANGUAGE:	9	Learned.
POPULARITY:	10	Wearable.
PERSONA:	10	Touch of class.
VOICE:	10	Friendly.
KNOWLEDGE:	10	"Can compare baseball and football as well as anyone," said *TSN*.
MISCELLANY:	10	Did network NBA, Big 10 football and basketball, and other NCAA hoops. In 1973, covered World Games, shot Moscow tourist photos, and was quizzed by the KGB. "The KGB got the film. I got to go home."
TOTAL:	85	(32nd place).

Merle had each player and umpire sign a scorecard laser print, retiring after three no-hitters, Joe Namath's Super Bowl III "guarantee," and 1974 World Football League. "I had so much to do with Merle Harmon Fan Fair [then-largest U.S. sports souvenir retailer]." Ultimately, the Mormon lay preacher went belly-up, had a heart attack, and beat both—each a breeze, he joked, vs. Finley, the lame-duck Braves, and Diz.

"Every day I do exercise on the treadmill," the still-nobleman mused. Richard Nixon said: "I get up every morning just to confound my enemies." Harmon got up to bless his friends.

LINDSEY NELSON

In 1876, the New York Mutuals folded after eight months in the National League. "How bad was this!" Lindsey Nelson conspired with memory. "Even the 1962 Mets weren't kicked out of the league." By 1882, two teams shared the Polo Grounds: the N.L. Giants and American Association Metropolitans. "The Mets! They were bonkers nearly a century before the team we recall!"

The expansion '62ers convened at St. Petersburg. "We got to work on the little finesses," said manager Casey Stengel. "Runners at first and second, and the first baseman holding a runner, breaking in and back to take a pickoff throw." New York lost, 17–1. Casey saw the light, not liking what he saw. "The little finesses ain't gonna be our problem."

Nelson's problem was how to mesh the 1962–78 Amazin's, 1957–61 NBC "Major League Baseball," 1952–65 NCAA football "Game of the Week," 1966–86 "NFL on CBS," and 1974–77 Mutual "Monday Night Football."

"I know you're a child of the Depression," a writer said, "but this was ridiculous. What didn't you do?"

"Rest," Lindsey said, once doing six bowls in ten days. "I missed the Derby and Indy 500. That's about all."

Strangely, the Methodist is tied to Catholic Notre Dame 1966–79 taped TV. In Green Bay, he and Vince Lombardi took a pre-game walk. "Here's the Notre Dame announcer!" a teenager yelled. Nelson laughed. "Vince was shocked to be overlooked. But Notre Dame was national."

A closet Papist, in the Bible Belt? "If you won't tell 'em, I won't," said the man whose lilt, country gabble, and sport coats—in time, nearly 350— forged a princeling/professor of radio/TV.

Born in Pulaski, Tennessee, in 1919, Lindsey soon moved to Columbia, near Nashville. At eight, he heard Graham McNamee call a fight so near that he could "reach out and touch the canvas." To Nelson, the rectangular box speaker—an Arbiphone—"looked like a question mark." His answer was the wireless.

Each Saturday, Graham called football. Each fall, a receiver in the school auditorium aired the World Series during recess. Lindsey found that he could hear it in class through a window. A teacher asked, "Who was that?" meaning Caesar. Lindsey: "Gehrig—doubled to right!" Baseball's fuel was hope. His generation ran on radio's.

In 1937, Nelson became a University of Tennessee student spotter. "The Station of the Grand Ole Opry"'s booth bisected the second deck. "It lacked a restroom. Once there, you were stuck, because coming down the ladder was worse than going up." Near halftime, WSM's Jack Harris, needing relief, told him to read statistics. Forty years later the spotter smiled. "Jack had a second cup of coffee that morning, and it was too much. One cup, and my life may have gone off in a different direction."

The journalism graduate joined the Army Ninth Infantry Division in Ft. Bragg, North Carolina. On December 7, 1941, he attended a football game in Washington. "During the game, the P.A. man kept asking members of the military establishment to report to their station." Naval officer John F. Kennedy watched quizzically from the stands.

Afterward Lindsey caught a train at Union Station. A stranger slapped him on the back: "Give 'em hell." Overnight his uniform had become a pass to anywhere. Ahead: Nelson's most vital, if not famous, job.

By 1942, Japan bestrode the Pacific. Dominoes littered Europe. Pledged Franklin Roosevelt: "Soon we and not our enemies will have the offensive." He cabled Churchill: "It is fun to be in the same decade with you." Nelson's was exhausting, and inexhaustible.

The publicist trekked to North Africa and Sicily, met the French Foreign Legion, and helped reporters like Ernest Hemingway. In 1945, U.S. and Soviet troops drank captured German champagne at the Elbe. A photo shows Lindsey, with Russian officers: "I oversaw inspectors—prepared me for Stengel." Another reads: "To Lindsey Nelson, a very busy man the day this picture was taken. Dwight Eisenhower."

May 8 was V-E Day. Nelson aired baseball in Linz, Austria: "Hitler'd grown up there. Now our occupying force put together big-league teams."

Released, he tried to resume pre-war life. "I wrote for a Tennessee paper. After Europe, I couldn't get excited about a drunk in city court."

Nelson recalled the Arbiphone, "how I liked radio," joining WKGN and WROL Knoxville. Next: Liberty's re-created 1950–51 "Game of the Day." By then, NBC TV's Bill Stern was a drug addict. "He'd lost a leg in an accident," said Tom Gallery. "Doped up, he'd disappear." One day Stern left a Dallas golf tourney, locked his hotel room, and left NBC awash.

In the soup, Gallery phoned a friend. "Know someone who can cover golf?" He did, in Tennessee. Tom asked: "Would it be possible for you to get to Dallas—like, tomorrow?" Hopping the next prop plane, Lindsey soon moved to NBC New York.

"I needed an associate," Gallery said. "Best damned phone call I ever made."

Five of Cooperstown's first six Voices then did baseball in the Apple: Allen, Barber, Harwell, Hodges, and Scully. Mel was a Peacock peer. "He did our big games," said Lindsey. The trouble: numbers. "*Enough* statistics!" Tom exploded. "Just do the game!" Once Allen grabbed the statistical *The Little Red Book*. Gallery hit him with a headset. "Didn't I *tell* you to leave statistics alone?"

Mel ferried *Events;* Nelson, *events,* as NBC *nonesuch.* "Allen overwhelmed you," said Tom. "Lindsey was perfect for continuity." 1952: They share college football. 1955: Red Grange joins Nelson (later, Bud Wilkinson and Terry Brennan). A bigger test lay 'round the curve. "For years Dizzy Dean killed us Saturday. Our outlets said, 'Without an answer, we'd might as well close down.' "

In 1957, Diz added Sunday. Gallery unfurled a *fiat*: baseball by Opening Day. Already CBS had bought eight teams' rights. Said Lindsey: "They tried to squeeze us, but missed Milwaukee," which won a pennant. He bought 11 Braves, 11 Pirates, two Senators, and two Cubs games: "manic, but we got it done." How many would now forsake Dean?

"Major League Baseball" began with a Dodgers–Braves exhibition. "From then it was whether you liked baseball with us, or song and dance with Diz." Dean rarely checked the monitor. His antithesis bound word and look. "If a cameraman tipped his lens to a gum wrapper on the floor," a producer said, "Lindsey would say the right thing about the wrapper."

Each Saturday he unloosed from Forbes Field, Wrigley Field, or County Stadium. In 1959, NBC began Sunday: at some point, it thought, even Ol' Diz must succumb. Nelson aired pro basketball, the Army–Navy Game, Bob Hope Desert Classic, and Cotton (also, at one time or another, Rose, Gator, Sugar, Sun, Liberty, and Poinsettia) Bowl.

Who would trade this for The Metropolitan Baseball Club of New York, Inc.? Lindsey Nelson would.

A major-league baseball Voice had the best job in the world, he felt. "The game has drama, tragedy, comedy. Plus, you spend one month in spring training and six afterward. The rest of the year's his own." NBC baseball had been blacked out in New York. "Many people, not knowing that, said, 'Why are they hiring a *football* guy?' " If this were Broadway, he replied, the tryout had run five years.

Like the Arbiphone, the question mark was the Mets. Nelson decided to shadow their manager. "Soon we're hiding between palm trees to avoid him. Casey was over 70 years old and running us into the ground!" Stengel spanned Tris Speaker and Tom Seaver. "At his age, he didn't care what you said. You had no identity."

All year Casey confused him and Bob Miller. One night the bullpen phone rang: "Get Nelson up!" he said. Joe Pignatano knew Lindsey was a broadcaster: "I also knew not to argue with Casey." He took a ball, put it on the rubber, and said, "*Nelson!*" Miller started throwing.

Yarns still stitch the '62 Metropolitans. "I tell them myself," said Lindsey. "But they were gruesome. Thank heavens for Stengel. He spread more happiness than anyone I've ever known—because he was doing exactly what he wanted."

It was, he said, a last age of innocence. "The Mets played for fun. They weren't capable of playing for anything else."

Their first game was Metsian: St. Louis, 11–4. Things went downhill from there. New York ended 40–120. Next year: 51–111. The Mets' first slam earned Rod Kanehl 50,000 trading stamps. Jimmy Piersall ran his 100th career homer *backward* around the bases. "The worse we played," said Nelson, "the more legendary we became."

Roger Craig was hardship's poster child: 15–46 in 1962–63. Another, *Marvin Eugene Throneberry*, yoked Alfonse at the plate and Gaston in the field. One mate dropped a fly. "What are you trying to do?" flushed Marv. "Steal my fans?" The umpire called him out for missing first base on a triple. Coach Cookie Lavagetto told Stengel, "Don't argue too long, skipper—he missed second, too.' "

Richie Ashburn was "a rarity," said Lindsey. "His talent wasn't in the past tense," hitting a team-high .306. The ex-Phil played center field. Frank

Thomas more or less filled left. Shortstop was Spanish-speaking Elio Chacon. They often met, without trying to.

"I got it!" Ashburn yelled. Thomas stopped as Chacon ran into him.

At sea, Richie approached bilingual Joe Christopher. "How you do say, 'I got it' in Spanish?" Joe said, "'Yo la tengo.' "

Soon a pop invaded the Bermuda Triangle. The triad merged. "Yo la tengo!" Ashburn screamed. Chacon stopped. *Thomas* ran into *him*.

Hobie Landrith was Stengel's first expansion pick. "If you ain't got no catcher," Casey said, "you get all passed balls." Even he wondered if New York would pass on the Mets. The '62–63ers drew 2,002,638—"amazing," Nelson said, "given our atrocity." The Perfessor surveyed one house. "We are frauds—frauds for this attendance. But if we can make losing popular, I'm all for it." By 1963, their WABC Radio/WOR TV audience beat the Yankees!— akin, said partner Bob Murphy, "to a mule lapping Man O' War."

That June, Stengel visited The Stadium for the first time since his 1960 firing. "The Yankees were world champions. Casey, like our fans, *hated* them," said Lindsey, whose wife and two daughters brought horns and bells to the Mayor's Trophy Game. "The Yankees confiscated it, like all noisemakers, at the gate. Fifty thousand people there that night, and forty-nine rooted for the Mets."

Sixth inning: Mets lead. Casey hails a reliever.

"[Vapid Ken] MacKenzie?" said a coach.

"No!" he boiled. "Carl Willey."

Nelson fell back on memory. "Casey used our best pitcher in an *exhibition*": Mets, 6–2. The Bronx aped Picadilly Circus. "David killed Goliath. That's what Stengel brought to the Mets."

The Polo Grounds closed in September: A pilgrim recalled a Mets sense of *deja vu*. Ashburn was voted 1962 team Most Valuable Player. He took the prize, a boat, out on the Delaware River, where it sank.

A 1964 *New Yorker* cartoon showed Mets entering the dugout. A fan says, "Cheer up. You can't lose them all." Game two of a twinbill at their new park, Shea Stadium, took 23 innings and a record 7 hours, 22 minutes. (Could they? Jints, 8–6.) "Pitch to Cepeda. Runners go," Lindsey said. "And it's lined to McMillan. And it is a double play! And it may be a triple play! A triple play!" Jim Bunning threw a perfect game. The Mets outdrew the Yanks by 429,959. Nelson telecast NBC's All-Star Game: N.L., 7–4. Under one-upmanship, a year later he spoke from a gondola over second base in the Astrodome.

"What about my man up there?" Stengel asked Tom Gorman.

"What man?" said the umpire.

"My man Lindsey. What if the ball hits my man Lindsey?" Gorman shrugged. "Well, Case, if the ball hits the roof, it's in play, so I guess if it hits Lindsey, it's in play."

"How about that?" Casey said. "That's the first time my man Lindsey was ever a ground rule."

Nelson commuted from Huntington, Long Island. Wife Mildred, named "Mickie," after Cochrane, grew up with baseball. Each daughter followed him to the park. "Sharon [the older, mentally and physically handicapped] knows things about baseball *I* don't. We ate the Mets at breakfast, lunch, and dinner," a blur of Mr. Met, Miss Rheingold, and the city's N.L. tilt.

In 1966, Stengel, now retired, made the Hall of Fame. Five times the 1962–68ers hit last. Finally they left the cellar, for how long Lindsey was unsure. "Personally, I thought forever." Instead, miracle and metaphysical, they climbed Jacob's Ladder.

"The Mets may endure a thousand years, as Churchill would say," Nelson said of 1969. "They may win a dozen championships, but they can only do it the first time once, and the first time was incomparable." Seaver pitched a near-perfect game. Ron Swoboda hit two two-run homers: Mets, 4–3, despite Steve Carlton's 19 Ks. On September 8, Chicago held a 2 1/2-game lead. "Before the first game a black cat crept toward their dugout, hissing the manager." The crowd did, too, singing, "Good night, Leo [Durocher]." Black magic soon helped the Amazin's take first.

They clinched on September 24. "That night," said Lindsey, "someone asked [manager] Gil Hodges, 'Tell us what this proves.' He sat back, stared, and said, 'Can't be done.' "What could: an L.C.S. sweep. Next: World Series vs. Baltimore. "We are here," said the Orioles' Brooks Robinson, "to prove there is no Santa Claus."

Games One–Two split: elves awoke. New York strewed four hits, 5–0: the North Pole warmed. J.C. Martin bunted in Game Four's tenth inning. The throw hit his wrist, scoring the 2–1 winning run: Santa primed. Next day the O's led, 3–2. "Al Weis hadn't homered at home since '65," said Nelson. He struck the scoreboard: 3-all. Cleon Jones and Swoboda doubles and a double error KO'd Baltimore, 5–3: Mets, set and year.

"The game was the most memorable event I ever covered—so far ahead I can't imagine what's second," said Lindsey. He aired NBC's post-game clubhouse show, then drove his family to Manhattan. "We saw dancing, confetti, cops going wild. It's a cliche, but this is, if there ever was, a once-in-a-lifetime happening."

Santa cleared the chimney. Said Casey: "They did it *slow,* but *fast.*" A ticker tape parade snaked through the island. Mets chairman M. Donald Grant was asked what it meant. "Our team finally caught up with our fans."

In 1962, Nelson stopped at a men's clothing store at 49th and Broadway. "Show me jackets that you can't sell," he told the owner, buying seven "gaudy, showy, awful" coats that Liberace wouldn't wear. "We were competing with the Yankees. I needed attention." Next month a cabbie said, "You're the guy who wears all those wild jackets!" Lindsey told a friend, "See, he doesn't know my name, but he knows what I do. It pays to advertise."

Andy Rooney served with Nelson in World War II. "Of all my old buddies," he said, "only he dressed better then." Murphy and colleague Ralph Kiner scavenged on the road. "If we saw a wild enough jacket, we'd tell him." Daughter Nancy bought a jacket in Ireland. Both were stopped at customs. The inspector, a Mets fan, joked, "*Nobody* would wear a jacket like this."

"My daddy will," she beamed.

In 1988, daddy made Cooperstown. Speaking, he gave his sport coat—12 colors randomly jigsawed into squares—to Hall head Ed Stack. It flanks other Mets bric-a-brac—"most about '69." 1970: Seaver K'd 10 straight Padres. 1972: Say-Hey returned. 1973: He retired, introduced by Nelson. "Willie, say good-bye to America," choked Mays, sharing another Mets' L.C.S. Its postlude resembled 1962, not '69: A's, in seven. Nelson and Curt Gowdy again did the Series.

Having swung from tenth to first, the Mets swung back in an Elio Chacon sort of way. The '77–78ers placed last. New York again became a Yankees town. Once Nelson coined three rules of life: "Never play poker with a man named Ace, never eat at a place called Mom's, never invest in anything that eats or needs painting."

In January 1979, he hatched a fourth: "Never stay at the fair too long."

Team business manager Jim Thomson was in his office when Lindsey began a speech that not even Marvelous Marv had prepared or conditioned him. "I have loved every minute of my association with the Mets. Even the bad times were memorable [losing an average of 91 games]. Despite that, I would like to be released from the remaining year of my contract," for reasons germane to the personal and real.

In 1973, Mickie died of a cerebral hemorrhage. Sharon lived in a residence near New York. Nancy was a University of Southern California graduate student. Wanting to be near, daddy also recalled Mel and Red. "They were bitter at the end. I didn't want the uniform cut off me." He aired the 1979–81 Giants, made the NSSA Hall of Fame, and was introduced by an old Army bud. "I am here," said William Westmoreland, "because I am a friend of Lindsey Nelson's."

For a decade the University of Tennessee had asked him to teach broadcasting. In 1982, Lindsey returned to the second cup of coffee that conspired to change his life. He lectured, wrote a memoir, did 1985–86 CBS baseball, and aired a 26th and last Cotton Bowl. "I hear Guy Lombardo says that when he dies he's taking New Year's Eve with him," mused a wag. Retiring, Nelson took January 1. Its yearly table has an empty chair.

Once he addressed the problematic. "Near the end of their life certain women say, 'Maybe I should have married John.' We do that with professions— 'Maybe I should have tried something else.' I never felt that way." Lindsey died in June 1995, at 76, of Parkinson's disease. Finally, he could rest.

LINDSEY NELSON

LONGEVITY:	10	30 years.
CONTINUITY:	8	Liberty "Game of the Day" 1950–51; NBC TV "Major League Baseball" 1957–61; New York N.L. 1962–78; San Francisco N.L. 1979–81; Cincinnati N.L. 1982; CBS Radio "Game of the Week" 1985–86.
NETWORK:	6	"Game" 1950–51 (Liberty). "Major League Baseball" 1957–61, All-Star Game 1964, and World Series 1969 and 1973 (NBC TV). "Game" 1985–86 (CBS Radio)
KUDOS:	10	Cooperstown 1988. NSSA Sportscaster of the Year 1959–62 and Hall of Fame 1979. Mets Hall of Fame 1984. ASA 1986, College Football 1988, Pro Football a.k.a. Pete Rozelle Award 1990, and University of Tennessee baseball and football Halls. Tuss McLaughry Service Award 1988.
LANGUAGE:	9	Allegro.
POPULARITY:	10	As Amazin' as Mets!
PERSONA:	9	Sport Coat Man.
VOICE:	10	Voltaic.
KNOWLEDGE:	10	At heart, an academic.
MISCELLANY:	10	Outlasted Polo Grounds, seven Mets managers, and 238 players from A (Ashburn) to Z (Don Zimmer).
TOTAL:	92	(10th place).

GENE ELSTON

Nelson evoked Manhattan. The Georgian Ernie Harwell defined Detroit. In Houston, an Iowan etched Texas-size disgust with limits of any kind. "We couldn't get over the hump," said 1962–86 Astros nee Colt .45s Voice Gene Elston. "If we didn't have *bad* luck, we wouldn't have any luck at all."

Luck carted him from hometown Fort Dodge (high school basketball) via World War II (Navy) through 1946–48 Waterloo and 1949–53 Des Moines (Three-I and Western League) to N.L. Chicago. Said Phil Wrigley: "We have a defeatist attitude"—understandably. The 1954–57 Cubs finished 258–357.

Roberto Clemente once plucked a bottle from the outfield wall. "He thought it a baseball," mused Elston. "It got caught in Wrigley's vines." In 1958, dumped for tyro Lou Boudreau, Gene plucked defeat from the jaws of victory.

He found refuge in Mutual's "Game of the Day." The state with its most outlets blared orchards and fields and streams, falling away in endless line. "Texas heard me," he said. "'Game' led me there." Elston found that selling the 1962 Colt .45s was even harder than the Cubs.

Nelson liked the 1961 expansion draft. "The Mets were great on paper, but paper doesn't play." By contrast, Houston G.M. Paul Richards offered to trade *rosters* with cellar Philadelphia. The Colts trained at Apache Junction, Arizona, near Superstition Mountain, where Indian spirits and a Dutchman's ghost were said to guard lost gold. "Geronimo's warriors roamed here," mused Elston. "The way we played, maybe he warred on us."

We forget that the '62ers outdrew New York: "characters," Gene explained, though none as iconic as The Marvelous. Jim Pendleton neared third base, stopped, and restarted. "His cup fell out when he rounded third, rolled down a pant leg, and was around his knee by the time he hit home." First baseman Rusty Staub, charging the plate, said, "Whatever you do, throw home." Pitcher Hal Woodeshick nodded, then almost hit him in the ear.

Dick (Turk) Farrell shamed Peck's Bad Boy. "He'd put snakes in lockers, give the hot-foot," said Gene. A drive smacked his head, caroming to out-fielder Jimmy Wynn for an out. Owner H. Roy Hofheinz made the team wear "western outfits with black cowboy boots in orange, black cowboy hats, and belt buckle embossed with a pistol with 'Colt .45s,' an orange tie, white shirts with red and blue baseball stitching." Mercifully, he deepsixed them.

"Explains a lot," said 1962–64 manager Harry Craft. Mysterious: Houston's reverse Midas luck. In the first inning of its first exhibition game, Al Heist stepped in a hole, breaking an ankle. Jim Umbricht died of cancer; Walt Bond, leukemia; Don Wilson, accidental asphyxiation. Left: Bobby Shantz, Robin Roberts, Nellie Fox, Eddie Mathews, Don Larsen, and Joe Pepitone.

"How come our whole didn't match the parts?" Perhaps Geronimo was not a fan.

In 1965, the Space City hatched a space-age home: baseball's first air-conditioned, domed all-purpose stadium. It had sky boxes, five tiers, and 5,000 roof plastic windows and steel grate guides a foot and half apart. "When a fly hit that jigsaw background," said Gene, "the light and dark made it impossible to judge." Hofheinz put blue translucent acrylic on the roof, greasing vision. Sunshine was cut, though, killing turf. By 1982, 11 of 26 bigs parks brooked artificial a.k.a. *Astroturf.* Suddenly, watching grass grow had a new appeal.

The Astrodome opened April 9, 1965, with a Yankees exhibition. "Look at all the players out of the dugout up on the rim," gawked Elston. "Just a magnificent sight." The scoreboard flashed, canon boomed, and cartoon cowboys rode upon a homer. In 1968, one in town for a film turned three sheets to the wind. Houston won, 1–0, in the 24th inning. "Longest complete night game and John Wayne didn't see it," said Gene, working near the Astrodome Club bar. "In the 23rd, they carry him out."

Thirty-five radio and 15 TV outlets, respectively, carried Elston from the Panhandle and Gulf to Biloxi and Baton Rouge. Partner Loel Passe coined "Hot ziggety dog and good ol' sassafras tea," "He breezed him one more time," and "Now you're chunkin'." His briefcase was even tangier. "It had the kitchen sink," said Gene. "In April someone put a hot dog there." Passe found it that fall.

"Loel was the entertainment, but Gene the key," said *Houston Post* writer Mickey Herskowitz. "Solid, trustworthy," giving skeletal plot and score, born in a place where hyperbole was thought curse, not core.

"Coming from Iowa, I didn't know if my style would work," said Elston. TV's Andy Taylor settled Barney Fife and Gomer and Goober Pyle. "That was Gene," said Passe. "An island of sanity in a nutty place."

In 1977, pitcher J.R. Richard said that he saw a bird: "He was evidently sent down by God and he told me to straighten up and win this game and that's why I turned things around."

Elston: "What kind of pitches did you use to make the change?"

"Shit, I'll tell ya," Richard said on air.

Later Gene interviewed J.R. on TV. "If you had to throw a pitch in a tight situation, what would you throw?"

"Well, I'd throw him a slider," he said, putting a hand on his groin. "I'd put it right in there, cock-high."

Houston got high much of 1980: record 2,278,217, N.L. West playoff victory, and 2–1 best-of-five game L.C.S. edge. Bad luck: The 'Stros took a 2–0 next-day lead—before Gary Woods left third early on a fly. It cost a flag: Phils, in 10. Houston led, trailed, tied, and lost Game Five in overtime.

"We'll climb the final step," chirped manager Bill Virdon. A quarter-century later, the Astros are still climbing.

Elston broadcast 11 no-nos. Nolan Ryan broke Sandy Koufax's record on September 26, 1981. "Two balls and no strikes to Baker. And a ground ball to third! Art Howe! He got it! Nolan Ryan! No-hitter Number 5!" Less abiding: sidekicks, blown to and fro.

In 1985, Milo Hamilton arrived from Chicago. Next season, new team head Dick Wagner fired the 'Stros original. "If they want somebody to phony

GENE ELSTON

LONGEVITY:	10	43 years.
CONTINUITY:	9	Chicago N.L. 1954–57; Mutual "Game of the Day" 1958–60; Houston N.L. 1962–86; CBS Radio "Game of the Week" 1987–95.
NETWORK:	8	"Game" 1958–60 (Mutual). World Series 1967 (NBC Radio). All-Star Game 1968 (NBC TV). "Game" 1987–95 and L.C.S. 1995–97 (CBS Radio).
KUDOS:	5	Houston Baseball Hall of Fame. Four-time Texas Sportscaster of the Year.
LANGUAGE:	8	Dry, like Lubbock.
POPULARITY:	9	Unlikely expatriate.
PERSONA:	9	Just the facts, ma'am.
VOICE:	8	Pleasant.
KNOWLEDGE:	10	Authored "Gene Elston's Stati-Score Baseball Scorebook."
MISCELLANY:	8	Did Eddie Mathews' 500th homer, Nolan Ryan's Walter Johnson–topping K, and Houston's first 1,600 games. Houston–Rice football cost No. 1,601.
TOTAL:	84	(37th place).

up some excitement, I can't change my personality," said Gene, skedaddling to CBS's "Game of the Week." Said analyst Larry Dierker: "As always, he was low-key, with plenty of room to get excited and take it up an octave."

His last play-by-play hymned 1997. Having braved a stroke, Elston left broadcasting's cattle drive, still waiting for luck to change.

RAY SCOTT

Elston's voice was flat, but strong. Jim Woods's turned whiskeyed, at the mike or bar. Ray Scott's crossed John Huston and Bishop Fulton Sheen. "When he intoned, slowly, profoundly, simply, 'First down, Green Bay,' " wrote *TV Guide,* "10 million spines would quiver."

From 1956 to 1974, Scott embodied the National Football League. We mimed his prose, watched his Packers, and never knew that another game lured.

In 2002, I asked son Preston which sport dad preferred. "My father said baseball, no contest." The choice said something about it, and him.

Born in Johnstown, Pennsylvania, Scott's flood of four Super Bowls and nine NFL title games began with the Pittsburgh Pirates. "How dominant was base-ball? The [now Steelers] team was named after theirs." Already the teenager had a radio show—"great training," Ray said of 250-watt WJAC. "I announced, did copy, sold ads"—and made $55 monthly.

One Friday football's Pirates crashed Johnstown for a game. That morning owner Art Rooney signed Colorado's Byron (Whizzer) White. "Paid 'im $15,000. The owners said his waste would ruin football!" Scott didn't care, landing White on his show. "When you're young, priorities smack of *me.*"

By 1947, Ray, now in Pittsburgh, aired each Steelers exhibition. "At Comiskey Park, we were put in the broadcast booth behind home plate. No respect." If lucky, he had a spotter, seat, and wire to the production truck. Pro football was akin to wrestling—except that wrestling had a niche.

In 1952, Scott had a brainchild—an NFL TV network, he crowed—except that "the three biggies wouldn't take it," leaving a tatter of the time. "The DuMont network was small, so it could dream big," adding football to "Demo-lition Derby," "Colonel Humphrey Flack," and "Rocky King, Detective."

Each Saturday, Ray did play-by-play. "*Primitive?* [Ex-Yale coach] Hermann

Hickman did color in studio. I was by myself." Not exactly: his audience mugged CBS's "Jackie Gleason." How sweet it was, and away Scott went.

DuMont died in 1955. On January 1, 1956, a legend primed for ABC's Sugar Bowl. At game time, Bill Stern reached the booth "doped up [cocaine]," said backup Scott. "No way he could go on."

Ray replaced him, brilliantly. In September, joining CBS, he helped tie Anaheim, Azusa, and Cucamonga—Jack Benny's famous litany—to Frank Gifford, Jon Arnett, and Bobby Layne. "Until now," he said, "America did everything Sunday *except* watch TV"—drive, see family, fill the beach. CBS changed how we spend the Sabbath—same time and channel, pro football, live.

"It was a funny format," said Ray. "Each team had a Voice [Chris Schenkel was the Giants; Chuck Thompson, Colts]." In Wisconsin, Hamm Brewing Co. bought the Packers. Braves Voice Earl Gillespie seemed a natural—except that Miller paid his salary. Hamm said, "Ray, if this works out, we'll give you a bigger market."

Then, in 1959, Vince Lombardi became coach. Straightaway Fordham's thirties "Seven Blocks of Granite" guard made granite steel. Personae blurred: "Run to Daylight"; Green Bay as Titletown; Scott, its Voice. "CBS's National Football League coverage didn't make a move to any big game without him," read *TV Guide*.

About this time, Ray added another sport. The Upper Midwest thought it a natural evolution.

Scott once aired NBC's "Major League Baseball" from Pittsburgh, where he lived. Years later, Ray couldn't recall who won. "That was the extent of my pre-1961 baseball." To Minnesota, it was enough.

Moving there, the ex-Nats asked Bob Wolff to remain. Partner Chuck Thompson stayed in the Baltimore area. Buying rights, Hamm persuaded Scott to move his wife and five children to Edina, a Minneapolis 'burb.

"Whether I do football again is questionable because of the overlapping seasons," Ray mused. "But I wouldn't pull up stakes with my family if I wasn't sold on baseball for the future." Son Preston nodded. "Dad did everything you can in football. The irony is that he was ready to give it all up for baseball."

The object of his ardor debuted April 11, 1961: Twins 6, Yankees 0. Their 30,637-seat triple-deck cantilever opened ten days later. Metropolitan Stadium had no posts, cows beyond the outfield, and a spartan look and feel. Farmers and businessmen and women in curlers merged.

Baseball was a drop-dead craze. Doing it, could Ray dodge death? "His football style was simple," said Wolff. "At first he didn't grasp how baseball, especially radio, needs more." Scott adapted. "People cut him slack," mused publicist Tom Mee, "so pleased to have this national celebrity as a local announcer."

The 1955–60 Senators drew 2.7 million people. The '61ers wooed almost 1.3. "Such a marvelous reception, like Milwaukee in the '50s," said Ray. In 1962, Wolff left for NBC. Griffith felt no need to even name Scott top dog.

"When the Senators left Washington," Scott recalled, "an expansion team replaced them." The new Nats Voice had called Mutual's 1956–60 "Game." Said John MacLean: "'Game' went everywhere. I just didn't expect it to perish." His Senators perished almost each day.

"Five years before," wrote Morris Siegel, "they'd have been great." Instead, hand-me-downs helped the '61ers tie for ninth in a new ten-team league. "In a case like this," mused MacLean, "you empty your bag of tricks." They included lauding the loyal oppositon.

"I found myself promoting Mantle, Maris, Kaline," he laughed. Partner Dan Daniels sympathized, arriving from Orlando, Jacksonville, and Birmingham. "D.C. was a tightrope. Government workers from elsewhere cheered for the enemy. On the other hand, most people pulled for the home team": 460–668 from 1962 to 1968.

In 1969, Robert Short became Senators president. One brainstorm was naming Ted Williams manager. Another: new Voices to hype what little there was to sell.

"We need something fresh," said Short, dumping MacLean and Daniels. Soon Shelby Whitfield drew "a beautiful day in Washington. Come out and see your Senators," as rain soaked the field. By 1971, the FCC made stations identify paid employees of a team.

That fall the Nats again decamped. "I'd listened to MacLean on 'Game,' " said Red Sox announcer Ned Martin, "and hired him in '72. But he had a stroke," was hospitalized, and died in August.

For the next 32 years, baseball in Washington did, too. "Next time you go to buy a club," John reflected, "made sure you have either a ballpark or a team." In Minnesota, Scott was lucky to have both.

By 1965, New York had won 14 titles since 1949. On July 11, the Twins trailed, 5–4. "The Yanks were aging," Ray mused. "We're in first, and had won two of a three-game series." Harmon Killebrew faced the Stripes' Pete Mikkelsen: ninth inning, one out and on. "Oh my, and imagine the season's only half over. One after another of games that go right down to the wire." Scott paused. "A drive deep to left! Way back! It's a home run! The Twins win!" The dynasty was dead; my radio seemed to quiver.

September 26 knotted new team/old town. "The Twins have won 98 games," Ray said in D.C. "Number 99 means the pennant. Here's the windup—and the pitch! Strike three! He struck him out! The Twins win! . . . Final score: the Twins 2, the Senators 1. The Twins have won the American League pennant!" Mudcat Grant went 21–7. Tony Oliva hit .321. Zoilo Versalles became MVP.

Scott and Vin Scully called the first Series of transplanted teams. Minnesota took a 2–0 game lead. L.A. then won three at home. Grant evened the Classic, 5–1. Game Seven turned on third baseman Jim Gilliam's third-inning two-on heist. "He doesn't rob Versalles, we score twice, Zoilo has a triple, and Sandy [Koufax, winning, 2–0] leaves."

Instead, Ray left for CBS's Ice Bowl, Super Bowls I–II, IV, and VI, Masters, and PGA. "With my network stuff, I really don't have time for baseball," he said. "I do it [1970s Senators, Twins, and Brewers TV] because it keeps me in the game." Keeping him in trouble was a composte of honor, rage, and pride.

In 1974, CBS fired its NFL Caruso. "I chose to speak out against the growing tendency to focus on the announcer, not event," Scott explained. Howard Cosell was "a mean and nasty man." Voices had become "vaudeville." Ex-athletes "have no talent whatever." ABC's "Monday Night Football" was "a sham."

The sham was Scott, being snubbed.

"The networks won't hire me," he said by 1988, reduced to cable TV golf, college football, and Pirates—"coming back, I guess you'd call it," to his early home and sport.

He entered the hospital for a triple bypass, then kidney transplant, knee surgery and hip surgery, and prostate cancer.

"I've got more artificial hips than baseball players on a team," he said in 1998, dying that March, at 78. Heaven is thought angelic. Proof reads: "Starr. Dowler. Touchdown. Green Bay."

RAY SCOTT

LONGEVITY:	8	25 years.
CONTINUITY:	6	NBC TV "Major League Baseball" 1960; Minnesota A.L. 1961–66, 1973, and 1975; Washington A.L. 1970–71; Milwaukee A.L. 1976–77; Pittsburgh N.L. 1982–93.
NETWORK:	1	"Major League" 1960 and World Series 1965 (NBC TV).
KUDOS:	10	NSSA Sportscaster of the Year 1968 and 1971 and Hall of Fame 1982. ASA Hall 1998. Twelve-time Sportscaster of the Year in Florida, Minnesota, Pennsylvania, and Wisconsin.
LANGUAGE:	7	Rudimentary.
POPULARITY:	10	Packers' tide, Twins' riptide.
PERSONA:	10	Upper Midwest's Lewis and Clark.
VOICE:	10	Perfect 10.
KNOWLEDGE:	10	"I should have paid to do the games, but got paid 10 times as much getting ready to do them. It's preparation."
MISCELLANY:	3	After CBS, did Penn State and Kansas City, Minnesota, and Tampa Bay pro football.
TOTAL:	75	(76th place).

HERB CARNEAL

"If he'd broadcast in New York," mused an admirer, "they'd build a monument." In 1996, Cooperstown built something better: a plaque to the Lochinvar of Boise and Bismarck and International Falls.

Herb Carneal joined baseball's northernmost franchise a year after the Senators left Washington. The capital thought the Twins a two-headed monster. Minnesota deemed its new Voice the quintessence of age and place.

Three 50,000-watt stations—WHO Des Moines; WOW Omaha; and flagship WCCO Minneapolis, "The Good Neighbor to the Northwest"— berthed a 55-outlet hookup and a weekend extra 15 in the Rocky Mountain area. WTCN keyed a seven-state TV orb.

"You'd go to the parking lot on Saturday or Sunday," said Herb, "and see license plates from Colorado, Idaho, Wyoming, Illinois." Announcer as metaphor: right man, right time.

Growing up in Richmond, the dean of A.L. mikemen loved the nearby Senators. From high school he sashayed to WMBG Richmond, Triple-A Syracuse, and Springfield, Massachusetts. In 1954, Carneal did Philly's last two-team year. "I was a swing man, doing 100 [A's and Phillies] games." Not enough: He wanted a 154-game slide.

In 1957, Herb bounced to Baltimore. "Ernie Harwell took me under his wing. His philosophy rubbed off." Clarify. Paint a picture. "'The radio listener doesn't know anything until you tell him.' " Carneal told: Hoyt Wilhelm's 1958 no-hitter, Rocky Colavito's four-dinger June 10, 1959, and 1960 near-miss Baby Birds. When Hamm lost O's rights, Herb lost a job.

In late 1961, he replaced Bob Wolff, Scott becoming boss. "We worked six years, and never had a disagreement," Ray said. "No pretension, down to earth. Herb knew the game—no screaming, yelling—priorities perfect for the area." Above all, he spurned a perceived Eastern urban gyp, scold, and scam.

Two days after Killebrew's Yankees-killer, Minnesota hosted the 1965 All-Star Game. Herb manned NBC Radio. "There's a high drive to left field! It is really hit! Way back! A long home run! It's . . . 5 to 5 on a tremendous home run way back into the left-field stands by Harmon Killebrew!" Might-have-been ensued. Same year: Series. 1967: last-day blown flag. 1969–70: L.C.S. loss to Baltimore. "Never all the way," Carneal said, "but amazing names."

Rod Carew averaged .328, won eight batting titles, and got 3,053 hits, including 2,085 with the Twins. Harmon's 500th homer bucked August 10, 1968. Cesar Tovar played each position in one game, but kept forgetting signs.

"I've got an idea," coach Vern Morgan finally said. "If we want Tovar to steal, I'll call his last name three or four times and that'll signal him to go to second on the next pitch." Skipper Bill Rigney nodded: "We've tried every-thing else. Let's give it a shot."

Tovar reached first base, whereupon Rigney flashed steal. "Tovar, look alive," Morgan began, "c'mon, Tovar, find your position—atta boy, Tovar, let's go."

Cesar asked for time. "Vern, I've been with this club for five years. How come you don't call me by my first name?"

"He had a genius for backing into the limelight," wrote Lowell Thomas of Lawrence of Arabia. Herb liked the footlights: "not interested," said 1967–69 partner Merle Harmon, "in getting his name in the paper." Most colleagues were.

Halsey Hall munched cigars, carried a liquor satchel, ate green onions in the booth, and claimed to say "Holy Cow!" before Harry Caray. "In 1915, I was a minor-league batboy and heard Billy Sullivan, a religious guy, use it." Hall seized the term, but never a check.

Once Ray Christensen mentioned on-air taking the Twins' bus to the park. Tuning white, Halsey shook Ray's arm at break. "For Pete's sake, don't say anything about a team bus. The station thinks I take a cab."

In 1974, colleague Larry Carlton said Minnesota would draw a million or "I'll return half my salary." On closing day the St. Paul *Pioneer*'s Pat Rickey grabbed Carneal. "Your partner might be in a little financial trouble today if the Twins don't draw 345,000."

By contrast, Herb bespoke "some quality," said Whittaker Chambers, "difficult to identify in the world's glib way, but good, and meaningful." Never was that more essential than when the 1982 Twins moved inside.

The Hubert H. Humphrey Metrodome wasted the region's clear, mild summer. A tarp topped its right-field wall. Sightlines cottoned to the football Vikings. One year the Dome planted gray-green Astroturf. "Great," wagged Carneal. "Now you can't see the ball." Greater: radio. You couldn't see the park.

The 1987 Twinkies won their first World Series. Cardinals fielders wore earplugs to blot Dome noise. Minnesota won another Classic in 1991. In 1994, Kirby Puckett retired with a .318 average. "I don't have a choice," he said of a damaged retina. In 1998, Herb chose to leave road coverage to John Gordon and Dan Gladden. In 2002, baseball nearly chose to contract the Twins. Their revenge: three straight A.L. Central titles.

A labor pact protects the franchise through 2006. At 80, Carneal signed

HERB CARNEAL

LONGEVITY:	10	49 years.
CONTINUITY:	9	Philadelphia A.L. and N.L. 1954; Baltimore A.L. 1957–61; Minnesota A.L. 1962– ; ABC/NBC TV The Baseball Network 1994–95.
NETWORK:	2	All-Star Game 1965 (NBC Radio). 1994–95 The Baseball Network (ABC/NBC TV).
KUDOS:	8	Cooperstown 1996.
LANGUAGE:	9	Shuns catchphrase and caricature.
POPULARITY:	10	One of us.
PERSONA:	10	As anchored as 10,000 Lakes.
VOICE:	9	Stolid.
KNOWLEDGE:	10	Unlike Hall, carried baseball books, not booze.
MISCELLANY:	7	Listened to Nats Voice Arch McDonald as child. "Good, but a lot of emphasis on style."
TOTAL:	84	(34th place).

a pact through 2005. "I would say realistically that might be it," he said, "but you never know." Wife Kathy had died in 2000. "The booth gives me something to do. I like to keep working."

In 1988, Herb hailed the 100th anniversary of "Casey at the Bat" by reciting it for the Minneapolis Symphony. The Twins' *real* Good Neighbor welds Mudville and Minneapolis-St. Paul.

HARRY CARAY

It might be! Baseball's Jackie Gleason, inhabiting another orb than Carneal's rural chalet. It could be! A half-century as Voice of the Cardinals, A's, White Sox, and Cubs. It was! God broke the mold *before* He made Harry Christopher Caray.

Recall the boozy Mayor of Rush Street. Hail the Maestro of the seventh-inning stretch. Sing "Take Me Out To the Ballgame." Holy cow! Caray lives, even now.

Ultimately, he defied the laws of probability, longevity, and cirrhosis of the liver. A caricature was the message; and the message, gold. Harry mined it at Sportsman's Park, Comiskey Park, and Wrigley Field: its alloy brass, verve, and cheek.

"Thank God I came along when I did," Caray said two years before his death. "With clubs hiring ex-jocks-turned announcers, a young me couldn't get a job." He bridged bobby soxers and the VCR, seeming truant across the land.

Here's to a life worth reliving. Mr. Mayor, this one's for you.

Caray was born of Italian-French and Romanian parents, orphaned at three, and raised by an aunt "more athletic than I was." Dad's name was Carabina. "It's Italian, so people'd say, 'Are you from the Hill in St. Louis?' I'd say, 'Hell, the Hill was Beverly Hills compared to where I came from' "—1909 LaSalle Street.

Selling papers, Harry used three cents to borrow books from a library. "I'd buy a sundae at a soda fountain and get halfway through the book." Next day Caray finished—and bought another sundae. After high school, he worked at day, began night college, and graced Sportsman's Park. "Nobody knows dad's age," son Skip said. "Whenever he takes a job, he lops five years off." In 1942, arguably 22, Harry solved a puzzlement.

Siren in the flesh, the Cardinals bored on radio. "Was I lucky—seeing

only great games—or was the announcer bad?" That France Laux! What a
drone! he decided, auditioning at KMOX. "I'm given a script about Puccini!
Puccini? Who's he? I stink, but get another try." G.M. Merle Jones helped him
start at WJOL Joliet and WKZO Kalamazoo. In 1945, Caray tried to enter
the military, but thick glasses kept him out. Hurt, he reclaimed radio.

"I get a WXOK talk show and go wild, 'Walter Winchellizing' like crazy." In
1945, Redbirds play-by-play opened. Directly Harry beat down the door. "I'm
with the sponsor head [Griesedieck Brewery] and he mentions a candidate he's
got in mind. 'I can listen to him, and read the paper at the same time.' "

Harry sat wide-mouthed. "'That's your problem!' I said. 'You're paying
hundreds of thousands of bucks, and what are you getting?' " People reading
the paper, ignoring his ads!

The boss phoned his ad director. "Get over here. I want you to meet our
new play-by-play man."

In every sense but score—Opening Day: Cubs 3, Cardinals 2—a season of
excess had come. Ex-catcher Gabby Street was Caray's WEW and WTMV sidekick—"the closest thing to a father I knew, outspoken, great humor." Only
home games were aired, riling owner Sam Breadon. In 1947, he sold 154-game
exclusivity to Caray–Street. Gabby died in 1951: "born forty years too early."

A 1952 team guide touted "the Cardinals network of over 80 stations."
Next season it moved to 50,000-watt KMOX. "Rumors said they were going
to leave St. Louis," said Caray, "so Gussie [Anheuser Busch Brewery head
August Busch] bought 'em for the city." He rebuilt Sportsman's Park, ditched
Griesedieck, and made Anheuser sponsor. For a time Harry feared being left
on the outside, looking in.

"Gussie was afraid that every time I said, 'Budweiser,' people'd think
'Griesedieck.' " Caray asked for a six-month trial. Ignoring Griesedieck, he
helped bankrupt it in Missouri and southern Illinois.

Tending America's then-western and -southernmost team, Harry became a
Roland or Arthur in Webster, Iowa, and Cleveland, Tennessee, and Lawton,
Oklahoma. "In the years when baseball stopped at the Mississippi, KMOX
built a network that brought major-league baseball into every little burb,"
said Bill James. "Harry's remarkable talents . . . forged a tie between the Cardinals and the Midwest that remains to this day."

Reverse praise formed its core. "Right at him! [St. Louis's Don
Blasingame] *Should* have made it!" Bobby Shantz walked a batter: "*What* a time

to lose control!" Reds rally, 8–7. "I don't know *how* you can lose some of these games, but we do!" The predator defended eating his young. "I have to inform the fan, even if it hurts a player." Say a batter K'd thrice. "What do you say? Good swing? I report, and if they do badly they get a bad report."

Webster's defines *fan,* derived from Greek *fanatic,* as showing "extreme zeal, piety, etc." Said a newspaper: "The greatest show, no ifs or buts, is to hear . . . Caray going nuts." He was "an inveterate fan," Harry mused, "who happens to be behind the mike." Ultimately, "It might be! It could be! It is!" upon a homer knit 124 stations. Ibid, his *primo* moniker.

In 1942, Phil Rizzuto caught a ball, threw wildly to second base, and screamed at Gerry Priddy, "Holy cow! You should have held it!" Harry sat nearby at Sportsman's Park. "Holy cow!" he repeated. It escorted him to every ballpark in the bigs.

One player Caray never knocked kept pilgrims trekking to Dodier and Grand. On May 13, 1958, Stan Musial needed one hit for 3,000. Home next night, St. Louis wanted it to happen there. The Man sits the bench: two out and on, sixth inning at Wrigley Field.

Manager Fred Hutchinson: "You want to go up?"

Musial: "Hell, let's win the game." The pinch-hitter banged a 2–2 pitch. "Line drive—there it is—into left field! Hit number 3,000!" said Harry. "A run has scored! Musial around first, on his way to second with a double! Holy cow! He came through! Listen to the crowd! Time is called! Standing ovation!"

St. Louis in July melds Capetown and Tripoli. After a steamy twinbill Stan signed autographs for an hour. "He didn't make a fraction of what guys do now. Didn't matter," said Harry. "In public he never make a mistake." Life began at 41: Musial hit .330 in 1962. In late 1963, St. Louis went 19–1 to pull a game back of Los Angeles, then hosted a three-set series.

Losing twice, the Swifties led, 5–4. "Here it comes!" Harry said of a ninth-inning pitch to the Dodgers' Dick Nen. A soul-wracking still ensued.

"Oh, my God," he said, finally. "It's over the roof." Soon St. Louis was over the cliff.

On September 29, The Man, retiring, singled in his last at-bat. "A hot shot on the ground into right field! A base hit! . . . Listen! Gary Kolb is going to replace Musial! There he goes!" St. Louis's infield had started the All-Star Game: Boyer, Dick Groat, Julian Javier, and Bill White. Caray thought 1964 might close the deal.

"I can't believe it!" he howled in April. "Roger Craig [doubling] has hit the left-center-field wall! The Cardinals are going to win the pennant!" Boyer became MVP. Lou Brock hit .348 after leaving Chicago. Harry aired the last day from a box. "If you've never heard Mr. Gussie Busch excited, you just heard him over my shoulder! . . . The pitch! A high pop foul! McCarver's there! The Cardinals won the pennant! The Cardinals won the pennant! The Cardinals won the pennant! Everybody out! Hey! . . . Mayhem on the field!"

In 1967, Orlando Cepeda became first unanimous league MVP. A year later, Bob Gibson led in complete games (28), shutouts (13), Ks (268), and ERA (1.12). Harry was asked his best left- and right-hand pitcher. "Koufax and Gibson. You can have the rest, and wouldn't have a chance." Televising the Series, his third on NBC, Caray never doubted that he would die behind the mike. "With my last gasp I'd say, 'Cardinals win!' "

Next month Harry did Missouri football, stopped at a hockey game, and headed to a hotel to eat. Crossing the street, he turned "to see what was coming from my left" and flew 40 feet in the air. Shoes landed 25 feet from the hotel. Nearly dying, Caray abided a broken nose, shoulder separation, and multiple fractures of both legs below the knees. The driver had gotten engaged a day earlier. "Maybe that's what caused him to drive so wild."

Harry mended at St. Petersburg Beach. Casing his bill, a Busch family member noted phone calls to the home of August Busch III. A bell went off. A detective stalking Caray found an affair with Busch's wife. "Not exactly the best job security," snorted Jim Woods. "Here he is, screwing the boss's daughter-in-law."

On Opening Day 1969, Caray walked on the field, shucking a pair of canes. Canned that October, "Hell, I preferred to have people believe the rumor than keep my job. I was so irresistible that a beautiful starlet would go for me over the 25-year-old millionaire heir to the crown. All I said was that I never raped anyone." The public knew that he was gone, not why.

"After 25 years I was expecting a gold watch. Instead, I got a pink slip," before slipping out of town.

In 1952, Ronald Reagan used Cardinals radio to plug his film *The Winning Team*. "Harry, I've had so much fun, but I have another appointment," said Dutch, leaving. In 1988, Reagan called a half-inning on WGN TV. "Harry, it's been so much fun," said the president, "but I have another appointment." In 1970, Caray was appointed Voice of the Oakland A's.

"I got Harry to sell baseball," said owner Charles O. Finley, axing him that fall. "That shit he put out in St. Louis didn't go here." Nothing sold the

56–106 1970 White Sox. Next year Caray became their Voice. "There were years," said Bill Veeck, rebuying them, "when Harry was all we had."

"Holy cow!" had owned St. Louis. He milked a fortune at 35th and Shields. "I took less money as a base—but the more they drew, the bigger bonus I got." In 1971, attendance nearly doubled to 833,891. The 1973 fifth-placers drew 1,316,527. The first seats to go were under Caray's booth. Looking up, you heard the only song that he knew.

"I've always sung it, but nobody heard me" before a 1976 seventh-inning stretch. Organist Nancy Faust began "Take Me Out To the Ballgame." Veeck saw Caray mouthing the tune. Next night he hid a P.A. microphone, booming Harry's voice above the crowd's. "I've been looking 40 years," Bill said, "and as soon as I heard you, I knew you were the guy."

Caray beamed. Veeck then stuck the lance. "As soon as I heard ya, I knew any fan knew he could sing better and'd join in. If you had a *good* voice, you'd intimidate them into silence."

Instead, holding the mike, Caray bellowed, "All right, lemme hear ya, everybody!"—never letting interest die, even when the Pale Hose *did*.

The Bicentennial Sox lost 97 games. In 1979, Veeck had visitors turn in disco records: using LPs as frisbees, hundreds gutted the field. Two rock concerts made its landscape approach Bull Run's. Only Caray kept the team from scuttling on Lake Michigan. "He owns the town," *The Arizona Republic* wrote of packed bars, forays on Rush Street, and bathing in the bleachers. If diamonds are forever, Caray seemed forever tied to Comiskey Park.

Then, suddenly, in November 1981, the Tribune Company revealed that he would announce its new subsidiary, the cuddly, lowly Cubs. "Each year I get bigger in the media," Harry later said. "I owe it all to [that year's Sox sale to] Jerry Reinsdorf and Eddie Einhorn. I never trusted 'em—snake-oil." Since 1968, the Hose had aired at least 64 free TV games a year. The new owners liked pay. "I kept thinking of their move to cable"—less than 50,000 Greater Chicago homes—"I'd be Harry Who." One day he picked up the phone and dialed Wrigley Field.

For a time the old warhorse shocked people by his presence. TV flung the Cubs' schedule into every corner of the city: "Bars, homes, my guys!" Increasingly, cable technology beamed it by satellite from Alaska to Key West. Soon WGN carried the Cubs to more than 20 million homes. "Once they belonged to the North Side," a columnist said. "Now even North America isn't big enough. Cable television has made the Cubbies more than a home-town team."

In 1984, baseball's munchkin dealt one image (sadder, not wiser, losers) for another (Our Cubs). In Idaho, Cubs Power fan clubs took root like spuds. The

Costa Rica Key Largo Bar flagpole flew the Cubs and City of Chicago pennants. In June, St. Louis crashed Wrigley: Cards, 9–8, ninth inning. "Sandberg hitting .327 now. The pitch. There it goes! Way back! It might be! It could be! It is! Holy cow! The game is tied! The game is tied! Ryne Sandberg did it! Listen to the crowd!"

Next inning St. Louis, having fronted, 7–1, re-led, 11–9. Again Ryne hit. "The [two-out, one-on] pitch. There's a long drive! Way back! Might be outta here! It is! He did it! He did it again! The game is tied! The game is tied! Holy cow! . . . Everybody is going bananas! . . . What would be the odds if I told you that twice Sandberg would hit home runs off Bruce Sutter?" An inning later Dave Owen singled. "Cubs win! [12–11] Cubs win! Cubs win! Holy cow! Cubs win! . . . I never saw a game like this in my life!" roared Harry. "And I've been around a long life!" We remember, even now.

The Cubs drew a record 2,107,655. The Loop traded "Hey, Harry!" for a gladhand and drink. "Cubs win!" Harry howled of one triumph. "The Good Lord wants the Cubs to win!" Deacons: Sandberg (MVP), Leon Durham (96 RBI), and Rick Sutcliffe (16–1). Paradise found: September 24, 9:49 P.M. "One more and it's over. The Chicago Cubs will be the new Eastern Division champs! Hey, it's in there! Cubs are the champions! The Cubs are the champions! The Cubs win! Rick Sutcliffe—his thirteenth in a row! He pitched a two-hitter! Let's just watch it! The fans are getting on the field! . . . Now our lives are complete!"

Not quite. Beer and sympathy: Chicago blew a 2–0 best-of-five-game L.C.S. lead.

"All my life, I've believed in miracles," said Reagan in 1984. "Now after 39 years of waiting, the miracle is happening." One more victory would have put the Cubs vs. 1907–08–35–45 Series foil Detroit. "Holy cow!" tried to atone with a miracle of his own.

For 41 years, Caray never missed a game. In 1987, he had a major stroke. For three months Bill Murray, Bill Moyers, and George Will, among others, did play-by-play. Harry then refetched the booth, like a long-playing record loved for long wear. "Clearly not as good—slower, more mistakes," mused Bob Costas. "But who cared? He was still Harry Caray, better at 50 percent than most guys at 100."

In 1988, Wrigley became the last bigs park with lights. A pact limited night games to 18 (30, by 2004) a year. "Good!" brayed Caray, "because don't forget what made the Cubs. Each generation a kid leaves home, gets on the el, gets off at the park, and sees the game. By six he's home and can you imagine his excitement?"

You could next year: Harry made Cooperstown. British Prime Minister

Margaret Thatcher said, "I may go on and on and on." We hoped nothing less for him.

Let some bozo urge Caray to pack it in. Wrigley bashed him like Marines storming Normandy. The Cubs neared 2000 hoping to forget the last century. Caray was looking forward to the next.

"Lots of guys doing games, kick 'em to see if they breathe. Who can't say, 'Strike one. Ball one'? It's not life or death. Make it fun. It's a game." Caray's ended in 1998. Dancing, he fell on Valentine's Day, had a heart attack, bore a coma, and died February 18.

Funerals stop traffic. Harry's stopped Chicago's. Thousands viewed his coffin at Holy Name Cathedral. WGN TV beamed his service and cortege. Passersby saluted. Workers removed hard hats. A wake filled Harry Caray's Restaurant. Flowers, hats, and cards blitzed Addison and Clark. At a statue outside Wrigley, Cub fan/Bud fan put a beer can in its hand.

"I was amazed," said grandson and new Cubs Voice Chip Caray. "How do you react with anything but total and complete gratitude?" Today VIPs pine

HARRY CARAY

LONGEVITY:	10	53 years.
CONTINUITY:	8	St. Louis N.L. 1945–69; Oakland A.L. 1970; Chicago A.L. 1971–81; Chicago N.L. 1982–97; ABC/NBC TV The Baseball Network 1994–95.
NETWORK:	8	All-Star Game 1957 (NBC Radio) and World Series 1964, 1967, and 1968 (NBC TV). Superstation 1982–97 (WGN TV). The Baseball Network 1994–95 (ABC/NBC TV).
KUDOS:	10	Cooperstown 1989. NSSA 1988, ASA 1989, and National Association of Broadcasters 1994 Halls of Fame. Seven-time *TSN* "Announcer of the Year."
LANGUAGE:	10	Got A in 10th-grade Spanish. Pre-stroke English as good.
POPULARITY:	10	Ain't no mountain high enough.
PERSONA:	10	"You can't beat fun at the ol' ballpark."
VOICE:	10	Irascible, indomitable.
KNOWLEDGE:	10	Called more than 8,300 bigs games, quoting another Harry, Truman: "I just tell the truth, and they think it's hell."
MISCELLANY:	8	Did football, including long-time Cotton Bowl. In 1960, Syracuse clinched national title on 87-yard pass. "[Ernie] Davis is going to go all the way! Touchdown!"
TOTAL:	94	(sixth place).

to carol "Take Me Out To the Ballgame" in the seventh-inning stretch. Unlike Harry, some can even sing.

Ethel Merman was asked if Broadway had been good to her. "Yes," she said, "but I've been good to Broadway." Baseball was good to the man who quaffed sundaes as a child. Towering, his memory is as good to us.

JACK BUCK

Jack Buck died June 18, 2002, of Parkinson's disease, lung cancer, and other disease. By reputation, he put forth irony, a fluent phrase, and brave front under pressure. The rep was right.

Buck called 11 World Series, 17 Super Bowls, and the 1954–2001 Cardinals. Expert at social intercourse, he was always ready with the winning gesture and winsome word.

Say Bob Wolff, and see a briefcase. Howard Cosell changed the parameters of his profession. Curt Gowdy mimed Jack Webb's "Just the facts, ma'am." Buck used humor vs. absurdity and incongruity.

As TV's *Matlock,* Andy Griffith said, "Ain't nothing easy." Nothing was easy for John Francis Buck. The wonder is that he made you swear it was.

Buck was born August 21, 1924, in Holyoke, Massachusetts, to Kathleen and Earle Buck, a railroad accountant who commuted weekly to New Jersey. Their third of seven children loved radio. "I was a Red Sox fan, and Jimmy Foxx was my hero," Jack mused. "I'd get Mel Allen, Red Barber on network." At night, from Havana, he heard Spanish play-by-play.

Ain't nothing easy: "Cereal for breakfast, soup for lunch, bakery leftovers for dinner." In 1939, dad got a job in Cleveland with the Erie Railroad. Next year he died, at 49, of high blood pressure. Already the teenager had taken odd jobs—"two, often three at once. Didn't leave much time." Baseball got the balance.

In 1935, Buck watched the All-Star Game: A.L., 4–1; Foxx homered. On July 17, 1941, the bigs' then-largest night crowd, 67,468, packed Municipal Stadium. "From the bleachers I saw [third baseman Ken] Keltner rob Joe D. twice," ending the 56-game streak. A year later Jack boarded a great Lakes iron ore boat as porter, painter, cook, deckhand, and crane operator.

Buck feared never seeing land again. Then, in 1943, he became a corporal and instructor with K Company, 47th Regiment, 9th Infantry Division.

On March 15, 1945, crossing the last (Remagen) bridge into Germany, Jack took shrapnel in the left leg and shoulder, earned the Purple Heart, and years later learned that Lindsey Nelson was also wounded—same spot, and day.

"I'd say, 'Yeah, but you weren't dodging bullets carrying a hand grenade on your chest,'" said Buck, who, almost losing his left arm, spent V-E Day in a Paris hospital. He supposed a prologue. "I've always had a fondness for Italian women. In fact, during World War II an Italian woman hid me in her basement for three months. Of course, this was in Cleveland."

In 1995, Jack visited Normandy's D-Day cemetery, where he felt not guilt, but gratitude, and tearfully penned a poem: "They chatter and laugh as they pass by my grave, and that's the way it should be. / For what they have done, and what they will do, has nothing to do with me. / I was tossed ashore by a friendly wave with some unfriendly steel in my head. / They chatter and laugh as they pass by my grave, but I know they'll soon be dead. / They've counted more days than I ever knew, and that's all right with me, too. / We're all souls in one pod, all headed for God, too soon, or later, like you."

In Germany, Buck had panted to be a paratrooper. Entering Ohio State in 1946, he panted to make up for lost time.

"If you want something done," said Lucille Ball, "ask a busy person." Jack paid for college by working at an all-night gas station. He graduated in three years, majored in Radio Speech, and took a course in football theory from Woody Hayes. A broadcast professor told him "to find something else to do for a living." At WCOL Columbus, he recalled the saw: Those who can't do, teach.

Buck's first game was Ohio State–DePaul hoops. Next: Ohio State football and Cardinals Triple-A Columbus. Joining WBNS, he met comic Jonathan Winters, did a variety show, but missed baseball. "Thankfully, the Cardinals had another Triple-A team." At a 1952 dinner, Rochester Voice Ed Edwards told a dirty joke. "Destiny or bad taste—I'm grateful for his lapse." Jack replaced him. "Like a player, I was working my way up."

In August 1953, Buck took the subway to the Polo Grounds. "The Cardinals didn't call it an audition, but hadn't asked me there to sell socks." Harry backed Chick Hearn. The future hoops star declined. Hired, Jack got a Caray tape. "'Copy him,' they said. I could no more do that than with any other guy." Harry treated calm like leprosy. His new aide tried to "get excited, but not lose control."

St. Louis did both. "I'd get letters from Oklahoma, Tennessee." Weekend lots paraded license plates: Kentucky, Georgia, Florida. "Skip Atlanta. *We're* America's Team," riding Anheuser's 14-state network Redbird wave of love. In 1958, the Bums and Jints left for California. "Suddenly, there's a void which Anheuser hoped to fill." A year later it aired 44 of their games on WOR New York: The city felt Buck deliverance. "I'd do 'em, then rejoin the Cardinals. The reaction in New York was bananas, but the Yanks started bitching about territorial rights."

The Apple series ended in late 1959. Ain't nothing easy: That fall the Cards cut Buck. "Bud Blattner, from St. Louis, needed a job and KMOX squeezed me out." At liberty, Jack bounded to ABC. The problem was CBS and NBC. "Each Saturday their 'Game' started at two o'clock. Ours began at four. It was overkill." Looking back, the fight should have been stopped on points.

Fired, the unhappy wanderer found a happy ending. "I'd got good notices on network baseball," he said. "Now KMOX wanted me." Also wowing: Buck's grasp of another sport.

In 1960, ABC handed Jack the new American (some said Almost) Football League. "A franchise cost exactly $25,000. Guys ran around with hundred dollar bills, paying cash to snatch college players [from the NFL]. I know because I saw it." The league seemed alien—more UFO than AFL.

A 1962 title game photo shows Buck, with mike, at midfield, reporting overtime's Houston–Dallas coin toss. "Abner Haynes won the toss, then stupidly said Dallas'd kick. Houston gets the wind—and ball," Jack said. Dallas won, anyway. Next year Buck switched to the NFL. "He prepared, but loosely," said then-CBS analyst Pat Summerall. "'This is not a funeral. We'll have fun, and hope people do, too.'"

Lite and bite: Buck aired the Bears and Cowboys. Twin peaks: Super Bowl IV (Kansas City 23, Minnesota 7), and Ice Bowl (December 31, 1967) at Green Bay's Lambeau Field. A hotel operator phoned at 7:30 A.M. "Good morning. It's 17 below zero." Pursed lips froze. Players developed frostbite. Said Jack: "Excuse me while I have a bite of my coffee."

Pack, 21–17. Buck's twin-engine plane leaves for Chicago. Wind chill reaches 50 degrees below zero. Suddenly, near New Holstein, Wisconsin, the front door opens. "Frank Gifford's in that seat and I've got my arms around him," said Jack, "and [analyst] Tommy Brookshier is shooting scotch in Gifford's mouth."

The plane lands, skids, and stops. Trembling, Buck saw a stand of wood 50 feet away. "We switched planes, got to Chicago, and believe me, celebrated New Year's Eve."

He had reason. Jack's sixties daybook listed hoops (Hawks), hockey (Blues), and bowling (with ABC's Chris Schenkel). He interviewed Eleanor Roosevelt, broadcast from the new Gateway Arch, and bloomed as emcee. "The best there ever was at a dinner," said Bob Broeg. His phrase "That's a winner!" seemed less applicable to the team. Six times the '54–'62ers failed the second division. "By August, pure drudgery," Buck said. By contrast, "Baseball's daily, so a winner [1964 and 1967–68] engulfs the city and lives through the winter. A wonderful thing to see."

In 1965, Buck called his first All-Star Game. Next year Busch Stadium, opening eight blocks from the Arch, hosted the Mid-Summer Classic. The field temperature read 130 degrees. "I must say," said Casey Stengel, "it [the park] holds the heat well." Easy? Ain't *nothing* easy. In St. Louis, Caray was still king.

"He had his moments, but he was the first to editorialize," Jack said. "When Harry and I were doing the game, we were as good a team as there ever was." To Skip Caray, "Dad [was] the voice of the guy sitting in the bleachers with his shirt off, and Jack the emcee for the guy dressed in a dinner jacket," hitched like "[Itzhak] Perlman and a violin."

Harry's firing made pickets froth. How could you *replace* him? *The Great Gatsby* dubbed style "an unbroken series of perfect gestures." Inside, Buck anguished. Publicly, he never broke a sweat.

In 1976, Jack left "the best baseball broadcasting position in the United States, but sometimes you have to take a chance," hosting NBC's new "Grandstand." Cool and wry, how could the natural miss?

"A question I still ask," he joked two decades later. Guesswork: network TV's iron hand: in at 54:10; out, 57:23; go to break; toss to remote. Local work was breezier. "You golf, swim, and shoot pool, go to the park and b.s., do the game, and go home." Bob Costas joined KMOX in 1974: "NBC's Buck was not the Buck we knew."

Axed, he repaired to St. Louis to raise money for cystic fibrosis, narrate Benjamin Britten's "Young Person's Guide to the Orchestra" for the St. Louis Symphony, and reclaim the Cards.

Bob Gibson became the second pitcher to fan 3,000. Lou Brock got 3,023 hits. Al Hrabosky stalked the mound, mumbled to himself, smacked his glove, and restabbed the rubber. "Jack did it all," said Costas. "I'd hang around, hoping to soak him up."

In 1982, Ozzie Smith arrived from San Diego, having reinvented shortstop. The season ended with Bruce Sutter K-ing Gorman Thomas. "That's a winner! That's a winner!" cried Buck. "A World Series winner for the St. Louis Cardinals." A 1985 flag pivoted on L.C.S. Game Five. Ozzie had never homered in 2,967 ups batting left. "Smith rips one into right! Down the line! It may go! Go crazy, folks! Go crazy! It's a home run, and the Cardinals have won the game, 3–2, on a home run by the Wizard!"

Buck did CBS Radio's 1976 All-Star Game, 1979–82 L.C.S., and 1983–89 Series, including the 1988 opener. L.A. trails, 4–3. Kirk Gibson limps to the plate like Walter Brennan, fouls pitches like Hank Aguirre, then swings. "And a fly ball to deep right field!" Jack cried. "This is going to be a home run! Unbelievable! A home run for Gibson! And the Dodgers have won the game, 5 to 4. I don't believe what I just saw!"

We did: Buck let us, every word.

To Buck, CBS Radio's 1979–97 "Monday Night Football" meant "telling where the ball is, giving the score." Baseball differed. "The audience knows its sport better because you're brought up on it. You give bright people inside dope you know because you're on the scene and they're not." In 1990, CBS TV began four-year exclusivity. "It pays a bundle to get baseball," said *TSN*'s Jack Craig, "then finds sales stink." The mikeman falleth: Buck replaced Brent Musburger. Surely Jack—modest and fatalistic, with a nice-guy air—would grease interest. Think again.

"CBS never got that baseball play-by-play draws word-pictures," he rued. "All they knew was that football stars analysts. So they said, 'Let [analyst Tim] McCarver run the show.' " The bug was wayward regular-season coverage: "CBS stands for 'Covers Baseball Sporadically,' " wrote *Sports Illustrated*. "Buck and McCarver may have to have a reunion before [their] telecast," added *USA Today*. Said Buck: "We never got a chance to fit."

In 1991, Bobby Vinton mangled the National Anthem before a playoff game in Pittsburgh. Jack lightly referred to Vinton being Polish. "The irony," said son Joe, "was that he trying to *help* the guy." Death threats rose. Buck found a footprint on his hotel pillow. Next day director Ted Shaker spotted him in the lobby. "You're in trouble," he snapped, then walked away. Solace: a see-saw/hold your breath/worst to first World Series.

"The ['90] Braves and Twins were last," Buck said. "Now both make the final." In Game Six, Kirby Puckett tripled, stole a dinger, and hit the Event's fourth overtime game-winning homer. "Into deep left-center! . . . And we'll see you tomorrow night!" Game Seven, 10th inning: Minnesota's Dan

Gladden reaches third base. Two walks follow. "Larkin is the pinch-hitter . . . the Twins are going to win the World Series! The Twins have won it! It's a base hit! It's a 1–0 10th-inning victory!"

Five, three, and four games were decided by a run, in extra innings, and in the last at-bat, respectively. "Great way to go out," said Phil Mushnick. "But what I recall is Jack trying to predict plays, as if to prove he was still on top." Sacked, he sported a what, me worry? front, visiting next spring's Irish Derby. "The Irish are so relaxed. If you buy a paper, they say, 'Do you want yesterday's or today's?'

"I say, 'Today's, of course.'

"They say, 'Come back tomorrow.' I like that attitude after the last couple years."

Ronald Reagan said of Thomas Jefferson, "I know that's true because he told me." Aging, Jack refused to age. "One good thing about you is you don't die young," he told Ernie Harwell in 1992. That season an old pal greeted another septuagenarian. "Take care of yourself," Caray urged Herb Carneal. "There aren't many of us left to lose."

Smith left in 1996. A year later Mark McGwire arrived from Oakland. Buck covered them despite diabetes, a pacemaker, vertigo, and Parkinson's disease. "I shook hands with Muhammad Ali recently," he joked. "It took them 30 minutes to get us untangled." Wife Carole asked what Jack would one day say to God. "I want to ask Him why He's been so good to me."

In 1998, the Cardinals dedicated a bust of Buck, smiling, hand cupping an ear: "Jack in his favorite spot," it read, "behind the microphone." McGwire ripped homer 60—"Wake up, Babe Ruth! There's company coming!"—then stalked Roger Maris. "Look at there! Look at there! Look at there! McGwire's No. 61, Flight 61, headed for Planet Maris! History. Bedlam! What a moment! Pardon me for a moment while I stand to applaud!"

Peroration: Buck called game 6,500. The 2001 Cards resumed a week after 9/11. At Busch, Jack read an original poem. "As our fathers did before, we shall win this unwanted war. And our children will enjoy the future we'll be giving." Ain't nothing easy. His face twitched, his hands jerked. Buck never stood so tall.

After December 5 cancer surgery, "He was doing fine," said Carole. "Everything was on track to do baseball in 2002." Next month doctors removed an intestinal blockage. Five operations, including brain surgery, shed Irish luck from a life begun hard. "I always told him how much I loved him," said Joe, visiting daily. "He and I didn't waste one second together."

Dad died on a night the home team played Anaheim. "Buck Dead at 77," knelled the page-one *Post-Dispatch*. The Swifties permanently lit his statue. Thousands viewed the casket, lined a freeway for Buck's cortege, and recalled him saying, "They talk a lot in football and baseball about not beating yourself. The same applies in life. Don't shortchange yourself." A city wept: Jack had not shortchanged *it*.

Churchill said of former British Prime Minister Herbert Asquith: "His children are his best memorial." Buck left his wife, five daughters, three sons, and 16 grandchildren. "He meant class," said Costas, "a guy who never talked down."

That's a winner! seems easy to apply to Jack.

Not easy: sport without a man who synthesized the Gaelic mix of grace, pain, and cheer.

JACK BUCK

LONGEVITY:	10	48 years.
CONTINUITY:	9	St. Louis N.L. 1954–59, 1961–75, and 1977–2001; ABC TV "Game of the Week" 1960; CBS TV "Game of the Week" 1990–91.
NETWORK:	10	"Game" 1960 (ABC TV) and 1990–91 (CBS TV). World Series 1967–68 (NBC Radio), 1983–89 (CBS Radio), and 1990–91 (CBS TV). All-Star Game 1965 (NBC TV), 1976 (CBS Radio), and 1990–91 (CBS TV). L.C.S. 1979–82 (CBS Radio) and 1990–91 (CBS TV).
KUDOS:	10	Cooperstown 1987. NSSA Hall of Fame 1990 and nine other Halls, including ASA 1990 and Radio 1995. Statue outside Busch Stadium 1998. Lifetime Emmy Achievement award 2000. Missouri Athletic Club St. Louis Citizen of the Year 2000.
LANGUAGE:	9	"That's a winner!" was.
POPULARITY:	10	Higher than Gussie Busch's.
PERSONA:	10	Grand stylist.
VOICE:	9	Ironic.
KNOWLEDGE:	10	Didn't fake, or cram.
MISCELLANY:	9	Did CBS TV 1963–78 "NFL on CBS" and Radio 1978–94 Super Bowl. "No sweat," he said of eight children. "They only took 10 minutes of work."
TOTAL:	96	(fourth place).

BOB PRINCE

Statistics cite number of, say, World Series. They cannot retrieve a ribbon of rococo prose. From 1948 to 1975, one radio after another aired a baseball original. A great play sparked "How sweet it is!"; dingers, "Kiss it good-bye!"; a Pirates' triumph, "We had 'em allll the way!" In an inning, Bob Prince might loop from U.S. Steel stock via golf with Bing Crosby to his favorite charity, the Allegheny Valley School for Retarded Children.

"Oh, by the way," he would note, "Clemente grounded out, Stargell flied out, and that's the inning." Prince's moniker was The Gunner. (Once he made a joke to a woman in a bar. Her husband replied by pointing a gun.) Some thought Bob a maniac. It is fair to say he was maniacally riveting.

The son of Army Colonel F.A. Prince, Bob was raised "by a mammy who had sayings like 'it's as quiet as a gnat pissing on a bale of cotton.' " His mother placed a word "under my breakfast cereal dish. When I came home from school that day, I had to know how to define and use it properly." Dad plunked the Army brat at six posts and 14 or 15 schools. He flunked out of four universities, got a B.A. at Oklahoma, and entered Harvard Law.

"I had three uncles, cousins, a grandfather and brother who were Harvard lawyers. I went so I wouldn't have to work." In 1940, Gunner, 24, read about a jurist who frequented a burlesque house. One night Papa Prince saw sonny, with a stripper, in a newsreel on the jitterbug. "You're wasting my money," dad phoned from Alabama, yanking him from school. "Here's $2,000. Go make a living." The Gunner had another aim in mind.

Bob's unwritten memoir read *I Should Have Never Danced with the Stripper.* He should have never been scarred by a polo mallet, kicked in a rodeo, or jailed for vagrancy—but was. A pattern emerged, worthy of a diffident respect. "Anything short of murder," he said, "I've been there." From Harvard, that meant Zelienople, near Pittsburgh, at his grandmother's home— "the only town where I could find a place to live."

Dad phoned again: "Throw that bum out of the house." Prince was to find a job. Instead, he found a wife.

"One day I see this nifty lady," Bob said of a local high school teacher. Betty married him in 1941. Having been a vagabond, Prince more or less settled on his career. "In the Army I'd played golf, polo, fenced. I'd swam at Oklahoma. All I'd been trained to do was loaf. Broadcasting was the next easiest thing."

By day he sold insurance. At night, like Caray, Bob began "Winchellizing" radio—in his phrase, "disputatious." One night Prince charged that boxer Billy Conn ducked opponents. Next week Conn hit him in the gut.

"I can't fight you," said Bob, "but I'll take you to the Athletic Club and swim you."

Conn later asked, "What would have happened if we'd fought in the pool?"

"I'd have drowned you." Instead, Prince profited from a man immersed in God.

In 1948, Bucs broadcaster Jack Craddock discovered the kindly light that led. "He resigned," Bob said, "and began to preach at revival meetings. [Rosey] Rowswell needs an aide." Owner and law school friend Tom Johnson proposed the Gunner.

"I'd never heard anything like this guy. We were bad, and Rosey'd trip the light fantastic, like a kid when he's tired." Prince asked why. "Sponsors deserve fans, and fans deserve a show," said Rosey. "Don't forget that just play-by-play gives 'em neither." Bob didn't.

Forbes Field had yawning turf, a right-field pavilion, and in-play batting cage. A brick wall enclosed the outfield. Bleachers lay beyond third base. "This is how we recall her," said 1955–76 G.M. Joe L. Brown. We recall Rowswell's caddy as neither cliched nor Talmudic.

Prince was partisan: "Come on, we need a run." The infield became an "alabaster plaster." "Give me the Hoover!" meant bases to be cleaned. Bob won a bet by waltzing from center field to home plate in stockings, pumps, neon jacket, bow tie, and red bermuda shorts. "I became controversial—controversial on the air, and in my jackets. Anything to establish a reputation."

Ultimately, Rosey got ill, slept in the studio, and had Bob re-create by ticker. Prince woke him if the Bucs took the lead. At Forbes, he pointed to a base or position. "That way he had some idea of the ball."

The 1950–57 Pirates finished last or next-to-last. "Here's to the Rosey Ramble," Bob said after Rowswell's death. His riposte: "Gunner's Gallop"— anything but the game.

Dale Long was an exception, homering in seven straight games. Next night in 1956 he took Carl Erskine deep for a bigs record No. 8. "Forbes about tumbled down," said Prince. "Long got such a standing ovation that he had to come out of the dugout for a curtain call." A curtain fell May 26, 1959.

"The final out of the ninth inning was . . . the eighth turned in by Haddix, and . . . he became the eighth pitcher in all the history of baseball to pitch a perfect no-hit, no-run game. He then went on to get 'em in the tenth, and the eleventh, and the twelfth," said Bob, "before a man got aboard, and then only on an error. One out. Batter, Adcock . . . There's a fly ball, deep right-center. It is gone! Absolutely fantastic!"—a term for the Bucs' annual percent of radio/TV sets in use.

One reason was Jim Woods, joining Prince in 1958. A year later what he called "the ugliest woman I ever saw" crashed the press box. "I want to see fucking [Jack] Brickhouse!" she barked.

A writer fingered Bob: "*There's* Brickhouse."

"Are you fucking Brickhouse?" The network carried every word.

Convulsed, Woods watched her leave. "Gunner, if you think *that* one was ugly, look at the broad she's sitting with!" Brown phoned: "You can't call women *broads* on the air." Jim countered: "*Broad* is the only thing you *could*."

Next year Bob called the Bucs' first post-1927 pennant. Cy Younger Vernon Law went 20–9. MVP shortstop Dick Groat hit a bigs-high .325. Bill Mazeroski patented the double play. A war then ensued of shock and awe. The Yanks won Games 2, 3, and 6 10–0, 16–3, and 12–0, respectively. Nova merge: Don Hoak's diving stops; Bill Virdon's leaping catch off Yogi Berra; Bobby Richardson's Series record 12 RBI.

Once Woods offered Gunner a drink. On the wagon, he demurred. "Don't worry! I'm just as crazy sober!" Game Seven left you feeling like a morning-after binge.

October 13 broke mild and bright. In the first inning, Rocky Nelson hit "a drive! Deep into right field! Back she goes! You can kiss that one good-bye!" Prince said on NBC TV. Pirates, 2–0. Low tide: Yanks rally, 7–4. High: Hal Smith's three-run "electrifying [eighth-inning] homer," read the *Pittsburgh Press*, "turned Forbes Field into a bedlam." Bucs, 9–7.

At 3:36 P.M., Mazeroski cleared the 406-foot mark: 10–9. The Stripes outscored [55–27], outhit [.338–.256], and outhomered [10–4] Pittsburgh. Bob didn't know—literally—how they lost. "In the ninth, I hear, 'Do the clubhouse celebration.' I get there, find the game tied 9-all," and refound the booth. A din promptly shook the yard. "Get back downstairs!" an NBCer yelled. "You win!"

Breathless, Bob interviewed manager Danny Murtaugh, N.L. head Warren Giles, and the mayor of Pittsburgh. "Everyone except the one guy in the world people wanted to see."

Finally Maz was maneuvered to the mike. "How does it feel," Bob asked, "to be a member of the world champions?"

"Great."

"Congratulations," he said. End of interview. The hero is led away.

"By the way, how *did* we win?" Prince asked at dinner.

Betty eyed him like Cyclops. "You must be kidding. Maz hit a homer." Bob suddenly felt less hungry than Rosanne after lunch.

Controversial on purpose: "I think it ridiculous," he told a dinner, "to honor here a man [Stan Musial] who made more than 7,000 outs." Or accident: Number 46, unlisted in the scorecard, pinch-hit. Intercom: "Will Rab Mungee report to the press gate?" Gunner: "Rab Mungee is the Houston pinch-hitter."

One day Prince ribbed several Bucs about baseball's sedentary tilt. Knocking his stick figure, Gene Freese said, "Here's $20 you can't dive into this pool." Bob made for his third-floor hotel room. "If he doesn't clear it [12 feet of concrete]," said trainer Danny Whelan, "strictly a blotter job." He did. "At least Freese paid. If I'd bet Dick Stuart I'd still be waiting."

A 1965 partier joked he couldn't wait to drop Prince from the 17th floor. "Half the room would have been for it and half against," replied a friend. On the bench a year later Whelan held a wiener painted green. "There," jibed Bob, "is a [TV] picture of a grown man pointing a green weenie at Lee May." May popped up. Trucks put the Weenie on their aerial. Serta Mattress made a model to help it last a doubleheader. In Calcutta, an Indian fakir played a pipe. The Weenie rose from his wicker basket. Controversial.

At Forbes, Pittsburgh faced the Dodgers. "Let's put the Green Weenie on [Don] Drysdale!" Prince told transistors. A roar commenced. Big D stood, sneering. Finally umpire Ed Vargo said to throw. "How can I pitch with these nuts going crazy and that skinny bastard up in the booth?" Vargo: "I don't know, but pitch." The batter tripled. Leaving, Drysdale shook his fist.

Bob flew to Dallas, changed for San Francisco, and began talking to an attendant, inadvertently saying "bomb." A sleep-challenged Gunner was released next day. The Black Maxers, a pack of Pirates fixated by World War I flying gear, named him Official Bombardier.

Would Prince, 50, ever settle down? "I am, or at least my wife thinks it's time I did."

Bob did NBC Radio's 1966 O's-Dodgers Series. Later he admitted to imagining in the Classic the man with four batting titles, a dozen Gold Gloves, and 3,000 hits. Bob asked Spanish for "let's go." Roberto Clemente said *arriba,* whose word he became, treating baseball, said Roger Angell, "like a form of punishment" on the field.

SI had called Prince "shaped so distinctly in his mold that every listener feels he knows him"—or was that No. 21 or even Poss, parting in 1969 after "a pissing contest with the station," said Bob. "They were only about $1,200 apart." Another friend left June 28, 1970, before 40,918, the Bucs' largest crowd since 1956. "I often come back," Prince later mused. "I love what Forbes had"—haze and horizon, pleasant, almost golden, with pews so near the field that, watching players, you could sense what they were like.

However vague memory may be, it knows why Three Rivers Stadium seemed K-Mart *sans* the charm. Gunner loathed its *faux* turf, concrete shell, and top deck in West Virginia. Willie Stargell—to Bob, "Willie the Starge"— hit it more than anyone. He owned a Kentucky Fried Chicken franchise in Pittsburgh's Hill District. Bob: "Let's spread some chicken on the Hill!" In 1971, Starge spread 48 dingers on the league. Pittsburgh took the L.C.S. Prince then did his last World Series.

It began Orioles 5–3 and 11–3, reviving in Game Four, the first Classic after dark. "Day games shut out working people," said Commissioner Bowie Kuhn. Over 60 million watched: Bucs, 4–3. In Game Seven, "Here is Bobby Clemente, who has had, if there has ever been a vendetta, this might be it," growled Bob. "And there's a ball hit very deep into right field! Going back for it is Frank Robinson! He's at the wall! He can't get it! It's gone!"

Pirates win, 2–1. *Arriba* hits .414. "Bobby Clemente continues to totally annihilate Baltimore pitching!" The question was how many wished to annihilate Gunner, too.

At Three Rivers, some bayed, "Shut up, Prince!" at the man in narrow tie and gaudy coat or shorts, a T-shirt, socks, and shoes—"my game uniform." Once, yapping "The hell with this. It's too hot," he worked in briefs. Most scent a sweeter bottom line: "without question," said ex-Mayor Joe Barr, "[helping] the underprivileged, sick, and disadvantaged more than any public entertainment figure in Pittsburgh."

Bob formed or chaired, said Poss, "more charities than a dog's got fleas." At Allegheny Valley School, he counseled parents, spent Christmas Day on campus, and got firms to donate wheelchairs. In Chicago, Gunner stopped at Kraft Foods to record "Little Red Riding Hood." The public man barred publicity. "He'd come in, play with a child," said a Valley domo, "and leave, saying, 'That's what I needed.' " Prince needed a handkerchief July 28, 1972.

"[Any] doubt that Prince fans outnumbered Prince detractors . . . was proven last night," the *Press*'s Bob Smizik wrote of "Bob Prince Night." School students made two lamps from popsicle sticks. "No home run," said Gunner, "hit me with such heroism." Another hero crowned September 30. "Everybody standing. They want Bobby to get that hit 3,000. Bobby hits a drive into the gap in left-center field! There she is! A double for Roberto!" The Bucs blew a 2–1 game playoff lead. New Year's Eve's loss was worse: *Arriba,* dead at 38, aiding victims of a Nicaraguan earthquake. "He *was* the Pirates," a fan said, "and they were different without him." Few thought of life without Prince.

In 1974, traveling secretary Art Routzong phoned from Atlanta. "We're coming home and haven't sold many tickets." Putting on his thinking cap, Gunner found a Slavic word. "We got Ladies' Night coming up. Why don't you wave your"—he blanked on *hanky*—"babushka?" Art steamed. "They won't know what you mean." Enough did to pack Three Rivers. "'Ladies, wave your babushkas,' and they go wild," he said. "We get a run. I say, 'That's what Babushka Power is all about.' "

The '74–'75ers were about taking the East, losing the L.C.S., and being lucky to lure a million. "Five divisions in six years," said Prince, "and we can't draw"—the park, football Steelers, or black stars in segregated Pittsburgh, who could say?

The Pirates considered those whyfores, and insanely chose another.

In 1968, a KDKA owner Westinghouse Company lawyer told Poss and Prince to sign "contracts so I can take them back to the office."

Bob: "Ready?"

Jim: "Whenever you are."

Each tore the paper. "There," Gunner said. "Take *those* back to your boss."

By the 1970s, Westinghouse accused Bob of putting show-biz above seminar: "too big for his britches," an official said. It began shrinking him: less promotion, less pre- and post-game time, more clients in the booth. Several turned up radios. "They were bombed," Prince said. "You could hear 'em in Erie." He turned off the mike, said, "Shut the hell up," was called a "mother-fucker," and slugged a thug. "Then I sat down, opened the mike, and said Westinghouse was making it impossible to do my job."

Prince misread power. "He thought he had the sponsors and team behind him," said partner Nellie King. On October 30, 1975, Westinghouse misread his niche, sacking baseball's Tri-State heart. Radio raged. Bars dumped sponsor Iron City Beer. "For many people," wrote Charlie Feeney, "the baseball world yesterday came to an end."

On November 5, a parade packed downtown Pittsburgh. Bystanders waved babushkas. Bob held a weenie. Stargell told a rally: "It's like the U.S. Steel Building falling down." Prince rued dancing with a stripper. The Bucs forgot to dance with their Astaire.

"There are people in the Tri-State area who think Prince is irreplaceable," said Feeney. He was.

The Astros quickly hired him. In early 1976, ABC added "Monday Night Baseball." Driving back from dinner, Bob, 60, pulled off the road. "I wouldn't say this to anyone else, but I'm worried," he told Woods, having never called a network series. Said Poss: "You can't *do* on ABC what you've done in Pittsburgh." A Rosey Ramble would get Prince busted to an affiliate in Nome.

"Bob knew he'd have trouble adjusting to network TV—promote this, say that." On June 8, "Monday" aired from Pittsburgh. The board welcomed Prince, handclapping all around. He waved a babushka, began to cry, and said, "I have to apologize . . . and turn over my mike." The *Post-Gazette* read: "Ratings are low, negative reviews rampant," Gunner battered and confused.

Dethroned that fall ("I hated Houston, and ABC never let me be Bob Prince"), he took a job with WEEP Pittsburgh ("How ironic"), did hockey (sample: "We have it. They have it"), and returned to baseball in the early eighties. "It's just cable, not as many homes. But you hang in there," more upset that baseball might not fit again in the region's emotional luggage.

KDKA rehired Prince in 1985. "Other than my family, you're giving me back the only thing I love." He had cancer surgery, did a game, reentered the hospital, and got lung dehydration and pneumonia. "It is a sad morning," Tom McMillan wrote June 11. "We walk to work. We shuffle our feet. A piece of us is missing. Bob Prince is dead."

In 2002, the Bucs left Three Rivers for downtown PNC Park: Gunner's Bar vaunts the legend's core. How sweet the gravel voice and rhetoric and sheer unpredictability were. Forget kissing memory good-bye. Prince still has us all the way.

BOB PRINCE

LONGEVITY:	10	33 years.
CONTINUITY:	10	Pittsburgh N.L. 1948–75 and 1982–85; Houston N.L. 1976; ABC TV "Monday Night Baseball" 1976.
NETWORK:	6	All-Star Game 1959 and 1965 (NBC Radio) and 1976 (ABC TV). World Series 1960 and 1971 (NBC TV) and 1966 (NBC Radio). L.C.S. 1969 (Robert Wold Radio). "Monday Night" 1976 (ABC TV).
KUDOS:	10	Cooperstown 1986. NSSA Hall of Fame 1986. Fourteen-time Pennsylvania Sportscaster of the Year. Pittsburgh Jaycees and Chamber of Commerce Man of the Year. Art Rooney Award.
LANGUAGE:	10	Vernon Law became "Deacon"; Don Hoak, "Tiger"; Harvey Haddix, "Kitten."
POPULARITY:	10	"I've got to get to the booth. A million people are waiting to turn me off [sic, on]."
PERSONA:	10	"You'd swear the man who invented the microphone had him in mind," said TSN.
VOICE:	10	Inimitable.
KNOWLEDGE:	9	Teaching Sunday school, turned David vs. Goliath into Philistines at Israelites.
MISCELLANY:	9	Did Steelers, Penn State, and NCAA football, Pitt, Duquesne, and NIT hoops, golf, boxing, wrestling, and opera—"not play-by-play. I introduced Igor Gorin on CBS."
TOTAL:	94	(seventh place).

MILO HAMILTON

George H.W. Bush was a conundrum wrapped in hard-to-get-a-handle-on. The Northeast Episcopalian liked country and western music. The patrician enjoyed horseshoes. Bush warred on language: "Deep doo-doo . . . Don't cry for me, Argentina." Yet old-shoe charm—"I'm president and I don't have to eat it [broccoli]!"—eclipsed Andover and Yale. Canned by the American people, he, I, and 400 friends left the White House in 1993. Milo Hamilton, who adored Bush, understood.

Hamilton called Stan Musial's record five homers in a 1954 doubleheader. In 1972, he did a twinbill in Atlanta. "Would you believe it? Nate Colbert hits five dingers, too." Next day Nate, a 1954 Knotholer, recalled having seen Stan's explosion at Sportsman's Park. *Eerie* daubs the junction—also, Milo's life.

Eight times, all but once involuntarily, he left one team for another. Said *League of Their Own*: "There is no crying in baseball"—and no guarantees. "Hamilton is as interesting as the weather channel, to which I would frequently dial when he was on," wrote Bill James. Even as a teenager, hearing him, I disagreed.

To me, Milo seemed bright, glib, and bookish, tying courtesy and hospitality. "The credit," Theodore Roosevelt said, "belongs to the man in the arena." Hamilton's led to Cooperstown in 1992.

In 1928, Charles Lindbergh endorsed Herbert Hoover, born in tiny (pop. 350) Cedar Branch, Iowa, for president. A song on the wireless hymned praise-by-association:

"You remember Hoover, back in the war.

"Saved us from the Kaiser, now he'll give us something more.

"He'll serve as the President of the land of the free.

"If he's good enough for Lindbergh, he's good enough for me."

Hoover was good enough for the Hamilton family of nearby Fairfield. Shy and leaden, he made a hash of radio. Milo loved it. "It was so ingrained in all of us"—like The Game.

"People clung to baseball," he said of the thirties. "Dad and friends'd talk at the cigar store." Each school district had a team. Each day Mom bought bread late to save a penny. At eight, Hamilton got his first 35 cent Spalding *Guide*; 18, joined the Navy, went to Guam, and did Armed Forces Radio; 22, left the University of Iowa for Moline, Illinois. That night he saw his first fight. "Worse, I *called* 16, too."

The Radio Speech major aired Iowa football, Tri-City basketball, and the Three-I League. Once, after hoops, he re-created an afternoon Quad City Quads twinbill. "At the studio I find there'd been 37 walks. Holy Toledo! How'd you like *that* finale to the day?"—a prologue to the Browns, Cards, and Cubs.

In 1953, Milo, 25, joined A.L. St. Louis. "I wasn't ready for the majors. Neither were the Browns," junking him before Baltimore. Two axings followed: 1955, for Joe Garagiola; 1958, Lou Boudreau, squeezing him at Wrigley Field. In 1961, he moved to Comiskey Park. "Bob Elson'd say, 'Save something for a thrilling finish. Go pell-mell earlier and you have nowhere to go.'" Not pell-mell nor thrilling, Hamilton was encyclopedic like a logue.

"He plays draftsman all winter," read a guide. "Just to prepare a book on home runs for the season took more than ten hours." Lindsey Nelson laughed: "No one has a bigger briefcase." Milo opened it on WCFL Chicago. "If the Sox weren't scheduled, we'd re-create, say, Senators-A's. Try that on your inspiration meter." It rose October 1, 1961.

The Hose season ended a day earlier, Saturday. Sunday Hamilton aired

Roger Maris's homer 61. "The ticker told me Roger tipped his cap, and I passed that on." Milo aired his next historic blast *live.*

From time to time, gossip had him replacing Elson. "What the hell do I say? 'Drop dead so I can have your job?' " He might have succeeded Bob—but for a Rebel yell.

In 1965, the Sox and Braves played an Atlanta exhibition. The General Finance Network had knit the South: "They knew my name, at least my voice." A pre-game luncheon treated Hamilton like Stonewall Jackson. That night, Milwaukee G.M. John McHale said, "That was some welcome. You ought to come down with us [to Atlanta] next year."

"I'd be interested," Milo said, "in just that chance."

Alabama's Mel Allen, 52, had seemed a lock. "There were rumors about him," explained McHale. "Drinking, drugs." Hamilton was young, fresh, and handsome. "We wanted a new image." At first it seemed that Atlanta had no idea what that image was.

"There'd be fifty thousand people and not a sound," said catcher Joe Torre. "Fans didn't know what to do—such a contrast to Milwaukee." Tony Cloninger—to Milo, "T.C." or "Top Cat"—lost the 1966 opener despite a 13-inning complete game. On July 3, he won, 17–3, belting two slams. "One day a guy goes all the way to lose. Next, he's Babe Ruth," laughed Hamilton. "Anyone who says they know baseball is nuts."

In 1969, it split into four divisions. Atlanta won the West, but lost the L.C.S. Next year Rico Carty batted a bigs-high .366. Increasingly, Atlanta warmed. In 1972, the Braves averaged a prime-time TV 27 rating and 56 share: higher than any team, "Game of the Week," or college and pro football. "Milo is one reason," said parent Cox Broadcasting's James Landon. Another: power.

In 1973, three players—Aaron, Darrell Evans, and Davey Johnson—hit 40 homers for the first time on a team. Hamilton named Hank "The Hammer": third all-time, games played and hits; second, times at bat; first, runs scored, RBI, total bases, and extra-base hits. The marquee number was 714. "Hank ended 1973 one short of Ruth's mark," said Milo. "All winter I thought about what I was going to say when he broke it. George Plimpton kept at me. I said, 'Gotta be spontaneous.' "

Hank's first 1974 swing tied the Babe. On April 8, a rainy night in Georgia, he crossed a most Ruthian line. "Sitting on 714," Hamilton began. "Here's the pitch by [L.A.'s Al] Downing . . . swinging . . . There's a drive into left-center field! That ball is gonna be . . . outta here! It's gone! It's 715!"

clearing the fence into reliever Tom House's glove. "There's a new home-run champion of all time! And it's Henry Aaron! Henry Aaron's coming around third! His teammates are at home plate! Listen to this crowd!"

Plimpton said: "Maybe you'd been rehearsing and didn't know it." Milo gaped: Maris, now this. "Only problem: We weren't drawing. Some real bow-wows on the field." In 1975, Hamilton ripped Atlanta for non-support: "This is . . . a big-league city or it's not." At the same time, higher-ups demanded he fudge. "I wouldn't shill. Folks could smell us all the way to *Chattanooga*."

Where could he report, look in a mirror, and still not self-destruct? Perhaps the bigs city where he began.

In late 1975, Jack Buck left St. Louis for NBC TV. "We were seriously talking," said Hamilton, until Jack got antsy: What would happen if his new "Grandstand" sank? The Cards agreed to his return. Milo bailed. "I wasn't going without a multi-year guarantee as No. 1." That December he left the guillotine for a noose.

"You could be Mel Allen or Red Barber here, and they couldn't replace Bob Prince," said the new Bucs Voice. "I have to be myself. I think it will work." Hoover had a better chance of beating FDR. "I was competing with a specter," he later mused, alone and in the dock. "I never tried to imitate him, but I couldn't *escape* him."

An edge bit his voice. "The average fan liked me, but the press, Prince's booze buddies, knifed me from the start." Gunner did play-by-play from Sid Caesar via Milton Berle. Milo did it by the book: "radio-school professionalism," sneered the *Post-Gazette*. He thought its jury tainted: "blubbering idiots. No way was I going back." Pittsburgh won the Series October 17, 1979. Next week Hamilton retrieved his past.

"Anybody in my place would jump at the opportunity," said the Cubs' once/again radio *duce*. Later he recalled being "guaranteed in blood" TV by 1982. "*Promised*? It was *announced*. Jack Brickhouse'd be retiring." In September 1981, Hey-Hey! called him "The Voice of the Cubs for years to come."

On November 16, a WGN exec phoned at 7:30 A.M. "Can you come to the office? We need to tell you in person." At 10 o'clock Harry Caray snatched Cubs TV. "Talk about history repeating itself," said Milo, though not in the way he expected, or hoped.

Holy cow! In 1955, Harry had shed him to accommodate Garagiola. A broken vow; Caray's gall; having to work next door—it was too much. In

1984, Caray conceded his affair with August Busch's daughter-in-law. "What a jerk," sniped Milo. "Saying on the air, 'Today I mailed alimony checks to all my ex-wives,' bragging about it, no wonder we never got along." The Cubs won the East. At season's end he was sent packing. "The station spent an hour praising me, then said, 'But the bottom line is that Harry doesn't like you, and he's more important.' "

Threads flank, part, and merge. Harry's son replaced Hamilton in 1976. In 1985, DeWayne Staats joined Caray *pere,* Milo replacing him in Houston. The new Astros Voice was unhip and unboutique, a family man, a fine Lone Star fit. "The Midwest gave him trouble," said a friend. "It took the Southwest to give the esteem he deserved."

Milo, in turn, esteemed 1986. Cy Younger Mike Scott led the league in shutouts, innings, ERA, and Ks. The kicker: September 25. "Now the hitter is Will Clark," Milo said. "He's 0 for 3. Swing and a bouncer! This could be it! Davis runs to the bag! A no-hitter! [Milo's seventh] Astros win the championship! Mike Scott throws a no-hitter and the Astros are the champions of the National League West!" Next: the L.C.S., where, up, 3 games to 2, New York trailed mentally.

"Scott had owned us twice," said now-Mets manager Johnson. "Lose Game Six, and we face him again." Ahead, 3–0, 'Stros lefty starter Bob Knepper entered the ninth. Holy Toledo! Johnson pinch-hit Len Dykstra. "Another lefty, and he triples!" The Mets tied, then led, 4–3, in the 14th. "Astros badly need a base runner," said Milo. "Full count. [Jesse] Orosco ready! Pitch to [Billy] Hatcher! There's a drive! It's gone! We're tied again!"

Scott lingered like a plume. Sixteenth: New York scored thrice, 7-4. Again Houston rallied: 7-6, full count, two out and on. The noise made indoor ball almost passable. Kevin Bass missed a breaking ball. Suddenly, Milo didn't miss a single pre-Deep in the Eyes of Texas stop.

"Rapture! Congratulations to all!" yamped the *New York Daily News.* Consolation: 'Stros. Losing the 1997–99 Division Series, they entered Minute Maid (then Enron) Field—its left-field porch, center-field berm, in-play flagpole, and 1860s lifesize locomotive and steel tender siring "a ballpark," read *SI,* "of idiosyncrasies and intrigue."

Milo liked idiosyncrasy. He was tired of political intrigue. The game still gripped, always had. "I'll be calling a play, and have to say, 'Ever see that before?' My partner'll say, 'Nope.' Mention one game. The memory triggers another, which leads to a story, then another."

In 2004, Houston split L.C.S. Games One–Four. Next day neared overtime. "Let's see if he can step on the clutch here. Two on, one out, bottom of the ninth," said Hamilton. "Isringhausen delivers. Driving, way back into left field! It's up! It's over! It's gone! It's gone! A big home run by [Jeff] Kent! Holy Toledo!" jolting St. Louis, 3–0. "What a moment," Milo later said. "The Astros, one game from a pennant," [where they stalled, losing the final two].

In 1992, he, Musial, and Bob Feller got to recalling the Depression at Cooperstown. "All of a sudden I start thinking of my parents." At that point Brooks Robinson and Johnny Bench began getting autographs of inductees and Hall of Famers.

The moment evoked boyhood: "grown men playing a kids' game with short pants." Suddenly, Fairfield, Iowa, and the recess of New York's Mohawk Valley seemed two veins from the same mine.

MILO HAMILTON

LONGEVITY:	10	49 years.
CONTINUITY:	6	St. Louis A.L. 1953; St. Louis N.L. 1954; Chicago N.L. 1955–57 and 1980–84; Chicago A.L. 1961–65; Atlanta N.L. 1966–75; Pittsburgh N.L. 1976–79; Houston N.L. 1985– ; ABC/NBC TV The Baseball Network 1994–95.
NETWORK:	1	TBN 1994–95 (ABC/NBC TV).
KUDOS:	10	Cooperstown 1992. Honorary Georgia American Cancer Society 1973 chairman. Houston Interfaith Charities 1991 "Mr. Sportsman." Texas Baseball 1994 and Radio 2000 Halls of Fame. Allen Russell Award 1996. Great Communicator Award 2000. Fred Hartman Service Award 2001. Radio Lifetime Achievement Award 2002. Quad City, Iowa, "Milo Hamilton Press Box."
LANGUAGE:	10	Elastic.
POPULARITY:	10	Last stop, best stop.
PERSONA:	10	Mr. Smooth.
VOICE:	10	Bigs' Mel Torme.
KNOWLEDGE:	10	A perfectionist.
MISCELLANY:	10	Beat leukemia in 1970s. Delta Airlines' 1966–75 Voiceover. Among others, did Big Ten basketball and Georgia Tech and Ohio State football.
TOTAL:	87	(24th place).

Been To Canaan (Modern Age, 1966–79)

Joe Garagiola

Chuck Thompson

Curt Gowdy

Ned Martin

Harry Kalas

CURT GOWDY

From 1953 to 1965, Mel Allen, Bud Blattner, Jack Buck, Dizzy Dean, Joe Garagiola, Merle Harmon, Lindsey Nelson, and Bob Wolff, among others, aired network baseball. In 1966, Curt Gowdy tried to replace them all. Unlike Mel, he roused no response to personality. Unlike Scully, Curt was a small-town boy. His bent was basic, like Wyoming youth. "The game is the important thing," Gowdy said. "A Voice is no better than his script."

He became a TV generation's sports paradigm: 16 All-Star Games, 13 World Series, 24 NCAA Final Fours, seven Olympics, eight Super Bowls, 14 Rose Bowls, Pan American Games, and "The American Sportsman." For a decade Curt called the bigs' whole network schedule. "The good news is how he prepared," said Blattner. Bad: "If only the Good Shepherd did play-by-play, *He'd* be overexposed."

In 1970, Gowdy won sportscasting's first George Foster Peabody award for radio/TV excellence. It led to Canton, Cooperstown, and Springfield, MA. "Putting a town into a piece about [him]," a writer said, "is like trying to establish residence for a migratory duck"—a Rocky Mountaineer who conjured respectability, good manners, and pluck.

Growing up, even radio seemed far away to the son of a Union Pacific Railroad superintendent. "Dad would say, 'Curtis, there's a big world out there. Someday I'd like to see a big-league game.'"

His mother liked the three R's. On Curt's must-do list: typing, elocution, and one book a week. An early swain was basketball till coach Jack Powell said, "You're off the team."

"What'd I do?" the senior yelped. As it happened, mom had seen the principal, discussed Curt's low English grade, and ordered him not to play.

"How can you do this?" said Gowdy, livid. "Basketball's my life. We'll be a great team this year"—and were, winning 31 straight games.

"Get your English up!" Mom said. He did.

In 1938, the All-Stater entered the University of Wyoming. Six letters later he graduated, joined the Air Force, and left with a ruptured spine. Back surgery failed: for ten months Curt fretted in a hospital. Finally, doctors sent him home. "More rest, no sports, and with luck you won't be a cripple."

In Cheyenne, the Cowboy eyeballed ghosts: pals had joined the service. "It was as low as I've ever been"—until a phone call lit a high.

Bill Grove managed Cheyenne's sole radio station, KFBC. "There's nobody else. I need you to call football," he told Gowdy. Tiny Pine Bluff and St. Mary's played a six-man game, before 15 fans and 14 players' relatives, without yard lines, sidelines, goal posts, or player numbers. Curt "stood on a soap box, guessed where the ball was, and made up names." For two years he aired basketball, football, Western Union baseball, and what passed in this time and place for "big events. We made a big to-do over Santa Claus's arrival for the Christmas season." In March 1945, chance found a place where Gowdy did not know a soul.

Driving through Wyoming, the owner of 50,000-watt KOMA Oklahoma City heard Curt do basketball. Soon, as sports director, Gowdy called Oklahoma A&M, Bud Wilkinson's football Sooners, and Triple-A Oklahoma City Indians—"the biggest break of my career." To Curt, the minors were a workshop: "all the demands of the sports broadcast business—ads, production, play-by-play—in one."

By 1948, business meant General Mills, backing 13 bigs teams, and account executive Frank Slocum, looking for "talent to sell its products"—Wheaties, above all. Frank needed a No. 2 Yanks announcer. Hearing Gowdy, "he asked for a brochure with tapes." The Cheyenne emigree met Allen. "I would have settled for nothing. Fortunately, I didn't have to." Curt married in 1949. His best man made him better. "I was intimidated by Mel. His timing, reading an ad, weaving it in the play helped me learn."

Class was public: Gowdy's, and the Yankees', flubs. No regular topped .287. Three Red Sox topped Yogi Berra's team-high 91 RBI. Boston had ex-Stripes skipper Joe McCarthy. The query would endure: how could the Towne team lose?

New York trailed by one game with two left: Boston, at The Stadium. "As long as I live," said Curt, "I'll never forget volleys back and forth of noise." Yanks, 5–4: race tied. Next day they held a 1–0 late-inning lead when McCarthy yanked Ellis Kinder. Four runs offset three in the Sox ninth. On the train back to Boston, Ellis slugged Marse Joe in the jaw.

In *The Old Man and the Sea,* Santiago tells Manolin, "Have faith in the Yankees, my son." Gowdy did: They won the 1949–50 Series. He also feared that Allen would never stop calling them. In 1951, Jim Britt left the Red Sox. The Cowboy got an offer. "Part of me knew this was my chance to be Number One." Another part loved New York. Mel said he would piggy-back Curt to Fenway Park. "Six states, great fans. Today I can't believe I was torn."

The Sox opened in the Bronx, Gowdy botching Boston-area names like Worcester and Swampscott. Telegrams blared "Yankee-lover, go back to New York." A day later, owner Tom Yawkey welcomed him: listening, Curt felt reborn.

"What kind of play-by-play do you want?" he said.

"No line drives made into pop-ups or excuses for errors, just give 'em the game."

In time, Yawkey became a father. Reinjuring his back, Gowdy missed all of 1957. "I don't care how long this kid misses, he's got a job here," Tom told a neurosurgeon. He was said to run a country club. "Bull!" Curt flared. "They were family."

The clan lost the flag, playoff, or Series the last or next-to-last game of 1946, 1948–49, 1967, 1972, 1975, 1977–78, 1986, and 2003. Losing bred doubt. It did not dim Number 9.

Ted Williams was loyal, profane, and drop-dead handsome—the ultimate inner-directed man. He tied a .344 average, team-high 521 dingers, six batting, four home run, and four RBI titles, 1946 and 1949 MVP, and 1942 and 1947 Triple Crown. "All this despite five years in the military," said Gowdy. "Otherwise Ted'd have every record."

Curt called him the most competent man he knew. "Best hitter, best fisherman, best hunter."

Once Ted roared, "There! Watch two ducks coming up at 3 o'clock."

Gowdy: "Where?" They appeared two minutes later.

John Glenn was Williams's Korea flight commander. "What kind of pilot was he?" Curt asked. Glenn: "Best I ever saw."

Gallup says we liked the 1950s. Not Boston: only the '55ers vied post-Labor Day. The Kid eased blight. Too, Curt's "ever so soothing and sensible voice, with its guileless hint of Wyoming twang," wrote John Updike, over WHDH Radio's 50-station and TV seven-outlet network.

"No great teams," said the Cowboy, "but what personalities!" It is no lie to say they were all the Red Sox had.

Could catcher Sammy White top Yogi Berra? ("Already has," joked a Nashua druggist. "Seven inches taller.") Was this the Biblical year to redeem post-1918? ("Sure," said Berkshirers, "the same year Vermont goes Democratic.") Name a better outfield than Williams, Jim Piersall, and Jackie Jensen. ("Can't," said the Plymouth housewife, "but where's the *pitching*?") Roseanne Roseannadanna: "If it's not one thing, it's another."

Jensen was 1958 MVP. Piersall trussed depression, shock, and resilience, if not recovery. On September 28, 1960, the Sox retired Williams's number. "He had an intense pride that every time up he wanted to produce a hit," said Curt, emceeing. "Not only for himself but for the fans at Fenway whom he secretly loved, who stood behind him amid ups and downs . . . the greatest hitter of all time, Ted Williams."

Moved, Ted said, "I want a copy. That's one of the nicest tributes to me ever."

"I don't have a copy," Curt said.

"Oh, shit," Ted said, then walked, skied to center field, and flied to right. In the eighth, Jack Fisher, 21, faced the twice-his-age Kid. "Everybody quiet now here at Fenway Park after they gave him a standing ovation of two minutes knowing that this is probably his last time at bat," said Gowdy. "Here's the pitch. Williams swings—and there's a long drive to deep right! That ball is going and it is gone! A home run for Ted Williams in his last time at bat in the major leagues!"

Leaving like a deity, Ted declined to tip his cap. "It just would not have been me." Updike drew an angelic gloss: "God does not answer letters."

The Cowboy would have settled for a card. "The longer I stayed, the more they were funny without trying." One spring Sarasota, Florida's mayor primed for the first pitch. At that moment the press steward asked Curt about a drink. "He was too far away to answer, so he wrote down a suggestion—a *milkshake*—and handed it to me." Gowdy misread the steward: "Here is the Mayor, Mike Shane."

In 1958, two pals telecast the Classic. Mel "talk[s] too much," a critic said. Curt was "restrained"—literally. "I wore a steel back brace with a painkiller prescription in my pocket. Maids thought I was nuts, sleeping on the floor." He did the NBA, college football, first 1959 All-Star Game—and 1964 Series. "There's a high drive to deep right! And forget about it! It is gone! The ball game's over! [2-1, Yanks] Mantle has just broken a World Series record. He now has 16 World Series home runs. He and Babe Ruth were tied with 15 apiece."

In 1962, ABC gave Gowdy the AFL. 1964: NBC bought it, and him. Next year the Jets signed Joe Namath. "Suddenly," said Curt, "the league didn't mean Upper Slobovia." To many, baseball meant CBS's 1955–64 "Game of the Week" thoroughbred. A year later, NBC bought ABC's 1965 variant of a mule. "We had the Series and All-Star Game. [1966–68's] 'Game' meant exclusivity," said sports head Carl Lindemann. "[Colleague] Chet Simmons and I liked him with the Sox and football"—also, getting two network sports for the price of one.

As analyst, Gowdy craved his pal. "[Lead sponsor] Chrysler said no when [Sears spokesman] Ted was pictured putting stuff in a Ford truck." Falstaff Brewery hyped Dean—"I said, 'I can't do "Wabash Cannonball." Our styles clash'"—then, Pee Wee Reese. "They figured he was fine with me, and they'd still have their boy."

NBC said okay. Would a generation to whom "Game" bespoke Diz?

To Lindemann, the answer was a gimme. What if Curt's voice was not a fever-swamp? He was fair, did homework, and had a Chip Hilton delivery. That would be enough—until Nielsen's 1966–68 "Game" and Series ratings fell 10 and 19 percent, respectively. Only the All-Star Game nixed the view that baseball was too bland for a hip and inchoate age. Almost half (48 percent) in a 1964 Harris Poll named it their favorite sport. Just 19 percent did a decade later.

Why?

Exclusivity, to begin. "Think of the last decade," said Nelson. "Mel, Buck, Diz—and one guy replaces 'em?" Viewers tired. *TSN* got so many letters— "atrocity . . . a pallbearer . . . baseball is not dead, no thanks to Gowdy"—it routed them to NBC. Curt frowned on hype and buzz. The late sixties and early seventies smiled. "As spectacle, baseball suffers on [TV]," wrote Harry Caray. "The fan at the park [talk, drink, take Junior to the john] rarely notices the time span between pitches. Not the same fan at home." Not responsible, Gowdy was held accountable, becoming, as he did, more visible than even Dean.

Before 1966, local-teamers called the Series. "NBC's contract changed that," said director Harry Coyle. "We intended to showcase our boy." Curt aired half of each set-to. In L.A. and Baltimore, Vin Scully and Chuck Thompson, respectively, did the rest.

Scully was incensed. "What about the road? My fans won't be able to hear me."

Game One evoked tit for tat. Vin did the first 4 1/2 innings. Gowdy then inherited a clunker made duller by Scully's refusal to say another word. Four years later, emceeing a dinner, "They'd'a killed each other," said Lindemann, "if we hadn't kept them apart." At Boston, Curt would have killed for a pennant. 1967: He called its Series. 1968: Detroit, in seven. A year later: Linguists still grope to explain how, and why.

"Until '69, 'Game' had ignored the Mets," said Gowdy, airing them weekly that September. Next he beamed their L.C.S. and Series. The Chinese discovered the 365 1/4 day solar year in 2300 B.C. The Mets discovered Canaan October 16, 1969. "There's a fly ball hit out to left!" Curt said. "Waiting is Jones! The Mets are the world champions! Jerry Koosman is being mobbed! Look at this scene!"

Suddenly the Mets seemed more Amazin' than even Cheyenne's hills, ravines, and ponds.

Later, Gowdy rued ubiquity. Then, a brigade at Utah Beach could not have persuaded him to recede. 1970 Series: Brooks Robinson augurs A&E's *Biography.* "Look at that grab! He's playing in another world!" 1971 Mid-Summer Classic: "That one is going—way up! It is—off the roof! That hit the transformer up there! A tremendous smash! [by Reggie Jackson, in Detroit]" 1974: "Von Joshua is up . . . Here, it could be—he [Gene Tenace] caught it. . . . The Oakland A's are the first team since the New York Yankees to win three world championships in a row!"

About this time, Jerry Lister termed "a week in Gowdy's life like a chapter in Jules Verne's *Around the World in 80 Days.*" He read 22 papers, traveled 350,000 miles a year, and spent them memorizing. Each January 1 he did the Rose Bowl; fall, NFL; winter, 1964–84 "Sportsman." Like Williams, the Cowboy thought outside inviolate. On March 27, 1972—"my greatest day"— Wyoming opened the Curt Gowdy State Park. Other days weren't bad:

November 17, 1968: NBC showed a movie instead of the Jets-Raiders' final minute. Only the West Coast saw Oakland, scoring twice, win. "I'm leaving when our assistant starts yelling, 'Gowdy! Here are earphones to the truck.' It says, 'Uh, uh, phone calls are blowing lines up.' I have to re-create the last-second scores" for the next-day "Today Show." The *Heidi* Game burnished football's rise.

January 12, 1969. "I guarantee a [Super Bowl III] victory," said Namath. The Colts were a 19-point lock. Jets, 16–7. Christmas 1971: Miami's second-overtime field goal beat K.C., 27–24. Curt renamed sudden death "sudden victory." December 23, 1972: Oakland, 7–6, with 22 seconds left. "I'd better congratulate the boys," says Steelers owner Art Rooney, leaving for the locker room.

Pittsburgh wins, 13–7, on a deflected pass. Pick 'em: "The Immaculate Reception" or The Kid's Last Swing as Curt's abiding call.

Each week Gowdy and Reese's successor, Tony Kubek, attended a pre-"Game" meeting in New York. On cue, the producer, director, and cameramen haggled. The star then raised a hand. "Yes, Gowdy," they sighed.

"What about the ball game?"

"Hell with the ball game. We have to have the opening and the close."

"Yes," said Curt, "but, fellas, we're here because of the game." Do your homework. Tell the score.

In 1972, hoping that "Monday will take off like football," wrote *Broadcasting* magazine, NBC began a 10-game prime-time schedule. Next year it beamed 15 straight. For a man who lived on numbers, the Cowboy's stalled: Saturday down; Monday barely up. Even crown jewels—L.C.S., All-Star Game, Series—seemed on autopilot. Another NBCer saw his chance.

Joe Garagiola did the pre-"Game" show. Baseball's angel was his boss. "He did Chrysler ads," said Lindemann, "and now wanted play-by-play." Meanwhile, baseball wanted cash. "Ratings couldn't get more from one network," said bigs media director John Lazarus, "so we approached another." Upshot: 1976–79 format of NBC, Saturday; ABC, Monday; and shared post-season/All-Star Game.

NBC added Garagiola to its last-year Monday coverage. "Looking back," said Lindemann, "this was the first shot in a campaign to get Curt off baseball altogether." He soon took one between the eyes.

By 1975, Gowdy had aired seven of sport's all-time 10 most-watched events. The year became a kind of *The Last Picture Show,* though he did not see it clearly. "Joe's great at throwing elbows," said Coyle. "For all his success [three homes and seven radio stations], Curt was a small-town kid."

Poignantly the Towne Team won the pennant. In the Series, Cincinnati led Game Six, 6–3. Two eighth-inning Sox reached base. "The pitch," said Gowdy on NBC Radio. "[Pinch-hitter Bernie] Carbo hits a high drive! Deep center! Home run! . . . Bernie Carbo has hit his second pinch-hit home run of the Series! . . . It came with two out. And the Red Sox have tied it, 6 to 6!"

Next inning Fred Lynn arced a bases-full pop. Third-base coach Don Zimmer screamed, "No, no!" Runner Denny Doyle misheard "Go, go!" Curt: "It is caught by Foster. Here's the tag. Here's the throw! He's out! A double play! Foster throws him out!" Cincy's Joe Morgan batted in the 11th. "There's a long shot! Back goes Evans—back, back! And what a grab! Evans made a grab and saved a home run on that one!"

At 12:34 A.M., Carlton Fisk hit his memorable, implausible, epochal blast. Ned Martin called it fair. Added Gowdy: "They're jamming out on the field! His teammates are waiting for him! And the Red Sox send the World

Series into Game Seven with a dramatic 7 to 6 victory. What a game! This is one of the greatest World Series games of all time!"

NBC plainly felt there was nothing else to say.

Memory, said Alexander Chase, is the thing we forget with. A decade later, Lindemann wanted to forget being odd man out. "Chrysler kept pushing. I was the only guy behind the Cowboy." That November, Gowdy filmed "Sportsman" in Maine. Carl flew to tell him—"Curt was shocked"—that he was through.

In 1978, Gowdy became a "roving [Series] reporter"—to Coyle, "humiliating, such a minor role." He did a final Rose and Super Bowl. One hoops Saturday, the spotter misidentified each starter: Curt, barely 60, soon put out to TV pasture, got the blame. CBS TV offered a three-year pact, dropping him in 1981.

CURT GOWDY

LONGEVITY:	10	29 years.
CONTINUITY:	9	New York A.L. 1949–50; Boston A.L. 1951–65; NBC TV "Game of the Week" 1966–75; CBS Radio "Game of the Week" 1985–86.
NETWORK:	10	"Game" 1966–75 (NBC TV) and 1985–86 (CBS Radio). All-Star Game first 1959, both 1960, second 1961–62, 1966–75, and 1978 (NBC TV). World Series 1958, 1964, 1966–75, and 1978 (NBC TV). L.C.S. 1969–75 (NBC TV) and 1980–81, 1983, and 1985–86 (CBS Radio).
KUDOS:	10	Cooperstown 1984. NSSA Sportscaster of the Year 1966 and 1969 and Hall of Fame 1981. Basketball 1973, ASA 1985, Pro Football 1993, and three other Halls. Long-time Basketball Hall President: broadcast award named in honor. John Bunn Award 1978. George Foster Peabody Award 1970. Numerous Emmy Awards for "The American Sportsman" and PBS's "The Way It Was." Chairman, American League of Anglers. Curt Gowdy State Park 1972.
LANGUAGE:	9	It's the game, stupid.
POPULARITY:	9	Loved in New England; respected nationally.
PERSONA:	10	Age's Voice.
VOICE:	8	Trustworthy.
KNOWLEDGE:	10	Mom's son never scrimped on study.
MISCELLANY:	6	Did 1970s NBC Radio show from Wellesley Hills, MA, home. Greatest thrill: 1998's "Casey At The Bat," with the Boston Pops, at Tanglewood.
TOTAL:	91	(11th place). *Scores based on 1–10 point scale.*

"It was an ugly, abrupt end," said Lindemann. "Neither Curt nor I know why." I first met Gowdy on 1960 Sox-Stripes wireless. Allen guided me until Albany: Eastward Cowboy-ho. In the 1980s, he spoke again on CBS Radio: the game, still the important thing; the voice, still as sturdy as a post.

"You look at McNamee, Husing, Allen," said Lindemann. "With networks dividing sports, nobody ever did what Gowdy did." It is a safe bet that nobody will.

JOE GARAGIOLA

"Kennedy was, whether for good or bad, an enormously large figure," Theodore H. White wrote of America's first Catholic president. "Historically, he was a gate-keeper. He unlatched the gate and through the door marched Catholics, blacks, and Jews, and ethnics, women, youth, academics, newspersons, and an entirely new breed of politician." Joe Garagiola, a large baseball figure, unlatched a gate for nonrural, -cornpone, and -native stock announcers. He was urban, ethnic, and as barbed as wire.

We learn to take our craft, not selves, seriously. Garagiola took himself, not his game. Caray tutored, then loathed, him. Nelson called Joe "the single most ambitious man I ever met," not necessarily meaning a compliment. On the other hand, he asked for little, worked like a dog, and helped found the Baseball Assistance Team.

Churchill termed Russia "a riddle wrapped in a mystery, inside an enigma." Intriguing people often are. Said Joe G.: "I went through life as a [1946–54] player to be named later." Ordinary on the field, he was extraordinary off.

Joe will always be boyhood pal Yogi Berra's ambassador without portfolio. "I'll ask him, 'What time is it?' Yogi'll say, 'Now?'"

"I get lost going to Yogi's home, and call. 'Where are you?' he says. I tell him. He says, 'You're not far away. You come this way. Don't go that way.'"

A woman mused, "Yogi, you look cool in that outfit." Berra smiled. "Thanks," he said, "you don't look so hot yourself."

What a card—or was Yogi Charlie McCarthy, mouthing a baseball Bergen's lines? "It's *his* humor," said Garagiola, growing wintry. "He thinks funny, and speaks what he thinks."

Joe's mother—"a dear, loving simple woman"—could not speak English. Dad worked in a brickyard. Born on Lincoln's Birthday, 1926, their son learned a salute-to-the-flag, catch-in-the-throat, tear-in-the-eye Americanism. Like Yogi, "a pickoff away" on St. Louis's Dago Hill, his universe was baseball. The exception was, oddly, soccer.

Berra took ill the morning of one game. "You look terrible," Garagiola said. "Why don't you go home?"

"If a guy can't get sick on a cold, miserable day like this he ain't healthy," Yogi shrugged. Try converting *that* for mom.

Growing up, both shared a glove, played in a Works Progress Administration league, and worked in a Cardinals training camp. In 1942, Joe graduated from South Side Catholic High School, signed for $500 with St. Louis, and bounced to Class-A Springfield, Triple-A Columbus, and the Army in Manila.

One day he heard the wireless etch a young, fast, and strong Cardinals catcher. "I turned to my closest Army buddy and said, 'If that guy's that good, I'm in trouble.'" The radio predicted Garagiola would fill Walker Cooper's shoes. As he said, it didn't say with what.

In 1946, joining his home team, Joe G. was assigned washing sanitary hose. "We used to always put on Stan Musial's socks 'TGIF'—Toes Go In First. Anything to help The Man." The Man helped by leading the league in seven categories.

Enos Slaughter had an N.L.-high 130 runs. Howie Pollett, Harry Brecheen, and Murry Dickson went 51–31. St. Louis was still made a 7-to-20 Series underdog vs. Boston. Games One–Two split. The Sox then won Fenway's first Series match in 28 years. To New England, Game Four seemed as long: Swifties, 12–3. Joe, Slaughter, and Whitey Kurowski each had four of a record-tying 20 hits.

"Here I am," he said, "living a kid's dream, and [Ted] Williams picks that day to beat the shift [three infielders right of second base]." Papers blared: "Williams Bunt!" Cards, in seven. Garagiola gloried in his .316 average. The hereafter was stickier: 1947, .257; '48, minors; '50, shoulder separation. Hurt, Joe began listening to Caray, "how he called the game, and I got to thinking about radio."

Dealt to Pittsburgh, he rubbernecked the 42–112 '52ers. "It was the most courageous team in baseball," said baseball's Letterman. "We had 154 games scheduled, and showed up for every one. We lost eight of our first nine games and then we had a slump."

Next year marked the ninth season of Branch Rickey's five-year plan. One day the Bucs' G.M. summoned Joe. "He looks at me with his big, bushy eyebrows. 'By Judas Priest,' he says, 'we're turning the corner. And you, my boy, figure in my plans.'" That week he was traded to the Cubs.

In 1954, the Giants claimed him off waivers. "I'd sit in the bullpen and say, 'Why the hell doesn't he throw the curveball?'" Joe said, retiring. "All I had to do to become an announcer was to take out the *hell*."

Hired by KMOX St. Louis, the Funny Man began making a virtue of necessity. "You can't imagine the thrill," Joe said of his .257 career average, "to walk into a clubhouse and wonder if your uniform is still there." Dago Hill became *terra firma*. "A door to door peddler told my mom I was the first boy from the neighborhood with a name ending in *a, e, i, o,* or *u* that gets his name in the papers and he no kill anybody."

Baseball wasn't "like going to church." Dead air: "I'm Italian. I like to talk." Strategy: "An idiot could pick up" the signs. St. Louis forgave his sharp voice. Caray taught using the diaphragm. "I had a lot of help, and needed it. Off my first play-by-play, I wouldn't have hired myself."

For Anheuser Busch, Joe emceed, spoke to B'Nai B'rith, the Holy Name, and Masonic Lodge, and bloomed as a ribster. He and Musial became godfather for the other's child. In 1959, he broadcast with the Cardinals from Japan. Back home, Yogi's pal taped, reviewed, and learned, becoming the Bob Hope of the resin bag.

His gate, unlatched, would soon open wide.

In 1960, Herbert Hoover and Indian prime minster Jawaharlal Nehru were introduced at the World Series. "You amaze me, Yog. You've become such a world figure that you draw more applause than either a prime minster or former president," Garagiola laughed. "Can you explain it?"

"Certainly," said Berra. "I'm a better hitter."

That season, Joe released the runaway bestseller *Baseball Is a Funny Game*. "One day I'm a dumb jock and suddenly I can write." NBC made him 1961 "Major League Baseball" colorman. Next year Bob Wolff began play-by-play. "You work your side of the street [interviewing players]," said Garagiola, "and I'll work mine."

Wolff liked Joe's pizazz. "He'd say, 'The guy stapled him to the bag.'" A runner's "smilin' like he swallowed a banana peel." The game preceded due diligence. "Afterward, we'd replay each pitch. 'I said this, you said that, and I shoulda said this.'" Soon Garagiola played "The Jack Paar Show" with Kaye Ballard and June Valli: "the first time a group of Italians have gotten together when there wasn't a senator present."

In 1962, he left the Cardinals full-time for NBC. Radio bound the 1963 Series, "Monitor," and "Joe Garagiola Sports Show." TV blared "The Tonight Show," "Match Game," "What's My Line?," and "I've Got a Secret." A writer said, "His words hit home runs." Caray's friendship, on the other hand, fanned.

Small world. The 1964 World Series matched Joe's Swifties and Berra's Stripes. Garagiola called it with, among others, "Holy cow!" Before Game One, Harry decided to say hello. "I hadn't seen him in a while. Joe walks toward me, I figure, for the same reason," barely acknowledging his pal. Caray boiled, having treated Joe better, he claimed, than even son Skip. "I called him every name in the book and I'm half-Italian myself. When you can help him, he's your friend. If you can't, he's not."

The Cards cut their seventh title. Yogi was axed as Yankees manager. As jaw-dropping: Mel Allen's firing. Joe augured "a more human Yankees image," wrote Kay Gardella. Inhumanely, they chose his time to crash (last, 1966). Garagiola understandably avoided when possible anything germane to score. "Once in a while you'd get lucky: the Yankees like they were." May 14, 1967: "Stu Miller's ready! Here's the payoff pitch by Miller to Mantle," he said. "Swung on! There she goes! There she goes! . . . Mickey Mantle has hit the [career] 500th home run!"

In 1968, Joe joined NBC "The Today Show" regulars Barbara Walters, Hugh Downs, and Frank McGee. Some foresaw a flop. Instead, he "indulged in diamond talk with Frank Robinson," Ben Gross wrote, "boxing with Muhammad Ali, poetry with Marianne Moore, and politics with Hubert H. Humphrey." President Johnson introduced him to a diplomat: "Turn on your TV set tomorrow morning and you'll see this fellow. I watch him every day."

Define New York: "The only four-letter word they object to is ROTC." Was Joe sentimental? "Give me the Queen of Spades and I'll bawl." A slider was "a curveball after taxes." A plane trip spawned "rope burns from my Rosary." Garagiola rose at 4:30 A.M., caught the 5:26 commuter train, and knew his niche. "I'm not Joe Show Biz, just a sweatshirt guy running at stop speed to stay even. Those guys on the bubble gum cards, they're mine."

By 1973, Joe's card listed "Joe Garagiola's Memory Game," "Sale of the Century," and Monday's pre-game "Baseball World of Joe Garagiola." Wife Audrie asked: "How many cars or suits do you need?" Leaving "Today," he called, with Gowdy, the 1974 All-Star Game. Next day Joe grabbed Carl Lindemann. "I can't work with him. He kept cutting me off. I couldn't say a word."

In 1975, he hosted NBC's "Next Year Is Here" and "First World Series of

Bubble Gum Blowing." A new gate soon opened. "Mr. Garagiola," read a network press release, "will do our [entire 1976] play-by-play [Tony Kubek, keeping color]." Political animals aren't limited to politics.

NBC hoped that Joe's charm and unorthodox dwelling on the personal would halt "Game"'s decade-long hemorrhage. Instead, ratings bobbed from 6.7 (1977) via 7.5 (1978) to 6.3 (1981–82). "Saturday had a constituency," said executive producer Scotty Connal, "but it didn't swell." Millions still missed Dizzy Dean. Local-team TV split the audience. By contrast, regulars awaited bits like a "Star Trek" groupie.

The '52 Bucs meant a belly laugh: "Once we had a rainout and we staged a victory party." Diction was a yuck. One year Yogi, Dean, and Garagiola joined the Missouri Hall of Fame. "What do you want? Good grammar or good taste?" "Game" mixed aplomb and nonchalance. "I'm an expert on two things—trades and slumps." How far did Yogi go in high school? "Nine blocks." If Howard Cosell lunched "with everyone he says he does, he'd weigh 720 pounds."

ABC's 1976 power grab was no laughing matter. "I wished they hadn't got half the package. Still, 'Game,' half of post-season—we got lots left." Billy Martin and Reggie Jackson fought in 1977. Next year New York again made the Series. Game Two: L.A., 4–3, ninth, two on. Reggie Jackson kept fouling off Bob Welch. Finally: "He gets him!" Joe cried. "What a battle!"

Garagiola never caught a no-hitter. In 1981, he called Nolan Ryan's fifth. "Pressure building! This may be it [game-ending grounder]!" A year later Vin Scully got play-by-play, Joe retaking color. Somewhere Gowdy was likely smiling.

"People couldn't wait for us to be the odd couple, always sniping at each other," Vin later mused. Once again Joe adjusted. Wolff, for one, was not surprised. "If I couldn't see who was warming up, he'd write me a note. 'Smith to the left, Jones to the right.' That way I could say it: Joe wanted me to look good." By late 1983, *The New York Times* observed: "That the duo of Scully and Garagiola is very good, and often even great, is no longer in dispute." Talking less, Joe was saying more.

"He understood the cash," a friend said of NBC's 1984–89 407 percent bigs hike. "Scully was the star"; Garagiola, Pegasus, the Peacocks' junior light. In 1984, he predicted a Series pitchout. "*How* did you know that?" Vin gawked. The fist sign, he said, hadn't changed since 1944. "He'd say the batter wiggled," said Harry Coyle, "so we'd put the replay on him, and the camera proved him right."

The eighties tied flag-waving, supply-side economics, and Ronald Reagan's remembered and/or reinvented past. NBC's fused: 1984, Jack Morris's no-no; 1985, Ozzie Smith's L.C.S. parabola; 1986, Buckner Series; late 1988, baseball's excising "Game." Joe resigned that fall—"I was trying to renegotiate, and they left me twisting"—returning to 1990–91's "Today." Cooperstown followed. "The Hall of Fame! My God, Rickey wouldn't believe it!" Miming Yogi, Garagiola thanked those who made the day necessary. "I couldn't hit my way in here. I talked my way in instead."

In 1993, the Smithsonian Institution hailed Joe's baseball world. "Tonight's honor might not be Mt. Rushmore," wrote Jack Paar of his folically-challenged friend, "but there's still a place on Mt. Baldie." Joe was Gerald Ford's emcee in the 1976 presidential campaign. Recalling another

JOE GARAGIOLA

LONGEVITY:	10	35 years.
CONTINUITY:	8	St. Louis N.L. 1955–62; NBC TV "Major League Baseball" 1961–64; New York A.L. 1965–67; NBC TV "Game of the Week" 1975–88; California A.L. 1990; Arizona N.L. 1998– .
NETWORK:	10	"Major League Baseball" 1961–64; World Series 1961, 1964, 1975–76, 1978, 1980, 1982, 1984, 1986, and 1988; All-Star Game second 1961, first 1962, 1963, 1965, 1974–75, 1977, 1979, 1981, 1983, 1985, and 1987; N.L. playoff 1962; L.C.S. 1975, 1977, 1979, 1981, 1983, 1985, and 1987; "Game" 1975–88 (NBC TV). World Series 1963 (NBC Radio).
KUDOS:	10	Cooperstown 1991. George Foster Peabody Award 1973. NSSA Hall of Fame 2004. ASA Humanitarian Award 1995. Freedom Foundation Award. Children's MVP Award, Jim Eisenreich Foundation. Baseball field, named in honor, Arizona's St. Peter's Indian Mission.
LANGUAGE:	9	"A 'dem and dose' kind of guy," he said.
POPULARITY:	10	Rivaled "Game"'s, and game's.
PERSONA:	10	Good wit, no hit.
VOICE:	8	Barbed.
KNOWLEDGE:	10	Veiled by humor.
MISCELLANY:	5	Exercised regularly. "In the banquet business, your legs go first."
TOTAL:	90	(15th place).

president, Jack termed him the only Voice to have slept in the Lincoln Bedroom before it became the Hollywood Hotel.

Garagiola moved to Phoenix, called the Angels and Diamondbacks, and hailed Arizona's first general manager: "My Rickey!" dad said of son Joe. Pop helped open a gate for former players: the Baseball Assistance Team.

By 2002, the average big-league salary, $29,000 in 1968, neared $2.4 *million*. "These guys," he snapped. "Where's concern for the players before?" A pitcher couldn't afford to bury his 11-year-old son. An ex-Dodger pondered a raffle to pay for an amputated leg. "Nobody cares about no pension then. Without them, guys today wouldn't be living like they are."

BAT paid bills, bought insurance, above all, gentled shame. Unlatching hope: a conservative, turned do-gooder; the hustler, aiding those whom life forgot.

Bob Dole told Richard Nixon that he was too complicated to be understood. "Aha!" Nixon enthused. "Now you're getting somewhere." Ibid, Yogi's chum. The final gate was knowledge.

TONY KUBEK

By 1939, Lou Gehrig was dying of amyotrophic lateral sclerosis, a hardening and collapsing of the spinal cord. On July 4, he gave baseball's Gettysburg Address. "Fans, for the past two weeks you have been reading about the bad break I got . . . but I have an awful lot to live for."

Game Seven, 1960 Series: A lesser break afflicts limb, not life. Gino Cimoli singles to start Pittsburgh's eighth inning. Bill Virdon grounds a 1–1 pitch to Tony Kubek. "A sure double play," said the Yanks shortstop, "except the ball hit something"—pebble, divot, or Forbes Field rough spot, no one knows—"and hit me [in the larynx]."

Tony fell, grabbed his throat, and began to choke and cough blood. NBC TV's Mel Allen empathized: "He wants to stay in, but Casey [manager Stengel] is saying, 'This is no time to be a hero.'" Kubek was carted to a hospital. En route, Bill Mazeroski swung.

In 1965, doctors found that Kubek had broken his neck. "The closest they could detect was what happened in Game Seven." Three vertebrae had fused: a collision could paralyze him. Ironically, the bad break spun identity: The average guy knew who Tony was.

Retiring, Kubek, 29, was to fly home to Milwaukee. "I was going to sell [Laughing Cow] cheese," he laughed. Instead, NBC poo-bah Dave Kennedy grabbed him at "Mr. Laffs," Phil Linz's Manhattan club. The Peacocks had just acquired "Game of the Week." Would Tony audition as backup analyst? At that moment he did not think of Gehrig. Unlike the Iron Horse, luck had bounced his way.

Kubek was curiously sensitive about 1960. Once 1983–89 "Game" partner Bob Costas referenced Virdon's smash. "Tony put his hand on my thigh to stop me. I relented so that circulation would resume." Doubtless he resented it kaputing his career.

In 1954, teams could still break the bank for a bonus baby. Each wanted Kubek, 17, "a painfully shy guy" who never dated in school. Papa took the longer view. "Forget a big deal," said the ex-Triple-A Milwaukee Brewer. "Their rules make you stay with the [parent] club." Dad wanted his stringbean to mature in the bushes. Agreeing, the Yanks gave him just $3,000 to sign.

By 1957, Kubek reached New York, became Rookie of the Year, and made the Classic. In Game Three, he homered twice at Milwaukee: Stripes, 12–3. "Local people called my parents, heckling them." Next year Tony played shortstop, third base, and entire outfield. "And in just one Series game! Casey liked to be cute." He was fired in 1960, making Kubek the daily shortstop. "He'll play there, period," new skipper Ralph Houk said, next year leading shortstops in chances per game.

"Don't write about me, write about *Kubek*," Roger Maris told a reporter. "He plays great every day, and fans don't know." Maris encored as MVP. He and Mickey Mantle had 115 homers. Whitey Ford went 25–4. "Ellie [Howard, catching] was a star. Moose [Skowron] at first, Kubek and Bobby Richardson up the middle, [Clete] Boyer at third," said Allen. "Ft. Knox had more holes."

In 1987, Kubek wrote *Sixty-One: The Team, The Record, The Men*, about a consortium impossible to forget. "For pure excitement, never a season like it." Nor, he added, a club like '61's.

Tony got married—"she's a social worker and has her master's degree"—was drafted, and entered the Army. On August 7, 1962, homering, he returned with the Switcher's flair. Thomas Wolfe thought he would never die. Kubek could not imagine the Yanks' meridian might end. Each year Mel and Red Barber invited him on their post-game show. Tony appeared once: the camera made him twittery. "I was the last guy you'd ever think of going into it." At NBC, he began by becoming ill.

New York, April 1966. About fifty baseball, network, and ad officials discuss "Game"'s first year. Strangely, its primary match—Detroit–New York, with Curt Gowdy and Pee Wee Reese—airs everywhere but there. "Blackout rules gave them the 'B' [backup] game," said Scotty Connal. Tony and Jim Simpson beamed Reds–Cubs into Motown and the Apple.

A rain forecast is read for Tiger Stadium. Another report says that Simpson has laryngitis. The crowd looks at Kubek. "If Simpson's got laryngitis and somebody thinks I'm doin' the"—gulp, *national*—"'Game' alone, I'll be in the bathroom 'cause I'm going to be sick." Weather cleared. Simpson healed. Tony reverted to the B's.

One Saturday morning the "A" game was rained out. "We learn the whole network is ours," said Charlie Jones, Simpson's sub. "I'm thrilled. Everyone'll see us."

Excusing himself, Kubek left the booth. "Thirty minutes before the game, no Tony. Twenty, no Tony. Fifteen, no Tony." Finally, Tony.

"Where you been?" said Jones.

"Throwing up. I'm not ready to go national."

By 1968, he was. "The problem," said Connal, "is being hidden on the backup." That fall a *good* Series hop found Tony's glove: he wowed as a field reporter. "He wormed his way around, but I wasn't bitter," said Reese, soon fired. "I just think if you don't have anything to say, you should shut your mouth."

Kubek had a lot to say, though he was gangling, stuttered, and talked too fast. "In the early seventies, Curt suggested that I work offseason on my delivery." Buying a recorder, Tony often read poetry aloud for 20 minutes a day.

One night, Monday "Game" guest Howard Cosell began trashing baseball. "No amount of description can hide the fact that this game is *lagging insufferably*."

"Baseball's athletes top everyone's," Kubek countered.

"No, my friend, try auto racing," smirked Cosell. Tony was almost speechless. It did not become a trend.

In 1973, NBC launched the "celebrity in the booth." Kubek panned it at a network luncheon. "Cosell? Bobby Riggs? Danny Kaye? A great guy, but come on." Why not Marcel Marceau, Harpo Marx, and Linda Lovelace? Designated hitter? "Dumb rule." Salary structure: "Completely irrational." Replacement players: "I'm a union guy. They'd have to be called scabs."

Tony called the 1969–75 All-Star Game and post-season. In 1972, knocked down, Oakland's Bert Campaneris threw his bat at Detroit's Lerrin LaGrow. "It's justified," Kubek said. "Any pitch like that," aimed squarely at Bert's legs, "endangers his career." Incensed, Motown's Chrysler Corporation phoned Bowie Kuhn, who called NBC, which pressured Tony. A day later he stiffed them all.

Would Kubek speak off-season? "Some guys write jokes for you. It wouldn't be me." National ads found the can: "I don't need the money." Winter meant family. "I go hunting, coach junior high basketball, and wait for baseball." To *TSN,* he had "really no sense of humor, speaks a little too often, and may be too much in love with his sport. Still, one listens," as in the 1975 World Series.

Cincy's Cesar Geronimo reached first in Game Three's 10th inning. Boston catcher Carlton Fisk then flung Ed Armbrister's bunt into center field. "Armbrister interfered [with the attempted forceout]"! charged Kubek. Plate umpire Larry Barnett disagreed. Joe Morgan plated the 6–5 winning run. Barnett blamed Tony for death alarum. Later the NBCer got 1,000 letters dubbing him a Boston stooge.

"It would be unfair to call him the last honest network broadcaster," wrote Jack Craig. "But he may be the most honest." For a long time that sufficed.

Tony called Gowdy his favorite partner. Garagiola changed "Game"'s tone and feel. "I grew up with a baseball of legend," said Lindsey Nelson. Antipodal: sport as job, not lore. "To players, it's a livelihood. That's how they treat it." Scully's and Caray's menu starred wine and beer, respectively. Joe's and Tony's listed meat and spuds.

"A great example of black and white," said Connal. A pitcher throws badly to third. "Joe says, 'The third baseman's fault.' Tony: 'The pitcher's.'" Media critic Gary Deeb termed theirs "the finest baseball commentary ever carried on network TV." In 1978, Kubek targeted another critic: Boss George.

"He's got an expensive toy," Tony said of George Steinbrenner. "Baseball's tough enough without an owner harassing you." Irked, the Yanks owner memoed each owner, Kuhn, and NBC about "biting the fan that feeds it."

Tony: "George likes to use people as pawns."

King George: No player will grant an interview.

"A lot of owners were ready to cave to Steinbrenner's bullying," said Kubek.

Diogenes was not.

Most Voices would kill for an Olympics. Tony's pact forbade it. He seemed as steady as 27 outs until the 1983 pact returned him to the B's. "I'm not crazy about being assigned to the backup game, but it's no big ego deal." NBC's tourniquet doubled salary to $350,000. Costas proved a newcomer, not neophyte. "I think my humor loosened Tony, and his knowledge improved me."

Increasingly, many preferred them to Vin's musings and Joe's asides. Then, in late 1988, Kubek went back to a future where he never expected to reside.

"I can't believe it," Tony said of NBC losing baseball. On September 30, 1989, he aired its 981st and last "Game" from SkyDome, having manned Canada's The Sports Network since 1977. "Kubek educated a whole generation of Canadian baseball fans without being condescending or simplistic," said the *Toronto Star*. In 1990, he joined the Yanks' Madison Square Garden Network. Steinbrenner's ode spurned joy.

"Kubek's style is not cuddly," wrote *The New York Times*'s Richard Sandomir. "His intensity costs popularity." Ask Ken Burns and David Halberstam: "I wouldn't talk with . . . interlopers coming in to take over our game." Peter Ueberroth: "To say that baseball's drug-free, the big-lie theory lives." George, firing Bucky Dent: "If you are really a winner," Tony said on MSG, "you should not have handled this like a loser."

After five years, "the last honest broadcaster" picked up a scorebook, scrapped a final $525,000 MSG season, and walked away. "I hate what the game's become—the greed, the nastiness. You can be married to baseball, give your heart to it, but when it starts taking over your soul, it's time to say *whoa*."

The decision stunned TV brass. What could he be *thinking*? Actually, priorities a sane man might cheer.

"I want to go home [Menosha, near Appleton] and spend more time with my family. They deserve it more than anyone. I don't need that ego stuff. I feel sorry for those who do."

Baseball's tough break (Tony, retiring) sprung from Kubek's good (life *sans* cant). Seldom had Forbes Field seemed so far away.

TONY KUBEK

LONGEVITY:	10	29 years.
CONTINUITY:	9	NBC TV "Game of the Week" 1966–89; Toronto A.L. 1977–89; New York A.L. 1990–94.
NETWORK:	10	"Game" 1966–89; All-Star Game 1969–75, 1977, 1979, and 1981; L.C.S. 1969–75, 1977, 1979, 1981, 1983, 1985, 1987, and 1989; World Series 1969–76, 1978, 1980, and 1982 (NBC TV). "Baseball" 1977–89 (CTV).
KUDOS:	5	Chairman, 1970s Presidential advisory commission, helping recently unemployed. National Polish-American Hall of Fame 1982.
LANGUAGE:	8	Sincere.
POPULARITY:	9	Unlike "Game"'s, grew.
PERSONA:	9	Honesty, best policy.
VOICE:	7	Untrained.
KNOWLEDGE:	10	Akin to Tim McCarver's now.
MISCELLANY:	7	Coming attractions. "Spewed with conviction," said Bob Wolff, on NBC TV's 1964 Series pre-game show. "He bristled with what he wants to say."
TOTAL:	84	(36th place).

CHUCK THOMPSON

At one time or another, Ernie Harwell, Herb Carneal, and Jon Miller called the Orioles. None denote Charm City. A child who learned it in a home that lodged Connie Mack does. "Chuck Thompson *is* Baltimore," mused Brooks Robinson. "Anyone will tell you that."

There was something special about the warm, beguiling voice. "Excellent flow, easy to hear," wrote John Steadman, "as old-shoe as a diner." Thompson credits grandma's renters house, near his Palmer, Massachusetts, birthplace for "giving me a love of baseball." Like Homer, Mack told tales to the hawk-nosed youth. The man later filled the air.

At 18, a friend dared an audition at WRAW Reading. Chuck became a singer, moved to WIBG Philadelphia, joined the 30th Army Division, and returned to Center City. In 1946, a balky elevator delayed the Athletics' Byrum Saam and Claude Haring. The tyro began talking. Impressed, the A's and Phils hired him—"Did each at home, no travel, as good as baseball gets"—too, hoops Warriors, football Eagles, then I.L. Orioles.

Thompson lived near an "avid golfer, but formal," who never swore on missing a putt. "I'd hear Bob [Sharman] in the yard, shouting a phrase I never understood." Intrigued, he borrowed "Go to war, Miss Agnes!" for the A.L. 1955–56 O's and 1957–60 Senators. Thrice D.C. dredged last. Once Chuck and a colleague recalled the grunge.

"As I remember," Bob Wolff said, "we rarely gave the score of the Senators games. That wasn't an oversight. It was well-planned, believe me."

Worse than watching the Nats drunk was seeing them sober. Future O's owner Jerold C. Hoffberger bought a table at the annual New York Baseball Writers dinner. "'I'm going to get some sleep. See ya tomorrow,'"Thompson said, hailing a cab to Toots Shor's. "All my Senators pals were there. We start drinking up a storm."

Near midnight, Hoffberger put a hand on Chuck's shoulder. "Kid, you got a hell of a bedroom."

"I feel there's not a better game than baseball, but it's tough to do. Every pitch you have to say in a different way,"he would say. Football, on the other hand, "is once a week. Prepare, you're fine. Just easier to call." Chuck was even better on first and ten than three and two, calling Albright, Temple, Navy, DuMont "Game of the Week," and the Baltimore Colts. As a boy, Miller watched CBS each Sunday. "'Lenny Moore gets five yards of real estate,'" he mimicked. "What a voice! It doesn't matter what Chuck says—as long as he says it."

If timing is all, December 28, 1958, had everything: John Unitas, the Giants' marquee defense, 50 million NBC viewers, and Thompson, doing Baltimore's 23–17 title victory, in the twilight, with a dreamboat denouement. The Colts reached the one-yard line in overtime. Suddenly the screen blackened. "The cable wire's loose," said Chuck. "No picture, and we're about to score." Saving the day, a man abruptly weaved across the field, making referee Ron Gibbs call time. The wire fixed, Alan Ameche scored over tackle. "We found the drunk was an NBC executive. He got the game stopped—and I hope got a raise."

Colts–Giants blessed football's ministry. In 1960, baseball was the sport. Chuck aired the Series on NBC Radio. Game Seven: Yanks, 7–6. "[Hal] Smith swings—a long fly ball deep to left field! . . . It is going, going, gone! [Pirates, 9–7, eighth inning] Forbes Field is at this moment an outdoor insane asylum! We have seen and shared in one of baseball's great moments!"

The ninth inning crowned another. "Well, a little while ago when we mentioned that this one . . . was going right to the wire, little did we know.

Art Ditmar [*sic*] throws. There's a swing and a high fly ball going deep to left! Back to the wall goes Berra! It is . . . over the fence, home run, the Pirates win! Ladies and gentlemen, Mazeroski has hit a one-nothing pitch over the left-field fence here at Forbes Field to win the 1960 World Series for the Pittsburgh Pirates, 10 to 0 [*sic*]!"

Neither glitch cut ice. "People didn't notice because they were berserk," Thompson said. A year later the Bucs asked if he wanted a voice-over correction on a souvenir LP. "Hey, it was a horrible mistake, but I said it, so keep it in." In 1985, a gauzy Anheuser Busch Series TV ad used his call. Hundreds phoned the brewery. *Ralph Terry*! *10 to 9*!

The flak endeared Thompson even more to Baltimore. Go to war, Miss Agnes! The city might, for him.

"For a long time breweries were baseball's big sponsor. They owned you, not the club." In 1957, the National Brewing Co. left the Orioles for Senators. In 1962, it, and Chuck, returned. September 1964 bunched the White Sox, Stripes, and O's. On Long Island, Bob Costas sat in a car, adjusted the radio, and fixed WBAL Baltimore. "If the Yankees played at day, I'd listen to the Orioles at night, and in truth I'd try to *will* them to lose."

Boston's Lee Thomas's ground-rule double rebounded on the field and was grabbed by a labrador retriever. "Well," Thompson said, "that was a dog-goned double." Saleable, he mused, "Mmm, ain't the beer cold!" upon an O's homer, save, or 4–6–3. Said Costas: "It seemed to sum up baseball so perfectly, a guy sipping a beer on his back porch, keeping up with his team."

In 1966, the team kept up with Chuck. "We were good until we got Frank [Robinson, from Cincinnati]," said Brooks. "He made us a winner": Triple Crown .316, 49 homers, and 122 RBI. Boog Powell added 34 taters. Luis Aparicio, Davey Johnson, and Paul Blair sealed the middle. Baltimore clinched September 22. The Dodgers won that "other league." B. Robby: "They looked at us like hired help." The serfs swept the Series.

They made another in 1969. "I've done a Classic," said Chuck, ceding NBC to his partner. Gawked Bill O'Donnell: "Name one guy who would voluntarily yield his sport's top event." Thompson's last Series were 1970–71 vs. Cincinnati and Pittsburgh, respectively. Said Brooks: "We won the two we should have lost [1966 and 1970], and lost the two we should have won."

Some players have children out of wedlock. In Baltimore, babies are named for a man mom never met. Brooks entered Cooperstown in 1983 holding records for best third base fielding average, chances, assists, putouts, and double plays. The '70 Series evinced his Velcro mitt. "Swing, ground ball, third-base side. Brooks Robinson's got it, throwing from foul ground toward first base! It is . . . in time! And the Golden Glove artistry of Brooks Robinson was never more apparent than on that last play." He "played a simple game," said Chuck. "Hit it to him and he'd catch it—on grass, turf, concrete, in a swamp. Throw it to him, and Brooks hit it": 2,848 hits, including 268 homers.

His last studded 1977. "It was a rainy night, 7,000 people." Brooks's pinch-dinger won the game. "Spectators then ran down to the field. Maybe they sensed this was Brooks's last blast. Whatever, the crowd made as much noise as I've heard at a World Series"—one course in a menu of plot and place. Thompson hoarded ballpark yarns like Imelda Marcos, shoes.

At Seattle's Sick's Stadium, "The away Voice looked down the first-base line. You could only see right of shortstop." Chuck hung a mirror for balls hit to left: "That way you refract the play." At Fenway Park, P.A. Voice Sherm Feller announced Neil Armstrong's 1969 moonwalk. Applause began. The umpire called time. Due to hit, Brooks asked what Feller said. Told, *he* started clapping. A fan warbled "God Bless America." Soon Fenway housed teary carolers. Caruso never sounded better.

One day Blair led off third base in Detroit. Swinging, F. Robby hurled a bat near the seats. Blair faced them—"worried," said Chuck, "about a fan injury"—whereupon catcher Bill Freehan tagged him.

"You're out," said the umpire.

"You can't do that," said Blair.

"Why not?"

"Because when I get back to the dugout, [manager] Earl [Weaver]'s going to kill me."

The O's bantamweight won six divisions, four flags, and one Series—"unique, like his double-billed cap," said Chuck, "so he could argue any way he turned." One day, homering, outfielder-turned-minister Pat Kelly touched the plate, raised an arm, and pointed skyward.

"What's this pointin'?" Weaver asked.

Kelly said, "Without the Good Lord, I wouldn't be able to do that."

Earl: "The Good Lord didn't do much for the guy who threw the ball."

Yogi Berra was mystified by a streaker's sex: "He had a bag over his head." An O's rain delay removed doubt—and dress. A man stripped, ran to second base, and slid on a tarp into third. Memorial Stadium security rushed him to the dugout. The man leaves for jail. Raising a hand, umpire Nestor Chylak separates his thumb and index finger by an inch. "There were 27,000 in the park," said Thompson, "and every one roared."

Once Al Bumbry tripled to left-center. "*Listen* to that guy!" a friend said of Chuck's staccato. "What enthusiasm!" In 1979, it described a pennant; '81, Eddie Murray, leading in A.L. homers and RBI; '82, Cal Ripken, Jr.'s debut at third. The last weekend Baltimore thrice beat Milwaukee: the A.L. East was tied; true believers packed Birdland's bowl. Weaver had announced retirement. Would a Series postpone it?

"Take our last game," Thompson said, "and we got a flag." Losing, the crowd wouldn't leave, chanting "Earl!" The '83ers won the Series. Chuck completed a decade with Brooks on WMAR TV: "Here's the 2–1 pitch . . . let's watch the outfielder . . . a mighty fine ballplayer is ____"—pick a name and year. He missed Weaver riding players and kicking dirt. A listener missed him, "retiring" in 1987. "Actually, the station had me do games each year. Guess I never left."

In 1991, Thompson helped close the O's beloved "ramshackle, beat-up old place [Baltimore *Sun*]." On October 4, Miller introduced him. The ovation volleyed, rocked the girders, shook the field. Two days later Ripken banged into a Memorial-ending double play. A limousine carted home plate to Oriole Park at Camden Yards. The field was cleared. Music began from "Field of Dreams." The first O's left the dugout: Brooks, for third; F. Robby, right field.

"Then came Jim Palmer pitching, Boog to first. This is how the team said good-bye—ex-players coming back. The crowd hadn't expected this. When it happened, they were stunned." More than 75 players ran in period uniforms to their position. "No introduction, just music rolling. I looked with binoculars at Brooks and Powell and we were all fighting to keep from breaking down."

Later, Thompson walked to his car through a sea of red-eyed love. "Whoever says, 'There's no crying in baseball' would that day change his mind."

Opening April 6, 1992, the O's new home was a pop fly from the Inner Harbor, near the Camden Railroad Station of the old Baltimore and Ohio. A brick facade mimed old Comiskey Park. Left field was triple-tiered like the Bronx. The 1,016-foot-long and 51-foot-wide 1898 brick B&O Railroad Warehouse enfolded the park, like houses around Wrigley Field.

Memorial was big band, blue collar, and National Bohemian Beer: Camden, less rowdy than a baseball salon. "It was hip," said Chuck, "but wasn't home." Cooperstown was, by 1993. "There is no way you can prepare yourself for the emotion of the impact of the moment," Thompson told the crowd. "You wanted it for me and I wanted it for you." For one day, Baltimore moved 340 miles north.

Later Chuck brooked eye disease, lost sight, and tried commentary. Said O's Voice Jim Hunter: "He still has the mind and voice." Retiring, he relished Chuck Thompson Bobble Head Day. "It's got the trademark fedora, the [jagged] nose," mused colleague Fred Manfra. "Push a button and hear the calls," including F. Robby's 500th homer.

Thompson converted to Catholicism, turning inward, but not bitter. Go to war, Miss Agnes! He found inner peace. Ain't the beer cold! "He's ours," said Steadman, "and that's enough," love as clear as a day behind the rain.

CHUCK THOMPSON

LONGEVITY:	10	44 years.
CONTINUITY:	7	Philadelphia A.L. and N.L. 1947–48; Baltimore A.L. 1955–56, 1962–87, and 1991-2000; Washington A.L. 1957–60; NBC TV "Major League Baseball" 1959–60.
NETWORK:	6	"Major League Baseball" 1959–60 (NBC TV). World Series 1960 (NBC Radio) and 1966 and 1970–71 (NBC TV).
KUDOS:	9	Cooperstown 1993. Six-time Maryland Sportscaster of the Year. Advertising Club of Baltimore 1966 outstanding TV personality. Orioles Hall of Fame 1995.
LANGUAGE:	10	Quick, clipped.
POPULARITY:	10	Statue should moor Inner Harbor.
PERSONA:	10	Real Lord of Baltimore.
VOICE:	10	Melodic.
KNOWLEDGE:	9	Forte personal, not statistical.
MISCELLANY:	10	Meeting on red-eye flight, Thompson and hero Bing Crosby reached L.A. at 5 A.M. Bing stood in terminal singing the old dance-bander a song.
TOTAL:	91	(13th place).

BILL O'DONNELL

Radio/TV often rewards the me-hymning, fast-talking, and fact-twisting con. Exceptions seem old-world in an eat-your-young field. Until his death at 56 of cancer, Orioles 1966–82 Voice Bill O'Donnell was such a gentleman.

"Never, ever, did I hear him say a bad word about anyone," said Chuck Thompson. "Never, ever, did I hear him utter one word of profanity." He was honest, kind, and civilizing. The combination is hard to find.

Bill grew up in the Bronx, entered Fordham Prep School, and at 14 became a *Times* copy boy. Later: Fordham University, the Marines, and *Navy News* editor. "After the war," he said, "I came back to find no room at Fordham." Ex-classmate Vin Scully joined Brooklyn. O'Donnell slogged to the *World Telegram and Sun, Utica Daily News,* WIBX Utica, and Mohawk Valley Community College.

In 1951, he called Pioneer League Pocatello, Idaho. A year later Bill returned to Upstate New York. Through 1965, he did the Triple-A Chiefs, hitched Syracuse University hoops and football, and was WSYR TV/radio sports director.

"I loved it, and tried not to get discouraged." At forty, he hadn't made the bigs—and might never have, without luck.

In early 1966, the Red Sox' Curt Gowdy left for NBC. O'Donnell, then Colts Voice, asked their ad agency for a plug. That day the O's added an announcer. Skip Boston: the agency proposed Charm City.

Football owned Baltimore. Baseball's stupor was contagious. A Tribe reliever threw two balls, was yanked by skipper Birdie Tebbetts, but got reinstated by the ump. "Birdie forgot the [minimum] one-batter rule," said Bill, "so starts doing the breaststroke, waving his arms to the dugout." Asked to explain, he said, "I was swimming through a sea of my own stupidity."

The 1966 Birds drew a record 1,203,366. "I'm not taking credit," said their rookie Voice. "I think maybe winning our first pennant helped." In 1968, he spurned the Yankees. By 1969, the Orioles 60-outlet network reached Maryland, Virginia, Delaware, Pennsylvania, and D.C. Baltimore reached the Series.

In Game Three, New York's Tommie Agee homered, made a fourth-inning backhand catch at the fence, and encored in the seventh.

"Here's a fly ball to right-center field!" Bill said on NBC Radio. "Shamsky with Agee. Agee dives—and he makes the catch!" Davey Johnson was the O's last Game Five—thus Series—hope. "Fly ball, deep left field! Jones is back at the fence! Jones is on the warning track! The World Series is over! The Mets have won it by a score of 5 to 3!"

The 1970 O's sought retribution. "Even when we won [its Series], we focused on '71," said Bill. "Win, and people talk dynasty." Again he called the Classic. Pittsburgh took a 3–2 game lead. Game Six went overtime. "Frank Robinson had bad legs. He walks, gets to third on a single, and barely beats the throw to third with a belly-flop."

Brooks flew to shallow center. Heaving, Frank slid between catcher Manny Sanguillen's legs. Pittsburgh took a 2–1 final. The Ming Dynasty was safe.

By now Bill did pro and college football, TVS Network hoops, and NBC's backup "Game." Travel braced, not bored. "In Boston, I'll focus on the restaurants; Chicago, long walks; Kansas City, golf; Anaheim, the beaches," he said. "Nothing comes to mind in New York"—just home. In 1979, new O's radio household WFBR began hyping "Orioles Magic." Aptly, they began winning games in an "Orioles Way." Wild Bill Hagy, a taxi driver in section 34, twisted his body to spell O-R-I-O-L-E-S atop the dugout. Recalling the empty-seat 1971 Series, you sang, swung, and swigged.

Overnight, Baltimore became a baseball town. Attendance hit 1,681,009. The O's won the East, took the L.C.S., but lost again to Pittsburgh. "We've got to stop playing them," O'Donnell said. Soon the A.L.'s longest radio/TV co-op nested in Birdland. "Seventeen years!" Thompson exulted. A reason: Bill.

"Broadcasters spend seven months, every day, with the same person," said

---

BILL O'DONNELL

LONGEVITY:	6	17 years.
CONTINUITY:	10	Baltimore A.L. 1966–82. NBC TV "Game of the Week" 1969–76.
NETWORK:	6	"Game" 1969–76, World Series 1969, and L.C.S. 1975 (NBC TV). World Series 1971 (NBC Radio).
KUDOS:	5	Court Grimes Television Award 1959. Greater Utica Sports Hall of Fame 1997.
LANGUAGE:	9	Exacting.
POPULARITY:	8	Eclipsed by Thompson's.
PERSONA:	9	Gentleman Bill.
VOICE:	9	Cultured.
KNOWLEDGE:	10	Like the O's, seldom unprepared.
MISCELLANY:	8	Did 1970–76 NFL on NBC. Once aired 24 high school hoops games in four nights, and 27 boxing matches in 8 1/2 hours.
TOTAL:	80	(56th place).

Chuck. "Some teams off the air are totally incompatible." By reckoning, he and O'Donnell ate 95 of every 100 dinners together on the road. Slowly, pain drove Bill off. He died, at Johns Hopkins Hospital, October 29, 1982, leaving wife Patricia and five children. Next year, Thompson moved exclusively to TV.

"Without this dear, sweet man," he said, "I knew radio wouldn't be the same." Chuck ferried the Orioles through 2000. It seldom was.

KEN COLEMAN

In 1940, only England stood between Adolf Hitler and a new dark age. "Let us therefore brace ourselves to our duties," said Prime Minister Winston Churchill, "and so bear ourselves that, if the British Empire and its Common-wealth last for a thousand years, men will say: 'This was their finest hour.'"

The Red Sox' post-1918 Everest was 2004. Until then, a Townie might cite another year. Bill Clinton could fall again, and Al Gore rise again. Martha Stewart could become a social worker, and the Rolling Stones retire. Bob Uecker could find the front row, and Madonna become a nun. All this would happen before a finer baseball hour than 1967.

The 1966 Sox finished ninth. Next year's 100-to-1ers wrote "one of baseball's great rags-to-riches stories," said Joseph Durso, by waving a last-day pennant. Pinching himself, Ken Coleman still did not believe it.

In the clubhouse, his suit oozed Great Western champagne. Outside, Red Sox Nation replayed an Ozymandian year. So we beat on, F. Scott Fitzgerald wrote, "boats against the current, borne back ceaselessly into the past." Coleman's past had never wandered far away.

It began in Quincy, a Boston suburb, eight miles from Fenway. Ken's ikon was Jimmy Foxx. At age 12, a BB gun accident cost an eye. Heroes were tradeable: Double X, for Fred Hoey. "We called him 'The man who does the games.'" Coleman's was baseball as a hopeful, awkward child.

In 1943, he left high school, entered the Good War, and was asked to call sports in India on Armed Forces Radio. "Try speaking with 12,000 troops lis-tening." Released, Ken majored in Oratory at Curry College, partly to con-quer fear. Next: Vermont's Northern Baseball League, Boston University football, and 250-watt Worcester outlet. In 1952, he took port at Cleveland Stadium. "Lindsey Nelson and I were Browns radio finalists." Nelson joined NBC; Ken, a 125-station network.

In 1954, he tried Browns video. I still recall, from their lakeside fort, Coleman's wise, knowing way. "When people mention him, they think baseball," said Jack Buck, "but he's the best football announcer I ever heard." Ken did the 1954–63 Indians. "My first year they won 111 games, then not much to tell." The exception was slugger Rocky Colavito.

In 1960, Cleveland dealt No. 6 for Harvey Kuenn. It took a while to forget Ohio's greatest pin-up since Boudreau. Humor helped. Once Rocky retreated to the wall. "Back goes Wally against the rock," Coleman said of the now-Tiger. Red-faced, he amended: "For those of you interested in statistics, this was my 11th fluff of this year. It puts me in third place in the American League."

Ken called his last Cleveland game January 2, 1966. "Also my eighth [Mutual or CBS/NBC TV] NFL title game [losing to Green Bay, 23–12]," leaving at the top for baseball's bottom. In March, Curt Gowdy left the Sox for NBC. You lucky stiff, Coleman told himself. "It was like a dream, going back to my roots, taking Curt's and Hoey's job."

The nightmare was the team. In 1965, 1,247 watched Dave Morehead no-hit Cleveland. Each 1966 pitcher had a losing record. Boston will win a title, said a fan, when Tiny Tim sings bass.

'Sixty-seven made baseball cool again, revived the Boston American League Baseball Company, and filled a funhouse of peals. Leonard Bernstein said, "Music is something terribly special. It doesn't have to pass the censor of the brain before it can reach the heart." Like music, the year cried *gotcha* to the soul.

Drawing 8,324, Fenway's opener sang anonymity. That week Billy Rohr pitched his first bigs game. "Eight hits . . . all of them belong to Boston," Ken's ninth inning began on WHDH Radio. "Fly ball to left field! Yastrzemski is going hard, way back! Way back! And he dives—and makes a tremendous catch!" The next batter singled. The rookie won only two more games. Later WHDH released the LP "The Impossible Dream." Of Rohr, Coleman said: "The fans began to sense it. This year was not quite the same."

July crossed the rubicon. The Sox swept a 10-game road trip. Pilots from Boston to Nova Scotia traced a West Coast game by lights in homes below. Wrote the Boston *Herald*'s Kevin Convey: "It is late on a late-summer night in 1967. The house is dark except for the flashlight beside my bed. It is quiet except for my transistor, in a whisper. Ken Coleman didn't just call baseball games. He called my summers."

Reggie Smith hit with the bases full. "A listener," Ken said, "refused to enter a tunnel. Soon hundreds of cars, listening, back up a mile." On August 13, 2 1/2 games bunched five teams. Tony Conigliaro was beaned. Two days later Boston trailed, 8–0: the Fens were mute; the bottom was falling out. Then: "Fly ball hit deep into left-center field, and it is a home run! Jerry Adair has hit his second home run of the 1967 season. And the Red Sox are now leading in the eighth inning, 9 to 8."

Ahead: "If I may add a personal note," Coleman would say, "the greatest thrill of my life."

By September 30, Minnesota led the Sox by one game with two left at Fenway. Stores closed. Churches opened. All knew the truth and consequences. Boston hit in the 2-all sixth. "And Scott hits one deep into center field! This one is back! This one is gone!" Ken cried. Sox: 6–4. Next day they dittoed, 5–3.

"[Afterward] the players came into the clubhouse. Some were crying, some yelling, and I was trying to interview." A radio aired in the background. Detroit could tie by taking a twinbill. Instead, it lost game two, 8–5, tying past and present in Blue Hill and Brattleboro and Wakefield and Woonsocket—Boston's first pennant since 1946.

The Boston *Record-American* cover blared "CHAMPS!" and a drawing of two red socks. Jim Lonborg went 22–9. George Scott hit .303. Carl Yastrzemski transcended myth: Triple Crown/MVP 44 homers, 121 RBI, and .326. Ken and Curt called each World Series game in Boston. "Talk about coming full circle," Coleman said of his predecessor. Another filled 1972–75: He moved to Sox WBZ TV, then Ohio—"both moves due to flagship changes."

Like 1954 and 1967, the good luck penny shone: Ken's '75 Reds met—the *Townies*! "I did their TV, Marty Brennaman radio, and he got the Series." In 1979, retaking the Logan Airport shuttle, he began a final decade in the Hub. Retiring, Coleman wrote five books, did Harvard football, and entered the Red Sox Hall of Fame, tracing the region's burgs, back country, and sunburnt hills.

Inevitably, a stranger mentioned Yaz and Boomer and Gentleman Jim. "People talk about upsets," Ken would tell them before his 2003 death, at 78. "They're nothing compared to '67." Convey recalled the flashlight beside his bed. "There will be other summers. And I will listen to other announcers. But I will never stop hearing Ken Coleman."

KEN COLEMAN

LONGEVITY:	10	34 years.
CONTINUITY:	8	Cleveland A.L. 1954–63; Boston A.L. 1966–74 and 1979–89; Cincinnati N.L. 1975–78.
NETWORK:	1	World Series 1967 (NBC TV).
KUDOS:	9	Red Sox Hall of Fame 2000. Eight-time Ohio Sportscaster of the year. Twelve awards, American Federation of Television and Radio Artists. Cleveland Press Club Hall of Fame. Founder, Bosox Club. Fenway radio booth named in honor.
LANGUAGE:	10	Never ended sentence with a preposition.
POPULARITY:	9	Unsurprisingly, peaked in '67.
PERSONA:	9	Gentleman/gentle man.
VOICE:	10	Silken, restrained—"a beautiful horn," said Boston Bruins Voice Bob Wilson, "and, oh, he played it well."
KNOWLEDGE:	10	A nicer Barber.
MISCELLANY:	8	Was second executive director of Jimmy Fund, New England's cancer charity.
TOTAL:	84	(35th place).

GEORGE KELL

If a baseball Voice is lucky, said Coleman, he becomes a member of the family. "The first year's the toughest," added Ernie Harwell. "Get past it, and you've got a lifetime pass."

Harwell got by the first year to call five decades at Detroit. In 1959, another Southerner of piety, charm, and blue eyes embarked. "People thought of us as soulmates," Ernie mused of Arkansas's George Kell, "but he did one medium [television] and I mostly did the other."

Their 1960–63 radio/TV co-op hatched a lasting glow. "I thought George Kell and Ernie Harwell was one word," wrote listener Rebecca Stowe. Their *de facto* name was work—what it wasn't to hear them on the air.

Compare third basemen. Brooks Robinson was the Human Vacuum Cleaner. Mike Schmidt became the Dayton Flyer. Kell mocked ballyhoo. Joe DiMaggio's liner once broke his jaw. George nabbed the ball, crawled to third, applied a forceout, and fainted.

"It's something you pick up in Arkansas. You made do." Leaving the minors, Kell, 22, made good as 1944 A's third sacker. Traded to Detroit, he batted at least .296 from 1946 to 1954. In 1949, his .342911 edged Ted Williams's .342756—first man at the position to win a post-1912 crown.

Next year hitched a league-high 56 doubles and 218 hits. Detroit finished 95–59. "I made [1947–51] All-Star Games. That was nice, but what I missed was a pennant." A.L. records grew like vines around a trellis: four times, assists and total chances; seven, fielding percentage; among the top 20 life-time in putouts and assists.

George started the 1957 All-Star Game as an Oriole, retiring that fall with a .306 average. Rounding the square: successor Brooks Robinson entered Cooperstown in 1983—with Kell.

In 1958, CBS TV gave him pre-"Game of the Week." George hoped to ask guest Casey Stengel about the batting order. He was asked how it went. "Fine. But in our 15 minutes, Casey didn't get past the leadoff batter." A year later, he replaced Tigers analyst Mel Ott, whose "death in a car crash stunned me." Ernie then arrived from Baltimore. "Detroit's tough," wrote Joe Falls, "and here you had two quiet voices, alien accent, but knew baseball" in a baseball-batty town.

Crosby, Stills, Nash, and Young sang "It's been a long time coming." Kell's family had waited a long time by 1963. "I've been away so much my boy says, 'yes, sir' or 'no, sir' at the dinner table." Business chafed, too. George owned a farm, insurance company, and Cadillac agency in Swifton (pop. 601, where he was born) or Newport (7,007, raised). "Whenever there were decisions to be made, I was in Detroit or on the road."

Kell spent 1964 in Arkansas, then trekked to Tigers video. "Twenty-two road trips a year from Swifton, most weekend. Rest of the time's my own." The '68 Tigers owned Detroit's: George beamed the Series. "I'm on NBC," he said, "and my team's barely breathing." Behind, 3 games to 1, Detroit received CPR. Bathed in bubbly, Kell hosted post-Game Seven's clubhouse shebang.

"As long as I live, I'll never forget this." His hope: a future bereft of flat champagne.

"Life is a people business," said the more-friend-than-celebrity. Kell nearly ran for Governor, chaired the Arkansas Highway Commission, and tended the Swifton home he and wife Charlene built in 1946. "If I had to choose between here and Tigers games, I wouldn't have to think." George never had to. "Any-body who doesn't know baseball means people is in the wrong game."

In 1993, Detroit acquired Eric Davis. Kell began pre-game 15 minutes later. "I'd tried to get to Sparky Anderson for quotes, but there was a mob." Knowing him, George invented five. "Yeah, that's probably what I've have said," the Tigers manager said later. "You read me pretty well."

Kell deemed Frank Robinson America's best post-war player. "He'd run over his grandmother if he had to." George would outwork her. "His secret was the guy at home," said Ernie, "who knew that Kell knew the game."

He retired to Swifton in 1997. "I'll never forget it," George said of Motown. A listener might say that about Harwell's Ozark kin.

GEORGE KELL

LONGEVITY:	10	39 years.
CONTINUITY:	9	CBS TV "Game of the Week" 1958; Detroit A.L. 1959–63 and 1965–97.
NETWORK:	5	"Game" 1958 (CBS TV). N.L. playoff 1959 (ABC TV) and 1962 (NBC TV). All-Star Game second 1962 (NBC Radio). World Series 1968 (NBC TV).
KUDOS:	8	Cooperstown 1983, inducted as player. Voted Tigers' all-time greatest third baseman. Michigan Sports Hall of Fame.
LANGUAGE:	6	Cracker-barrel.
POPULARITY:	9	Approached Harwell's.
PERSONA:	10	Arkansas Traveler.
VOICE:	8	Easy listening.
KNOWLEDGE:	10	Working meant learning.
MISCELLANY:	5	Grew up in Cardinals country. In 1968, felt like "I was rooting for the enemy."
TOTAL:	80	(55th place).

HARRY KALAS

The face belongs in the Vienna Boys Choir. The voice evokes a bass, lead cello, or wrecker razing cars—to Bill Conlin, "a four-Marlboros into a three-martini-lunch baritone." Harry Norbert Kalas woos the Delaware Valley. A minister's child spreads the Phillies' Word.

"It's like Harry had opera training," said team vice president Larry Shenk. "No one can call a moment like him." To the Main Line, Brandywine, and Center City, "Long drive! . . . It's outta here! Home run!" is outta sight.

In 1944, Kalas, eight, raised near Chicago, visited Comiskey Park for his first bigs game. Rain halted batting practice. "The Senators stunk. I'm praying weather clears, so the Sox'll win. I go near their dugout," where Mickey Vernon sat Harry on the bench. At that moment he pledged to hit, or call, the curve.

At the University of Iowa, Kalas majored in speech, radio, and TV. A blind professor said, "You have a voice that could take you a considerable way." He was drafted, became a broadcast specialist, and re-created P.C.L. Hawaii. "Road trips were too costly to do live." The bigs team hiring him was no bargain at any price.

The Colt .45s were a hero of every dog that was under. In 1965, they got a new name (Astros), park (Astrodome), and Voice, but not team. Doug Rader used the clubhouse as a driving range. Larry Dierker explained— "They wanted to live"—why no one took his clubs. Once Rader, Joe Morgan, Kalas, and his father golfed. Increasingly, Doug's language turned blue.

"Ease off," said Morgan. "Don't you know Harry's dad is a [Evangelical United Brethren] minister?"

"Mr. Kalas, I didn't know that," Doug brightened. "Jesus Christ!" Scales fell from pop's eyes like Saul on the Damascus Road.

In 1787, Benjamin Franklin wondered during Philadelphia's "long hot summer" whether the sun painted on the president's chair was rising or setting. "But now at length, I . . . know that it is a rising not a setting sun." In 1970, the sun set on Connie Mack Stadium. Many wondered when decent baseball would rise.

April 1971: Veterans Stadium opens. Kalas, replacing Bill Campbell on Phils radio/TV, finds the city up in arms. "Bill Giles had been [V.P.] in Houston. Coming here, he offered me a job," not saying whose. "Bill was very popular. For several years my confidence level faltered." He was not bolstered by the 1971–73ers, dredging last.

"You kept hoping pieces'd merge," said Harry. One day Greg (Bull) Luzinski drove deep in batting practice. "Wow, that's way out of here!" gawked Larry Bowa. Nearby the new Voice stood: "It's outta here!" began. Like Kalas, another piece braved a rough initiation. "He came up [1972], and you saw the skill. But he'd miss wildly, make an error at third, and sulk."

In 1975, Mike Schmidt and Luzinski combined for 72 homers. Bowa made shortstop hermetic. "Two-thirds of the world is covered by water," wagged broadcaster Ralph Kiner. "The other third is covered by [center fielder] Garry Maddox." Philly placed second.

Byrum Saam retired, making Harry lead announcer. Finally, the sun began to rise.

Even Napoleon, said Danny Ozark, "had his Watergate." The Phils skipper and a player had "a wonderful repertoire." Morality, he said of team morale, "is not an issue here." The '76 Bicentennial was. Philly won the East—first title since 1950. "Even then," Harry rued, "our luck wasn't great." Two men reached base vs. St. Louis's Al Hrabosky. Maddox smoked an out. The shortstop caught Schmidt's liner, sprawling. Hrabosky deflected and retrieved the Bull's game-ending smash. "We had everybody played right," joshed manager Red Schoendienst, "except maybe Al was a little shallow on Luzinski."

Cincy swept the playoff. Next year Philadelphia led L.C.S. Game Three, 5–3, in the ninth: two out, none on; 63,719 shook the Vet. "Maybe we were thinking World Series," said Harry. L.A. scored thrice. A day later Phils ace Steve Carlton lost, 4–1, ending the playoff. By now Harry the K distilled a region's hope, hurt, and fatalism.

Already he had done, or would, Notre Dame, DePaul, Marquette, Southwest Conference, Big Ten, and Big Five basketball, Irish, University of Houston, and Westwood One's network football, and NFL Films, as co-host/voiceover. Also: videos, team highlight reels, and U.S. Mint, Sears, Campbell's Soup, and Dilbert's animated cartoon.

"All stemmed from Harry's baseball stage," said Shenk. When would Philly, filling it, shake a rep as Red Sox South? The '80ers again took their division on Schmidt's next-to-last-day blast. The L.C.S. against Houston followed, an 8–7 final aping jai-alai. "Finally, after all these years, a Series!" Kalas chortled—the Phillies' first since 1950. There was, as they say, a hitch.

Baseball's then-policy barred local-team Classic coverage. "So NBC gets a petition of thousands of names," said partner Andy Musser. "'Let Harry broadcast on [flagship] KYW!'" The Peacocks demurred. Next season, too late for Kalas, the radio ban ended. "I understood NBC," he said. "I just wish I could have done something I'd dreamed of since a kid."

It commenced by accentuating the positive: Philly, 7–6 and 6–4. Kansas City won twice, led Game Five, but blew the ninth inning, 4–3. Back home, the Nationals took a 4–0 edge. In the ninth, Tug McGraw filled the bases. Frank White fouled near the first-base dugout. Catcher Bob Boone touched but dropped the ball. Lunging, Pete Rose caught it barehanded.

At 11:29 P.M., the Phils, 97, won title one. "World champions of base-ball!" Kalas, re-creating, roared. "It's pandemonium at Veterans Stadium! All of the fans are on their feet. This city has come together behind a baseball team! Phillies are world champions! This city knows it! This city loves it!" Rising sun: A million Quakers jammed the victory parade.

"The [50-day 1981 players'] strike killed our championship momentum," said Harry. In 1983, a lesser club won the flag: Kalas did the Series in customary white loafers and blue slacks, cigarette in hand, filling a homemade score-sheet. Rose hiked to Montreal. Carlton skipped to San Francisco. Remaining: "There's a smash down the third-base line! What a stop by Schmitty! . . . Struuuck him out! . . . Watch that baby go!" In suburban Wallingford, a ninth-grader penned a "favorite person essay." Kalas's voice "is sleepy and invigor-ating all at once," Rich Beck, 15, wrote. "It is a beautiful thing."

In 1986, Schmidt won a 10th Gold Glove, led the N.L. for the eighth time in homers, and took his third MVP. Next April 18, he faced Pittsburgh's Don Robinson. "Here's the pitch. . . . He takes a shot at it! There it goes! It is outta here! Michael Jack Schmidt has hit his five-hundredth home run! What a spot! What a spot! And the entire team comes out to greet Schmitty! He puts the Phillies in front, 8 to 6! For Mike Schmidt, his five-hundredth homer!"

In the clubhouse, mates cried "We want Harry!" then four times replayed his call. Rising/setting: The Phils twice plunked last; the '93ers won the East. Kalas brayed "High Hopes," his favorite song. Once the team's pear-shaped, green-haired, elephant-nosed mascot crashed the booth, scaled a ledge, and mugged his way around the bowl. "What does it say," partner Richie Ashburn asked Harry, "that you're one of our biggest stars—and the [Phillie] Phanatic is the other?"

For $120, the Vet proposed marriage on the scoreboard. Kalas swooned like a schoolboy for 2002. "I'm on cloud nine," he said of Cooperstown. "For a kid who fell in love with the game at ten, to be going in . . . is mind-bog-gling." A full house at the Vet, including Mickey Vernon, got bobble head dolls of Mr. K and now-late Ashburn. Harry toured the field in a convertible: said the *Daily News,* "as much a local figure as cheesesteaks, the Art Museum, and the Summers Strut."

In July, Philly fanatics filled another field near the Hall of Fame. "This is the ultimate honor," Kalas began. Tearing, he imagined Richie's twist: "Hard to believe, Harry!" ending with a poem that read, "Philadelphia fans, I love you!"

From the distance a voice yelled, "And we love you, too, Harry!" At such a time, "It's outta here!" seemed less chant than definition of his appeal.

HARRY KALAS

LONGEVITY:	10	40 years.
CONTINUITY:	9	Houston N.L. 1965–70; Philadelphia N.L. 1971– ; ABC/NBC TV The Baseball Network 1994–95.
NETWORK:	2	TBN 1994–95 (ABC/NBC TV). L.C.S. 1984 (CBS Radio).
KUDOS:	10	Cooperstown 2002. 18-time Pennsylvania Sportscaster of the Year. Board of Governors Award and Lifetime Achievement Award, Philadelphia Sports Congress, 2002. First Legacy of Excellence Award 2004, Philadelphia Sports Hall of Fame. In 2004, restaurant Harry The K's opened in Phils' new Citizens Bank Park.
LANGUAGE:	9	Minimalist.
POPULARITY:	10	More phenomenal than the Phanatic's.
PERSONA:	10	Links Delaware, southeast Pennsylvania, and western New Jersey.
VOICE:	10	Resonant, transcendent: soothes, then explodes.
KNOWLEDGE:	10	Eclipsed by pipes.
MISCELLANY:	7	Cut CD "Rain Delay" for Philly band Marah. Son Todd Tampa Bay Devil Rays announcer.
TOTAL:	87	(25th place).

RICHIE ASHBURN

Supreme Court Justice Potter Stewart observed, "I can't define it [obscenity], but I know it when I see it." Radio/TV chemistry is what you see, hear, and sense. Philadelphia's 1971–97 alloy was two chemists with a needle. "We anticipated one another," mused Ashburn. "It's nothing you can work on." Said Kalas: "Our rapport—it was always there."

Richie had mixed elements since 1948: .308 lifetime average; 1955 and '58 batting titles; four-time league-high in walks and on-base percentage. The five-time All-Star was a paladin in center field. Said *The National Pastime*: "Each year he would catch about 50 balls that Mays wouldn't get to"— hungry, smart, and fast as a deer.

In 1963, the towhead—ergo, "Whitey"—swapped jockstrap for jockocracy. "Those first few years, I had a lot to learn." By Kalas's arrival, he had.

Born in Tilden, Nebraska, 140 miles from Omaha, Ashburn was twice signed by 18. "The Indians and Cubs gave me deals, but technicalities messed up the contract." He got it right leaving Norfolk Junior College: a $3,500 Phils bonus. Next: the Army, Eastern League, and perpetual National League second-division team.

In 1948, Whitey hit .333, became *TSN* Rookie of the Year, and wowed Ted Williams. "That kid has twin motors in his pants." Nine times Philly's captain led the league in chances and had 500 or more putouts—5-10, 170 pounds, and looking for an edge.

Once Richie kept whining about pitches.

"All right," umpire Jocko Conlan said. "You umpire. I'm letting you call the next pitch."

"You're kidding," he replied.

"Nope, you call the next one." The next pitch was a foot outside. Ashburn said, "Strike."

Conlan signaled, called time, and went out to dust the plate. "I gave you the only chance a hitter ever had in history to bat and umpire at the same time," he said, looking up. "You blew it. That's the last pitch you'll ever call. You're not gonna louse up my profession."

For a long time the Phils kept lousing up their own.

The '49ers finished 16 games behind Brooklyn. Philadelphia had not won a post-1915 flag. In 1950, it led by a game with one left at Ebbets Field. Whitey threw out Cal Abrams in the ninth inning to keep the score 1-all. Dick Sisler's three-run dinger won the pennant. A decade-long free fall then started. Ashburn remained a Merlin, hitting one season ticket holder in the head. She took a stretcher to the hospital. Next day he went to visit. The woman's leg was in traction from the roof of the bed.

"Gee," said the Samaritan, "I knew I got you with that foul ball, but what on earth happened to your leg?"

"Richie, you won't believe this," said Alice Roth, "but as they were carrying me off on the stretcher you hit *another* foul ball that hit me and broke a bone in my knee."

One day a Cub neared the batting cage. "Whitey, you hit a lot of foul balls. My wife, Madge, and I aren't getting along. You know where the wives sit here [at Wrigley Field]. Why don't you take a shot at her your first up?"

Obliging, Ashburn lined toward Madge. Her spouse waved a towel: "Whitey, two rows back and one to the left and you got her."

The Cubs got Richie in 1960. Next year he was plucked by the expansion Mets. "Ashburn brought a . . . curiosity about life and people with him to the ballpark," said Stan Isaacs. "He had style." Radio/TV seemed a next step. Problem: the silken player was burlap-rough. "Boys, this game looks a lot easier from up here," he said. It wasn't.

"You've got so much time to fill," Richie rued. The '64ers helped, though that was not their intent.

Later, as Bull bulldozed, one skipper said, "Nobody makes a *scrapgoat* of Frank Lucchesi," and another, Dallas Green, won a Series—Ashburn and Kalas became, by any norm, the team.

"We were friends immediately," said Harry, "and best friends, eventually." Added Whitey: "We knew how lucky we were not to have a real job." Baseball is routine. A listener soon anticipated theirs like a pet book or favorite film: Ashburn, cap and piped blacksmith's son; Kalas, the piano man— "George Burns," said the *Inquirer,* "to Whitey's Gracie Allen."

Last day, 1992. Phils finish next-to-last. "What are they going to name their highlight film?" said Harry.

Richie: "How about, 'The game's not so easy.'"

Another night. "Harry, you know I did something Babe Ruth never did?"

"What's that, Whitey?"

"Hit a home run in Dodger Stadium."

"Yeah, Whitey, I guess that Babe Ruth wasn't the player he was cracked up to be."

Ashburn knocked pitchers, baited umpires, and bayed, "Oh, brother" and "Bet the house on it"—a fine squash, golf, and gin rummy player, 1974–91 *Bulletin* and *Daily News* columnist, and the *Inquirer*'s "most beloved Philadelphian in the world."

Getting an award, Richie told the City Council: "I always wanted to be an institution before I went into one. The race is pretty close." Tri-Staters loved his barb and view: like Kalas, a pal at the corner bar.

In 1995, 50,000 watched Harry's best friend enter Cooperstown. Two hundred buses drove from Philadelphia. Phillies red dyed the crowd.

"Do I have to treat you any differently now?" said Kalas.

"Yeah, with a little respect."

Jest can prick a funny bone. Truth can break a heart. On September 9, 1997, in a 5:45 A.M. phone call from Phillies trainer Jeff Cooper, Harry learned that "Whitey just died of a heart attack." Stunned, he sat and sobbed.

Three days later the K gave a eulogy. "Never in [Philadelphia] history . . . has there been such an outpouring of love and affection for our beloved departed friend," Harry began, voice cracking. "Why this overwhelming reaction? Because Don Richie Ashburn was Whitey: gentle and easy as a country breeze, down home, biscuits and gravy, Norman Rockwell come to life."

Each night, touching a plaque honoring Whitey, he recalls Ashburn "wonder[ing] aloud on air if the people from Celebre's Pizza were listening." Invariably, pizza reached the booth. Problem: Celebre's was not a sponsor.

A light came on. "I'd like to send out very special birthday wishes," Richie said, "to the Celebre's twins—Plain and Pepperoni."

Seldom had chemistry seemed so pure.

RICHIE ASHBURN

LONGEVITY:	10	35 years.
CONTINUITY:	10	Philadelphia N.L. 1963–97. ABC/NBC TV The Baseball Network 1994–95.
NETWORK:	1	TBN 1994–95 (ABC/NBC TV).
KUDOS:	8	Cooperstown 1995, inducted as player. Philadelphia Baseball Hall of Fame 1997. Number 1 retired by Phillies 1979. Forty-year award 1988. Pennsylvania Sportscaster of the Year 1991.
LANGUAGE:	6	Jocular.
POPULARITY:	10	"In friendship," said Kalas, "he was perhaps the richest of men."
PERSONA:	10	Whitey a.k.a. "His Whiteness."
VOICE:	6	Redolent of the Plains.
KNOWLEDGE:	10	Thinking man's player.
MISCELLANY:	9	To Bill James, "His [center field] stats [were] the best to ever play the game." Phillies' center field concourse named Ashburn's Alley.
TOTAL:	80	(53rd place).

DICK ENBERG

"The country is most barbarously large and final," William Bammer wrote in *The Gay Place*. "It is too much country . . . so wrongly muddled and various that it is difficult to conceive of it as a piece." Dick Enberg has been large, various, and of a piece, including, but eclipsing, the World Series, "Game of the Week,"

Wimbledon, college and pro football, and NCAA basketball. Don Drysdale was Big D. Enberg's cool evokes Mr. C. "Oh, my!," to use his moniker.

As a boy, Dick loved how Detroit's Ty Tyson "used the language." Later he worked as a $1-an-hour janitor at Central Michigan University's radio station, left for hills heavy with farmland and towns shot by Ansel Adams, and got two degrees in health sciences at the University of Indiana.

In 1961, Enberg took his doctorate, left for California State University at Northridge, and began a teaching and coaching job. "I wanted to be the best professor around—that, and never give the same test twice. Sportscasting was just a way to supplement my salary."

Gradually, he became a boxing and Western Hockey League announcer. Soon Dick left seminars and blue books, play-by-play now "in my blood." It is fair to say he never tried to cleanse it.

In 1969, Enberg, 34, added Angels baseball to Rams radio and UCLA TV basketball. His new park lay hard by Disneyland. The San Gabriel Mountains hued the backdrop. Palm trees swayed beyond center field. Arriving, Dick thought it Anaheim's *second* magic kingdom.

"Never in contention," he said, "so you looked for the bizzare." One batter hit between shortstop Jim Fregosi's legs. "That error by the Dago?" mused skipper Harold (Lefty) Phillips. "Water *over* the bridge." In 1970, Alex Johnson won the Halos' sole batting title. Phillips fined (five times), benched (29), and suspended him. A judge called Johnson "emotionally incapacitated." How different, Alex mocked, was the team?

Then, in 1972, California got a Mets pitcher for Fregosi. Through 1975, Nolan Ryan no-hit four teams, including Detroit. "I'm in the booth where I'd visited as a kid," Enberg said of 1973, "and Nolan's on a tear." Norm Cash thrice went hitless. Next up, he ditched his bat. "He had a leg from a clubhouse chair as a substitute. The home plate ump didn't notice" till the first pitch was thrown.

"Get a bat," he said.

"Why?" Cash huffed. "I'm not gonna hit Ryan anyway."

By now, Dick had hit the big time with TV's syndicated "Sports Challenge." Each show, ex-jocks turned panelists. "The people on these programs were idols to me as a kid. Now I'm asking them questions." He produced PBS's "The Way It Was," aired the game show "Battle," and joined NBC in 1975.

Suddenly, the classroom seemed far away.

Gowdy was the Peacocks' then-apotheosis: "Name it, he did it," said Scotty

Connal. Dick ousted him on NCAA hoops, Super Bowl, and 1980s Grand-daddy of Them All, worked "Sports World," and made the analyst look good. "Only he could work with us at the same time," said Al McGuire, "and keep everything sane." Not even Gowdy kept so many balls in the air.

Paradise cost: Enberg divorced his wife, a playwright. "She'd critiqued every broadcast. I'm grateful for her part in my development." Ibid, sched-uling: Dick left the Angels in 1978. In 1982, he did NBC's "Game" and Brewers–Halos L.C.S. "I kept recalling the fifties, when Milwaukee was everything. When things move me, it's clear to viewers." Series play-by-play, with Joe Garagiola, followed. Dick was warm, kind, and open, unlike net-work dominoes.

"No room for me," he mused upon Vin Scully's hiring. "'Game' had enough for two teams a week." In 1985, Enberg refetched Angels video. Even friends asked why. "I gave the most honest answer I can—I love the game. I miss it."

Casey Stengel said of baseball, "Not too hard, not too easy." Dr. Dick

DICK ENBERG

LONGEVITY:	5	13 years.
CONTINUITY:	7	California A.L. 1969–78, 1980, and 1985; NBC TV "Game of the Week" 1982.
NETWORK:	2	"Game," L.C.S., and World Series 1982 (NBC TV).
KUDOS:	10	Four-time California and 1979–81 NSSA Sportscaster of the Year. ASA Sportscaster of the Year 1984, 1986–87, and 1990. Three Halls of Fame, including NSSA 1996. Eclipse Award 1984. Thirteen Emmy Awards, including "The Way It Was" and Life-time Achievement: only broadcaster to win Emmy as sportscaster, writer, and producer. Star, Hollywood Walk of Fame 1998. Ronald Reagan Media Award. Victor Award, as top sportscaster of last 25 years.
LANGUAGE:	10	Poetic.
POPULARITY:	10	Nice-guy manner.
PERSONA:	10	Romantic in unromantic field.
VOICE:	10	Lyric.
KNOWLEDGE:	10	Academic, still teaching.
MISCELLANY:	10	Aired Orange, Rose, and Super Bowl, NCAA basketball, French Open, Wimbledon, Ryder Cup, Masters, PGA, NBA playoff and All-Star Game, Breeder's Cup, 1972, 1988, 1992, and 1996 Olympics. In 1973, first sportscaster to visit People's Republic of China.
TOTAL:	84	(38th place).

struck the balance, never giving the same test twice. Today his wit and schoolboy awe stud CBS TV. Large and various, it lacks the bigs' final piece.

In 2002, Enberg was flying from Buffalo to Los Angeles—"ironically, after football"—when he learned of the Angels' first pennant. Quietly he began to weep. Fearing trouble, a woman in the adjacent seat caressed her Crucifix and held his hand.

Laughing, Dick explained. "I told her why it meant so much—the Angels—after all these years!"

One religion, meet another.

Oh, my!

BOB STARR

1930s Oklahoma. Wind buried farms in a halfmoon of sand. Most of the state crossed Dogpatch and Hades. Bob Starr knew little of economics. Growing up, what he knew was a craving to get out.

One day, a Braves scout invited him and a friend to a tryout in nearby Kansas. Hitchhiking, they spied a sideboard truck with a winch and pulley system. Bob couldn't recall why it seemed familiar. "Little 'en, you get in the front," the driver said. "Big 'en [Bob], in the back."

Boarding, Starr retrieved his youth. "This is a dead animal truck and this horse is expired and his aroma is pungent and little things are crawling on it that don't look too neat." The trip resumes. Bob mounts his suitcase, leans over the edge, and inhales. He fantasizes an autobiography: *Forty Miles on a Dead Horse* or *Dead Horse Scrolls.*

From 1972 to 1997, Starr was too busy with the Cardinals, Angels, and Red Sox to pen a memoir—also, bluff, dry, and unafraid. "What I remember," said Sox partner Joe Castiglione, "is his voice," piercing a listener like the thirties, Oklahoma. More lovable was a gentle William Bendix kind of charm. Bob lumbered into jams even Ripley would disbelieve.

In 1972, he joined the NFL St. Louis Cardinals. "The only football guy I ever saw working without a spotting board," said Jack Buck. "He'd know the name, number, and information. Incredible." As unlikely was the big leagues' wishing upon a Starr.

"I'd never done baseball," he said. "I get here and the Cardinals need a number two." That March, Bob joined Buck and Mike Shannon. Nightly Lou

Brock, Bob Gibson, and Keith Hernandez shone. Bob Costas put Starr above each for "providing baseball's greatest broadcast moment, topping Russ Hodges's call of Bobby Thomson's homer or anything else."

National Dairy Day, 1977: the Swifties host the Cubs. Starr, Buck, and Shannon call the fourth inning. Costas, 25, stands nearby. Bored, Jack hails the Dairy president. He precedes a buxom belle in high heels, bathing suit, and "Miss Cheesecake" sash. Below, Ken Reitz flies to left. The lass gives each Voice a cheesecake. A *Rashomon* moment nears.

Bob says that Buck asked, "Do you like cheesecake?" Starr said, "Yes, very much." Jack: "How do you like *this* cheesecake?" meaning dessert. Bob: "I haven't had any yet, but it looks good enough to eat."

Costas recalls a rawer script. "Hey," Buck asks, "what do you think of Miss Cheesecake?" Starr thinks that Jack said "*this* cheesecake." He replies: "I'll tell ya, I'd like to try a piece of that right here."

In Pittsburgh, the Cardinals crowd the hotel bar. Starr is keeping Napa Valley in the black. At 11 P.M., he leaves, goes to bed, and dreams of morning golf. Nature calls near 2 A.M. Adrift, Bob finds the toilet, leaves, and opens the front door. "Before I knew it, it slams behind me." Starr is standing nude.

At first he considered knocking on doors and asking a samaritan to hail a key. Instead, Bob told a bellhop, "I have a little problem here." The worker found a coat, got a key, and returned the jaybird to his nest.

Starr tells his tale at breakfast. Buck phones KMOX talk host Jack Carney, who bares the naked truth. Bob's wife Brenda is listening. Later, recalling Miss Cheesecake, she kids her husband, "Tell me I didn't hear what I just heard on the air."

Afterward: In 1979, an ABC TV exec, in town for "Monday Night Baseball," spots reporter Nancy Drew next to Brenda. "Who are those good-looking babes," he said, "in the KMOX booth?"

Team publicist Jim Toomey never missed a beat. "You won't believe this, but that's Nancy Drew and Brenda Starr."

A year later Don Drysdale left the Angels for ABC. Replacing him, Starr joined a team pining for Prince Valiant. The Halos had never won a flag. "I loved [owner] Gene [Autry]," said Bob, called *Oklahoma Crude, Crude,* or *O.C.* after his childhood and 1973 film. "I wanted it to be like the movies—white hats win."

California blew a 2–0 game 1982 L.C.S. advantage. In 1986, four days before turning 40, Reggie Jackson's 537th homer passed Mickey Mantle for sixth place all-time. "What a thrill," he said, "being mentioned in the same breath." The Halos often left Starr breathless. That was not their aim.

The '86ers took another division. The playoff, sadly, mimicked 1982's. Boston won its first winner-take-all game with a title at stake since 1912. "You know what the poets say," mused Sox manager John McNamara. "'Hope springs eternal in the human breast.'"

It was a poem, and thought, with which either team could sympathize.

On August 6, 1989, Carl Yastrzemski joined Ted Williams, Joe Cronin, and Bobby Doerr on Fenway Park's right-field facade. Their retired numbers scrawled 9-4-1-8—Boston's last crown for 86 years. Some felt Starr's musical taste as vintage. Said Castiglione: "He'd wear those plaid dotted shirts, loved golf, and thought 'Walking in the Rain' topped the charts."

Rather switch than fight: Bob joined the Olde Towne Team in 1990. "Some Okie I am," he laughed. "Just a bi-coastal guy." In 1993, Starr returned to "a franchise," wrote the *Los Angeles Times,* "that hasn't recovered [from 1986]."

Before long, the chain smoker began to feel chest pain. He took a leave of absence, fought cancer, and died August 3, 1998, at 65, of pulmonary fibrosis.

"Never did get a pennant," Bob mused, riding a dead horse truck far from Oklahoma. Nude, clothed, or eating cheesecake, the "big 'en" was easy to digest.

BOB STARR

LONGEVITY:	9	26 years.
CONTINUITY:	6	St. Louis N.L. 1972–79; California A.L. 1980–89 and 1993–97; Boston A.L. 1990–92.
NETWORK:	1	In effect, the Redbirds' arrangement was.
KUDOS:	3	"He'd just sit there with a flip card roster," said Bob Costas. "The best radio football guy [Cardinals, Rams, and Missouri] I ever heard."
LANGUAGE:	9	Forthright.
POPULARITY:	9	Endearing, unconventional.
PERSONA:	9	Redeemed, *sans* saving, teams.
VOICE:	10	Deep, interior.
KNOWLEDGE:	10	Knew baseball, not The Beatles.
MISCELLANY:	9	"Over four thousand games and no pennants. I must have loved the game."
TOTAL:	75	(77th place).

LON SIMMONS

"You don't get a Yaz at Fenway for their whole career anymore," said Peter Gammons. "Free agency changed things." Vin Scully becomes the Dodgers' MVP—Most Valuable Person. The 2002 Phillies sell out one game—Harry the K's. Jack Buck's funeral befits a captain or a king. "The boys of summer come and go," wrote Jayson Stark. "The voices of summer stay with you for a lifetime."

The Giants hiked west in 1958. Lon Simmons did them until 1973, then in 1976–78, and 1996–2002, jumping to Oakland from 1981 to 1995. His history is largely the Bay Area's history. It began after Simmons got hurt, became a carpenter, and decided that to make the major leagues he needed a different kind of resume.

Tall, blond, and handsome, with a Kirk Douglas jaw, Lon heard a Dempsey–Tunney fight at four, grew up in beautiful downtown Burbank, lettered in baseball, track, and football, and planned to attend USC. Instead, after World War II, he joined the Phillies' system, K'd the side his first inning, and tore a shoulder muscle the next. The injury cashiered the bigs.

Trying construction and carpentry, the ex-pitcher made $1.90 an hour. Hating it, he prayed for rain. "Then I'd feel guilty because my family needed money." The memory segued into radio. "You'd think, 'Why should I stay *here?*' Then I'd think how it had been. It's good to keep in mind from whence you came."

The 1954 champion Giants drew just 1,155,067. "New York was changing. At the Polo Grounds people'd get mugged." Simmons was getting started in Elko, Nevada, Marysville, California, and KMJ Fresno. In 1957, KSFO San Francisco made him sports director. Gigs included the 49ers and Giants—"if we could lure baseball."

On September 20, the Jints lost their Polo Grounds finale. A two-foot-square piece of sod was transplanted west. Also moving: Voice Russ Hodges. "When you're young, everything means more," said Lon, then 33. "You couldn't get closer to my emotions than the Giants' first years."

The '58ers played in steep-rowed 22,900-seat Seals Stadium. "On the street you heard baseball from a dozen directions," said KSFO's Stu Smith. "A restaurant had the radio on. It flooded offices and bars. People at the opera'd wear ear plugs." A holdout muttered, "Good God! People will think we're *Milwaukee!*"—a then-synonym for baseball chic.

Seals opened April 15, 1958: Giants, 8–0. Upon each homer, Lon cried, "Tell it good-bye!" Baghdaders cheered their own. "Unlike Willie Mays, Cepeda [Orlando, a.k.a. Baby Bull], Felipe Alou, and Jim Davenport weren't New York's," said Simmons. Attendance almost doubled to 1,272,625.

Cepeda's swing was quick and wild. Willie McCovey's spun from longer gams than Lauren Hutton's. On July 30, 1959, he reported from Phoenix, hitting .372. Stretch debuted 4-for-4, batted .354, and became Rookie of the Year. The third-placers filled 81 percent of capacity.

"There was an innocence to this bandbox. People loved it," said Lon. Their next home earned more contempt than a Don Drysdale duster.

No park had more pseudonyms: the Stick, Cave of the Winds, North Pole. Few seemed more antithetical toward charm. How did Candlestick Park become baseball's most reviled abode? The old-fashioned way, earning it.

Candlestick opened April 12, 1960, on a point above San Francisco Bay. "Immediately you asked why it was put near water." The park froze at night. Birds dive-bombed the pitcher. Wind blew in from left-center field, then out to right. "The irony is that O'Malley persuaded Horace Stoneham to come here—'a gold rush.' Walter gets Dodger Stadium, and we get a dump."

The trick was looking past. It was easy in 1962. "Here's a liner straight to Richardson!" Lon cried on NBC Radio. "The ball game is over and the World Series is over! Willie McCovey hit it like a bullet. A line drive straight to Bobby Richardson. Had that ball got out of his reach, the Giants would have been the winner! Now, it's the Yankees! . . . The Yankees win it, 1 to 0!"

Stretch's 1986 Hall of Fame plaque lists 521 homers. Juan Marichal '83 high-kicked like Gwen Verdon meets Gower Champion. Mays '79 made Cooperstown. Cepeda's 379 dingers joined him in 1999. "There's one! You can tell that good-bye!" Lon said. "It's way out of here. He just waited on that pitch and mashed it."

Most clubs would "kill for a star," wrote Bob Stevens. "It was hard to keep ours straight." Looking back, you almost forgot the weather.

For a time, Stoneham mimed Nostradamus. Then, in 1968, the A's invaded Oakland. Jints attendance fell. Canaan became Cannery Row. A pen called Simmons dull. Reply: "That's part of my basic charm." Some games become a toss-up. Lon: "This is a throw-up." The scoreboard read: "Happy birthday, Debbie." Lon: "Too bad she left in the third." Another game turned official "as we go into the bottom of the fifth. Boy, I wish I was at the bottom of the fifth." Listeners roared. Stoneham fumed.

"Horace didn't mind if I told the truth early on," Simmons smiled. "Later, he didn't like what he called my getting on the players." Mays, Marichal, and Cepeda retired. Hodges and Lon's wife Ann died. He left, unsure "if I were coming back." Then, in 1976, the Jints were sold to two local businessmen. Rehired, Simmons denoted their ex-blue chip niche.

By 1979, KSFO had built the Giants since Lon's carpentry. Succeeding it, KNBR tapped Lindsey Nelson, who found replacing him uphill. In 1981, Simmons joined the A's, crazies terming him "that Giants SOB." Easier to take: bottom-line marketing. Oakland played "Billy [Martin] Ball." The NFL Raiders became L.A.'s. "We made the Oakland [-Alameda County] Coliseum a baseball place. Whichever team won drew"—e.g., 2,900,217, hailing a 1990 A's flag.

Lon planned to retire in 1987, "thirty years enough in radio." Instead, his investment firm lost $400,000. Widowed again, "He put his energies into broadcasting," said then-partner Wayne Hagin, "because he had nothing else." Mark McGwire and Jose Canseco forged the "Bash Brothers." Dave Stewart won 20 games a fourth straight year. Rickey Henderson's 130 steals set a single-season record: Career No. 939 topped Lou Brock.

"Brock was a great baserunner," said Rickey, "but today I'm the greatest of all time." Lon's Oakland time was ending. "I find that kids screaming, messing around on the bus, bothers me more than it did. I'm not the same"—or was he? Simmons paid a $4,000 team dinner bill. In Baltimore, learning that Hagin had never visited Washington, he brought a limousine to the A's hotel.

"He's exceedingly generous, but in many ways an introvert," said ex-colleague Bill Thompson, "working out crises by himself." The '93–94ers finished last. Next year the Raiders returned, added 22,000 seats, and made a hash of baseball. The farce compounded Lon's sense of wanting to come home.

Simmons recrossed the Bay in 1996. A listener admitted a crush since childhood. Winked Lon: "You must have been terribly deprived." Another told of falling asleep, radio in bed, to his baritone. "That's okay. A lot of people fall asleep listening to me." In 1997, native Jon Miller arrived from Baltimore. Wrote a columnist: "Miller and Simmons in the same booth is like McCovey and Mays."

Once pitcher Robb Nen struggled. "It looks like he's trying to overthrow it," said Simmons. "Which is fine, if you're pitching against a government." The bases were loaded. "And I wish we were, too."

In 1999, Candlestick's last game capped "Tell It Good-Bye Week." The Stick was contrary to the end, voiding a teary eye or twitching jaw. Most were glad to see it go.

Pacific Bell Park opened April 11, 2000, by San Francisco Bay. Next year, Barry Bonds hit homer 60, tying Ruth, ending with a record 73. "As I recall," mused Lon, "it was a little cooler day when [Babe] hit his 60th." The '02ers won the flag. "It's great, but nothing rivals when you're young."

At 80, retiring, Simmons moved to Maui. "I wish you could broadcast baseball," a woman gushed.

"That's what they used to tell me in the broadcast booth, too," he said, in reality not wanting to. "I've found the last several years I prefer going to the ballpark and, say, sitting with McCovey than being on the air."

In 2004, Lon made Cooperstown on a huge Hall website vote. "I don't think I belong," he demurred, feeding peanuts on a Maui porch to the cardinal he named Stan Musial. Knowing better, the Bay helped complete the resume of a gentle, humane, and modest man.

Try telling *that* good-bye.

LON SIMMONS

LONGEVITY:	10	41 years.
CONTINUITY:	10	San Francisco N.L. 1958–73, 1976–1978, and 1996–2002; Oakland A.L. 1981–1995.
NETWORK:	1	World Series 1962 (NBC Radio).
KUDOS:	7	Cooperstown 2004. Pac Bell's radio/TV booth, a.k.a. the Hodges–Simmons Broadcast Center.
LANGUAGE:	10	Light, sharp. Upon a stinker: "Boy, am I glad *that* stretch is over!"
POPULARITY:	10	"He is in [the Hall], at last," wrote the *Mercury News*'s Tim Kawakami, "which means that so are we."
PERSONA:	10	A region's idealized self-image: "San Francisco," wrote Leonard Koppett, "to the core."
VOICE:	10	Bigs equivalent of opera.
KNOWLEDGE:	10	49ers 1957–80 and 1987–88 Voice grasped football, too.
MISCELLANY:	8	Queries so complete that guests said, "That's right, Lon." Phrase became his nickname.
TOTAL:	86	(29th place).

MONTE MOORE

We shun *apologia* in our me-first age. Never look back. Never express regret. I am sorry by what I once wrote of Monte Moore. What made me deem the Voice of the Oakland (nee Kansas City) Athletics radio "Caligula's Horse"? The local media mugged him. Employer Charles O. Finley bought mule Charlie O.: the real jackass was plain. The Oakland Coliseum sunk baseball in the East Bay. I did not distinguish among image, boss, and park.

Monte forged an iron streak (2,801 straight games), did three network Series (more than Lindsey Nelson), and aired the A's from Bobby Del Greco to Mike Gallego. Later NBC and USA TV capped a career unworthy to be flushed down the drain.

Vin Scully recalls pitcher Don Bankhead chiding a Dodgers teammate. "You're not only wrong," he said, "you're loud wrong." Jackie Robinson was not alone.

Moore started in radio at Duncan and Lawton, Oklahoma, Hutchinson, Kansas, University of Kansas, and Kansas City. Finley bought the A's in 1960. Next year, Monte joined flagship KMCO's four-state 20-outlet network. By 1964, the American League told Finley to sign a lease or lose his team. Cruel and cheap, he grasped baseball like a farmer senses rain. Catfish Hunter signed a $75,000 bonus. John (Blue Moon) Odom got $64,000. Sal Bando, Reggie Jackson, and Rick Monday launched the free-agent draft. Charlie was less able to win and woo.

Only the Yankees drew. "What a social occasion," writer Ernie Mehl said of a visit. "People from Mid-America came by car, bus, and train." Inevitably, envy flowed. Q: Why did the Stripes win? A: To Finley, The Stadium's 296-foot right-field line. "Only Charlie would make the tie!" said Moore, or build an identical "Pennant Porch." The bigs mandated 325. Finley complied, then indented it to 296 feet away.

About this time some began calling Charlie the voice behind his Voice.

"Charlie had his ear," said partner Lynn Faris. Another, George Bryson, said: "Hey, the A's *needed* someone to cheer." Moore outlasted 16 play-by-playmen. "I wasn't Finley's mole," sniffed the native Okie. "I *did* understand him. Maybe that's why it worked."

One year, Finley built a children's zoo of China golden pheasant, Charlie O., peafowl, dog named Old Drum, rabbits, and Capuchin monkeys. The

Farmers' Market kept them happy. Tigers pitchers fed the monkeys Vodka-soaked oranges. Finley gave one Nebraskan a tour of the zoo. Said shortstop Bert Campaneris: "They took a wrong turn and wandered on the field as a pitch was being thrown."

Daily, Charlie listened by radio from Indiana. Style was home style: born poor, he felt for umpires. "Finley disliked how they had to carry baseballs," said Moore. Enter Harvey the Mechanical Rabbit, holding a basket, buried behind the plate. On signal the ballboy pushed a button. The hare rose, unloaded stock, and vanished in the ground.

Finley even sired "Little Blowhard," a compressed air jet, to clean the plate. Not everyone knew the brainchild. Once, the air jet hissed; a startled batter fell. The A's, falling too, skipped town in late 1967.

The Midwest stirs more or less a blend, among other things, of duty, propriety, and individualism spiked by plain-speaking. Oakland—"liberal, avant-garde," Monte said—marched to a different tune. The cement Coliseum was built for football. Foul ground reached to San Mateo. A bleacher deck trimmed the outfield. A hill lay beyond. "Given the sterility," read the *Oakland Tribune,* "you focus on the hill, not field."

Moore fixed on coping. "In Kansas City you reported. This was Raiders country. We had to sell." Finley hoped to grow the market. Instead, he and the Jints divided it. On May 8, 1968, 6,298 saw Hunter's perfect game. In 1971, the A's won the A.L. West—and placed seventh in attendance. "Empty seats, though we bloomed through Charlie's talent." It peaked in 1972.

Hunter won 20 games for the second of five straight years. Reliever Rollie Fingers wore a handlebar mustache: "Charlie says, 'No raise, but you get a year's supply of mustache wax.'" The A's fought like most teams played pepper. Unwowed: giant KNBR Radio, orphaning them to college station KEEN. "Our flagship!" said sidekick Jim Woods. Recompense: that fall.

"Tony Taylor moves up to the plate. The count is two balls, two strikes," said Monte in L.C.S. Game Five. "There are two down, there's a runner at first base. Vida [Blue] gets set. . . . There's a drive into center field. Back goes Hendrick. He is under it! The Swinging A's have won the American League championship [2–1, over Detroit]! The Oakland A's are champions!"

Next: Cincinnati. Twice Oakland's Gene Tenace went yard in the Series opener. Next day Joe Rudi robbed Denis Menke of a game-tying dinger. Moore aired NBC TV/Radio. "Curt Gowdy happened to be on [Game Three] when Bench got fooled." Manager Dick Williams pointed to first. Fingers readied a two-out/on pitch. Big John: "I thought they were putting me on" till Rollie kicked, Tenace crouched, and Bench took strike three.

The A's won the title. Williams and Charlie partied by kissing their wives atop the dugout. "Mr. Finley has been wonderful to me," said Dick. Forthwith, the skipper yearned to punch him in the nose.

The film *The Way We Were* lit 1973. The A's aped *One Flew Over the Cuckoo's Nest*. MVP Jackson led the league in homers, RBI, runs, and slugging. Finley finally drew a million—1,000,763. Fewer heard on KEEN. The A's radio network girded Arizona, California, Colorado, Hawaii, Idaho, Nevada, Oregon, Utah, Washington, and Wyoming. "Monte, who cares 'bout *Hawaii?*" jibed a caller. "You're invisible *here!*" On occasion, Moore wished he was. "A lot of newspapermen have criticized me and if they've got a right, I've got a right to criticize them," he said, knocking writer/official scorer Edgar Munzel.

Highlight: He did another Series. Low: Charlie disqualified infielder Mike Andrews, who sued him for libel and slander. Trailing 3 games to 2, Oakland twice beat the Mets. Said Williams, resigning: "Finley's a raving maniac. A man can take only so much."

In 1974, seven A's took to second base. Fingers and Odom clashed: Five stitches closed a cut on Rollie's head. "The record is 15," he said, "held by many." Moore and Vin Scully called the less gripping all-California Classic. In Game Five, the Coliseum crowd began pelting L.A.'s Bill Buckner. Reliever Mike Marshall stopped warming up to watch.

"In a case like this," said Rudi, "you expect the pitcher to throw a fastball." Marshall did. Joe found the seats: A's, 3–2. Monte had now called more 1970s World Series than anyone but Curt Gowdy. The road ahead was about to fork.

"Three straight titles! ['72–74]," Finley hailed the first three-peat since 1949–53's Yankees. "Take that away!" Baseball tried. Hunter became a free agent, claiming unpaid bonus. Campy, Fingers, Jackson, and Rudi left. Suddenly, their unswinging Voice seemed a last link to the Swingin' A's.

"Monte is a homer," read a *Chronicle* letter, "but he tells me what's happening." Another added, "[Want] a solution to California's pollution? Install a catalytic converter in Monte Moore's mouth." Texas scored five first-inning runs. "Throw [it] out," he said, "and we'd have a great ballgame here." In 1976, KNBR re-signed the A's. The concord didn't last.

That November, Moore and 10 players, including three free agents, took a free cruise to Mexico. Returning, he found a Blue Cross bill, for back surgery, that the A's had always paid. "It's nobody's business if Monte's fired," said the boss man. Axe The Loyalist? Had the man, not mule, no shame? "A misunderstanding," he amended. "Monte is the greatest announcer in baseball." It didn't keep KNBR: The '77ers lacked a flagship Opening Day.

Having never missed an A's exhibition, regular-, or post-season game, Monte left, bought a Porterville, California, radio station, and joined USA TV's Thursday "Game of the Week." The series knit the outlands: "like radio in fifties Oklahoma." It ended in 1983, Moore repairing to family, church, and NBC's backup "Game."

From 1989 to 1991, he called *another* three straight A's flags, then retired in 1992, avoiding guilt by association: a year later, Oakland placed last. Today you recall decency, humanity, and The Mustache Gang eclipsing a prairie twang.

MONTE MOORE

LONGEVITY:	9	27 years.
CONTINUITY:	8	Kansas City A.L. 1962–67; Oakland A.L. 1968–77, 1987, and 1989–92; USA TV "Game of the Week" 1978–83; NBC TV "Game of the Week" 1977–78 and 1983.
NETWORK:	6	World Series 1972–74 (NBC TV/Radio). "Game" 1977–78 and 1983 (NBC TV) and 1978–83 (USA TV).
KUDOS:	5	Founder, "Big League Golf-a-Rama" for Porterville youth.
LANGUAGE:	8	Root for the home team: Dick Green's play was "miraculous"; Joe Rudi's .305 average, "phenomenal."
POPULARITY:	9	Keener than KEEN's.
PERSONA:	10	Sane Voice, insane asylum.
VOICE:	9	Chirpy, wearable.
KNOWLEDGE:	10	Approached Finley's.
MISCELLANY:	6	Aired basketball Big 8, West Coast Conference, and pro K.C. Steers.
TOTAL:	80	(54th place).

BILL KING

For Moore, a son of Mayberry, the early 1960s seemed to extend Ike's 1950s. By contrast, the new administration in Washington drew "a picture of total urbanity," said a writer, "the first true reflection in the Presidency of America at the turn of mid-century, a country of city dwellers, long gone from Main Street."

Little in the Kennedy White House ran counter to self-congratulation. Pablo Casals played the cello. JFK had Stravinsky perform. A group of Nobel Prize laureates became "the most extraordinary collection of talent . . . ever gathered together in the White House—with the possible exception of when Thomas Jefferson dined alone."

Much was show. Jackie called Kennedy's favorite song "Hail to the Chief." Three time zones away, Bill King grasped what *Le Figaro* of Paris termed "a certain feeling of possibility." He already felt it.

Near the end of World War II, the high school baseball star left for Guam, where an Armed Forces radio tryout pivoted his life. King nixed a minor-league pact and college scholarship for a 250-watt outlet in Pekin, Illinois. "I had the bug," he said, carrying it via Peoria baseball, Bradley basketball, and Nebraska football to the Bay Area in 1958.

For two years, Bill helped Russ Hodges and Lon Simmons. "The Giants'd just moved and played mostly in the afternoon. I got to exploring other things." He read Russian history, attended opera and ballet, painted and sailed, and bought a 31-foot boat. "Some people in the game get stuck in the game. I never find enough time *outside* it to do what I want."

King tried. "When we met," said friend Nancy Stephens, "he didn't know a thing about classical music. Now he knows more than me." The Young Man and the Sea sailed her to Hawaii, Canada, and down the Coast. The gourmet had peanut butter and onions on warm tortillas. "You see so-and-so is 57 or 32 and create in your mind an image of what a 57- or 32-year-old looks like," said Bill, 32 turning 21.

Ultimately, a generation matured hearing him do its three major sports. Kennedy touted "vigah." Flaunting cool and humor, King made his active the unconventional life.

"Holy Toledo!" (Bill's trademark) He drove a battered car, banned a telephone at home, and hated socks and shoes. Giants mikemen wore a coat and tie in the late 1950s. On hot days, feeling like "I'd showered in my pants," King ditched them for skivvies. G.M. Chub Feeney entered the booth to see him peeling. Said Simmons: "He almost had a heart attack."

Soon Bill grew a handlebar mustache and Van Dyke beard. "A beard in

America of 1976 is not . . . unusual," said the *Examiner*'s Art Spander. "But he was wearing a beard in 1962."

King did the 1962–83 NBA Warriors, 1966–92 Raiders, and University of California. "At his peak," a writer said, "[he could] do play-by-play, wax eloquent about the flow of the game, and decry officiating, all without missing a beat."

George Blanda became "King of the World"; fumble recovery, "a Holly Roller"; Stabler to Casper, "The Ghost to the Post." Hoops was glitzier: "His words burst free," said *TSN,* "like bullets from a machine gun." Baseball, on the other hand, seemed—what—Rockwellian. For 18 years the two boats passed. Then, in 1979, the A's drew 306,763. "We need some jazz," said a honcho, giving King radio/TV. Lon had just crossed the Bay. "Once, doing a TV Warriors game, I told the audience, 'If I were watching, I'd turn off the sound and hear [him] on radio.'"

Bill's first-year A's made the 1981 L.C.S. A year later, King made history: in Milwaukee, spying the beard and mustache, an elderly woman grabbed and proclaimed him the devil. "That's Bill—flair, panache," laughed Jon Miller, growing up near Oakland. Incredibly, recalling KEEN, A's radio became the last word, not last choice.

"By the eighties," said partner Ken Korach, "Bill was the sole guy in America doing basketball, football, and baseball." A newspaper chain named

BILL KING

LONGEVITY:	9	26 years.
CONTINUITY:	8	San Francisco N.L. 1958–59; Oakland A.L. 1981– ; ABC/NBC TV The Baseball Network 1994–95.
NETWORK:	1	TBN 1994–95 (ABC/NBC TV).
KUDOS:	4	Most are non-bigs.
LANGUAGE:	8	Staccato.
POPULARITY:	10	Tops sport.
PERSONA:	10	Renaissance man/own man.
VOICE:	9	High, sharp, a.k.a. "The Golden Voice of Guam."
KNOWLEDGE:	9	Non-baseball more intrigues.
MISCELLANY:	8	"His passionate descriptions," said a columnist, "[were] nothing short of Shakespearean."
TOTAL:	76	(72nd place).

him "[among the area's] 50 most influential sports figures of the century": to Spander, "a renaissance man who can explain a duet by Puccini or a double play by Spiezio."

The A's talk of moving to nearby Santa Clara. "Who cares?" a fan laughed, putting perspective in season. "Even if they leave, we'll still hear Bill King."

MARTY BRENNAMAN

'Twenty-seven means Murderers' Row; 1934, Gas House Gang; 1961, "M for Murder." The 1976 Big Red Machine owned the road. "I don't manage this team," said Sparky Anderson. "It's managed by Rose and Morgan and Bench and Perez." Upon each victory, Marty Brennaman bayed, "This one belongs to the Reds"—actually, to Louisville and Zanesville and Muncie and Marietta.

The seventies Reds won four flags, two World Series, and a timeless moniker. 'Seventy-six was the peak. Five regulars hit over .300. Tony Perez drove in 90 or more runs for the 10th straight year. MVP Joe Morgan had .320, 60 steals, and 111 RBI. Pete Rose led the league in three offensive categories and head-first slides.

Cincy took the West, swept the L.C.S., and crushed the Yankees. Catcher Johnny Bench shaped the Series: .533, six RBI, and MVP. Brennaman covered it for NBC. "Swung on," he said. "High fly ball to left-center! Should do it! There's Foster! And the 1976 world championship belongs to the Cincinnati Reds."

Later Marty called them "an All-Star team"—four Hall of Famers (Anderson, Bench, Morgan, and Perez), one might-be (shortstop Dave Concepcion), and one might-have-been (Rose). At the time, he asked how life could get better. On July 23, 2000, in Cooperstown, it did.

Growing up, Jack Brickhouse loved Bob Elson; Jack Buck, Jack Graney; Marty, Nat Allbright. "In Little League, I wasn't much of a player," he said of Portsmouth, Virginia. "They stuck me in right field on a team called Chubby's, which was a restaurant. We had little TV baseball, so I got stuck on radio," falling asleep to Nat's Brooklyn Dodgers.

Chapel Hill '65 began in High Point, Salisbury, and Norfolk. By 1971, he joined the ABA Virginia Squires and Triple-A Tidewater. In late 1973, Al Michaels left Cincinnati. The Tides sold Brennaman. "Radio was important to us," said Reds assistant G.M. Dick Wagner, "because we had a big [120-plus-station] WLW network and because we didn't have much TV."

Marty knew history: Cincinnati's, not Al's. "Everywhere I hear, 'You got big shoes to fill.'" The buzz grew in Florida. Braving game one—"It went well. Finally people see I can cut the mustard"—Brennaman worked next day at Tampa's Al Lopez Field. "Good afternoon," he began. "From Al Michaels Field . . ." Mustard soaked his face.

"It's March," sidekick Joe Nuxhall said at break, "and I got material for the banquet circuit." Next month Cincy rallied to win a game. Marty used "a phrase that caught on—'This One Belongs To The Reds.'" After a day game in Montreal, Bench invited him to a honky-tonk. "I should have had dinner," said Brennaman, who instead got gassed.

Waking at seven—"incredibly, no hangover"—the Voice taxied to Jarry Park, found Sparky, and began praising No. 5. That Bench! what a guy, showing me the town. "Is that right?" muses Anderson. "Exactly," the rookie says. Sparky finds John, in the training room, with a 102-degree fever.

"I understand you took Marty out last night," said Anderson.

"Yeah," Bench said, "but that doesn't have anything to do with the way I feel."

"I don't care if today goes 25 innings, you're catching every inning," the skipper reddened. Bench hit 389 dingers. One beat the Expos hours after Sparky's fit. "I was so stupid that first year. So many players helped me through," said Brennaman. Advice: Don't tell the manager what you do.

Marty smiled. "Bench has since forgiven me."

"After I got the job," he said, "I was told they liked my voice, enthusiasm, and could keep a consistent bit of chatter." For a time the Reds consistently lost in postseason: 1970 and 1972–73. "People were saying we couldn't take the big one"—till 1975.

Every regular had more than 45 RBI. Jack Billingham, Don Gullett, and Gary Nolan each won 15 games. "We had some bullpen," said Anderson, meeting Boston in the Series. The Reds took a 3–2 game lead. In Game Six, Nolan faced the A.L. MVP. "Fly ball deep into right-center field!" Marty said on NBC Radio. "Griffey is back at the bullpen and it is gone, a home run! Freddie Lynn has hit one out of here to deep right-center field with two men on base!"

By the eighth, Cincy led, 6-3. Shooed to the clubhouse, Brennaman watched Carlton Fisk's blast. "People ask how it felt to see it. Beats me. Ask TV." Next night, his team won its first Series since 1940. The '76ers drew a record 2,629,708. Machine parts left: Perez, to Montreal; Rose, Philly; Morgan, Houston. Sparky was sacked. Successor John McNamara did Marty's WLW "Reds' Line" show: off-season, it turned off-color.

An alleged *Ohio* magazine reporter meets Marty at the studio. The show starts. A caller suggests a trade. As Mac replies, the woman reporter bares her bosom. "Marty, *help,*" he pleads. "Pal," Brennaman roars, "you're on your own."

Later the plotter surfaced: WLW talk host Bob Trumpy, having hired an exotic dancer. The adjective bore little likeness to the '82–83 last-place Reds.

Rose became player/manager in 1984. He batted vs. San Diego on September 11, 1985. "There it is! There it is!" bayed Brennaman. Nuxhall could be heard: "Get up! Get up!" Marty: "Hit number 4,192! A line drive single into left-center field! A clean base hit! And it is pandemonium here at Riverfront Stadium! . . . The kind of outpouring of adulation that I don't think you'll ever see an athlete get any more of." Bottle rockets lit the night. Rose embraced son Pete. "Clear in the sky, I saw my dad, Harry Francis Rose, and Ty Cobb. Ty Cobb was like in the second row. Dad was in the first."

In 1988, Pete was bounced for shoving umpire Dave Pallone. Radios ferried Marty's rage—"Pallone is a horrible umpire"—through Riverfront Stadium. Debris choked the turf. Ordered to New York, Brennaman and Nuxhall met Commissioner Peter Ueberroth and league head A. Bartlett Giamatti. "Here I am, a lowly announcer, blamed for a riot," said Marty, apologizing, "in my case, for some of the inflammatory things I said."

Next spring Ueberroth began an inquiry into things Pete might have done. "We were in St. Petersburg when the story hit," said Brennaman. Rose arrived, raised a hand, and said, "Fellas, can't talk. I've got a [daily 'Rose Report'] radio show to tape."

In the clubhouse, Marty addressed the elephant in the room. "We can't not talk about gambling."

"You have to ask, ask. I'll answer the best I can."

The probe ended in a *nolo contendere* plea: Giamatti, now Commissioner, barring Pete for life. Some sniped good riddance. Many could not forget his 3,562 games, 14,053 ups, and 4,256 hits. *"Frailties?"* Marty said. "Pete was, is, and forever will be an amazing human being." The 1990 defending champion A's were thought a dynasty. Amazingly, Cincy swept the Series.

Pleased, Reds owner Marge Schott was also presumably grateful that stupidity is not a crime. She treated dog Schottzie like a dear aunt or lost child, "coos to her, put her in the team photo," said a player, "lets dogshit stain the field—sick." Later, baseball banned Schott for racial "insensitivity." Increasingly, an ex-Reds cheerleader banned rooting from the booth.

"I once told Jack Billingham, 'We had a great win.' He said, 'What's with *we*? How many hits did you have?'" Stung, Brennaman turned anti-homer. Wagner replied by "auditioning" another announcer—in a game. In 1983, Marty set a mid-August contract extension deadline. Wagner: "I can't be intimidated." Voice: "Me neither." Dick was axed that July. Spared, Brennaman soared.

"All I've got," he mused, "is credibility." Unmoved, a pitcher's wife beefed to Schott, who bashed Marty dining with a "hostile" reporter. Aware of his pull—a *Cincinnati Enquirer* poll asked: "Do you like Brennaman and Nuxhall?" Yes won, 2,442–16—the Virginian sniffed that he would pick his friends.

"Dad's in an envious position," said son Thom. "There aren't many guys with his editorial freedom," nor kids who more sound like dad. Ohio University '86 began at WLWT TV, did the Reds, joined WGN's Cubs, then left for a long preseason. "Arizona began in 1998. I arrived there in '96. Two years to put their broadcast package together"—and join Fox TV baseball and football, Midwest Conference basketball, and Fox Sports Net's "ACC Sunday Night Hoops."

"[Nepotism] gets you in the door," said Thom, "but you don't last if you're not doing your job." His spurned the Marty-speak of papa's idiom. "Frog strangler" meant tense game; "Grand Tour," dinger; "hit of the two-base variety," double; "right-now fashion," pronto. The Reds became "Redlegs"; Mets, "Metropolitans"; and Astros, "Astronomicals." Dad wanted the listener to have fun, never feeling like he had at Al Michaels Field.

In 1997, Marty built an "Elvis Shrine" in the booth. Entering Cooperstown's, he urged the Hall to induct "yes, by God, Peter Edward Rose." In the audience, Bench blanched: "Inappropriate," he said, quitting WLW's "Brennaman and Bench on Baseball Show." By then, Ken Griffey, Jr., son of another seventies Reds star, had been traded to Cincinnati. You recalled Sparky Anderson: "It never occurred to me that we might lose."

The revival failed. One night Marty blistered Jr. for not hustling. Next day Griffey swore at him before the game. "I was here before you were," said Brennaman, "and I'll be here after you're gone." We should not be shocked. Machines like the 1970s Reds drive once, if that. Be grateful for the memory. *That* one belongs to *us*.

MARTY BRENNAMAN

LONGEVITY:	10	31 years.
CONTINUITY:	10	Cincinnati N.L. 1974– ; ABC/NBC TV The Baseball Network 1994–95.
NETWORK:	3	World Series 1975–76 (NBC TV/Radio). TBN 1994–95 (ABC/NBC TV).
KUDOS:	8	Cooperstown 2000. Four- and 12-time Virginia and Ohio Sportscaster of the Year, respectively.
LANGUAGE:	9	Irreverent, idiosyncratic.
POPULARITY:	10	"One of the few people in the organization," said former G.M. Jim Bowden, "who has a great year every year."
PERSONA:	10	Last link to the Machine.
VOICE:	10	Compelling.
KNOWLEDGE:	9	Statistics ladder, not crutch.
MISCELLANY:	7	Did 2003 ESPN Reds–Yanks "Living Legends" game. Like son, hoops junkie: ACC, SEC, Kentucky, 15 NCAA regionals, and 11 Final Fours.
TOTAL:	86	(31st place).

JOE NUXHALL

"Home is the place," Robert Frost wrote, "where when you have go there, they have to take you in." Cleveland took in ex-pitcher Herb Score as a mikeman; Detroit, Harry Heilmann; Milwaukee, Ernie Johnson.

"If they liked you as a player," Johnson said, "they'll give you the benefit of the doubt in the booth." Joe Nuxhall would agree, having pitched for and called the Reds for more than a half-century. Each broadcast cited hearth: "This is the Ol' Lefthander rounding third and heading for home."

Home was named for the Society of the Cincinnati, a group of Revolutionary War officers founded by George Washington. The society honored the Roman patriot Cincinnatus, who returned to farming after serving his city in battle. Born in Hamilton, 26 miles from Cincinnati, Nuxhall at 15 began to serve his.

By 1944, castoffs and rookies ruled major-league baseball. Rosters pulsed 4-F. Most players were at war. On June 10, the bigs' youngest-ever faced St. Louis. "'Holy smoke! I'm in trouble now,' I kept thinking," said Joe: two outs, five walks, a wild pitch, two hits, and five earned runs.

Nuxie re-entered high school, toiled seven years in the bush, and rejoined the Reds in 1952. Solace is where you find it. He went 135–117, won as many as 17 games, and made two All-Star teams. In 1956, Cincinnati crashed a record-tying 221 homers. Joe's luck crashed, too.

"In all," he said, "my baseball career spanned 23 years"—all but one in the Reds system. In 1961, Nuxhall was dealt to Kansas City. Cincy won the pennant.

April 1, 1967. The *Cincinnati Post* scrawls a non-April Fool's screed: "Nuxhall Retires, To Air Reds Tilts [WCKY color]." Next year added play-by-play; 1970, subtracting Crosley Field. Home plate was helicoptered to the Ol' Lefthander's antithesis: Riverfront, cold and trendy; Joe, less hip than Cincinnatus. "He mangles prose, has a rough voice, and little training," wrote *TSN*. Each homer sired "Get up, get up, get *outta* here!"—to the Rhineland, soothing like the Ohio.

In 1974, Marty Brennaman attached to Nuxie like ticks on a hound. "I'd been a big fish in a small Virginia pond. My first year, I shadowed Joe like a shadow." In time, chatter included Marty's tomato plants, Nuxhall's golf hook, and food that showed each as, uh, not exactly a gourmet. "We'll talk for hours," said Brennaman, "God knows about who the hell knows what."

Joe was prim; Marty vaguely naughty. Tying a tape machine and monitor, engineer Mike Markward put Nuxie's straightness to the test. "The Reds lead [the TV game], 4–2, and here's Joe Nuxhall," says Brennaman from San Francisco. Mike pushes a button. The monitor shows the X-rated *Deep Throat*. "Joe panics," laughs Markward. "He fears an electronic glitch—this is being seen in Cincy!"

Later Nuxhall unearthed the hoax. Less puzzling was his product, which could hit, pitch, and lure. Eight straight years of two million attendance. Tom Seaver, tossing Riverfront's first no-hitter by a Red. Six Redlegs, to mime Marty, becoming MVP in the seventies. The next decade needed a less conventional come-on. "Believe in the WWF [World Wrestling Federation]," Joe told his partner. "You're not a good American otherwise."

Crashing the booth in dress and cape, Randy "Macho Man" Savage tore a life-like poster of Hulk Hogan. Marge Schott hit the roof. "So we find something else," mused Nuxie, using a shrug, gesture, or raised eyebrow to commune. "Each knows where the other's going," said Brennaman's wife, Sherri. "They have a special relationship."

Entering Cooperstown, Marty cited "Hamilton Joe," then stopped, unable to speak.

In 1992, Nuxhall beat prostate cancer. In 2001, he had a heart attack, healed, and was named all-time Reds most popular player. "This is better than being in Baseball's Hall of Fame, for Reds fans have honored me." In 1950s Indiana, David Letterman trudged with dad to Crosley. Later, on CBS TV, he recalled a *Sports Illustrated* story.

"After each game," Dave said, "Joe Nuxhall would have a six-pack of Michelob beer and . . . these big quarter-pound sticks of Cracker Barrel cheese." Laughing, Nuxie amended *SI*. "I had three beers, and . . . Dick Wagner jumped on me, because Stroh was then our sponsor!" He confessed liking cheese. "Any kind. The doctor said, 'I can't tell you had a heart attack.'"

Joe could—also, 2003 cancer. That May he and Marty had a Bobble Head Night. Next year, retiring, Nuxie aired sixty games—"one for each I've been with the club. I want to go on, but they want me out. I had to get it [the reason] off my chest."

In October 1990, the champion Reds visited the White House. Then-President George Bush ended his talk with "rounding third and heading for home." The Ol' Lefthander's bronze likeness now guards the entrance to Cincy's new Great American Ballpark. Almost every bystander takes Joe Nuxhall in.

JOE NUXHALL

LONGEVITY:	10	38 years.
CONTINUITY:	10	Cincinnati N.L. 1967–2004.
NETWORK:	1	For many years Reds network baseball's largest.
KUDOS:	6	Reds Hall of Fame 1968. Cincinnati's all-time most popular player 2001. "Rounding third and heading for home" inscribed on new park's exterior. Sixtieth year in organization award 2004.
LANGUAGE:	4	Friendly, homespun.
POPULARITY:	10	"The most beloved man," said Brennaman, "in Cincinnati sports history."
PERSONA:	10	Local boy stayed good.
VOICE:	2	Unschooled.
KNOWLEDGE:	10	Seven decades of watching.
MISCELLANY:	4	Began Joe Nuxhall Character Education Fund.
TOTAL:	67	(95th place).

VINCE LLOYD

William F. Buckley said famously that he would rather be governed by the first 100 people in the Boston telephone directory than by Harvard University's faculty. As a child, I would rather Vince Lloyd list them than hear most Voices do a game.

He engaged his people, had a throaty cloud-nine voice, and defined the Friendly Confines. "I remember trying to tune in Cubs broadcasts from deep in Missouri," wrote Mike Isaacs, then in college. "Once I could hear Vince's voice, I was home."

Born: 1917, South Dakota. Graduated: Yankton College. Early stops: Sioux City, Bloomington, and Peoria. Arrived, WGN Chicago: 1949. Unknown: Why did the 1950 and 1954–86 Cubs announcer bloom eight miles from Wrigley Field?

"Luck of the draw," said the 1957–64 White Sox broadcaster. "Wasn't that much success on Chicago's North Side." On the South, '59's Hose won a pennant. The '60ers drew a franchise record 1,644,460. A photo of John F. Kennedy and aide David Powers at the 1961 Sox opener shows them reading *The Sporting News.* On WGN TV's "Leadoff Man," JFK became the first U.S. president interviewed on television at a baseball game.

Lloyd: "Mr. President, have you had an opportunity to do any warming up for this, sir?"

Kennedy: "Well, we've just been getting ready here today."

Lloyd: "Throwing nothing but strikes? Very good."

President: "I feel it important that we get, ah, not be a nation of just spectators, even though that's what we are today, but also a nation of participants —particularly to make it possible for young men and women to participate actively in physical effort."

Leaving, Lloyd asked about Mrs. Kennedy. JFK smiled and said, "Well, it's Monday. She's home doing the wash."

One day Roger Maris agrees to "Leadoff Man." Taking the air, Vince finds him MIA. "I need a guest," he tells Whitey Ford, who grabs Yogi Berra, who nabs Mickey Mantle. Lloyd gapes: "I've got three great names." Suddenly, Maris makes it four. "I just got a call from my wife in Kansas City. She gave birth to a son!" The post-game show was sponsored by Hair Arranger conditioner. Vince gave a bottle to guest Jim Rivera. The outfielder said, "Gee, thanks a lot," thinking it shaving lotion. "I use this very time I shave my face."

Often the Cubs wanted to cut their throat: Ernie Banks, an exception. Mr. Cub hit a record five slams one year, whaled 48 homers in another, and became two-time MVP. Once, hit by a fastball, he left on a stretcher.

"Ernie, how can you be so dumb as to get hit in the nose?" teammate Hank Sauer jibed.

"If that ball hits *you* in the nose," said Banks, "it carries for a homer."

Lloyd telecast the 1954–64 Wrigleys. In March 1965, their radio Voice was killed when his car skidded nearly 200 feet into a truck. Jack Quinlan had played baseball, spurned a Dodgers contract, and graduated from Notre Dame. Three years later he made Chicago via Tuscola and Peoria. "Twenty-eight," Jack said in 1955, "and I'm with the Cubs." In 1960, he did NBC Radio's World Series.

"He had the big sound which brought the station greatness," said WGN sports editor Jack Rosenberg. "His voice possessed the firmness of a heavy handshake. The resonance of a finely tuned harp. The clarity of a starry night. The quality of a prayer." Jack Brickhouse likened his death to losing a younger brother.

"[Cubs analyst] Lou Boudreau was my best friend," said Vince. "He said he'd quit if I didn't take Quinlan's job." Lloyd succeeded, if not replaced, him. Lip helped: new skipper Leo Durocher. In July 1967, the Cubs took first that late in the year for the first time since 1946. More typical: blowing August 1969's 9 1/2-game lead.

Anybody can have a bad century, Lloyd said. He didn't know that the 1970s would be worse.

By 1975, the Cubs had been lousy since Harry Truman's first full year as president. Pittsburgh won a game, 22–0. Next year, the Mets' Dave Kingman hit the third frame house on the east side of Kenmore Avenue. "A little higher," said Lloyd, "and the ball goes through a window and smashes a TV set [tuned aptly to Wrigley Field]."

When a Cub went deep, Vince rang a cowbell and yelped, "Holy Mackerel!" Said Isaacs: "It felt like a pennant-winning shot the way he called it, rather than the last hurrah of a team going nowhere." The '73–83ers only once made .500. The optimist sees half a glass of water and says, "It's half-full."

The pessimist says, "It's half-empty."

The Cubs fan says, "When's it going to spill?"

1983: The booth crams Boudreau, Harry Caray, Milo Hamilton, Steve Stone, and Lloyd. "Too many!" said Vince, trading play-by-play for "Leadoff Man," postgame radio, and back-room deal.

"[50,000-watt] WGN is so strong, we used to figure, 'Hey, anyone who wants to hear the Cubs can there.'" Differing, their new owner, The Tribune Company, had Lloyd build a 60-outlet radio network in Illinois, Iowa, Wisconsin, Michigan, and Indiana.

"The first year away from play-by-play was hardest," he said, "sort of a phased withdrawal." In 1986, the last phase began: Vince retired to South Dakota, dying in 2003 of stomach cancer.

"I was lucky to do both Chicago teams." We were, hearing him.

VINCE LLOYD

LONGEVITY:	10	34 years.
CONTINUITY:	10	Chicago N.L. 1950 and 1954–86; Chicago A.L. 1957–64.
NETWORK:	1	Berthed pre-SuperStation WGN.
KUDOS:	5	First Voice to interview U.S. president at baseball game.
LANGUAGE:	8	Earthy.
POPULARITY:	10	Appreciated more by fans than front office.
PERSONA:	10	Holy Mackerel! Cubs' silver lining in tarnished years.
VOICE:	10	Roughhewn.
KNOWLEDGE:	9	No showboat.
MISCELLANY:	8	A.k.a. "The Voice For All Seasons." Long-time Voice of Big Ten football. Born Vince Lloyd Skaff.
TOTAL:	81	(49th place).

ERNIE JOHNSON

Free local-team TV was baseball's once-foundation. Pay-cable mostly seemed a distant possibility. For a fee, the customer could bloat their programming menu. "The problem," said Mel Allen, "was that cable systems only existed in some places, not others." Satellite could link them. Ted Turner pined to please—thus, grow.

In 1976, Turner bought the Braves, upped their TV schedule, and decided to rename WTCG Atlanta SuperStation WTBS. "The Braves'll tie the sticks to the big-time," he said, sagely. It was an offer that even Don Vito Corleone could not refuse.

Eventually, cable bulged baseball's stage. In turn, baseball swelled cable's audience. The pivot was 1982. "'TBS was just one offering," said Ted. "People weren't aware how it could sell the Braves a world from Georgia." Atlanta won a bigs record first 13 games: suddenly, people were.

The streak, one said, was "the 'two-by-four' that hit America between the eyes." A Storm Lake, Iowa, sign read "The Atlanta Braves: Iowa's Team." In Valdez, Alaska, a Braves Fan Club chapter pooled cash, bought a screen, and renamed its bar "The Braves Lounge." In a decade, WTBS households leapt 7,000 percent.

"The greatest thing to happen [to baseball] since Bat Day," the *Philadelphia Inquirer* called cable. Harry Caray, Skip Caray, and Tim McCarver became its billboard. A soft-spoken Vermonter became its first star.

"He isn't a controversial broadcaster because he isn't a controversial person," a columnist said of Ernie Johnson. "Easy-going and folksy, his manner is such that the listener can sense he's that way off the air as on." The son of Swedes who met in America, he signed with N.L. Boston, pitched in the Eastern League, entered the Marines, and served in Okinawa. By 1945, returning to Brattleboro, Ernie, 21, asked a former cheerleader at his old high school for a date.

"What do you do?" Lois Denhard asked him.

"I play baseball."

"I know, but what do you do for a *living*?" They married on November 15, 1947.

In 1950, his living made the bigs. Annual Boston City Series: Ernie curves The Kid. "Great decision. In seconds it's rolling to the Hotel Kenmore." Skipper Billy Southworth consoled the rookie. "Don't worry. He's hit them off better pitchers than you."

In 1952, veteran Vern Bickford faced Ted in Bradenton. Williams made out his first up. "Ted's up this inning," Vern later said. "Let's see how far that big donkey can hit one."

"What you gonna do?" said Johnson.

Vern: "Lay it in there 3/4 speed and see what happens."

Knowledge can spawn strain. "In batting practice," said Ernie, "if a guy sees a lollypop he'll get antsy and screw up." Ted hit the right-center field light tower.

"We're roaring as the inning ends. Bickford comes back, shakes his head, and says, 'I got my answer.'"

The 1952 Braves hit .233. In 1953, they hit the road. "I'd pitched in Milwaukee with the [1949 and 1951 Triple-A] Brewers," Johnson said. "A small town. Fans wouldn't let a Brave pay for gas or milk." Daily he drove to County Stadium past the Allen Brady Tower Clock, hovering like a sun. The 1957–58 first-placers shot the moon.

Warren Spahn won more games than any other lefty (363), all but seven for the Braves. Once he threw to first base, picking off the runner, umpire, and fielder. "We'd kid his big nose. 'When you move your head, your nose hypnotizes the runner.'" Spahn, said Ernie, once picked a runner off—and the batter swung.

In 1958–59, the Braves and Orioles, respectively, axed the career 40–23 starter/reliever. "Here's how bad I'd become. Del Crandall said to forget a spitter because 'It's so slow it's dry by the time it hits the plate.'" The Tribe invited him to 1960 spring training. A warmup catcher was 18 years old. "Don't worry, dad. Throw anything you want; I'll figure it out on the way down."

Retiring, dad hosted a Milwaukee TV talk show. In 1962, he became Braves' WTMJ TV analyst and post-game host. "The Senators with Cox beat the Yankees," Ernie began one program. He never so wanted a power failure. "People thought it hilarious that it would happen to this happy married, religious sort of guy."

In 1963–64, Johnson added Braves publicity. Next year he aired 17 and 53 games, respectively, on Atlanta WSB TV/radio—"a tease for 1966 when the Braves'd move." That fall, after 13 years—so few, they seem almost spectral—the team left for a region still asking a recount of Gettysburg.

"You think of thin air, the park's nickname [Launching Pad], Henry Aaron," mused Georgian Ernie Harwell of Atlanta. Unlike Babe Ruth, the more-marathoner-than-sprinter never hit 50 dingers in a season. The Hammer did nail 30 and 40, respectively, 15 and eight years.

1971: number 600. "Perry delivers to him. A fly ball, left field! Back goes Henderson! It is gone!" said Johnson.

July 21, 1973: "A huge turnout in the left-field seats bringing nets hoping to catch a home run! . . . Drive—deep left field! . . . This ball is gone! Seven hundred for Hank Aaron—only the second player in this great game ever to do it!"

Next year, Hank's first swing attained the unattainable. "Billingham pitches. Swung on! Drive—deep left field! Back goes Rose! He's at the track! This ball is going—and it is gone! 714! . . . Over 50,000 on their feet! And the whole team coming to home plate!"

Ernie aired each on radio, Hank whacking "in the third or seventh—my only non-TV time. Marconi'd have loved him"—if not his club. Seven times the seventies' Atlanta placed last or next-to-last, reminding the ex-pitcher of a yarn. The first baseman whiffs in the first. A blowhard behind the dugout starts yelling. He fans in the fifth. "You can't hit," says the man. "Go back to the minors!"

Again K-ing, the hitter scales the dugout. "Just listen," he tells the man. "As a boy I treated a jackass we had on the farm horribly. My dad'd tell me, 'Don't whip that jackass so bad. The way you're hitting him, someday his spirit'll come back to haunt ya.' I never believed my daddy until today."

In 1976, Ernie replaced lead announcer Milo Hamilton, invoking "pops that bring rain," skippers "opening a can of pitchers," or "give that one a blue star"—a paladin of a play. Skip Caray became No. 2. "Here with the play-by-play, the Voice of the Braves, Ernie Johnson." During break, Ernie said, "If you don't mind, we're all the Voice of the Braves." Decent and deep-going, he sketched the South's courtesies and codes.

'Eighty-two rewarded them. Atlanta won the N.L. West, next year wiling a record 2,119,935. A letter to *TSN* thanked cable "for getting baseball *back* in the hearts of rural America." Unchanged: the 1977, 1983, and 1986 Georgia Sportscaster of the Year, even as, retiring, he enjoyed Ernie Johnson Night.

"We'd gotten awful," said Caray. "Last place, less than a million. Then this"—42,020, 1989's largest crowd, from Savannah and Swanee and Siler City. Son Ernie Jr. joined TNT. Johnson *pere* returned to launch Fox's SportsSouth (Sports Net South). "People tell me, 'I thought you'd retired!'" dad laughed. "'What are you going to do? Give back all your gifts?'"

October invoked 1957–58: The nineties Braves made five World Series. Only 1995's unfurled a title flag. Ernie's Crabapple, Georgia, home flew the Marine Corps's—"Next to family, there's nothing I'm prouder of"—from a pole in the front yard.

In 1999, Johnson, 75, retired for good, his voice still falling lightly on the ear. Dixie's *paterfamilias* would grandfather the entire region if he could.

ERNIE JOHNSON

LONGEVITY:	10	35 years.
CONTINUITY:	10	Milwaukee N.L. 1962–65; Atlanta N.L. 1966–91 and 1995–99.
NETWORK:	5	In sense, each WTBS SuperStation game national.
KUDOS:	6	Three-time Emmy Award and Georgia Sportscaster of the Year. Braves Hall of Fame 2001.
LANGUAGE:	8	Casual.
POPULARITY:	10	Mr. Brave, succeeding Aaron.
PERSONA:	10	Face and voice of America's Team.
VOICE:	8	Soft, receding.
KNOWLEDGE:	10	Even as pitcher, mastered craft.
MISCELLANY:	6	Did sole Series on 1992 Braves Radio. "Skip Caray had me call three innings. Nothing like completing the resume."
TOTAL:	83	(43rd place).

NED MARTIN

Fred Hoey taught New England baseball. Jim Britt played English like a harp. Ken Coleman was born 15 minutes from Fenway Park. Curt Gowdy became a network flagship. More than any Red Sox Voice, why was Ned Martin beloved?

My view is personal, not parochial. Much of Red Sox Nation, I suspect, would cheer Martin's choice. In 1961, he arrived at Fenway. Fired in 1992, Ned left a pre-2002 death void.

Quoting Hamlet, he mourned, "When sorrows come they come not [as] single spies, but in battalions." Critics felt Martin goof-prone. Wiser, the Nation prized him in a way too deep for applause.

"Mercy!" Ned would say. His quality, seldom strained, still droppeth from memory today.

Raised 18 miles from Center City, Martin was fated *not* to be in Philadelphia. He entered Duke University, joined the Marines, and stormed Iwo Jima. "I'm not one of the guys that you see raising the flag." Courageous under pressure, Ned grew up fast. Later he spurned talk of heroism—or war.

"It is always that way with the guys who saw the real bitter action," said writer Clark Booth. "He never bragged, needed praise, and hated shtick and self-promotion." Martin returned to Duke, a not-so-young man in a hurry, to major in English, read Wolfe and Hemingway, and—what? For a while he didn't know.

In 1950, Ned worked on the Pennsylvania Turnpike, "hearing the Series as the Whiz Kids lost." Next: advertising and publishing—"fabulously unsuccessful" —before recalling college radio. "I'd worked at the station, where Bob Wolff critiqued my tapes and became my hero," then helped his friend crack Rockville, Maryland's country music—"then 'hillbilluh'"—WINX.

Martin began play-by-play in Athens, Georgia, moving to Triple-A Charleston in 1956. The next five years were harder than Iwo Jima's ash and stone. "I kept bothering people, sending tapes to big-league teams." In 1960, Sox Voice Bill Crowley decided to head publicity. That summer, Boston visited the Potomac. Ned fled Charleston to call an inning and a half.

"We didn't call it an audition," said Curt Gowdy, "but it was." Next January, Martin visited New England's bandbox bijou.

"The only time I'd even *seen* Fenway was film of the 1948 playoff." Ned left the Kenmore Hotel, crossed railroad tracks, and saw "what looked from the outside like a brickyard, not at all like a park."

Opening Day blared two rookies: Martin and Carl Yastrzemski. Yaz hoped to replace Ted Williams: Ned, cleanse the Katzenjammer Kids. First baseman Dick Stuart got a standing O for picking up a wrapper. Some said shortstop Don Buddin's license plate should read "E-6." Others felt he had no license to *play*.

In 1962, the team bus stopped in mid-Manhattan. Gene Conley and Pumpsie Green got off, asked a restroom, and vanished. Three days later Gene tried to buy a plane ticket to Israel. "If you can't find the promised land here," said Ned, "go abroad."

Through 1966 Boston placed as low as ninth, but made history come alive. "I got one good fastball," Tracy Stallard told Ned October 1, 1961. "I don't want to walk him, and I'll throw him the fastball. More power to him if he hits it." Roger Maris did—No. 61.

In 1953, Martin saw a childhood hero perform in Washington. "That hesitation pitch was still getting people out." Satchel Paige last pitched in 1965: one hit in three innings vs. Boston. Later they retrieved the past at a dinner. "'If you think I'm gonna throw any place but the letters, shame on ya!' he'd tell the hitters."

Edwin Martin, Jr.'s shame was the Phils: loving, he despaired of, them. In September 1964, they led the N.L. by 6 1/2 games. Ned visited dad before the

Red Sox' last trip. "He'd had two heart attacks, but I said good-bye": in Detroit, learning of pop's death. Returning home, the son found a letter from the crypt.

"Baseball had been our bond. When I last saw him, dad predicted the Phillies' collapse [losing 10 straight games] that had now come to pass. He then wrote this letter: 'I don't see how they can win the pennant. They pitch Short and Bunning on panic and no one else. I'm afraid they're going to crash.'"

Distraught, Ned rejoined a team which already had. Baseball, Mike Barnicle wrote, is not a matter of life and death in Boston. The Red Sox, he added, *were*.

"Maybe '67," Martin laughed, "was God's way of making up for years before." One August Sunday augured Oz-in-the-making. Boston led, 4–3: ninth inning, one out. "Berry, a fast [Chicago] man at third," Ned said on WHDH Radio. "Wyatt looks at him and throws. And there's a little looper to right field. Tartabull coming on, has a weak arm. Here comes the throw to the plate. It is—out at home! He is out! Tartabull has thrown the runner out at the plate, and the ball game is over!" Before 1967, Jose would not have got Aunt Maude.

It ended vs. Minnesota. Yaz batted in the penultimate game: Sox, 3–2, two on. "Deep toward right field! This may be gone! It's outta here! Home run!" Next day, "Lonborg is within one out of his biggest victory ever, his twenty-second of the year, and his first over the Twins. The pitch is looped toward shortstop. Petrocelli's back, he's got it! The Red Sox win [the flag, 5–3]! And there's pandemonium on the field! Listen!" As the last out settled in Rico Petrocelli's glove, students and working men and housewives on the field became a wave, hundreds of bodies rocking, collectively and ecstatically.

Success didn't last. Interest did. "The garrison finish revived the franchise," said the man who read poetry like Alan Ginsberg's, had politics like John Wayne's, and loved Richard Nixon. Milhous thrice lost Massachusetts: it revered Ned, anyway. One moment he called the Splinter "Big Guy." The next evoked the Bard: "Good night, sweet prince. May flights of angels sing thee to thy rest."

Martin closed bars, haunted book shops, and treated Fenway's workforce like royalty. "The complete package," Booth said, included disdain for radio jack, sham, and fools.

Mercy! The '71ers lost a doubleheader. Ned heard traveling secretary Jack Rogers say, "Be on the bus in 40 minutes." He blurted, "Bullshit," unaware of an open mike. "It was outrageous to happen then," said Martin, nearly fired. "Now it'd be a nursery rhyme." One memo knocked him for working *sans* necktie—in 100-degree heat. Another told Coleman to bar Ned if "not attired in accordance with company rules." Martin threatened to wear a tux. "Given how many clowns he offended," Booth wrote, "it's a wonder he lasted 30 years."

In 1971, Coleman dealt wireless for TV. Martin become *radio's* big guy. Partner Jim Woods arrived in 1974. Next July, Boston led second-place New York, 1–0, at Shea. "Drive to left-center field. May be a gapper! Lynn is running, Lynn is going! He's got it in a great catch! Oh, mercy, what a catch by Lynn! Red Sox fans are going ape out here! This is World Series time!" Ned crashed the bigs at 37. In October 1975, age 51, he made a Classic. "Next year, the new Series TV contract banned local guys. I snuck under the wire."

A horde wired NBC Radio/TV: Ned, Marty Brennaman, Sox video's Dick Stockton, and Joe Garagiola, Tony Kubek, and Gowdy. Martin likened Curt, Tony, and himself to "Winkin', Blinkin', and Nod." Game Six still blinks: 12th inning, 6-all, Carlton Fisk up. "The one-oh delivery . . . ," Ned said on radio. "He swings. Long drive, left field!" Memory freezes Fisk employing hand signs and body English to push or force or pray the ball fair. "Home run! The Red Sox win! And the Series is tied, three games apiece!" The Fens were alive with music. The Towne Team lived.

The Sox, being the Sox, lost Game Seven, 4–3. Fisk's blast was their, and Martin's, peak—"arguably the greatest [pre-2004] moment in franchise history." Game Six became "a keeper," and Ned, comer: to Jack Craig, "a quality announcer of pure gold." He and Ernie Harwell did CBS Radio's 1976–78 A.L. playoffs. To know him, though, meant returning to Fenway Park.

Who else could weld Rousseau, Reggie Smith, and Dizzy Gillespie and Dean? Radio's twits and toads did not know what they had. In late 1975, Boston signed a record $450,000 pact. Next year, flagship WITS (then WMEX) launched a spree of pre-Home Shopping Network *in*-inning ads. "More and more," said Ned, "we were told to shill and schmooze VIPs." The Nation was unaware. *Its* worry eyed the field.

In July 1978, the Townies led New York by 14 games. Ahead: "the apocalyptic Red Sox collapse," wrote Dan Shaughnessy, "against which all others must be measured. A four-game set—"The Boston Massacre"—began Thursday, September 7. The race was tied by Sunday: Yanks, 15–3, 13–2, 7–0, and 7–4. Boston fell 3 1/2 games behind, then turned. October 2 broke crisp and light—the first A.L. playoff since 1948. WITS had already dropped the shoe. "Fans didn't know," said Martin, "but this was Jim's and my last Sox game."

Dorian Gray led off inning two. "Long drive, right field, this may be out of here! It is . . . a fair ball, [Yaz] home run. Red Sox lead, 1–0!" Later they scored again. The Stripes then began turning screws. Lou Piniella caught Lynn's twisting drive (otherwise, 4–0). Bucky Dent fouled Mike Torrez's seventh-inning two-on/out pitch off his foot. Turn: Mickey Rivers ditched the broken bat for another. Reggie Jackson's earlier drive to left had dropped off a shelf. The wind now blew *out*. Dent swung. "I saw Yaz looking up," said Fisk, "and I said, 'Oh, God.'"

Each team scored twice: Yanks, 5–4. In the ninth, the final turn of "the Red Sox–Yankee competition," wrote Peter Gammons, "reached a peak of intensity rare even in that legendary rivalry." Blinded, Piniella snagged Jerry Remy's one out/on bounce liner to stem a flag-waving inside-the-park homer. Two men roosted. Jim Rice flied out. Yaz tried on his final chance for a World Series ring.

"A high popup to the left side!" said Martin. "In fair ground is Graig Nettles! In foul ground is Nettles! And the Yankees win the pennant!" Battalions of sorrow still shroud the yard.

"Martin's firing created such an uproar," Craig wrote, "that the fellow who fired him [WITS' Joe Scallon] was soon gone as well." Ned replaced TV's Stockton. "Dick was going to CBS, so why not try it?" Said Coleman: "He could paint a word-picture, frowned upon on television. TV's glitzy, not his kind of crowd."

In 1986, only NBC's local ban kept Ned from adding Bill Buckner to Game Six. Later he left free TV for cable's New England Sports Network. "The Sox bounced him around," said Booth, "making him feel indebted to have" a job. Errant, some began to muse. The Nation shrugged; we forgive those we love. In 1992, Ned got a week's notice, put Thoreau in a duffel bag, and retired to an old farmhouse in southwest Virginia. He showed a visitor family photos, Civil War cartoons, and a mass of books—the Squire, at peace and home.

In 2002, Martin entered the Red Sox Hall of Fame. The room shook on his introduction. "Until then," said Joe Castiglione, "he never knew what he meant." No. 9 died that July. Ned went to Boston for a service. "He'd had a bad back and knee and hip replacement, but wouldn't miss it," said son Roley. "He loved the videos, and Field of Dreams song, and taps."

Next morning Martin, 78, flew to Raleigh-Durham Airport, caught a shuttle bus, and had a heart attack. "Those who always feel the 'good old days' were better than the present," wrote the *Globe*'s Bill Griffith, "might . . . this time . . . be right." Daughter Caroline defined dad's mercy: "His love was his family [wife Barbara, of 51 years, three children, and nine grandchildren] . . . the country, his dogs, and cat Emily."

After all, Ned Martin was the cat's meow.

NED MARTIN

LONGEVITY:	10	32 years.
CONTINUITY:	10	Boston A.L. 1961–92.
NETWORK:	4	World Series 1975 (NBC TV/Radio). L.C.S. 1976–78 and 1981 (CBS Radio).
KUDOS:	6	Red Sox Hall of Fame 2002.
LANGUAGE:	10	Reflected "a subtle, controlled, and educated man," said MSNBC TV's Keith Olbermann, "from Duke to Iwo Jima."
POPULARITY:	10	The equivalent of 1967's.
PERSONA:	10	New England's.
VOICE:	10	Lucid.
KNOWLEDGE:	10	Got life, and game.
MISCELLANY:	9	Broadcast Fran Tarkenton's minor-league no-hitter, Yale, Dartmouth, Harvard, and Patriots football, and more bigs batting titles than anyone (12).
TOTAL:	89	(21st place).

JIM WOODS

A 1960s Avis ad yapped, "We're Number Two. We try harder." Jim Woods was 1953–78 Number Two to Mel Allen, Red Barber, Russ Hodges, Bob Prince, Jack Buck, Monte Moore, and Martin. Being top gun elsewhere seldom crossed his mind. "Jim didn't want the paperwork," laughed Ned. Not trying harder, "He wanted to have fun."

In 1956, Enos Slaughter, seeing Woods's buzz cut, gibed, "I've seen better heads on a possum." Betty Prince called Jim's wife "Mrs. Possum." Was Poss and Prince baseball's deuce—or was it Woods and Martin? Did any trio match Jim, Mel, and Red? "It's no coincidence," said Allen. The common tie was Woods.

Jim was a Kansas City Blues batboy, University of Missouri journalism major, and freshman dropout. "Dad hated me leaving," he said. "I said, 'You won't when I get to Yankee Stadium.'" Woods joined KGLO Mason City, *The Music Man*'s "River City." Robert Preston sang, "Ya gotta know the territory." In 1937, Ronald Reagan swapped his, Big Ten football, for Hollywood.

"Nothing like succeeding a prez!" crowed Poss. The Gipper's voice soothed, like a compress. Woods's slapped you in the face. "Gravelly, whiskeyed," marveled Ned, "leaping through the radio." Mel called him "the best-ever sidekick, superior to most Number Ones." Shunned by Coopers-town, Possum's void appalls.

In 1948, Ernie Harwell left Triple-A Atlanta for Brooklyn. Poss replaced him from WTAD Quincy, Illinois. Next season, the Crackers became the first team to telecast its entire schedule. In 1953, a voice even surpassing Woods's called Georgia. "Mel asks me to New York, I walk into his suite, and he's on the phone talking to Joe DiMaggio about Marilyn Monroe." Poss knew he was in the big leagues then.

That fall, Red fled Flatbush for The Stadium. "Add Jim," he said, "and it may have been baseball's greatest threesome." Woods respected, but feared, The Voice. "One day I described Mickey Mantle foul a ball on top. Mel had a habit of snapping his fingers if I did something wrong. 'What'd I do?' He said, 'On top of what?' I said, 'The roof.' 'Then say the roof and complete your sentence.'"

The rook's Yanks won a fifth straight Series. In August 1956, they released Phil Rizzuto, who began angling for a job. One day, Poss found G.M. George Weiss staring at the floor. "'Jim, I have to do something I've never done— fire someone without a reason.'" Ballantine Beer had ordered Phil's hiring. Stunned—"it's a funny business. Things happen"—Woods, 39, joined the Giants' Russ Hodges.

In 1958, Hodges left for San Francisco, where new sidekick Lon Sim-mons knew the territory. Jim moved to Pittsburgh—his third team in as many years. "It's like I needed a home," he said, "and here it was." Through 1969, Poss and Prince seared sameness like a laser cuts dead cells.

"Everyone said, 'Prince is out of control, you'll never get along,'" Woods mused. Instead, they gilded KDKA Radio with a pencil and scorecard. "That was it," said the Gunner. "We'd do play-by-play—or tap dance if the game stunk." Jim then turned off his mike. "Enough a' that! Booze!" A drizzly Friday, Ken Coleman arrived in Pittsburgh for "Game of the Week." Prince said: "'Poss, I wish they'd call the game so I could get home and watch that John Wayne Western.' So different from anything I'd heard."

Spying a lass, Bob howled, "Check that one out in black!" You're on the air, Woods said. "Geez," Prince replied, "when I think what I *coulda* said!" Once Poss evoked Bob's famed dive from a third-floor window. "How'd your act check out here?" Prince: "One way to find out," knifing from the ledge.

In 1960, Pittsburgh won its first World Series since 1925. Even a Yankees fan recalls its leaves and hues and spooked-up days. Woods recalls KDKA buying sixties rights from Atlantic-Richfield Company. "They began to hem us in, said we wandered." By late 1969, he demanded a pay hike: owner Westinghouse refused.

"I'd never got enough money. So when an offer for more came, I jumped." Landing in St. Louis, Poss soon regretted it.

"Great baseball city, my ass," he laughed without mirth. "The front office, Buck's ego, how you were afraid to smile." Woods couldn't wait to beat a 1972 path to Oakland. "Monte Moore liked to stay at home, didn't gamble: me, where's the track?" The A's took that fall's L.C.S. "[Detroit's] Fryman is set," Jim said in the clincher. "Here's the pitch to Tenace. Line drive into left field—this may be tough to score on. The ball is dropped—ball is dropped by Freehan. And Oakland moves into the lead, 2 to 1, on Gene Tenace's first hit of the playoff."

Poss's A's won two Series. In November 1973, Charles O. Finley told Woods that he liked homers more than him. "I was loyal to the man, never criticized him, but Finley loved the Midwest style where you scream at a foul ball," he said. "'Jim, you're a great announcer when something happens, but when nothing is going on you're not.'"

Weiss, St. Louis, Finley: Woods pined for Pittsburgh. Instead, he signed with Boston in early 1974. That same morning, the phone rang. "I've thought this over," said Finley, "and I'd like you to come back."

"Charlie," Jim said, "I've obligated myself to the Red Sox for the next two years."

"Shit," Charlie snapped, "everybody knows those contracts aren't worth the paper they're written on."

"I'm tied up. I'm not coming back to Oakland." Hanging up, he joined Martin on WBZ Radio. Their road show soon bagged New England: Poss, a megaphone; Ned, bemused and wry.

"Gunner and I were Ringling Brothers," said Woods. Martin was old-shoe, like a slipper. "Sox fans like it toned down. If I did a Prince I'd have been run out of town." Each knew the game, played off the other, and refused to toot his horn. "They had the same philosophy," said NESN's Bob Whitelaw. A listener hoped for rain: their stories held you fixed.

"Was it ever better," wrote Clark Booth, "than when Ned and Possum did a game on an August night when the pennant race was just beginning to simmer and the mood was evocative of the fifties?" In 1975, Carlton Fisk returned from a broken wrist. "Way back!" growled Poss. "Back! It is gone! . . . His first home run of the year! And look at him jump and dance! He's the happiest guy in Massachusetts!" The L.C.S. swung on Game Two. "Fly ball, left field! Rico Petrocelli has homered into the screen! Boston leads [the A's], 5–3, and Fenway Park is an absolute madhouse!"

For a time I thought that "the best play-by-play combination," Booth said, "in the history of American sport" would last. Silly me.

As we have seen, WITS Radio wanted company men, not good company. "Hit parties, ooze oil," Woods said. "I couldn't, nor would Ned." The poet and peripatetic refused to prostitute or pimp.

Retiring, Poss surfaced on USA TV's Thursday "Game of the Week." His last stop began February 20, 1988, at 71, of cancer. "Leave it to Jim," said a friend. "He had to go to Heaven to find a better boss than Ned or Prince."

JIM WOODS

LONGEVITY:	10	31 years.
CONTINUITY:	5	New York A.L. 1953–56; NBC TV "Major League Baseball" 1957; New York N.L. 1957; Pittsburgh N.L. 1958–69; St. Louis N.L. 1970–71; Oakland A.L. 1972–73; Boston A.L. 1974–78; USA TV "Game of the Week" 1979–83.
NETWORK:	2	"Major League" 1957 (NBC TV) and "Game" 1979–83 (USA TV).
KUDOS:	7	Array of awards.
LANGUAGE:	10	Declarative, like anvil.
POPULARITY:	10	Often rivaled No. 1's.
PERSONA:	10	The Possum.
VOICE:	10	Boomed, like the Queen Mary.
KNOWLEDGE:	10	Grand on name, place, or date.
MISCELLANY:	9	Spurned Cardinals minor-league pact. "I couldn't see myself as a player." Did NBC's first weekly baseball: 1957 Brooklyn–Milwaukee exhibition.
TOTAL:	83	(40th place).

6

Al Michaels

Jerry Coleman

Bob Uecker

Bob Murphy

Phil Rizzuto

AL MICHAELS

Thomas Wolfe wrote of baseball, "Almost everything I know about spring is in it." Al Michaels's knowledge of baseball sprang from growing up near Ebbets Field. "My school day went until only noon," he said: Dodgers game, at 1:30. A quarter and a G.O.——General Organization——card bought a left-field seat.

Each weekend, Al's clan walked hand-in-hand to seats high behind home plate. "My first remembrance in life is looking down into the booth at the back of Red Barber's head and saying, 'What a job. Can you imagine seeing every game for free?'"

In 1953, Vin Scully succeeded Barber. The Dodgers scamped to Los Angeles in 1958. By coincidence, so did Al's agent dad. "Baseball's best two Voices," said Michaels, "and I get to hear 'em both."

Al had not studied Clough: "Westward look, the land is bright." He did share the view. In 1968, the Arizona State radio/television major flew to Hawaii, never paying to see another game.

Michaels re-created the P.C.L. Islanders from a downtown Honolulu studio. A Cuban refugee ran the board. From the road, "all depended on the press box to send balls and strikes." One night Al preps for three innings vs. Tucson. Minutes lapse: No report. Finally, he speaks: "That's it. Here's Ken Wilson with the fourth," then leaves. In November 1970, at 26, Michaels swapped Oahu for Ohio.

That year's Reds won the pennant. The 1972 L.C.S. linked river towns. Pittsburgh led its final: 3–2. "The [ninth-inning] pitch to Bench. Change—hit in the air to deep right field!" shrieked Al. "Back goes Clemente! At the fence—she's gone! Johnny Bench—who hits almost every home run to left field, hits one to right! The game is tied!"

Two Reds singled. The flag led off third. "In the dirt—it's a wild pitch! Here comes Foster! The Reds win the pennant!" The voice rose an octave. Al did his first Series—or Scully's ninth? "When he is sitting in your living room talking about the nation's best-known baseball broadcaster," wrote Wells Twombly, "he sounds identical." You couldn't tell.

"It was subconscious from all the years I'd heard him," Al surmised. "When I discovered I sounded like Vin, I stopped listening." Celebrity, in turn, began. "He was more exciting than Waite Hoyt," said Joe Nuxhall, "and more of a homer than later," riding the Big Red Machine in seven midwest and southern states.

They heard: Joe Morgan, winning with his glove, bat, and legs. Dave Concepcion, siring the bounce throw to first. Pete Rose, "giving me a baseball Ph. D." Johnny Bench, 1972 MVP. "Growing up, we called catching the tools of ignorance. John changed that," said Al, like 1970s Cincy changed him.

"My time there made me." His unmaking: the Reds then-vice president.

In 1973, Michaels asked for $119,150. Aghast, Dick Wagner knocked a "figure quite high for a baseball announcer with three years of major league experience. At thirty, [he] needs some maturing." Screw you, Al replied. "I have known Dick Wagner for five years and have come to the conclusion that his definition of maturity is total subservience."

That fall, Michaels joined a team whose attendance approximated the swallows at Capistrano. One night he announced the crowd. "Mr. and Mrs. Jim McAlpine, Palo Alto." Another: "That's 1967. There are 1967 people here. Don't worry, folks . . . that's a great year . . . 1967 . . . a great year for Inglenook Wine. Not so good for the Giants, however."

San Francisco was greased for sarcasm. Al inherited much to be sarcastic about. "The score at the end of six is San Diego 9, the Giants 9. Unfortunately, the Giants are playing in German." Their mid-seventies resembled Stalingrad. "It has been said, not altogether humorously," wrote Twombly, "that the reason the Giants are last in home attendance is because everybody stays home and listens to Michaels."

ABC Sports head Roone Arledge hired him in 1976. In 1980, Al did his second hockey game—"No one at ABC had done any"—Lake Placid's Olympic Miracle on Ice: U.S. 4, Soviets 3. "Do you believe in miracles? Yes!" he bayed. Punier was "Monday Night Baseball"'s backup niche. The hitch: lead Voice Keith Jackson's idyll was South Bend or Happy Valley, not Fenway Park or Wrigley Field. "A football guy, on baseball!" *TV Guide* huffed. "It was no secret that Al was miffed that network execs took their sweet time making him No. 1 announcer."

Michaels debuted June 6, 1983, with ex-O's Jim Palmer and Earl Weaver. Flammable on the field, they fizzled above. Earl quickly left. Replacing him: the gadfly who left school (New York University), fifties ABC Radio ("SportsFocus"), and 1962–63 Mets radio (pre-game) for "Wide World of Sports," TVS boxing, and "Monday Night Football." In 1985, slamming ABC, Howard Cosell released *I Never Played the Game*. Already he and Al had fought off-air. Now Tim McCarver replaced him on the Series.

"Howard had become a cruel, evil, vicious person," said Michaels. "He's always had some of those traits, but they've now manifested themselves in spades." Al manifested play-by-play. Dane Iorg's Game Six hit tied the Classic. "And there's a blooper to right field for a base hit! Concepcion scores! Here comes Sundberg! Here comes the throw! He scores [Royals, 2–1]! And we go to the seventh!"

Next year Michaels went to "the greatest of all the thousands of games I've done"—Game Five, American League L.C.S.

Ahead, 3 games to 1, California trailed, 2–1, until Boston outfielder Dave Henderson, nearly catching Bobby Grich's drive, knocked it over the wall. In the ninth, up 5–4, the Angels were one out from the pennant. Gary Lucas's first pitch plunked Rich Gedman. Relieving, Donnie Moore went 2-2 on Henderson. The Red Sox had one strike left.

Champagne iced the Halos clubhouse. "The pitch . . . deep to left and Downing goes back! And it's gone! Unbelievable!" Michaels yelled. "You're looking at one for the ages here! Astonishing! Anaheim Stadium was one strike away from turning into Fantasyland! And now the Red Sox lead, 6 to 5! The Red Sox get four runs in the ninth on a pair of two-run homers by Don Baylor and Dave Henderson!" Effect: Man bites dog.

"This is supposed to happen *to*, not *by*, us," a Soxaphile said. It almost did in the ninth inning: 6-all, bases full, Grich up. Steve Crawford got him and Doug DeCinces. Boston: 7–6. "So many twists," Al said 18 years later. "Take Crawford, ninth guy on a 10-guy staff, trying to save a pennant. Afterward, he says, 'If there was a bathroom on the mound, I'd have used it.' What an unlikely hero. One day: Crawford's moment in the sun."

Michaels's dawned: college football and basketball, "Wide World of Sports," "The Superstars," 1986– "Monday Night Football," multi-Super Bowl, three-time Olympian and National Sportscaster of the Year. Slow in coming, ABC baseball slowly went away. By 1986, "Monday" aired 13 games vs. 1978's 18. Wrote *TSN*: "ABC pays baseball *not* to make it televise the regular season. The network only wants the sport for October, anyway."

Al's third Series was baseball's first inside (1987): its "decibel levels," a writer said, "associated with jets in aircraft takeoffs." His next felt another jolt. October 17, 1989, was clear and warm in San Francisco: "by local notion, earthquake weather," said Michaels, a resident. At 5:04 P.M., Pacific Time, on the pre-game show, he shouted, "We're having an [7.1 Richter scale] earthquake!" then fell with McCarver and Palmer to the floor. For 30 seconds the Bay Area rocked.

Ruptured gas lines lit the Marina. Part of the Nimitz Freeway collapsed. A Bay Bridge upper span section hit the lower level: 67 died. At Candlestick, generators revived the TV picture. The crowd filed out quietly. Michaels won a *news* category Emmy. "His hockey made him a celebrity sportscaster," said Craig. "The earthquake showed he could handle everything else."

A month earlier, Bart Giamatti had died of a heart attack. Successor Fay Vincent now postponed for 10 days "our modest little sporting event," braving an all-time low 16.4 Series rating. Next season, CBS began exclusivity: "tough to accept," Al said, "because baseball was such an early stepchild at ABC and had come such a long way."

In 1994–95, he surfaced on The Baseball Network. "Here Al is, having done five games since 1989," said Palmer, "and steps right in. It's hard to comprehend how one guy could so amaze."

Michaels retrieved "Monday Night Football," Stanley Cup, NBA final, and 1998 NSSA Hall of Fame. "I don't want to believe in reincarnation

AL MICHAELS

LONGEVITY:	7	21 years.
CONTINUITY:	7	Cincinnati N.L. 1971–73; San Francisco N.L. 1974–76; ABC TV "Monday Night Baseball" 1976–89; ABC/NBC TV The Baseball Network 1994–95.
NETWORK:	10	World Series 1972 (NBC TV) and 1979, 1981, 1983, 1985, 1987, 1989, and 1995 (ABC TV). "Monday" 1976–89; L.C.S. 1976, 1978, 1980, 1982, 1984, 1986, 1988, and 1995; All-Star Game 1980, 1982, 1984, 1986, 1988, and 1995; Divisional Series 1995 (ABC TV). TBN 1994–95 (ABC/NBC TV).
KUDOS:	10	Three-time Hawaii Sportscaster of the Year. 1986, 1989, and 1995 Emmy. 1980, 1983, and 1986 NSSA Sportscaster of the Year and Hall of Fame 1998. National Journalism Review Sportscaster of the Year 1991. ASA Sportscaster of the Year 1995.
LANGUAGE:	9	Connective.
POPULARITY:	9	Mr. Smooth.
PERSONA:	10	ABC Baseball.
VOICE:	9	Emphatic.
KNOWLEDGE:	10	Try naming last mistake.
MISCELLANY:	8	Grasps bigs fit: "like doing a jigsaw puzzle and finding all the pieces."
TOTAL:	89	(22nd place). *Scores based on 1–10 point scale.*

because God has been so good to me this time around that I'd probably come back as a cockroach in Cameroon."

What Al knew of spring was still in baseball. To the public, other sports and seasons were now more in him.

BOB UECKER

Johnny Carson dubbed him "Mr. Baseball." Wrote *Sports Illustrated*: "He is the funniest man in sportscasting"—Joe Garagiola with hair. A Boys and Girls Club of Milwaukee photo shows him making rabbit's ears behind a member. Text reads: "And some of our kids never grow up."

Bob Uecker grew up to be a cult clown, film/TV actor, and Brewers and "Monday Night Baseball" prosopopeia. Ah, those fans, he said, "I love 'em." They love the man as memoir: the *Catcher in the Wry*.

To know Uke meant grasping "my lunch-bucket family type, Eastern European kind of place." Twenties emigrants to Milwaukee included Sue and Gus Uecker, a Swiss homemaker and tool and diemaker, respectively.

One night Michaels asked about Uecker's father. "He came from the old country" and played soccer, Bob replied.

Did dad play goal?

"Oh, he didn't play anything. He just blew up the balls. That's where I get a lot of my talent."

Uke blamed his 1962–67 Braves, Cardinals, and Phillies .200 average on Milwaukee's Boys Club's pool. "They made me swim without a suit. I kept backing up against the wall, and they had those old iron radiators. I got too close. Explains a lot."

Mr. B was born January 26, 1935, on "Mom and Dad's oleomargarine run to Chicago because we couldn't get colored margarine in Milwaukee," he joked, in an exit area, "sort of a Nativity-type setting, the light shining down and three truck drivers present." By eighth grade, Uke made a team. Trying to help, Mom "made me a protective cup from a flour sack." Dad "was a fan. He booed me, too." Each feared that junior was not the brightest bulb. "Friends are still amazed I made something of myself. They think back on those three years in the pen—oh, never mind."

Uecker learned boxing—"The way I played ball, I had to defend myself"—devolving into a sandlot pitcher. In 1953, the Braves arrived from

Boston. A tryout ended after Bob was told to toss a fastball. Reply: "I was." He became a catcher, got a tiny bonus, and signed in a "swanky" restaurant. "Dad was thrilled, but so nervous he rolled down the window and the hamburgers fell off his tray."

Bob began at Class C Eau Claire. "Talk about vision. An early manager suggested I announce." By 1962, Milwaukee's first native Brave became minors Player of the Year—"not bad, considering it was my second big-league year."

The Cardinals acquired Uke in April 1964, losing every game involving him till July. Two college students formed the Bob Uecker Fan Club (membership, 500).

"I had to fight guys to get in games," he said, "and fans who wanted to get me out." Fans won: St. Louis made the Series.

Before Game One, three bands played at Busch Stadium. Bob grabbed a tuba, declined to blow—"Nothing to prove. Folks knew I had hot air"—and used it to catch flies. Most struck brass. "Cheap? The Cardinals charged me for a tuba!"

Leave it to Mr. B. You'd expect him to avoid Sandy Koufax. Instead, he hit .400 off baseball's Robespierre. "There he was, the greatest stuff since Doubleday, and I'd hit a home run or double." That alone, Uecker said, should have kept Koufax out of Cooperstown.

The Who sang, "Won't Get Fooled Again." Uke wasn't, planning post-retirement. He talked into a beer cup in the bullpen. "My managers didn't want me in the game. Heck, they didn't want me on the bench. Kids ask which clubs I played for. 'Nobody, but I sat for a lot.'"

Uke rued his 1965 trade to Philadelphia: "fans so tough, they go to the airport to boo bad landings." One cop fined him $50 for being drunk and $400 for being a Phillie. On the other hand, manager Gene Mauch "understood me," crying "get a bat and stop this rally." The third base coach turned his back on Bob at bat. "Worse, the catcher skipped the sign to the pitcher. He'd just yell what to throw."

No respect: Uke, batting in the ninth, saw rival players dressed in street clothes. A bigmouth fan "said awful things. The problem is, he was right." Bob finally dove into the seats. "Figured I had the edge with my chest protector and shin guards on. Even so, the guy hit me and they arrested him for assault." Police then arrested Uecker for impersonating a *player.*

In 1967, rejoining the now-Atlanta Braves, the mimist retired when manager Luman Harris snapped, "No visitors in the dugout." Uecker sashayed to their speaking bureau, wowing Nashville to Naples. "I did stuff about my career—anything for a laugh. Even when I was just getting started, anyone who ever saw me play knows I had plenty of material."

Once Bob slayed friend Al Hirt's *Atlanta* night club. Soon TV's "Merv Griffin," "Mike Douglas," and "The Tonight Show" called. How do you catch a knuckler? he asked Carson. Wait till it stops rolling and pick it up. Who held the record for passed balls? Uecker did. "But it had a good side. I got to meet a lot of people in the box seats."

Soon he began filling them at the Braves' old home.

In 1970, the Seattle Pilots moved to Milwaukee. A year later, Bob joined Brewers WTMJ Radio/TV. "Hard to believe, but his problem was finding stuff to say," said partner Tom Collins. Uke repeated count and score, puffing one cigarette after another. "I'd never done play-by-play, unless you count beer cups."

The greenhorn did each bottom of the fifth inning. One night Collins and Merle Harmon left him alone. "I look up and they're gone!" Surviving, Bob joined ABC's new "Monday Night Baseball" in 1976. Said Roone Arledge: "It'll take something different for it to work"—i.e., curb yawns and lulls. The real difference, he hoped, was Uke.

"I thought we'd be great," said Mr. Baseball. Instead, colleagues Warner Wolf and Bob Prince flopped. Uke, Cosell, and Keith Jackson did the A.L. playoff. "Bob," said Humble Howard, "was the only person in the series to have his reputation helped," calling it through 1981.

Once Cosell, saying *truculent,* claimed that the ex-jock couldn't possibly know its meaning.

"Sure, I do, Howie," said Uke, deadpan. "If you had a truck and I borrowed it, that would be a truck you lent."

Cosell hated athletes-turned-announcers. Bob was the exception. "The man's bigger than the game, bigger than the team, bigger than the league, bigger than the sport," Howard gloated. "They talk about a new commissioner. If I had my pick, it would be you, Bob Uecker."

"Howard," he sighed, "I wish I had time."

Time ran through: TV's "Mr. Belvedere," as a harried writer/dad, "Hee Haw," "Late Night With David Letterman," "Saturday Night Live," "Superstars," "The

Midnight Special," "Bob Uecker's Wacky World of Sports," "Bob Uecker's War of the Stars," and "Battle of the Network Stars," fleeing the Atlantic in a double-breasted jacket. Films *Major League I, II,* and *III* starred Uke as well-sloshed Harry Doyle. "Juuuuust a bit outside," he called a pitch to the lower deck. A batter "crashed one toward South America." Above all, 1980s Lite Beer for Miller personae—the poor soul, the hapless naif—spun fame beyond the game.

Even now, ads seduce. "Wow! They're having a good time in there!" cries Uke, banned from a bar. "So I lied," trying to crash it by claiming to be Whitey Ford. "One of the best things about being in the big leagues is getting free-bies to the game. Call the front office—*bingo*!" he heads for a box. Barred, Bob hallucinates, "Oh, I must be in the front rooow!" Not exactly. "Good seats, eh, buddy?" he says from the upper deck.

"His caricature [as] the poor knucklehead who keeps getting locked out of bars and dumped on by fans gave him . . . a cult following," wrote *SI*'s William Taaffe. "Outside the booth, Uecker's shtick is he's so dense and such a blowhard, yet so . . . out of it—after all, he doesn't even *know* that people are on to him—that he's lovable." An ad showed Bob howling, "He missed the tag! He missed the tag!" Missing: anonymity. Added Taaffe: "Uke is the man who made mediocrity famous."

Uke became Brewers lead Voice in 1980. "On stage he's funny," said broadcast head Bill Haig. "People who know his comedy are surprised he's not like that on the air." The '82ers surprised by taking the L.C.S. and an 11–0 Series opener. Paul Molitor had a record five hits. Robin Yount twice got four. St. Louis won Games Six–Seven at its Parthenon. "A stadium rally will welcome the Brewers home," read the Milwaukee *Sentinel.* Yount entered on a motorcyle. A chant rose: "It just doesn't matter."

What did: loyalty (1974–93), durability (2,856 games), and longevity (3,142 hits). "Growing up, I saw guys play their career in one city," said Bob. "Not with today's bucks. One of the last one-town players will be Yount," driving his Harley to County Stadium. "You see hibachis, wed-dings, a sense of community—and Robin helped make it," like the team's other Mr. B.

"I'm not a Hollywood guy," Uke kept insisting. "Baseball and broadcasting are in my blood." *His* type was radio.

"You paint a picture in the mind. It's better than TV, where you can't get away with much. Nothing like saying, 'Man, there's a homer to deep right,' then see the shortstop grab a pop." A real dinger spawned Uke's "Get up, get up, get outta here, gone!"

In 1983, a franchise-high 2,397,131 jammed the front row. Next season Bob got a replica of County's worst seat: 9, row 20, section 29. Juan Nieves's gem capped the '87ers' 13–0 start. "A swing and a drive to center!" said Uecker. "Robin is chasing—a long run—he's got it with a diving catch! A diving, sensational catch by Robin Yount to preserve the no-hitter! Nieves is being mobbed! What a play by Robin—the final out of the game!"

Milwaukee's final act reclaimed its 1953–65 league. "Wow! I get to cover teams I rode the bench for"—connecting tissue, then and now.

"Planted a new crop," a letter began.

Another: "Son got married."

He read them on the air—"even ones that say, 'You stink.'" Larry Haney was a 1977–78 Brewer. Two decades later, Uke K'd his boy in a father–son game. "He was seven. I'm proud of that."

Called: NBC's 1995 and 1997 World Series. Suffered: a 1998 back operation, replacing four discs, from "too much time sitting on the bench." Retired: from network baseball, due to rehabilitation. Named: escaping a rundown; winning a game by walking with the bases full; watching from the upper deck; making most games; and hearing games on radio that Uke didn't.

"My greatest thrills. Some life, huh?"

Bob helped emcee County's September 28, 2000, closing. Next year, Milwaukee's new field opened, selling 106 obstructed fourth-level "Uecker seats" for $1 each.

In 2002, Miller Park housed the All-Star Game. Uke threw out the first pitch, regressed to his 40-foot boat on Lake Michigan, and missed the 7-all tie. "Ran out of pitchers! My teams said they ran out of catchers—and I wasn't even in the game."

Cooperstown became Ueckerstown in 2003. "I got a call from Saddam Hussein, but I haven't heard from the President yet." On Induction Day, Bob told the crowd: "I am honored. But I still think I should have gone in as a player." Pointing to 44 nearby Hall of Famers, he added, "A lot of them were my teammates but won't admit it."

Anyone with ability could make the bigs. "To trick people year in and year out is, I think, a much greater feat." Some kids never grow up. Ah, we fans, we love 'em.

BOB UECKER

LONGEVITY:	10	35 years.
CONTINUITY:	10	Atlanta N.L. 1969; Milwaukee A.L. 1971–97; ABC TV "Monday Night Baseball" 1976–81; ABC/NBC TV The Baseball Network 1994–95; Milwaukee N.L. 1998– .
NETWORK:	10	"Monday" 1976–81 (ABC TV). L.C.S. 1976, 1978, 1980, and 1982 (ABC TV) and 1995–96 and 1998 (NBC TV). World Series 1977, 1979, and 1981 (ABC TV) and 1995 and 1997 (NBC TV). All-Star Game 1976 (ABC TV) and 1994 and 1996 (NBC TV).
KUDOS:	10	Cooperstown 2003. Five-time Wisconsin Sportscaster of the Year. Wisconsin Performing Artists Hall of Fame 1993. Wisconsin Broadcasters Association Hall of Fame 1994. "Big B.A.T." Award 1995. Wisconsin Sports Hall of Fame 1998. Radio Hall of Fame 2001. Brewers Walk of Fame 2003.
LANGUAGE:	9	Ukespeak.
POPULARITY:	10	Cosell, right: "bigger than the game."
PERSONA:	10	Mr. Baseball.
VOICE:	7	Eternally optimistic.
KNOWLEDGE:	9	Minimizes inside baseball.
MISCELLANY:	6	Owner Bud Selig sent pre-radio Brewers scout to Northern League. "What kind of a scout is this?" raged G.M. Frank Lane, throwing down Uke's report covered with gravy and mashed potatoes.
TOTAL:	91	(12th place).

JERRY DOGGETT

In an "I Love Lucy" episode, Ricky Ricardo loses his job. He calls himself a "has-ran," then "also-been." Lucy corrects him: "has-been." For a long time Jerry Doggett feared being an also-ran. "I wasn't even a has-been," he laughed. "Hadn't done enough."

In 1930, Jerry, 14, moved to Iowa from Missouri. Herbert Hoover said, "We in America are nearer the final triumph over poverty than ever before in the history of any land." He was wrong. Men on benches ("Hoover bed"), near a rabbit ("Hoover dog"), slept under a paper ("Hoover blanket"). You would do anything for a job.

Doggett soon joined his mother in Chicago. "I'd wanted to write about sports," he said, "but I didn't have the ability, so I tried to talk my way through." Radio school and a *Broadcasting* magazine ad snagged

Longview of the East Texas League. "Eighty dollars a month. In 1938, it seemed like a million."

For three years, Doggett coveted the Texas League. "I wanted [and in 1941, got] its Dallas team." Jerry's right arm was teletype: "You'd make up hits like you were at the park." In 1948, rights spun to KLIF. Gordon McLendon wanted Dizzy Dean, whose greed saved Doggett's job.

"When Diz's talks collapsed, it took me a while to react. I wasn't used to a happy ending." He had less time to grasp McLendon's *wunderkind.*

In 1950, Jerry became Liberty Broadcasting System's "Game of the Day" travel, scheduling, and play-by-play director. On September 30, 1951, it ferried Gordon, live from Boston (Giants, 3–2), and Doggett, re-creating from Philadelphia (Bums, 9–7) Jackie Robinson's sprawling catch and 14th-inning homer. Enter Bobby Thomson.

"Great coverage," Doggett said, "and Voices—Curt Gowdy, Lindsey Nelson. I hoped we'd go on forever." Instead, it went to Chapter 11. Paul Stuki sang, "I would not give you false hope." Shedding his, Jerry retrieved the Texas League. In 1952, Lindsey called an NBC golf tourney, Doggett rendering grandly as an aide. Tom Gallery remembered when Brooklyn phoned in 1955.

"Desmond's drinking again," blurted vice-president Buzzie Bavasi. "We're replacing him, and I've got four finalists' tapes." Jerry's began. "Don't bother with the others," Tom interrupted. Finally, after the bus rides and fleabags, success—or was it? Doggett was to join Vin Scully in February 1956. A month earlier Connie got another chance.

Dazed, Jerry recouped jobs just resigned—"the weirdest being Dallas baseball. A Giants team, and I'm talking with the Dodgers!" That August, Bavasi called again. Connie had flunked: Could Doggett hop a plane? "I arrive, look at New York, and figure I'm out of my league." In October, he returned to Texas, an also-ran no more.

The team bought a 44-passenger plane: "looking back," said Jerry, "for long road trips from L.A." Doggett, Scully, and Al Helfer sang a season-long adieu. The Dodgers packed for California. Would the not-yet has-been join them? Walter O'Malley nodded.

On April 19, 1958, a then-N.L. record 78,682 filled the Coliseum. Its successor rose in 1962. "I'll never forget my first visit," Jerry said. "I'm sure hearts were breaking back East. But I talked with Walter, and he was as pleased as a person could be."

Dodger Stadium smelt red clay, a view of downtown, and a Brooklyn twist. "The foul poles were in foul ground. How could you hit a home run?" Jim Murray wrote. The plate moved a year later so that the poles were fair.

L.A. won four Series through 1981. Old habits die hard. It lost in 1966, 1974, and 1977–78. Doggett etched the first switch-hitting infield. Chavez Ravine led the league in name-dropping: Sinatra, Danny Kaye, Doris Day. The biggest name made baseball lush and humming, a place to leave the world behind.

"I worked with the best broadcaster to come down the road," Doggett said of the bigs' then-longest radio/TV team. "We haven't got married yet," mused Scully. "We've got to pick out silver and get ready." Did Caruso have an *alter diem*? Barrymore, opening act? We recall the star, not cast.

Jerry knew that would apply to him. He had made it; that sufficed. "I was an average announcer whose greatest break was to work with Vin," he said, retiring in 1987, a decade before death. "My life shows it pays not to give up"—also, to be second banana to the biggest banana on the tree.

JERRY DOGGETT

LONGEVITY:	10	34 years.
CONTINUITY:	9	Liberty 1950–51 "Game of the Day"; Brooklyn N.L. 1956–57; Los Angeles N.L. 1958–87.
NETWORK:	2	"Game" 1950–51 (Liberty). All-Star Game first 1961 (NBC Radio).
KUDOS:	3	Largely local.
LANGUAGE:	6	Direct.
POPULARITY:	8	Courtier, not clown.
PERSONA:	8	Bigs' Ed McMahon.
VOICE:	8	Dulcet.
KNOWLEDGE:	10	18 years in minors teach much.
MISCELLANY:	7	Navy veteran and Northwestern graduate did football and Ryder Cup.
TOTAL:	71	(88th place).

ROSS PORTER

Derived from the Greek word for static, statistics can numb. *"Statics?"* barked Dizzy Dean, who hated them. By contrast, Ross Porter used numbers like Roy Acuff a mandolin. He prepped for five hours, called a game, and hosted

KABC's post-game "Dodger Talk." Listeners vented. "The Stat Man" replied. "Much of the audience knows as much as you do, if not more. You can't sit on past preparation."

At three, Porter sat on daddy's knee. "He'd read baseball stories, pique my interest." Gradually, the Oklahoman fixed play-by-play. "I'd sit in the family car at night listening to games." His hero, ironically, was Harry Caray, who preferred even sobriety to stats.

In 1953, Ross, 14, joined Class D Shawnee. He graduated from Oklahoma University via WKY Oklahoma City to KNBC L.A., doing, among other things, high school hoops. "Sandy [Koufax] had turned down a scholarship, knew basketball, and was under contract to NBC. They didn't know what to give him, so he got color with me."

In 1977, Porter joined another first-in-his class. "I thought, wow, with Vin Scully, the Dodgers'll make me run water!" Instead, he saved the best for first.

"Some start," Ross said, dryly. L.A. won a flag, became the first team to draw three million, and met the Yanks for the first time since 1963. The 74th rounders title of North America began October 11. CBS Radio tapped Porter. Reggie Jackson batted in Game Six. "Here's a drive to right deep and deep! Smith going back! It's gone!" Next up he swung again. "Drive to right field and deep! Way back! Going, going, gone! Another home run for Reggie Jackson!"

Later Charlie Hough tossed a knuckler. "Jackson, with four runs batted in, sends a fly ball to center field deep! That's going to be way back! And that's going to be gone! Reggie Jackson has hit his third home run [on three straight pitches] of the game!" Ninth inning: New York, 8–4. "Bunt—popped up! Torrez has got it! And the Yankees are the world champions for the 21st time—and for the first time in 15 years."

Seventy-eight reran the plot: pennant, Series loss, and Ross on CBS. By 1981, the Dodgers had dropped a playoff or Classic five times in 15 years. Mocking type, they won the L.C.S. L.A. then again played the Yanks.

"We had the feeling," said Jerry Reuss, "this might be our last chance." New York took a 2–0 game lead. "We're too good to lose again," added Davey Lopes. The Dodgers then won four straight: pride precedeth the unfall.

Porter resurfaced on CBS's 1984 N.L. playoff. In 1987, Jerry Doggett retired, bumping him to Number Two. Ross made data animate. Scully moved from Camus to Cey. Their new arrangement hiked contrast: each broadcast by himself.

"Today broadcasters chitchat," said the *Los Angeles Times*'s Larry Stewart. "Only the Dodgers announce solo, no interplay with a colleague." Their holdout evoked a radio-only age. "Red Barber taught Vin to stress the relationship with the person listening to you," said Porter. It helped him survive August 23, 1989.

Vin had waived the trip to Montreal. No. 3 Voice Don Drysdale was away expecting his wife's baby. The scoreless game reached overtime. "I was talking to the audience," Ross noted—and himself. Finally, Rick Dempsey homered: L.A., 1–0, in 22 innings. Game time: 6 hours, 14 minutes. Stats rarely seemed so shrewd.

"I got back to the hotel," he conceded, "and the voice seemed a little tired." Soon Dodgers tradition did. The O'Malleys sold the team. Buying it, Fox ordered blue game jerseys, loud music, and attitude. Ross's was tested in 2001 by a cerebral spinal fluid condition. He spent the offseason on the Internet: "the greatest invention for research."

Increasingly, Vin did television; Porter, radio. "You cannot be behind or get down on the game," Ross stated. Nothing in the stats said that his number was up. The Dodgers, however, did, canning him after the 2004 season.

ROSS PORTER

LONGEVITY:	9	28 years.
CONTINUITY:	10	Los Angeles N.L. 1977–2004.
NETWORK:	3	World Series 1977–78 and L.C.S. 1984 (CBS Radio).
KUDOS:	9	Two-time Oklahoma Sportscaster of the Year. Los Angeles Golden Mike Award 1969, 1972, and 1977. Greater L.A. Press Club Award 1969–71 and 1974. Associated Press TV Award 1970 and 1972–73. Four-time best sports talk show host, Southern California Sports Broadcasters Association. Two-time Emmy Award. Tom Harmon Special Achievement Award 1990.
LANGUAGE:	7	Matter-of-fact.
POPULARITY:	8	With Scully, got graded on the curve.
PERSONA:	8	Solid.
VOICE:	9	Strong.
KNOWLEDGE:	10	The angel's in the details.
MISCELLANY:	6	Did NBC 1970–76 NFL, 1974 NCAA hoops title, and 1975–76 Rose Bowl.
TOTAL:	79	(61st place).

DON DRYSDALE

"I hate all hitters," said Cooperstown Class of '84. "I start a game mad and I stay that way until it's over." Don Drysdale as Gentle Ben? The notion seems ludicrous. It was, however, true.

The 1956–69 pitcher hunted heads. The 1970–93 Voice was content not to turn them. "I'm not bigger than the game, just part of it," Don said, calmly and approachably. Constraint upped wearability. It also shrunk marquee.

"Batting against Drysdale," said Dick Groat, "is the same as making a date with a dentist." Return to an announcer, less Sinatra than Bennett, who was more fluorescent than drill.

Van Nuys, California, a small farming town in the San Fernando Valley, 1952. Two naturals, Big D, 16, and friend Robert Redford pitch hay, load squash and onions, and put baseball above classmate Diane Baker. Film's Roy Hobbs played infield/outfield. The future Hall of Famer manned second base. "My dad [Scott] had briefly played minor league baseball," said Drysdale. "He didn't want me pitching and hurting my arm."

A year later, Van Nuys's American Legion Post 193 pitcher failed to show. Its skipper turned to Don: "Dad told me to get the ball over." Next season the 10–1 high-school righty signed, then hit Bakersfield, Triple-A Montreal, and Ebbets Field. "In Brooklyn, baseball was the conversation." Big (6-foot-6) D sustained buzz with a) bullpen play-by-play; and b) a 17–9 1957 record. The team reversed his eastward hike. Throwing its 1958 opener, he reveled in going home.

Drysdale led the league in Ks, shutouts, and hit batsmen. "To win, you had to own the plate," he said. "Knock two of our guys down, I'd get four." The trick, added Orlando Cepeda, was to hit Don before he hit you. N.L. head Warren Giles fined him $100 for head-hunting: "my purpose pitch." Big D tried to pay in pennies. Catcher Bob Uecker rated him from 5 (chin music) to 10 (hummer in the ribs). Don's best tune was 1962's.

"It all came together," mused catcher John Roseboro. "The curve, speed, control." Tall, dark, and handsome went 25–9, won the Cy Young award, and led baseball in TV spots. Which was he: stopper, matinee idol, or son of a bitch? Big D never felt he had to choose. "On the field, he had to work harder than Koufax, but was 100 percent meaner." In one year or another, Don had a 2.18 ERA, hit seven homers, and opened a Series (1965). "Sandy would have, but begged off due to Yom Kippur." L.A. trailed, 7–1, when Walter Alston pulled him. Said Don: "Bet you wish I was Jewish."

In 1966, he and Koufax held out for $1 million. "I got $105,000, a lot then. Series checks meant something. Now they wreck your taxes."That fall, Drysdale cashed his last. Sandy retired. In 1968, the last Brooklyn Dodger threw a bigs record six straight shutouts and 58 2/3 scoreless innings. Next year he tore a rotator cuff.

"It's all over, baby," Don said, retiring after 209 victories, 2.95 ERA, five Series, 10 All-Star Games, four straight years of 308 or more innings, 29 homers, beanballs, spitballs, and record 154 hit batsmen—to columnist Lyle Spencer, "the John Wayne of ballplayers." D's dogma lingered: "I've got one way to pitch righties"—pause—"tight."

By now, Drysdale was perhaps "the first active millionaire pitcher in . . . history," said the *Times*: oil, avocados, and thoroughbreds, a breeding ranch, and "more property than the eye can see." Once Alston mused, "If you wanted one guy to win a big game for you, you'd look to him." In Big D's next life, not every game was big. "I've listened for years to different guys' styles, how they enunciate, and so forth." Etc. meant voice, mug, and name: Drysdale was the package.

In March 1970, he left a Hidden Hills ranch near Los Angeles for Expos English CBC-TV, training daily with a recorder. "No, sir, there's no way you're going to hear it," Big D told a reporter. "I feel back in the minors of the broadcast league." Later he joined Dick Enberg on Angels radio: "I'm here to work at this." Gene Mauch felt him already good—"particularly for a guy who spent most of his life with two fingers in his mouth."

Liking players, Don disliked "asking questions I already knew the answer to." In 1978, ABC's answer gave him "Monday Night Baseball," "Superstars," and "Wide World of Sports." It soon found that he was not hip or edgy—and that Southern California didn't care. The 1979 Halos drew a record 2,523,375, but lost the L.C.S. to Baltimore—and Don full-time to ABC. "My thing is to talk about inside things. Keith [Jackson] does play-by-play. Howard's role is anything, since anything can happen in broadcasting."

As proof, ABC released, then rehired, him in 1981. "If there is nothing to say, be quiet," he explained. Cosell would sooner remove his wig. 1982: Big D joined the White Sox. 1984: He made the Hall of Fame, did the N.L. playoff and, in a twist of irony, got beaned. "Competent, not outstanding," said *TSN*. "Cliches tumble from his tongue." Jim Palmer was ABC's new poster child "[of] superior looks and . . . popularity from underwear com- mercials." Tim McCarver's hiring returned Don to Comiskey Park. The damnest thing is that he didn't care.

One day the divorced Big D met ex-All American basketball player Ann Meyers, who mistook him for Don Meredith. "What would you do," he shortly said, "if I asked you to marry me?" They had three children; to his shock, Drysdale became a Ward Cleaver dad. "Life's a puzzle," he said, and laughed. The final piece was 1988's: he joined Scully at Chavez Ravine.

In August, L.A.'s Orel Hershiser began 59 straight scoreless innings. Voice and executioner: Vin called Don's record's end September 28. "A fly ball to right! Gonzalez backs up! . . . And Hershiser has the record!" Big D nabbed Orel in the dugout. "Oh, I'll tell ya, congratulations. . . . And at least you kept it in the family."

"He'd never been happier," said Meyers. "Working where his memories were, with Vinnie, away from network TV, his life picture-perfect"—except that pictures can break. In Montreal, where 37 years earlier he roomed with Tom Lasorda, Don, 56, had a fatal 1993 heart attack. Scully, red-eyed, opened that night's game. "Never have I been asked to make an announcement that hurts me as much as this one. And I say it to you as best I can with a broken heart."

DON DRYSDALE

LONGEVITY:	8	24 years.
CONTINUITY:	6	Montreal N.L. 1970–71; Texas A.L. 1972; California A.L. 1973–79 and 1981; ABC TV "Monday Night Baseball" 1978–81; Chicago A.L. 1982–87; Los Angeles N.L. 1988–93.
NETWORK:	6	"Monday" 1978–81; All-Star Game and L.C.S. 1978, 1980, 1982, 1984, and 1986; World Series 1979 (ABC TV).
KUDOS:	8	Cooperstown 1984. Number 53 retired by Dodgers 1984. Washington Touchdown Club Clark Griffith Memorial Trophy 1969. L.A. Mount Sinai Lifetime Achievement Award 1990.
LANGUAGE:	5	Regular-guy boiler-plate.
POPULARITY:	10	Residue from mound.
PERSONA:	9	Flame-thrower turned warm shower.
VOICE:	9	Mellow.
KNOWLEDGE:	10	Ted Williams wrote *The Science of Hitting*. Big D knew art of pitching: "The plate's divided into three parts. The batter only gets the middle."
MISCELLANY:	7	Don and Ann Meyers believed to be only husband and wife in sports Halls of Fame.
TOTAL:	78	(63rd place).

Drysdale flew back to a California so different from the Van Nuys of his youth that it is hard to believe that it existed. A memorial service lured a coalition of the loving. Hershiser termed him "a modern-day hero." Enberg, speaking, wept.

"He first saw light here," a 1973 eulogy to Lyndon Johnson said. "He last felt life here. May he now find peace here." Big D's biggest game lay ahead.

DAVE VAN HORNE

Save Brooklyn, the bigs' first foreign game was April 14, 1969, at Montreal's Jarry Park. The audience wore Gallic garb, ate corned beef and pastrami, and sang "The Happy Wanderer" in French. The P.A. announcer was bilingual, seats largely backless, and binoculars a must: women were the most ooh-ah in the league. Modern banks flanked old churches and European shops and inns. "The experience was otherworldly," said Dave Van Horne—Venus to baseball's Mars.

Network radio ferried the Expos' long-time Voice to Quebec, Vermont, eastern Ontario, and upstate New York. The English-TV Canadian Broadcasting Corporation carried him to Brandon, Calgary, and Dawson City. "They were Canada's team," said outfielder Ken Singleton, "long before the Braves called themselves ours."

Be careful what you wish for—a larger place than Parc Jarry. In 1977, the Expos left Canada's Ebbets Field for a baseball tomb. "Looking back," said Dave, "the team and I were made and broken by a field."

Wes Westrum cracked, "Baseball is like church. Many are called, but few are chosen." At one time few called Montreal a big-league city. Then, in 1967, Canada's centennial, "Man and His World," dwarfed New York's 1964–65 World's Fair. "Suddenly," mused Gerry Snyder of the Montreal Executive Committee, "baseball saw cosmopolitan, not sticks."

The National League gave Montreal a team "on condition that a suitable site is found." In 1968, league president Warren Giles and Mayor Jean Drapeau OK'd a 3,000-seat plot. Capacity swelled to 28,456. Jarry would work—till when? Next April 8, *L'Expos* opened in New York. Six days later, "frost hadn't left the ground," said Van Horne. "Yet nobody cared our opener was like standing on a sponge. What a moment: game one outside America."

SRO hailed an 8–7 home squeaker. Next week, Bill Stoneham no-hit the

Phils. "Some guys never call one. I knew then that whatever the franchise was, it wouldn't be dull." Born in Easton, Pennsylvania, Dave had schooled in Richmond, called Atlanta's 1966–68 Triple-A Richmond, and joined the Expos. Balding, "I looked older than my age. At first their novelty kept me young."

Once at 2 A.M. he promised "an autographed Expo ball to the listener writing farthest from St. Catherine and Peel Streets." More than 400 wrote. Many recalled Montreal as Brooklyn's 1939–60 conveyer belt. Ex-Bums colormen included Duke Snider, Don Drysdale, Pee Wee Reese, and Jackie Robinson, going blind from diabetes.

"Dave," he said, nudging the monitor, "just point to the ball, so I'll know where it is when I'm talking about replays."

A Quebecer still replays the age.

Early-seventies Montreal had a 1,214,300 population. The '69–73ers *averaged* 1,263,452. "Our percentage of seats filled was 60 percent," said Van Horne, "with the Mets and Cubs highest in the league." The Expos acquired red-haired Rusty Staub—*Le Grand Orange*. Skipper Gene Mauch parlayed George Patton and John McGraw. "Steve," he told pitcher Steve Renko, "I see the sideburns are down and the ERA is up."

Each year the jig seemed up for Jarry Park. "The league said we needed a dome with our awful weather," said Dave. "We couldn't wait to leave." Attendance fell. "How stupid that we talked ourselves into calling it antiquated," added Staub. Last game: September 26, 1976. Van Horne soon yearned for home.

His new haunt, 60,000-seat Olympic Stadium, suggested a space ship: walls bowed out, then in, curving back to almost meet. Three tiers loomed a province from the mound. An interior fence tied the poles. The back wall loomed beyond. "In between was a blackness between the field and building shell," said Dave.

Its no-man's land nicely characterized the park.

Le Stade Olympique opened for baseball April 15, 1977. A retractable roof that froze when wind hit 25 miles an hour wasn't finished till 1987. Ultimately, a faulty generator kept it closed. For a while it didn't matter.

In 1981, "A fly ball to center! Dawson is under it! He's got it! Charlie Lea has pitched a no-hit, no-run ballgame!" cried Dave. "The first ever for a French-born pitcher!" The Expos finally made an L.C.S. Like the Big O, its final broke your heart. "Fly ball, center field!" said partner Ron Reusch in the 1-all ninth.

"Dawson going back! . . . That ball is a home run! That ball is out of here . . . and the Dodger bench clears to congratulate Rick Monday!"

Found: a 1983 home record 2,320,651. Lost: mascot Youppi—"the only warm thing about the Expos," wrote *La Presse*—ejected from a game. Part of a 55-ton concrete block in the upper deck collapsed. Said Van Horne: "You began to ask if the franchise was collapsing, too."

Seals in a pre-game circus refused to leave the field: grounds help, chasing them, was heckled by the crowd. An 18-wheel truck in a parade took a U-turn through the fence. "I'd see the plaque and statue of Jackie Robinson," Dave mused, "and wonder what he'd think."

He would likely wonder about 1994. Van Horne has, ever since.

Venus: That August 12, the Expos' .649 percentage led the bigs. Mars: A labor stoppage killed the Series. "We didn't know it then," said Dave, "but it killed baseball in Montreal." The strike cost the club nearly $16 million. Next season it finished last.

Van Horne aired 1994–95's The Baseball Network. "Regional coverage, so I did the Expos." In 1997, he got the Canadian Baseball Hall of Fame's Jack Graney Excellence in Broadcasting Award. It didn't aid attendance. Only a new park could keep the Expos out of *les Etas-Unis.*

In 1999, new owner Jeffrey Loria touted a 36,287-seat den. It went nowhere. Upset, he yanked baseball off TV and English radio. Dave fell to Cyberspace: "You're listening to baseball on the Internet!" Privately, he told a friend, "I'm broadcasting daily, and I might as well be dead."

Fish swim upstream. In 2000, the Palm Beach Gardens, Florida, resident took his home run call, "It's up, up, and away!" to Miami. A year later Loria traded the Expos for Van Horne's new team. Florida won a 2003 wild card. Next: Division Series. Down, 3 games to 2, the Giants trailed, 7–6. "A line drive out into left field. Conine . . . up with it, the runner's waved. Here's the throw to the plate . . . Pudge [Rodriguez] is waiting! He tags him, gets knocked over, holds on, and the Marlins win the game! . . . And the Marlins are headed to the National League Championship Series!"

Venus: The Cubs took a 3–1 game L.C.S. advantage. Mars: The Marlins won the pennant at Wrigley Field. The Series emptied their pocketful of miracles: Florida, beating the Yanks in six.

"What a run," said Dave. "Who says all good things must end?"

Recalling Parc Jarry, Montreal does each day. *L'Expos* left for Washington in late 2004.

DAVE VAN HORNE

LONGEVITY: *10*   36 years.

CONTINUITY: *9*   Montreal N.L. 1969–2000; ABC/NBC TV The Baseball Network 1994–95; Florida N.L.
                     2001– .

NETWORK: *4*   English Network 1971–89 (CBC TV). The Sports Network 1990–2000 (TSN TV). TBN
                     1994–95 (ABC/NBC TV).

KUDOS: *6*   Three-time Virginia Sportscaster of the Year. Jack Graney Award 1997. Canadian
                     Sports Hall of Fame 1999.

LANGUAGE: *9*   Literary.

POPULARITY: *10*   Why would Expos pull his plug?

PERSONA: *10*   Canada's Voice.

VOICE: *9*   Urbane.

KNOWLEDGE: *10*   Bright in any tongue.

MISCELLANY: *5*   1999 Expos first bigs non-wireless team since 1938.

TOTAL: *82*   (44th place).

DENNY MATTHEWS

In 1969, the American League expanded to Kansas City and Seattle. Through 1975, Middle America heard Bud Blattner. Partner Denny Matthews then "succeeded, not replaced him," said the Royals still-liegeman behind the mike.

By 1980, Matthews keyed the A.L.'s largest radio network—120 stations, in 11 states, from New Mexico to Florida. Illinois Wesleyan '66 is now the longest-but-Vin Scully Voice of any big-league team.

"As a kid, I'd listen to Jack Brickhouse," he said of 1950s downstate Illinois. Baseball often means a team. If "Hey-Hey!" conjured the Second City, to many Denny bespeaks the Royals.

As a child, he walked, not talked, the game. In high school, the Giants gave a tryout. Later Matthews and Doug Rader manned Wesleyan's middle infield. In football, Denny's receiving yardage topped Otis Taylor's. "He was the Natural," added Rader. "What couldn't he do?"

September 1968. Having never called an inning, Matthews asked the Cardinals if he can tape a game. "A lot of people [over 300] are going to apply for the K.C. job," a friend cautioned. "It's not enough that they like your tape. They gotta *remember* you."

Schlitz Beer vended the Royals' KMBZ Radio/KBMC TV network. Denny found a dealer, got several dinner menus, and stole a Schlitz-logo serving tray. An ad filled the outside flap. "The inside was blank, for the place to put its menu." Matthews printed his resume, put a menu on the tray, and enclosed a tape. "Here," he wrote Schlitz, "is my final pitch for the Royals' job."

Some deem baseball a universal language. Soon Denny found that its universe surpassed English. Daily he hosted a pregame show. By August 1969, each player except utility infielder Juan Rios had appeared. Magically, Juan gets three hits. Denny names him next-day Star of the Day. Shortstop Jackie Hernandez offers to interpret. The interview begins.

"Jackie," Matthews said, "ask Juan about last night." In Spanish, Rios seems a chatterer. Denny thinks that "There must be some terrific stuff." Rios then hands Hernandez the mike.

"Juan said he feels great," says Jackie. Producer Ed Shepherd drops his recorder. Matthews drips with sweat. "This guy has just told his life story and that's it"—five seconds in translation.

July 2, 1970. English again works undertime. Guy's Foods is a local sponsor. The third inning starts. Denny's mind begins racing. "For those of you planning a Fourth of July picnic, take those good Guy's potato chips." Pleased, he smiles. "And, fans, while you're in the store, be sure to grab Guy's nuts."

Bud's face whitens. Matthews prays for a seven-second delay. Surprisingly, Guy's head Guy Caldwell howls. By 1973, all hailed the sole 1962–91 new big-league-only site. Royals Stadium's 12-story scoreboard in a fountain, waterfall, and pool complex lit a dead-end age of ballpark handiwork, spurring defense, alley pop, and speed.

In 1976, Denny rolled 7: first K.C. title/first year as Voice. Through 1978 the Yanks stood in the L.C.S. door. Then, in 1980, George Brett hit .390. The Royals took a 2–0 game playoff lead. At the Bronx Zoo, No. 5 hit in Game Three's seventh: Stripes, 2–1. "Gossage ready. Swing and a high fly ball!" sidekick Fred White said. "Deep right field! There she goes!" Royals Stadium's scoreboard used more than 16,000 bulbs. Brett's three-run titian still hangs in lights.

"Making the Series," said Denny, "threw off all that frustration." Renewing it: Philadelphia, in six. "For us, this was climbing another step." Ahead: the final rung.

Matthews climbed one in 1982, calling his first network L.C.S. The Stadium again hosted Kansas City July 24, 1983: Brett, homering for a 5–4 victory; called out for illegal pine tar on his bat; then bolting from the dugout like a lynx on speed.

In 1985, he averaged .333. K.C. trailed the expanded L.C.S., 3 games to 1. "Before that year we'd have been dead," said Denny, "but we used our chance," beating Toronto three straight.

"The War Within the State" followed. St. Louis took a 3–2 game lead. Behind, 1–0, Jorge Orta led off the Royals' next-game ninth by rolling to first base. Pitcher Todd Worrell beat him to the bag—until Don Denkinger ruled him safe. Steve Balboni popped foul—until Jack Clark lost the ball. A passed ball and walk preceded Dane Iorg's winning hit.

"It's a situation," he said, "you dream about as a child." In Game Seven, Bret Saberhagen threw a manly gem. "One out to go in the ninth inning!" Denny said. "Eleven to nothing. The one–oh pitch. Fly ball! Motley going back to the track! No outs to go! The Royals have won the 1985 World Series! And they converge on the mound in celebration!"

Two decades later, he would like to celebrate again.

Ageless: Brett, winning batting crowns in 1976, 1980, and 1990—"only guy ever," said Denny, "to lead in three decades."

Peerless: the 13-time All-Star, getting his 3,000th hit September 30, 1992 vs. California.

Timeless: the small-market Royals felt financially strapped.

In 1997, Matthews touted realignment. "Create four geographic divisions," he told the owners. "We'd be with the Cubs, White Sox, and Cardinals." Instead, the bigs eyed "contraction." In 2001, Denny contracted to 130 games a year. "It recharges the battery. You get away from it for a few days and come back strong," reaching Salinas and Ft. Smith and Yuma and Dodge City.

In 2004, Matthews telecast his first play-by-play since 1986. "I had to remind myself you don't need to paint the picture." He had outlasted 16 managers, 139 trades, and five Royals named Jones, but not doubt. Wrote columnist Joe Posnanski: "Where's the love for Denny Matthews?" Partner Ryan Lefebvre mused how he could walk through K.C.'s Plaza Hotel without someone offering a glad-hand or brew.

Denny hated to schmooze or self-promote. "It's not my job to scream. I tell what happened and then you can scream." Some Voices think the hymn "How Great Thou Art" means them. To Matthews, story-telling meant team, not self. "You don't learn about his life," said White: once working out with the Packers, catching passes from Len Dawson, or hitting a receiver in a touch football game.

"Denny, thank you," said Rush Limbaugh, eyes moist. "That was the first touchdown I ever had."

Why wasn't Denny beloved?

He was, quietly, like himself.

Better late than never.

In 2004, the Royals held Denny Matthews "Talking Bobble Head" Day, named him to their Hall of Fame, and helped fill a special K.C. to Wellington, Kansas, train.

Denny's granddad had worked for the Chicago and Alton Railroad. Matthews became a "train nut"—and Midwest grade crossing safety spokesman. "The crews were terrific," he said of the thank-you ride. "The only problem was that they wanted to talk baseball—and I wanted to talk trains!"

Denny loved their lure—also the flat, tall-grass, and endless Plains'. "That alone would keep me here." He would wait for symmetry to reassert itself: Matthews, a Hall of Fame candidate: the Royals, again king of baseball's hill.

DENNY MATTHEWS

LONGEVITY:	10	36 years.
CONTINUITY:	10	Kansas City A.L. 1969– . ABC/NBC TV The Baseball Network 1994–95.
NETWORK:	3	L.C.S. 1982 and World Series 1985 (CBS Radio). TBN 1994–95 (ABC/NBC TV).
KUDOS:	4	Royals Hall of Fame 2004.
LANGUAGE:	9	Technical whiz.
POPULARITY:	9	Bobs with Royals'.
PERSONA:	9	Voice of Cardinals Nation's Radio Free A.L.
VOICE:	10	Clear, masculine, and Middle American.
KNOWLEDGE:	10	Bright enough to avoid Guy's Nuts.
MISCELLANY:	7	Could subtly rip. Umpire Greg Gibson once blew a call. Said Denny: "You might want to tell [him] to take off his sunglasses."
TOTAL:	81	(47th place).

TOM CHEEK

Raised on J Street on the west side of Pensacola, the Toronto Blue Jays' first and still-only Voice formed a stickball league, used broom handles for bats, and played and called baseball. Pre–air conditioned Florida opened doors and windows. "Like it or not, the whole neighborhood heard me."

Tom Cheek's family bought its first TV the year that a neighbor got a tape recorder. The conflux let him describe, say, Auburn–Alabama. Tom's heroes were Curt Gowdy, Mel Allen, and Dizzy Dean. No one asked what he wanted to be.

In 1957–60, the U.S. Air Force sent Cheek to San Antonio, Cheyenne, rural New York, and Africa. More than 10,000 died in an earthquake in Morocco's resort of Agadar. To stop rats and flies, the military dropped corrosive lime and bulldozed rubble: Tom knew people buried alive. Discharged, a shaken motormouth missed his neighborhood. The bigs never looked so good.

In Burlington, Vermont, Cheek aired college football and "a few Expo games [1974–76]." Once he visited Toronto. The city was renovating Exhibition Stadium. "I'm standing on Lakeshore Boulevard, and I tell [wife] Shirley, 'I've put in time. I'm going to be part of a team there some day.'"

In 1891, Toronto's first team had left organized baseball. Six years later the Eastern League moved to nearby Hanlon's Point. The city's minors died in 1967. In 1977, the A.L. finally granted an expansion club. A baseball bonanza, eh?—except that Exhibition had a football core.

Foul lines, bases, dirt squares, and plastic grass garbed the Canadian Football League Argonauts' home. "Almost none of the seats," said skipper Roy Hartsfield, "even faced the plate." A contest chose the Blue Jays' name. Tom, 37, won CKFH Radio's audition. Like Toronto, he resolved to make up for lost time.

Opening Day 1977: Jays 9, Chicago 5, before 44,649. Dinging twice, Doug Ault is seldom heard from again. The wind chill hits 10 degrees Fahrenheit. Snow off the lake covers the entire field. The hockey Maple Leafs' Zamboni repeatedly clears the turf. Any Canadian could share: CBC TV linked Halifax and Ketchikan.

Bust soon linked each year. Cheek had a saying: "Win a little, die a lot." Hartsfield's went: "If they beat us today, we'll strap 'em on again tomorrow." Tom did, beating hoarseness, laryngitis, and even pneumonia. "At four in the morning I wondered if I'd see the light of day." Would the Jays?—last through 1981.

One night a young man dropped a foul. The next pitch was popped there, too. Lunging, his girlfriend caught the ball. "Can you believe it?" Cheek boomed. "*He* boots it and *she* catches it." Cooed sidekick Early Wynn: "She probably knows all about his hands."

Each year Wynn drove a motorcoach from Florida. Looking out the window in Coon Hollow, Tennessee, he saw his front wheel rolling beside the road.

"Your life must have flashed before your eyes," Cheek said. "What was going through your mind?"

"Tom, I recalled the lines of that song," popular in the 1970s. "'You picked a fine time to leave me, loose wheel.'"

The something loose was a screw in pitcher Mark Lemongello. Once he threw an ashtray at team president Peter Bavasi. Hartsfield told him to walk a batter intentionally. The righty threw a pitch 15 feet to the right of catcher Rick Cerone. A loyalist blessed any wheels staying on: Tom's included ABC TV's 1980 and 1984 Winter Olympics.

In 1985, Toronto lost a 3–1 game L.C.S. lead. The '87ers blew a last-week division: win a little, die a lot. Exhibition Stadium closed May 28, 1989. As usual, the seventh-inning stretch tooted a homey number. "Okay-okay, Blue Jays-Blue Jays. Let's play—let's play BALL!" Cheek would call it two miles and a roof away.

The first stadium with a retractable roof convened that June. Eight Boeing 747s could fit in SkyDome. The first homestand, it began to rain. The roof jammed without closing. Another night, millions of gnats forced umpire Don Denkinger to put the top down. The bugs were not a monkey wrench: Ontario loved its new-age digs.

Toronto won the East. In 1991, it hit a bigs-first four million attendance. Joe Carter batted in the ninth inning, October 2. "A fly ball will win it!" Tom said. "The winning run ninety feet away. The pitch—a swing—and a base hit! And the Blue Jays are the champs of the American League East!" Some edge: Like 1989, they lost each L.C.S. north-of-the-border game.

By contrast, Dave Winfield, 40, became the oldest 100-RBI man in 1992. On October 14, beating Oakland, 9–2, Toronto took its first flag. The Series bound an ump-blown triple play, first non-U.S. team, and Winfield's Game Six 11th-inning up. "A base hit down the line!" said partner Jerry Howarth. "White scores! . . . Alomar scores on Dave Winfield's two-base hit!" Blue Jays, 4–3: Win a little, win it all.

"Everywhere people were thanking you," said Cheek, more thankful in

1993. Again Toronto made the Classic. Game Four welded *Nutcase* and roller derby: record score (Jays 15, Phils 14), runs (29), and time (4:14). In Game Six, hits splattered around the Dome. The Jays trailed, 6–5, two on, one out, in the ninth.

Mitch Williams threw would-be strike three. "A swing—and a belt! Left field! Way back! Blue Jays win!" cried Tom. "Joe Carter hits a three-run home run in the ninth inning as the Blue Jays have repeated as World Series champions! Touch 'em all, Joe! You'll never hit a bigger home run in your life!" Carter leapt around the bases. Tom celebrated by becoming a Canadian citizen.

"It won't last," said Leafs head Cliff Fletcher, correctly. Hockey's hub hugging baseball was a gas while it did. North America's largest McDonald's moored the on-site 348-room SkyDome Hotel. One couple kept blinds open, making love. "Forget my play-by-play," said Cheek. "The crowd liked *theirs.*" Security applied the kibosh, like the bigs' 1994 work stoppage.

"We didn't have baseball roots," he mused, "so it hurt more than, say, Boston." The '93 Blue Jays drew a still A.L.-high 4,057,947. Now tickets lingered for a game. In 2003, I visited SkyDome: fewer than 10,000 paid. Even the motormouth worried. "Anyone who loves this sport wants to see others love it, too."

TOM CHEEK

LONGEVITY:	10	31 years.
CONTINUITY:	10	Montreal N.L. 1974–76; Toronto A.L. 1977– ; ABC/NBC TV The Baseball Network 1994–95.
NETWORK:	1	TBN 1994–95 (ABC/NBC TV).
KUDOS:	5	Jack Graney Award 2001. Jays Level of Excellence 2004.
LANGUAGE:	9	Keeps it simple.
POPULARITY:	9	"The only thing better than a winning baseball team," he said, "is a losing hockey team."
PERSONA:	9	Dr. Spread the Game.
VOICE:	10	Stentorian: Boston's Cambridge School of Broadcasting alumnus.
KNOWLEDGE:	10	Eclipsed majors. "Give me music with a message. Sinatra, Diamond, a little Waylon [Jennings] and Willie [Nelson]."
MISCELLANY:	9	Has broadcast for eight prime ministers and six U.S. presidents.
TOTAL:	82	(46th place).

Next year life, unlike love, changed. Cheek's father died, ending a 4,306-consecutive-game streak. Ten days later, like a Hardy plot, Tom braved brain tumor surgery. The Jays named him to their Level of Excellence—only the third non-player. Voice cracking, Cheek hailed people he had never met. "'Thank you [cards and calls] and God bless you.'"

As a child, Tom deemed baseball "my main course." Many now preceded theirs with a prayer.

DAVE NIEHAUS

August 1960. John F. Kennedy arrives two hours late for a flight from Washington to Hyannis Port. The Democratic presidential candidate enters the plane, kisses his wife and sister, and shakes aides' hands. A stewardess brings clam chowder. A barber begins cutting hair. "It was almost as if those around him were figures in tableaux who came alive only when Kennedy was in place at the center," wrote Richard Reeves. "He was an artist who painted with other people's lives."

Dave Niehaus grew up in a 1950s Indiana of farms and fields and boys playing basketball. Often he visited the Palace Pool Room in Princeton, current pop. 8,175. Each inning a man, dipping chalk into water, posted a tick-ertape score on the chalkboard. Dried, it illumined, say, Cardinals–Cubs. "I can still see the brilliant white against the dark."

At night, Dave sipped lemonade, caught fireflies, and heard Harry Caray on the porch. In 1957, he graduated from Indiana University, joined the military, and did Armed Forces Radio. "I'd call games from Yankee Stadium," then Dodger Stadium and Big A. Taking an apartment in North Hollywood, Niehaus befriended unknown actor Jim Nabors: surprise, surprise, surprise.

In 1977, Dave fashioned the Mariners' Northwest Opening—their first/still-only Voice. "It's been a wild, woolly Pier Six brawl," Niehaus said one night, "and the bullies so far have been the Kansas City Royals." Number One on *this* Dave's List: shunning muted tints for bold pastels.

"Say Dave, you think Seattle," said Caray. Many recall his rowing before the expansion M's set sail. In 1969 and 1973, Niehaus and Don Drysdale, respectively, joined Dick Enberg. Their Halos' Magi worshiped a deity. "Scully started the West Coast tradition of don't cheerlead or make excuses," said Dave. How good were they? "Three of us opposed Vin—and lived to tell the tale."

"I'm going to have dinner tonight at Singer's house," Drysdale once said, apocryphally.

"Bill Singer, the pitcher?" Niehaus said.

"No, Dave," said Big D. "The Singer is Frank Sinatra."

In 1977, the bigs reclaimed Seattle. "[Owner] Danny Kaye knew Dave on the Angels [also, Rams football and UCLA hoops]," said Dick, "and offered him the job." He balked. Kaye persisted. Dave finally embraced Puget Sound. "I sit on my deck watching boats on the lake [Sammamish], listening to birds. It comes to us from God." Godawfulness sprang from what Niehaus dubbed The Tomb.

"A large mausoleum that gives . . . the impression of being a poorly lit, damp basement with a beat-up old pool table in the middle," *Newsday* dubbed the Kingdome, opening April 6, 1977. "People ask my favorite memory," Dave said. "It's that night—against the Angels." Later the roof leaked. Balls struck speakers, hit support wires, and entangled streamers.

The ceiling was built to dim the echo of dinky crowds. Designers knew their team. "It was so quiet," said outfielder Jay Buhner, "you could hear fans knocking you." Most slowly warmed to Niehaus. "People had wanted a local guy." He never blamed Seattle. "People knocked us as a baseball town. I'd say, 'You fans don't owe us anything, we owe you a team.'"

Dave's "My, oh, my!" rose at Anaheim. His early tater call was duller: "It's gone!" In 1978, hearing Seals and Crofts, he affixed "Fly Away" to each M's dinger. S&C also sang "Summer Breeze." Lenny Randle's turned personal. A batter bunted toward third base. "Lenny knew the Kingdome's flat on the base paths. So he gets on all fours trying to blow the ball foul."

"We might be stuck in traffic or mowing the lawn," the *Post-Intelligencer* said, "but where we really are is the Kingdome because Niehaus takes us there." Refusing to fly away was the Mariners' ill-wind.

Seattle flunked .500 its first 14 years. "Oh, for a place like Fenway," Dave dreamt amid the mourning. "I genuflect when I walk through the gates. You see where Ted Williams played." In 1980–81, he saw M's manager Maury Wills.

Once the not-exactly-a-workaholic spotted Dave and partner Ken Wilson entering the clubhouse. "Fellows," he said, "why don't you write me up a batting order for tonight." Later Maury left an exhibition to fly to L.A. "He wanted to be with his girlfriend," said Niehaus, "and left us without a manager."

Another skipper closed a year with four straight victories. Dick Williams wasn't fooled. "Know what?" he told a friend. "We're still horseshit." Their announcer was a stud. "[Despite] virtually nothing to recommend them," said a writer, the M's percentage of radios in use was baseball's best.

"I've had offers to leave, but why be miserable in New York or Chicago?" said Dave. "I want to be here when we turn around." Williams was more prosaic: "When today stinks, you look to tomorrow."

In 1989, Seattle called up Ken Griffey, Jr., 19, son of the Reds outfielder. Two years later, the Mariners finally made .500, drew a record 2,147,905, and vaunted Junior's franchise-high .327. Griffey smacked 40 homers before the August 1994 strike. A year later, the Mariners asked the state legislature to build a park. Pols snorted a belly laugh. "We had no leverage," said Niehaus, who found that in its 19th year a team's luck could turn.

Gutting a 13-game Halos lead, the M's won an A.L. West playoff. Briefly the Northwest forgot the NFL Seahawks. The Division Series began in New York, Seattle losing twice. Dave threw out the first ball at the Kingdome's post-season inaugural: Randy Johnson, 7–4. Next day Edgar Martinez slammed: 11–8. In two weeks Seattle had become a baseball town. The final showed why.

Eighth inning: M's tie. Ninth: Manager Lou Piniella inserts Randy. "He'd pitched two days earlier. But he was the best we had." Eleventh: Yanks retake a 5–4 edge. Payback followed. "Swung on and lined down the left-field line for a base hit! Here comes Joey, and Junior to third base . . . and they're going to wave him in! The throw to the plate will be late! The Mariners are going to play for the American League championship! I don't believe it! It just continues! My, oh, my!"

That winter the legislature OK'd $320 million. "Once in a while, I'll think of what saved baseball here," Niehaus mused in 2004. "1995."

No longer was Dave a Monet, etching a paint-by-number team. In 1996, he brooked two angioplasties, abandoned vodka, steak, and Marlboro cigarettes, and drew shortstop Alex Rodriguez's first full season akin to Cronin, Wagner, and Banks. Griffey became the A.L.'s ninth unanimous MVP. The '97ers drew 3,192,237, many from Idaho, Oregon, Utah, and Montana. "For the first time," added Niehaus, "we became a regional team."

Johnson and Junior left for Houston and Cincinnati, respectively. A-Rod got an A+ deal: $252 million from Texas, then New York. "Damndest thing," said Dave. "They leave, we win"—a 2001 record-tying 116 games. MVP

Ichiro Suzuki hit .350. The Kingdome imploded. Its replacement, Safeco Field, strutted arched windows, bleachers, and look from its upper deck of Elliott Bay, Mount Rainier, Olympic Mountains, and ferries, ships, and sunsets from Albert Bierstadt.

Outside, the Burlington Northern freight whistle invoked rural Indiana. "These trains going by are the park's signature," said Dave. "To me, it's a romantic sound." Another knit the stands. Johnson was "humming along." A strike "had some hair on it, baby." Enjoy "a nice little pitchers' duel." Blurted ESPN's Jon Miller: "It's all here, it's gorgeous, it's got Niehaus, it's open air!"

Dave could be forgiven for feeling he had been paroled.

In 2000, he became the first member of the M's Hall of Fame. "I really feel as if I know each . . . of you," Niehaus told the crowd. "My, oh, my!" graced a banner, forged a chant, and was drawn by grounds help in the dirt. "[He] could take an ordinary losing game and make it a poetic winner," said Enberg. *Sans* fielder "loping," runner "lumbering," or ball "belted! Deep to right field! Upper deck time! Yes!" would there have been a team for Safeco to even house?

DAVE NIEHAUS

LONGEVITY:	10	36 years.
CONTINUITY:	9	California A.L. 1969–76; Seattle A.L. 1977– ; ABC/NBC TV The Baseball Network 1994–95.
NETWORK:	1	TBN 1994–95 (ABC/NBC TV).
KUDOS:	9	Two-time Washington Sportscaster of the Year. Honored by Washington State House of Representatives 1997. Mariners Hall of Fame 2000. *Seattle Times* Top 10 "Most influential people of century."
LANGUAGE:	10	Grand slam sires, "Get out the rye bread, Grandma, 'cause it's grand salami time!"
POPULARITY:	10	A 2004 *Sports Illustrated* survey asked Washingtonians their favorite announcer: 36 percent said Niehaus; next, John Madden, 8 percent.
PERSONA:	10	Household names leave. Dearest stays.
VOICE:	10	Throaty, bubbly.
KNOWLEDGE:	10	Bright enough not to flaunt it.
MISCELLANY:	8	*SI* poll's favorite team: Mariners, 56 percent; Seahawks, 10 percent. "The biggest reason," said an M's official, "is Dave."
TOTAL:	87	(26th place).

Some ask which Voice most loved baseball. Niehaus makes the cut. "Finally," he says, "what a joy to call good players in a great park!"The 1930s bred the HudsonValley school of painting. Dave's school still swabs the Sound.

JERRY COLEMAN

Few wreath America's oldest and greatest talking game like Jerry Coleman. "I used to worry about Colemanisms," he said. "Now I figure they add to my sex appeal."

Jesus Alou is "in the on-deck circus." Cy Younger Randy Jones was "the left-hander with the Karl Marx hairdo." Recall "Winfield going back . . . back . . . he hits his head against the wall. It's rolling toward second base!" Hail the man "sliding into second with a stand-up double."

Sit back, "put a star on that baby," and laud the 1960 CBS TV and 1976–97 radio, 1963–69 Yankees, 1970–71 Angels, and 1972–79 and 1981– Padres Voice. Think of evolution, going yard. "Sometimes big trees grow out of acorns. I think I heard that from a squirrel."

Born September 14, 1924, our linguist knew the way from San Jose. His road led to high school in San Francisco, Yanks' Class D Wellsville, Pacific Theater, and The Stadium in 1949. A year later, the second baseman became Associated Press Rookie of the Year. "He can throw backwards [on the double play]," said Casey Stengel. "He must have a mirror hanging down his neck."

In World War II, a B-29 mirror helped spot Japanese. Soon the pilot of 57 bombing missions added 63 in Korea. "Feller and Williams were right," he said. "What you do for America [13 Air Medals, three Navy citations, and two Distinguished Flying Crosses] counts most." Retiring in 1957, Coleman became Yanks personnel director. His CBS TV "[pre-] Game of the Week" began in 1960. Instantly it almost closed.

Jerry was interviewing Cookie Lavagetto when the "Star-Spangled Banner" started. "Better keep talking," the apprentice thought, and did through the Anthem. Letters swamped CBS. "Believe me," he later said, "when the Anthem starts I stop, whether I'm taping, talking, or eating a banana."

By 1963, Coleman made Yanks radio/TV, having never even kept score. He was scheduled for a full inning. Instead, 12 men hit in the top half. "I think you've had enough," said Mel Allen. Jerry agreed. "I went over to the corner, got into a fetal position, curled up," and stayed.

Life on the point. "You're so insecure at first that you need someone to pat you on the back." Instead, a sadist mailed a record "Famous Jungle Sounds," writing, "Listen to yourself." A road twinbill upped angst. Tribe lefties Sam McDowell and Jack Kralick are to pitch. Game One's starter blanks New York inning after inning. "Sam was a strikeout guy with erratic control," Coleman gawked, "but his control this day was astounding."

In the sixth inning, he learns why. WPIX New York telephones the booth. "Is that McDowell?"

Jerry turns to Indians Voice Bob Neal. "Who's pitching?"

Bob lip-synchs: "Kralick."

Four decades later the face still dropped. "They were similar in build," Coleman said. "But even that doesn't explain how we had the wrong guy pitching."

Mary Poppins moaned, "Things began to happen to me." Jerry's never stopped.

"I guess you ladies wear the pants when your husbands are gone," he told Dave McNally's wife. She smiled: "And we take them off when they come home."

One warm day Coleman stripped to shorts in Kansas City. A woman complained. "So I had to put my pants back on. Not that I took them off that often, anyway."

Jerry took off in 1970 for Angels television. In 1972, inheriting a hemophiliac, he tried to staunch the blood. The 1974 Padres were nearly sold to a Washington, D.C. buyer. Saving them for San Diego, McDonald's founder Ray Kroc snatched the P.A. mike Opening Day: "This is the most stupid ballplaying I've ever seen." Next day he apologized. Jerry couldn't grasp why.

Coleman managed the 73–89 1980 Pads. "There's a generation gap between Jerry and the players," rued Gene Tenace. None split Jerry and his cult. In 1980, he returned to radio, "where I'm probably more comfortable. Most players think I was born at 45."

At about that point "all this stuff began about me being nuts."

It angers friends that Colemanisms cloud smart prose, a fine voice, and decency. "Beloved," said the White Sox' John Rooney. "Sure, he has screwups, but the biggest will be if he doesn't make Cooperstown." Many Voices blur. Jerry struts identity. "He'd be excellent in any event," said Bob Costas. "Goofs make him unforgettable"—Ol' Diz via Casey Stengel to George W. Bush.

"He's [John Grubb] under the warning track." A hitter lined "up the alley . . . oh, it's foul." Dave Winfield led off first—"always a threat to grow." Nolan Ryan has "the most elastic arm ever made by human hands." The Pads waived

Glenn Beckert. "Before he goes, I hope he stops by the booth so we can kiss him good-bye. He's that kind of guy."

Coleman denies saying: "'Rick Folkers is throwing up in the bullpen.' I said, 'He's throwing them up.'" Undeniable: "This is the only afternoon day game in the National League"; "Next up is Barry Carry Garry Templeton"; "Pete Rose has three thousand hits and 3,014 overall"; and "There's a hard shot to LeMaster—and he throws Madlock in the dugout."

Put a star on these babies:

- "Redfern won't be 22 until October. Hey, he's only 21."
- "Whenever you get an inflamed tendon, you got a problem. Okay, here's the pitch to Gene Tendon."
- "It's swung on and Gamble sends a long fly to right, but Gamble goes back to the wall and makes the catch."
- "They throw Winfield out at second, and he's safe."
- "Swung on and fouled to the backstop. Wait a minute, that was a wild pitch and the runner moved over to second."
- "Reggie Smith of the Dodgers and Gary Matthews of the homers hit Braves in that game."
- "And the final score: Chicago 8, the Cubs 5."

The envelope, please:

- "Gaylord Perry and McCovey should know each other like a book. They've been ex-teammates for years."
- "Urrea had Owchinko in a hole, oh–two, but now the count is even, three–two."
- "Over the course of a season, a miscue will cost you more games than a good play."
- "Ron Guidry is not very big, maybe 140 pounds, but he has an arm like a lion."
- "From the way Denny's shaking his head, he's either got an injured shoulder or a gnat in his eye."
- "Royster has gone six-for-seven against Shirley this year . . . and there's a single that makes him five-for-eight."
- "Well, folks, that's it for the ninth inning. We're heading on into the 12th."

God bless them, every one:

- "Young Frank Pastore may have just pitched the biggest victory of 1979, maybe the biggest victory of the year."
- "The way he's swinging the bat, he won't get a hit until the twentieth century."
- "Bob Davis is wearing his hair differently, short and with curls like Randy [Jones] wears. I think you call it a Frisbee."
- "Shortstop Ozzie Smith was so stunned with the news, he lost his appetite right over the dinner plate."
- "[George] Hendrick simply lost that sun-blown pop-up."
- "Here's the 2–1 delivery. Strike 3, he's out!"
- A drug prevention ad ends. "Hats off to drug abusers everywhere."

Finally:

- "Hi, folks, I'm Jerry Gross."

In 1979, Winfield nearly made a leaping catch. "If he had made that play," said Jerry, "they'd be throwing babies from the upper deck." They fell in 1984. San Diego drew a record 1,983,904, won the N.L. West, and drew America's Cubs in the L.C.S. The pivot was a Game-Four poke. "Hit high to right-center field! Way back! Going! Going! It is gone! The Pads win it!" Coleman cried. "In a game that absolutely defies description, Steve Garvey, in the ninth inning, hit one over the 370-mark, and the Padres beat the Cubs, 7 to 5! Oh, doctor, you can hang a star on that baby!"

In the Series, Detroit mimicked Stengel's Yanks. Punks burned cars, smashed windows, and assailed passersby upon its end. Motowners rushed the field. Jerry aired a post-game show. "At Tiger Stadium it's only 30 feet from the field to the booth—so somebody picks up the idea of target practice." Dodging trash, he nearly charged the dry cleaning bill.

Next year Coleman added "Game of the Week" to CBS Radio's postseason. "He hadn't broadcast in the East since the sixties," said Costas. "People heard what he could do." At 68, he took up skiing. By then, Tony Gwynn had batted .394, Benito Santiago hit in 34 straight games, and L.A.'s Orel Hershiser broke Don Drysdale's record 58 straight scoreless innings. The last 10 stung the Pads. "There's a drive to right field!" said Jerry. "He's going to put it away! Oh, doctor! History was born right here at San Diego!"

The 1993 N.L. L.C.S. matched Atlanta and Philadelphia. "It was a fantastic game last night," he told CBS. "I'm still trying to figure out who did what, and why." The '98 Pads wrote another flag. The Series again fizzled: a pinstriped sweep. A year later Gwynn got hit 3,000 at Montreal. "Right-center field! Base hit! And there it is! Oh-ho, doctor, you can hang a star on that baby! A star for the ages for Tony Gwynn!" One Mr. Padre swings. Another speaks.

In 2002, Jerry, 78, became the bigs' oldest full-time Voice. The '04 Pads gave him an open-ended pact. On-deck circus. Karl Marx hairdo. Sliding stand-up double. Babies tumbling from the upper deck. "Sometimes big trees grow out of acorns." The legend grows, too.

JERRY COLEMAN

LONGEVITY:	10	42 years.
CONTINUITY:	7	CBS TV "Game of the Week" 1960; New York A.L. 1963–69; California A.L. 1970–71; San Diego N.L. 1972–79 and 1981– ; CBS Radio 1985–97 "Game of the Week"; ABC/NBC TV The Baseball Network 1994–95.
NETWORK:	9	"Game" 1960 (CBS TV). L.C.S. 1976–83, 1985, 1988–93, and 1995–97; World Series 1984 and 1988; "Game" 1985–97 (CBS Radio). TBN 1994–95 (ABC/NBC TV).
KUDOS:	6	Air Force Lieutenant Colonel. Number retired in honor, 1999. Padres Hall of Fame 2001.
LANGUAGE:	10	Supercalifragalistic.
POPULARITY:	10	Put a star on his.
PERSONA:	10	One of a kind.
VOICE:	10	Strapping.
KNOWLEDGE:	10	Can finally score.
MISCELLANY:	7	In 1981 strike, called Tokyo–Taiyo game for U.S. syndication. "Colemanisms even work in Japanese!" said partner Lindsey Nelson. Called more batting titles than any N.L. Voice: Tony Gwynn (eight) and Gary Sheffield (one).
TOTAL:	89	(19th place).

MEL PROCTOR

Driftless is the lot of a bigs broadcast man. He leaves the plane, finds his hotel, and migrates to the park. Dugout talk precedes the game. Tedium succeeds it.

Ernie Harwell visited pals in every city. Harry Caray never met a bar he didn't like. Bob Wolff made a list of celebrities to meet: in Kansas City, near Independence, he phoned Harry S Truman out of the blue.

Fearing *feeling* blue, Mel Proctor used travel to act and write. Proctor was a tour guide and reporter, respectively, on TV's "Hawaii 5-0" and "Homicide." In 1995, he authored *The Official Fan's Guide to The Fugitive*.

"I identified. He was a loner, and so was I," Proctor said of ABC's 1962–67 series. "It was fun to learn about David Janssen, a social animal who loved wooing gorgeous women." He forged a half-smile, memory pleasing him. Writing evoked a magical time.

"We feel things more deeply when we're young," Mel mused, sounding eerily like Lon Simmons. Raised in Denver, he doted on the Double-A Bears. Bill Reed was a swell. "Re-creating, he'd sound like he was at, say, Nicolet Field in Minneapolis."

Proctor attended The Colorado College, did the World Football League and University of Hawaii, and aired the 1973–78 Hawaii Islanders. Like Reed, he made radio art, not Armageddon: not easy, nor necessarily on time.

"Sometimes guys forgot to call from location, so you imagined things like a streaker," chased by cops, running near the mound. Would the phone ring? If not, sick people got attended to, rain began, the grounds crew turned cavalry. In 1978, Mel got married. Ceremony: 9 P.M. Game time: 7:30. The re-creation ended at 8:36.

Proctor's last game "had every sound effect conceivable"—fire engines, sirens, cannon. "A lion's roaring in the jungle, must be the pen. Any other time, I'm fired." Instead, he bounced to the NBA Bullets. "D.C. wasn't what I knew—too trendy." Nearby blue-collar Baltimore was. In 1984, the O's cable-TV network Home Team Sports tapped Mel and a fruit loops of a man.

Their first game ex-outfielder John Lowenstein hailed a vendor: "Give me a sandwich and lots of mustard." Years later Wade Boggs's affair with Margo Adams soaked tabloids. Mel mused how the superstitious Boggs had wife Debbie cook chicken before each game.

"Who cooks his chicken now?" asked Brother Lo.

"I don't know," said Proctor, "but we know who's cooked his goose." In the mid-to-late eighties, the Orioles' seemed fried.

Seat Cushion Night, Memorial Stadium. "Hold up your seat cushions," P.A. mikeman Rex Barney said. Lowenstein threw *his* toward the field. Like lemmings, the crowd obeyed. Play was stopped, John reproved. It was a feeling the last-place 1986 and '88ers could share. "I take it seriously," Proctor said. "But I also learned—John taught me—that baseball's a *game*. If people sense *you're* having fun, *they'll* have fun watching."

Mel watched Camden Yards open, Cal Ripken, Jr. pass Ernie Banks for most homers by a shortstop, and Baltimore draw a single-season high. He spiced pro/college basketball, TNT/TBS boxing, and Mutual, Turner, and NBC football, and wrote a sequel to *The Fugitive*—increasingly, feeling one himself.

As Orioles owner Peter Angelos sent players, skippers, and general managers packing, Mel got out while the getting was good. By 1997, he joined ex-boss Larry Lucchino in San Diego. Later a group including Lucchino bought the Red Sox. Proctor left the Pads for Fox TV.

"The more you do, the more you find you can do," said Lucille Ball. Mel still does by habit. "I'm writing a new book," he said in 2004. Screentests welcome, too.

MEL PROCTOR

LONGEVITY:	7	21 years.
CONTINUITY:	6	Texas A.L. 1980–81; Baltimore A.L. 1984–96; San Diego N.L. 1997–2001; Fox TV "Game of the Week" 2003.
NETWORK:	1	"Game" 2003 (Fox TV).
KUDOS:	5	Three-time Maryland Sportscaster of the Year.
LANGUAGE:	8	Restrained.
POPULARITY:	8	Try besting the O's Jon Miller, then Jerry Coleman.
PERSONA:	8	David Janssen was a doctor. Mel's house call casual.
VOICE:	9	Unflappable.
KNOWLEDGE:	9	Weaned on Billy Reed.
MISCELLANY:	6	Other TV gigs included "The Young and the Restless," "Homicide," and "SportsNight." Now anchors CBS Palm Springs affiliate.
TOTAL:	67	(96th place).

MARK HOLTZ

Like Jack Brickhouse, he was born in Illinois (Elmhurst, 1945). Like Gene Elston, he went to school in Iowa (speech major, Wartburg College). Like

Milo Hamilton, he left the Midwest for the Lone Star State. Unlike them, Mark Holtz lived an unfinished life. TV's Texas Rangers demanded justice. Shorn of it, the Rangers' Voice died of leukemia at 52.

In 1965, Holtz, 20, was paying for Wartburg by selling shirts at Chicago's Marshall Field's. On a bet, he asked Alice Rudge, a store clothing model, for a date. They married in 1967. Graduating, Mark meandered to Scottsbluff, Nebraska, Omaha, Peoria, and Denver.

"I paid my dues," he said. "That's why I was full of myself when I got to do some Rangers TV games [1981]." In Detroit, assigned a pre-game interview, Holtz approached the trainer wearing ego and a smile. "I'm Mark Holtz. Where's [starting pitcher] Danny Darwin?" The trainer pointed to the dugout. Holtz found a man in jacket and ear muffs sitting on the bench.

"I'd like to ask a few questions," he said.

"Glad to," said the man, "except there's one thing you should know."

"What?"

"I'm not Danny Darwin," said Charlie Hough.

Ultimately, the knuckling Hough retired as Texas's all-time winning pitcher. In 1981, he was an ex-Dodgers hack. "I didn't really want to interview him," said Mark, "but it was near game time and I couldn't find Darwin, so we begin."

Holtz asked about the American League. "I don't know," said Hough. "I've only pitched in two games."

A.L. parks: "Don't know. I've only pitched at home." Detroit: Did the ball travel? "Don't know. I've never pitched here."

Q & A ends. Mark finds the booth, head between his legs. *"Charlie Hough?"* rasped the WAP Radio producer. "If Darwin goes nine innings, we won't have a word."

In the third, he pulls a muscle. Relieving, Don Zimmer picks the least likely starter. Amazingly, Hough apes Cy Young. The interview proudly runs. "Ability is fine," said Napoleon, "but give me commanders who have luck." Holtz seemed to have it. The team did not.

"Most years, we were dead by July," Mark rued. The miasma spread. Partner Eric Nadel, opening his attache case, spilled a Coca-Cola cup. "It had all his baseball records. Eric's face was terrified. An entire career consumed by foam."

In 1989, a group led by George W. Bush bought a franchise short of fizz.

Attendance broke 2 million—first of five straight years. That April Nolan Ryan first pitched for Texas. On August 22, lost in thought, he drove past Arlington Stadium. "Never happened before. Guess I had a lot on my mind."

At 8:42 P.M. Central Time, Ryan got K 5,000. Later, leaving the club-house, Holtz spied him on the stationary bicycle.

"I can't believe you're not out celebrating!" Mark gaped.

"I'm in my forties," Nolan smiled. "If I don't ride this bicycle, I won't get ready for my next start."

"Can't you skip this one?"

"Nope. Got to ride a bike for 45 minutes after everybody leaves the day I pitch."

Holtz joined the Texas Baseball Hall of Fame in 1990. Ryan later joined Cooperstown: 27 years, 324 victories, and 5,714 Ks. In 1993, the Rangers lost their last game at Arlington Stadium. Ahead: The Ballpark at Arlington. Few would confuse them.

"Arlington was a minor-league park," said Mark, "built in stages." Bush built The Ballpark like Caesar out of Marco Polo by way of Sam Houston because this, after all, was Texas. Nooks summoned Fenway Park; right field, Detroit's overhang; a sign, "Hit It Here and Win A Free Suit," Ebbets Field. A four-story office building of Cajun twist, steel trusses, wrought-iron decor, and glass abutted center field.

Opening April 11, 1994, the new home housed a better club. "Hello, win column!" Holtz cried after each victory, the future suddenly as green as winter oats. "He was copasetic," said Alice, "the losing about to end." In August, a strike ended the division-leading Rangers' year.

Usually, the homebody would have tended his dog, friends, and Alice and daughter Cindy. "My life totally revolves around family," he said. "When Alice was diagnosed [1989, of cancer], I thought I would be left alone." Now Mark himself was diagnosed with a bone marrow disease, myelodysplasia.

"His blood-forming cells don't function normally," said Alice. "He takes medication, but the pain is awful." The soldier soldiered on. In February 1997, he began blood transplants and hormone injections. "He could barely lift a cup, or talk for thirty seconds," said Nadel, visiting in the hospital. "The handshake was wasted," like his life.

On May 22, Mark called his peroration. "I'd give anything to have another game, but I know my situation. It's over." Next month he entered Baylor University Medical Center for a bone marrow transplant. A huge card, signed by thousands at The Ballpark, flanked the bed. "Mark took care of me all those years," said Mrs. Holtz. "Now I'm taking care of him."

Her husband died September 7. Alice followed in 1999. "The place of justice is a hallowed place," said Francis Bacon. *In*justice is always hollow.

MARK HOLTZ

LONGEVITY:	6	17 years.
CONTINUITY:	10	Texas A.L. 1981–97.
NETWORK:	1	CBS Radio "Home Team Inning."
KUDOS:	5	Eight-time Texas Sportscaster of the Year. Texas Baseball Hall of Fame 1990.
LANGUAGE:	10	"Beautiful word pictures," said Nadel.
POPULARITY:	10	TV 1981 and 1995–97 and radio 1982–94 Voice liked prime rib and chocolate cake, rued not meeting Groucho Marx, and lived favorite film, "It's a Wonderful Life."
PERSONA:	8	"Fan with the ultimate voice," said Rangers G.M. Tom Grieve.
VOICE:	10	Deep, velvet.
KNOWLEDGE:	10	Devoured baseball stats and books 12 months a year.
MISCELLANY:	4	Called Bradley, Colorado, and Illinois football or basketball—also, Dallas Mavericks and Denver Bears.
TOTAL:	74	(82nd place).

HANK GREENWALD

Baseball is a game of stop and start. Put another way, a broadcaster must cross a sea of dead air. "There's not a lot going on," said Hank Greenwald. "You must create the illusion that there is." A nine-inning game may put the ball in play only 10–12 minutes. "Baseball is not an inherently exciting sport. It's interesting, subtle, contemplative, but tough to broadcast"—even tougher, without wit.

Greenwald was born in Detroit, raised in Rochester, and weaned on Harry Heilmann and Mel Allen. At Syracuse University, he met Jim Brown, joined the campus radio station, and decided to junk the law.

In one class Hank waited six months to appear.

"May I help you?" said the instructor.

"I'm in the class," he said.

"What's your name?
"Greenwald."
"Where you been, Greenwald?"
"I couldn't find the room."

Graduating in 1957, he began calling the Orange—Ernie Davis, Jim Nance, Floyd Little. "They made you sound good"—NBA Nationals, and I.L. Chiefs in 1960. In 1962, visiting San Francisco, Hank, 29, fell for a loop. "I did what any level-headed mature individual would do—quit my job," heading unemployed to California. Said a friend: "If you're going to starve to death you might as well do it in a place you love."

Bart Giamatti was once asked about pro basketball. "Young woman!" he huffed. "You want me to talk about thumpety, thumpety, thumpety, *swish*?" Greenwald loved a game less hip-hop than today's. By 1965, he did Frisco's Warriors and P.C.L. Hawaii. The Honolulu radio booth had four phones. "If line four rang, it was a wrong number because no one knew how to reach us."

One day it rang. Answering, partner Lyle Nelson presumed an errant call. "Ball one," said Greenwald. Then: "Who is it? Anyone we know?"

Lyle shook his head: "You know anyone named Clem?"

"Only Bill Klem [1905–40 umpire who said, "I never made a wrong call, at least in my heart"]. Maybe it's him," said Hank.

"No, it couldn't be Bill Klem," Nelson said. "He never made a wrong call." Greenwald finished the inning on the floor. A wrong number still makes him reel.

Hank spent a decade calling charging and traveling. Then, in 1979, KNBR San Francisco hired him and Lindsey Nelson. Each had a Down's syndrome daughter. Nelson's warmth leapfrogged the lines. "Don't get caught up in wins and losses. If you do, and you're with a bad team, you'll sound like them." Nodding, Hank was caught up with baseball. "Prepare yourself for the worst game ever played, then hope you never have to use it. The best way to learn is to watch, read," and act like the devil is your guide.

In Montreal, Greenwald yamped at mass smoking. "When you ask for the non-smoking section, they send you to Buffalo." Philadelphia: "It's such a rabid baseball town, even trucks are named for Connie Mack." Ken Caminiti left another game with "stomach problems." Hank couldn't help himself: "Why shouldn't the guy with all the hits and RBIs also have the runs?"

One day Pedro Borbon reached first base. Billy North singled him to third. Checking his scorecard, Greenwald looked up to find Pedro MIA, not LOB. "Borbon is missing," he told the audience. "I don't know what's going on, but I'll try to find out." The press box solved the puzzle: out on appeal, for missing second.

Some Voices fail trying to be funny. Not trying, Hank was. Said a writer: "The only failing broadcasting grade anyone would give Greenwald is an F in ego."

Five times, the 1980–85 Giants placed last or next-to-last. Hank's real bane was the pregame show. "There's not one of us who doesn't hate sorting, gees, who'm I gonna get today?" Visiting a bar, he and partner David Glass were hustled by a prostitute. "For $100 I'll do anything you want."

Glass missed not a beat. "How about the pregame show for a week?"

Greenwald turned 50 in 1985. "It's funny," he said. "When the season started I was only 43." One foul hit a sea of empty seats. Hank gave the section number. "Anyone coming to tomorrow's game might want to stop and pick it up." San Francisco drew 1,632 on September 3. "Sixteen thirty-two! That's not a crowd. That's a shirt size."

In 1986, the Yanks laundered a five-year $30 million WABC pact. "I had problems with KNBR management," he said, joining New York next year. Its problems were a bad team; Billy Martin, drinking; and George Steinbrenner, meddling. "Any criticism, he'd phone you." Greenwald stuck it out. "It's amazing how a couple of years with the Yankees can validate your career."

Hank rejoined San Francisco in 1989. "KNBR still didn't want me, but the Giants did. WABC'd tried to keep me on the cheap." Frisco made the Series. The '93ers won 104 games—but lost the West. One night he taped an open: "Good evening, everybody, I'm Hank Greenwald, along with Duane Kuiper. We're here at Three Rivers Stadium. . . ."

The producer tells Hank to shorten it. He tries. The producer asks again. "Good evening, everybody, I'm Hank Greenwald, along with Duane Kuiper. We're here at Two Rivers Stadium. . . ."

September 1996: Hank aired his 2,798th straight game, retired, and turned traveling man. His fixed *idee,* Douglas MacArthur, had returned in 1944 to the Philippines by wading ashore at Leyte Gulf. A picture by wife Carla shows hubby splashing toward the beach. In Rome, he held a sign in front of the Colosseum: "I need tickets." Greenwald schlepped the Canadian National Railroad, Johannesburg to Capetown Blue Train, and Eastern and Oriental Express, and took a two-month freighter to Australia. "All this *before* I retired. Watch me now."

Once he watched son Douglas Aaron, named for MacArthur and another hero, Henry Aaron, batboy at Shea Stadium. Brett Butler fouled a bunt. "Doug gets the bat, waits to give it to Butler, then swings it." Pitcher Rick Aguilera mistook him for the 5-foot-9 Brett. "He's about to throw at my kid in the batter's box. Thank God the ump intervened."

Doug followed pop to play-by-play. "At least one of us is working. He has to so I can stay retired." In 2004, Hank followed his past to Bay Area A's TV. "Okay, enough retirement," he said, lauding two truisms:

1) In baseball, often not a hell of a lot happens.
2) "The more I laugh," sang the actor Ed Wynne, "the more I'm a merrier me."

HANK GREENWALD

LONGEVITY:	7	20 years.
CONTINUITY:	7	San Francisco N.L. 1979–86 and 1989–96; New York A.L. 1987–88; ABC/NBC TV The Baseball Network 1994–95; CBS Radio "Game of the Week" 1997; Oakland A.L. 2004– .
NETWORK:	3	TBN 1994–95 (ABC/NBC TV). "Game" and L.C.S. 1997 (CBS Radio).
KUDOS:	3	Fewer than he deserves.
LANGUAGE:	9	Said of Yanks: "My greatest thrill wasn't working at The Stadium. It was walking out and finding my car still there."
POPULARITY:	9	Critics' Choice.
PERSONA:	9	Did he just say that?
VOICE:	10	Sharp.
KNOWLEDGE:	10	Still caught up with baseball.
MISCELLANY:	9	Carted enough fare for landing at Anzio: cigars, pencils, sharpeners, black suitcase, three-ring binder, and baseball pins, ties, and clippings. Super Bowl press box announcer.
TOTAL:	76	(73rd place).

JOE ANGEL

Announcers can be deacons, dirtbags, beggarmen, and/or thieves. "We're different behind a mike," said Harry Caray. "Why should broadcasters be the same away?" Pew, bar, or library: they loved diversity before diversity was cool.

A bilingual Voice has called the Giants, Athletics, Twins, Orioles, Yankees, Marlins, The Baseball Network, ESPN, and Jints and O's again. "I can play it either way," said Joe Angel of English and Spanish. "Just tell me how to play it."

In 1956, the native Colombian, eight, moved to San Francisco. Later, Joe hosted talk radio, was a 49ers fill-in, and replaced Al Michaels. "What could be better? Home team, home town." In 1979, a new Giants flagship made the City College of San Francisco grad odd man out: local boy without a job.

Next year a new owner bought the A's. Hiring Angel, Levi Strauss tried to gussy them up. "In '79, one game'd drawn 653." Plus: attendance tripled. Minus: the suddenly chic A's changed flagships, too. "I'd wanted to be a Giant. Now the Bay's other team dumps me." Security seemed as fickle as the curve.

Joe repaired to golf, his children, and Bay hoops and football. Daughter Natalie became a CBS reporter. Actor son Jonathan rang NBC's "Saved By the Bell." Minnesota's saved dad's. In 1984, "missing the involvement of a team," he joined WCCO's Herb Carneal. Their workplace was the Hubert H. Humphrey Metrodome, whose roof made each fly an adventure.

Snow postponed one game. Wind and rain stopped another for nine minutes. In 1985, Dave Kingman popped toward the ether. "When the ball gets past a point, you lose it and look at fielders." Mickey Hatcher began circling first base. "Soon the whole team's running around. Nobody could locate the ball!"

In time, umpires found it above a false ceiling, clearing ventilation holes barely larger than the ball. Kingman got a ground-rule double. Later Mickey decided to catch a ball dropped from the roof. "The law of gravity. What goes up comes down."

The quarry darted and knuckled. Raising his glove, Hatcher missed. The ball didn't, hitting his toe. "Sometimes, you can't win," he said. Unlike Joe, the Twins were about to.

On St. Patrick's Day 1986, Hatcher arrived for an exhibition game with his face, neck, arms, and hands painted green. Mates roared. Is he a package, or what? Mickey's skin began to burn. At the hospital, doctors removed the paint. "It was killing oxygen," said Angel. "Since then I stick to finger-painting." Next year, change fingered Joe, kicking him to Baltimore. "They say war is hell. Play-by-play's a close second."

The 1988 Orioles began a record-breaking 0–21. As sad: Angel's 1991 hiatus in the Bronx. "I couldn't say no to that tradition. But I didn't like the city." Partner John Sterling didn't help: "It was a clash of styles. Joe does everything by rote." Next year he returned to Baltimore, still pining for No. 1. "With Jon Miller on radio, it wasn't going to happen there." It might, however, in an expansion year/bilingual city.

On March 6, 1993, the Marlins began a four-hour ride to Homestead, Florida, for an exhibition. Manager Rene Lachemann's bus burst a tire. The players' bus kept going. "I wanted both to arrive at the same time," said Rene, who, reaching the second bus, U-turned it and begged a soda. "Our traveling secretary," Joe laughed, "had forgot soft drinks."

Belatedly, each bus found the park. The club slept overnight at a hotel. At 3 A.M., Angel awoke to bagpipes on his floor. "A convention, and in their long boots and short checkered shirts they're blowing up and down the hallways." Opening Day seemed an eon away. Actually, it arrived April 5.

That morning, a storm hit south Florida. Clearing, the sky dimmed Joe's hirings and firings and changes and moves. "I'd waited so long. I knew we'd be bad, but couldn't wait for the season." Introducing each Marlin, he called reliever Bryan Harvey "a man with almost as many saves as John the Baptist."

A month earlier Charlie Hough, 45, threw Florida's first-ever pitch. "[He's] into his motion," Angel began the exhibition, "and [it's] a knuckleball, high *and* low, ball one." Hough's first Real McCoy now knuckled a foot outside the plate. Ump Frank Pulli called strike: 42,530 roared. Hough threw one wider: strike two. "Anywhere the pitch was, Frank was going to inaugurate this place with a strikeout."

Jose Offerman K'd. Hough won, 6–3. Florida drew 3,064,847. By 1996, only 1,746,767 dotted Joe Robbie Stadium. "We can still make it," said owner Wayne Huizenga, buying Bobby Bonilla, Moises Alou, Alex Fernandez, and skipper Jim Leyland. Next year, adding TV, Joe doubted he would make it through the opener. "I do nine innings [not six] now. My voice is 'going, going, gone.'"

The wild-carders made the Series. Each Marlins dinger sired "*Hasta la vista,* baby!" Game Seven built through climaxes. In the ninth, Craig Counsell's sacrifice fly tied Cleveland. "Each pitch was the universe," said Angel. "There's nothing like it in broadcasting—easily, the highlight of my career."

Bases full, 11th inning, two out and all: Edgar Renteria singled past Indians pitcher Charles Nagy's glove. "A five-year-old child has become king!" Joe bayed on the Marlins' network. Their reign was briefer than summer in Saskatoon.

Huizenga iced the Fish in a 1998 fire sale, then sold to a commodities trader. "Either people don't go to [renamed] Pro Player [Stadium]," said John Henry, "or they cheer the opposition." Suddenly, Miami seemed as camp as Glenn, Mitch, and Mrs. Miller combined.

"The situation was so chancy," Angel conceded. "No wonder I was let go. The upset is that I stayed so long." On the road again: from 2001 ESPN, Joe's wound to Pac Bell Park. "It took me 24 years to get my heart back, but I've got it back," rejoining Miller. "I debuted a Giant and with some luck I'll retire one."

In early 2004, his road picture improbably led back to Baltimore as lead announcer. "What's the good of a home, if you are never in it?" said a 19th-century British singer and comedian.

Angel hopes to be in this home a while.

JOE ANGEL

LONGEVITY:	8	22 years.
CONTINUITY:	4	San Francisco N.L. 1977–78 and 2002–03; Minnesota A.L. 1984–86; Baltimore A.L. 1988–90, 1992, and 2004– ; New York A.L. 1991; Florida N.L. 1993–2000; ABC/NBC TV The Baseball Network 1994–95; ESPN TV "Major League Baseball" 2001.
NETWORK:	2	TBN 1994–95 (ABC/NBC TV). "Baseball" 2001 (ESPN TV).
KUDOS:	3	Hurt by turnover.
LANGUAGE:	9	Pick 'em.
POPULARITY:	9	Survives peregrination.
PERSONA:	10	Baseball's U.N.
VOICE:	10	Deep.
KNOWLEDGE:	10	Merits time to flaunt it.
MISCELLANY:	10	Galileo High School quarterback threw to receiver O.J. Simpson.
TOTAL:	75	(79th place).

LANNY FRATTARE

In *Hamlet,* Banquo's Ghost hovers like a cold front: actors respond for good or ill to exterior things at play. Like Janus, the Pirates' Lanny Frattare's ghost was two-headed. Would outliving mean excising them?

Frattare grew up to their north and east. "Look at big-league guys from Rochester," he said. "Greenwald, Pete Van Wieren, Fox's Josh Lewin." Each watched the Cardinals', then Orioles', Triple-A affiliate. Lanny wasn't picky: any bigs aviary would do.

"I'd look at the booth and think, 'This must be the best seat in the house.'" His hero ruled the Yanks'. "Everywhere you'd hear Allen. I got a tape recorder and imitated him." Mel's voice was rich, clear, and urgent. Lanny's was deep, stout, and calm.

At 20, the Ithaca College student met two local announcers "who got me in the market." In 1974, airing Triple-A Charleston, he overnighted at Steve Blass's home in Pittsburgh. Bob Prince asked Frattare—dirty, hair askew, having blacktopped Blass's driveway—to do an inning.

"If I never get to the majors again," he said, "they can't take this away." In October 1975, the Pirates took Prince's job. From 65 applicants, Lanny and Milo Hamilton succeeded Bob and Nellie King. Their problem was Pittsburgh's psyche. The Gunner filled its core.

Prince's ghost was as real as any relative. "Ironically, Bob'd buck me up, say to get involved in the community," said Lanny. A second specter, Forbes Field, draped the Bucs' new home. "At Three Rivers, charm had to come from the team, not park." In Pittsburgh, both meant Pops. Where Willie the Starge led, even umpires went.

In 1977, manager Chuck Tanner put Stargell's name in the fourth and sixth lineup spots. Alvin Dark waited till Willie doubled and the second Stargell hit.

"We got two Wilver Stargells!" San Diego's skipper told Doug Harvey.

The ump eyed his scorecard. "Mr. Dark, I know who Wilver Stargell is and he's not at home plate now. No matter what the card says, Stargell's hitting fourth and this man up for the second time is hitting sixth—and I don't care *who* he is!"

Next season ended at home against Philadelphia. "We're trailing the Phils," said Frattare, "but sweep a twinbill": two games left, 1 1/2 behind. A day later radios tuned to KDKA at a University of Pittsburgh football game shook on Pops's first-inning slam. "That's what baseball is about—a whole city riding on each pitch."

Pops headed the Pirates family. In 1979, southwest Pennsylvania's melting pot—Slavs, Poles, Blacks, Germans—sang Sister Sledge's "We Are Fam-i-lee." Pittsburgh won the Series vs. Baltimore. Sadly, it banned local radio till 1980.

"We came from 3 to 1 [games] behind," said Lanny. "It'd have been great to call the Classic." Next week, another kind of call cleared his line.

"Even during the Series, I knew Milo wasn't going to extend his contract. He was done trying to replace the Gunner." Up: Frattare replaced Hamilton, not Prince. Down: Bob began local cable-TV in 1982.

The '84ers finished last. Next year a flailing franchise rehired an ailing god. "I never call myself the 'Voice of the Pirates,'" Lanny said on the Gunner's KDKA return, "because Bob always will be," even after his death in June. Frattare still hears pleas to sound, well, like Prince.

Bob roared, "We had 'em all the way!" Lanny wags, "There was no doubt about it!" George H. W. Bush once said, "I'm not Ronald Reagan. I couldn't be if I wanted to." Ultimately, Lanny less persuaded than gentled ambiguity.

The 1990 Bucs rallied on Memorial Day to beat Los Angeles. A year later to the day, they edged the Cubs. "It's Memorial Day all over again!" Frattare whooped. Assets: Pittsburgh made three straight L.C.S. Twice Barry Bonds became MVP. Debits: The late-'90ers lost audience and attendance.

In 2000, Stargell threw out the confluence's last first pitch. Sister Sledge sang two Anthems—America's, and "We Are Fam-i-lee." Three Rivers imploded in 2001. Lanny took its digital-timer box to 38,365-seat PNC

LANNY FRATTARE

LONGEVITY:	10	29 years.
CONTINUITY:	10	Pittsburgh N.L. 1976– ; ABC/NBC TV The Baseball Network 1994–95.
NETWORK:	1	TBN 1994–95 (ABC/NBC TV).
KUDOS:	5	Bob Prince Award 1989. Three-time Vectors Club award. Western Pennsylvania Sports Hall of Fame. Pittsburgh Radio/TV Club outstanding achievement in radio award 2003.
LANGUAGE:	8	Basic, with "statistical-heavy style," said Associated Press.
POPULARITY:	9	Shedding ghosts helps.
PERSONA:	8	Like Pittsburgh, solid and stable.
VOICE:	9	Clean, crisp.
KNOWLEDGE:	10	Has scorecard of each Bucs game broadcast—more than 4,000.
MISCELLANY:	6	U.S. Presidency student and memorabilia collector.
TOTAL:	76	(71st place).

Park. Light towers, corner pens, and a flat-green roof conjured Forbes. Downtown rose across the Allegheny River. Behind right field, homers flowed slowly to the Mississippi.

"I've waited all my career for a real baseball park," Frattare pined. Lady MacBeth cried, "Out, out damn spot." Lanny's had.

PHIL RIZZUTO

In 1941, a first-year Yankees shortstop entered the General Manager's office. "I didn't know Ed Barrow," said Phil Rizzuto. "I did know that the man being shaved by a guy whom he kept calling Goulash was Barrow."

Rizzuto waited silently. "Young man," Barrow snapped, "what is your trouble?"

Phil's was money. "I give you this, and no more!" the G.M. flushed. "If okay, sign! If not, get the hell out of here!" Goulash applied talcum powder. Rizzuto signed.

Red Ruffing, Bill Dickey, and Joe DiMaggio gave Phil the cold shoulder. Hurt, the 5-foot-6 new kid on the block approached another star. "Relax, they're not snubbing you," Lefty Gomez said. "They just haven't seen you yet."

Later, DiMag became a friend. "If you forget Phil was so tiny as a player, it's because his reputation was so huge."

You gotta be kiddin'! What a huckleberry! Smaller than the game, Rizzuto made baseball larger than it was.

Leave it to the Scooter—Fiero Francis Rizzuto, a trolley car conductor's son—to be born in Brooklyn. At 16, he tried out for the Giants and Dodgers. "Go get a shoe box," sniffed Brooklyn's Casey Stengel. "That's the only way you'll make a living." Phil then phoned the Yanks. Signing, he went to Bassett, Virginia.

"*Bassett!*" said Rizzuto. "Sounds like I'm swearing at somebody." Holy cow! Cows draped its hill. "The players told me that the front legs of the cows were shorter than the back because they were always on the hill. And I believed them. With my short legs, I've always had an affinity with cows." Billy Hitchcock named him "Scooter": "Man, you're not runnin', you're scootin'."

In 1941, the rookie reached the Bronx. Hitting .307, he replaced Joe DiMaggio at a Newark firemen communion breakfast. "Joe had a family illness, but they were still expecting him. So I get booed—at a communion breakfast!" Embarrassed, a fireman asked him home for coffee. Daughter Cora Esselborn then entered the room. Half a century later, Phil's blood ran, not scooted: "Those legs, her red sweater, those blue eyes." They married June 23, 1943.

By then, Rizzuto, in the Navy, had served or would in the Philippines and Australia, anchor Pee Wee Reese's team, and get malaria. Released in December 1945, he saw "a seminal American invention," Ron Fimrite wrote of Babe Ruth, break down. In June 1948, the Stripes retired No. 3. Said Phil: "He was so sick [of cancer], it took two men to lift him."

Ruth leaned on Bob Feller's bat like a cane. "Any time you want me to come to your house for Holy Communion, I'd be glad to do it," said His Eminence Cardinal Spellman.

Babe smiled. "Thank you, but I'd rather come to *your* place."

Rizzuto's place was pressure: "It didn't take long," said Ted Williams, "to see that in big games he was at his best." Phil hit a 1942 Series-high .381. His 1949 last-day triple eluded Williams to help win a pennant. A year later he got 200 hits, scored 125 runs, and was named MVP. "My best pitch," said Vic Raschi, "is anything the batter grounds, lines, or pops in his direction."

Scooter knew how to field, bunt (Joe D.: "the greatest I ever saw"), hit behind the runner, and win (four All-Star teams, nine flags, and six titles). "Those years I made more money from Series cuts than I did from my salary for the whole year." 1953: now-skipper Stengel benched him. 1954: Phil hit .195. 1955: the Yanks held his Day. 1956: the Stripes hung a noose.

"We've got a chance to get Enos Slaughter. What do you think?" said George Weiss.

"Boy, getting him would be a help," said Rizzuto, taking cyanide. Enos replaced him on the roster. Holy cow! Released on Old Timers' Day, the Scooter, 39, was unemployed. "From a damn good living, suddenly I didn't have anything." Mel Allen had him call a half-inning here or there. The Orioles offered radio. Phil was torn, not wanting to leave New York.

As Richard Reeves writes of politics, broadcasting magnifies charm and institutionalizes seduction. By late 1956, Rizzuto had charmed Ballantine Beer head Carl Badenhausen, who told Weiss to hire him. "Can you picture a thorn between two roses [Mel and Red Barber]? I wouldn't have hired myself!" he laughed. The joke was on them: stomaching each other, they resented Scooter.

"They were pros," said axed-for-Phil Jim Woods. "Rizzuto'd write down stories in the dugout, go on the air, and hide the paper." Interrupting, he stole one sign—"Oh, my God! He's going to steal home!"—as Allen called a pitch. Another game Mel and Red left the booth, forcing Phil not to halt, stumble, and brook dead air.

"Kansas City Ath-a-letics," he would say.

"No, Phil, it's Athletics," Mel corrected him on air. Scooter accepted it. Mother Rose detested it. Gradually, the two pros warmed. In 1957, the thorn caught a bouquet: CBS Radio's thrice-weekly five-minute "Phil Rizzuto On Sports." On October 1, 1961, he got another.

"Fastball, hit deep to right!" Scooter yapped. "This could be it! Way back there! Holy cow, he did it! Sixty-one for Maris! Look at 'em fight for that ball out there! Holy cow! What a shot!" Maris had expunged a ghost. "And they're still fighting for that ball out there! People are climbing over each other's backs. One of the greatest sights I've seen here at Yankee Stadium!"

Mel called the Series vs. Cincinnati. Phil called upon aspirin. "I screamed so loud on Maris's homer, I had a headache for a week!"

At first he did two innings daily. "He'd leave in the seventh or eighth," said Allen. "Red and I'd finish." One game went overtime. "And now to take you into the tenth, here is . . . here is": Rizzuto was already on the George Washington Bridge. "He became famed for leaving early," added Bob Costas. "Even when he stuck around, you'd hear him hooking the mike into the stand announcing the final score."

June 24, 1962: Yanks at Detroit. Inhaled by 35,638: 32,000 hot dogs and 41,000 and 34,500 bottles of beer and pop, respectively, during 600 pitches, three seventh-inning stretches, and a seven-hour game: New York, 9–7, on Jack Reed's 22nd-inning blast.

"I've got to leave," an Ontario writer said two innings earlier.

"Where are you going?" said a colleague.

"My visa just expired."

Leaving in the seventh, Phil flew to LaGuardia Airport, headed to Jersey, and turned on the radio. Time: 7 P.M. The 1:30 game should have ended by 4. "I drop my jaw. Red's starting the 19th": Mel has TV; neither can take a leak. "I'm on the bridge and say, 'What am I gonna do? Should I turn around and fly back to Detroit? No, that doesn't make sense.'"

He arrives home, kisses "my bride" Cora, and turns on WPIX TV. Allen's warm-voweled lilt never seemed so cold.

The 1964 Yanks won the pennant. Next year's flunked .500. Mel and Red both left. "They had Jerry Coleman, Joe Garagiola came, but Rizzuto was the guy," said Phil Mushnick. "Homework? Stick around? He's the Scooter!"—increasingly, his own best subject matter. An inning, George Vecsey wrote, might link "birthday greetings, movie reviews, golf tips, war memories, frequent psychosomatic broodings, fearsome predictions of rain, sleet, snow, thunder, lightning, tornadoes, waterspouts," and allergies and insects: one dragonfly drove Scooter from the booth.

In 1974, The Stadium began a $100 million facelift. Slumming at Shea, the 1976 Stripes returned to win a flag. NBC aired the Series. "Under its new pact, local Voices couldn't broadcast," said Costas. Phil broke the rule, in his artful, artless way.

Later Bob probed Rizzuto's scorecard. A slash bespoke a K. "WW" seemed to mean a single and sacrifice. Puzzled, he said, "I've seen a lot of ways to keep score. What's WW?"

"Wasn't watching?"

A 90-year-old woman writes a letter. "Before it gets too late," Phil replies, "she might not be with us the whole game"—going to bed or the great beyond, he doesn't say.

The camera spots a lovely teenage girl.

Rizzuto: "She reminds me of that old song, 'A Pretty Girl Is Like a Memory.'"

Partner Bill White: "Scooter, I think that's 'Melody.'"

"Really. How do you know her name is Melody?" Cora says that everyone has a trap door at the back of the head. "When a thought reaches the door, the brain asks if I should say this. My door is always open."

In 1985, the Yanks marked Phil's birthday by presenting a convertible, golf clubs, and a cow named Huckleberry, who stepped on Rizzuto's foot, decking him. Later he begins waving from the second deck. "You know, Mussolini used to do this." A visitor arrives from San Jose. "San Jose? I love San Jose. What's that song?" Someone begins Dionne Warwick's tune, "Do you know the way . . . ?" Phil amends: "No, it isn't San Jose. It's Phoenix."

A grounder finds the hole. "They'll never get him! They got him! I changed my mind before he got there, so that doesn't count as an error." At The Stadium, he vows to drive north to Philadelphia, then recalls Benjamin Franklin inventing lightning. A sidekick starts laughing. "You know what I meant," Rizzuto says. "I didn't mean that Franklin invented lightning. I meant he discovered it." Among other things, he describes putting grits in his pocket on visiting the South. "My first time there. It looked like oatmeal. I didn't know what to do."

A Hindu "or Indian or something" wrote a letter "beefing about that holy cow," said Scooter. "He said in India the cow is sacred, and I shouldn't say such a thing."

Love that Phil. If it's sacred, he answered, what's wrong with "Holy cow"?

In 1987, Rizzuto cut lyrics for Meat Loaf's "Paradise by the Dashboard Light." He didn't know that it hailed teenage sex.

"Meat Loaf said, 'I've got this song for you.' I thought it was a singing part—all Italians love to sing." Phil attended the recording session. Meat Loaf says: "It's a talking part."

"Where's the band to accompany me?"

Meat Loaf: "We'll put it in later."

By and by his son said, "Dad, you're a rock star!" Six times pop reran the album, finally grasping its core. "I never knew, so help me. My priest gave me hell"—Scooter amusing, diverting: a character, not drone.

"Any idiot can call a great game," the Cubs' Jack Quinlan claimed. "It takes a different tack—tell a joke, explain making moonshine, anything— with a game that's dull."

Was Phil a professional? He never *feigned* to be, said columnist Will Grimsley, "[attracting] a broader spectrum of the audience, nonbaseball people who might overwise be watching," say, A&E—the most popular broadcaster to ever darn the Stripes.

In 1994, the Veterans Committee belatedly drove him into Cooperstown. "For years baseball wanted me to sing the Anthem the day players were inducted," said the Metropolitan Opera's Robert Merrill. "I said, 'Not till Rizzuto's in.'"

Scooter's daughter phoned Induction Eve. "Mr. Merrill, Dad's so nervous, he's losing his voice." Merrill gave her lozenges. Later, Phil: "Where do I get those drops?" The Rizzutos got a trip to Europe that fall from the Yanks. At the Vatican, Pope John Paul II changed his schedule for an audience. "I'll tell you," said Phil, 76, "that's as close to God as you can get."

Next August roused another sense of time running out. Mickey Mantle's death of alcohol-induced cancer "just hit me. I started thinking of my family." The funeral was in Dallas. Phil aired a game from Boston. "When I saw the [TV] service, I realized what a big mistake I had made [not going]." Distraught, he left in the fifth inning, retired, returned in 1996, and retired again.

In 1997, Richard Sandomir wrote, "Where are you, Scooter? The MSG Network's Phil-free games miss his mirth." Bad game, good game, Scooter meant a fun game: more playactor than play-by-playman, baseball's *paisan* with *pizazz*.

PHIL RIZZUTO

LONGEVITY:	10	40 years.
CONTINUITY:	10	New York A.L. 1957–96.
NETWORK:	3	World Series 1964 and 1976 (NBC TV). "Phil Rizzuto on Sports" 1957–76 (CBS Radio).
KUDOS:	9	Cooperstown 1994. American League Most Valuable Player 1950. Hickock Belt 1950. Number 10 retired by Yankees 1985. Pride of the Yankees Award 1981.
LANGUAGE:	10	Welded William Faulkner and Curley Howard: "A day without cannolis is like a day without sunshine."
POPULARITY:	10	No. 10, No. 1.
PERSONA:	10	Bodacious, not faceless.
VOICE:	7	To the *Daily News*'s Bob Raissman, "sandcastles in asphalt, a summer sea breeze down the Grand Concourse."
KNOWLEDGE:	8	"Rizzuto reciting stats," mused the *Denver Post*, "would be like Jim Carrey doing Shakespeare."
MISCELLANY:	10	Superstitious. Once kept gum on hat till Yankees lost. "Nobody would sit next to me on the bench. It smelled awful but I wouldn't take it off."
TOTAL:	87	(27th place).

BILL WHITE

"He seems to hit a baseball on the dead run," wrote *Time* magazine. "Once in motion, he wobbles along, elbows flying, . . . shoulders rocking. . . . He is not only jack-rabbit fast, but about one thought and two steps ahead of every base-runner in the business."

Jackie Robinson broke the color line in 1947. In 1965, he became the bigs' first black analyst on "Game of the Week." One Saturday, Robinson listened by earpiece to producer Chuck Howard. "Chuck said something," mused Voice Merle Harmon, "and Jackie said, 'Okay.' You heard it on the air."

Braving diabetes, Robinson died, at 53, in 1972. "He had a high, stabbing voice, great presence, and sharp mind," said Howard. "All he lacked was time."

"Here is a man," said Branch Rickey, signing Jackie in 1945, "whose wounds you could not feel or share." In 1997, baseball retired No. 42 on the golden anniversary of his debut. "No one could grasp his trial," said Bill White, baseball's first black play-by-playman, "but at least I got a sense of the loneliness he knew."

As a boy, the son of a steelworker and Air Force clerk left Florida for Ohio. Picking Hiram College, Bill hoped to practice medicine. "Baseball was only for money for my pre-med courses."

In a 1952 tryout, White, 18, sprayed Forbes Field's vast depths.

"Get him out of here!" yelled Giants skipper Leo Durocher. "If [then-Bucs head] Rickey sees this kid, he'll get him."

Bill joined Carolina League Danville, Virginia. Segregation soiled towns like Greensboro, Durham, and Winston-Salem. White abided "colored-only" restrooms, was barred in hotels and lunch counters, and stayed with black families on the road. One crowd stoned his bus. "The uglier people got, the more I turned to baseball—and the harder I hit the ball."

The Giants first basemen led 1956 N.L.ers in putouts and assists. Drafted, he quit the Army post baseball team. "All I remember is a guy calling me a nigger." The Jints moved to San Francisco. Joining them, he met a wall: Orlando Cepeda. A 1959 deal to St. Louis posed another: Stan Musial. "The minors' hate—now this!"

White won the 1960–66 Gold Glove, four years had at least 100 RBI, and got the 1961 Redbirds to leave a segregated St. Petersburg hotel. Players' wives began a color-blind day school and kindergarten. "Training camp actually became a tourist attraction," said *The New York Times*. "People [drove] out of their way to see and gawk at the [then and there] remarkable sight of integration." St. Louis won a pennant in 1964.

"So good-bye, dear," wrote Cole Porter, "and amen." In 1966, the five-time All-Star went to Philadelphia, later rejoined the Cards, and retired in 1969.

The decision was less lonely than inevitable. "When you hit .211, you know it's time to change your job."

In St. Louis, he did a weekly KMOX Radio five-minute show. "I'd told Harry Caray, 'Broadcasting's easy.' 'Oh, yeah, try it,' he said. He was right." In 1970, Philadelphia ABC TV outlet WFIL began a nightly segment. Howard Cosell, hearing White call basketball, phoned Yankees head Michael Burke, who proffered play-by-play.

"I got the job because they wanted a black," said Bill. Baseball's pilgrim knew the stakes: failure might sink others. "My first year I was terrible. The next year I was a little less terrible. The Yankees could easily have fired me." Blanche DuBois relied on the kindness of strangers. White relied on his work, not team.

The 1971–73 Yanks finished 241-238. "It'd have been nice," he allowed, "to still have Mantle and Maris." Instead, commuting two hours from Bucks County, outside Philadelphia, "he critiqued his taped segment of every game on radio," said partner Frank Messer, "something I never did even when I started." Slowly, White improved. A cause: Rizzuto, becoming Costello to his Abbott.

"Some guys just click," Phil chimed. Jon Miller revived Ken Coleman. Tim McCarver renewed Ralph Kiner. Phil unlocked Bill's wit. White stirred his eccentricity. "You wouldn't think so, but deep down they were alike," said Messer—ex-jocks, minorities, latecomers to language.

If the Yanks couldn't interest you, Phil and Bill might.

"I love to listen to Rizzuto," White said. "He makes me laugh." Phil starts reading a long list of birthdays. Bill interrupts: "Hey, don't you have a name in there that doesn't end in a vowel?" Rizzuto begins another telecast. "Hi, everybody, this is New York Yankees baseball. I'm Bill White. Wait a minute! I swear to God I didn't." The straight man—to Scooter, always "White"— laughed. "How'd you like to work 18 years with a guy who still doesn't know your first name?"

Viewers heard White's on ABC's "Monday Night Baseball," CBS Radio L.C.S. and Series, and October 2, 1978, A.L. East playoff. Boston led, 2–0: seventh inning, two out and on. "Deep to left!" Bill cried on WPIX TV. "Yastrzemski will not get it! It's a home run! A three-run homer by Bucky Dent! And the Yankees now lead by a score of 3 to 2!"—winning, 5–4.

New York made the Series. "Popped up behind the plate!" White said. "Coming back, Munson! Throws the mask away! He's there! It's all over— the Yankees charge out on the field! They mob Goose Gossage! The Yankees have won their second straight world championship!" The '80 Stripes drew a record 2,627,417. The '81ers again reached the Classic. George Steinbrenner named/axed Billy Martin a fifth/final time.

Bill rarely sweat hiring/firing. "I do my best. If they don't want me, I'll go somewhere else"—anywhere to fuse game, frill, and time. His 40-foot trawler on Chesapeake Bay lured like a hanging curve. "The Yankees took a trip to the West Coast. I worked a game in Seattle and then flew to Alaska and fished for five days," jetted to Oakland, did a game, fished four more, then heard Peter O'Malley suggest he toss leisure in the can.

The Dodgers owner headed the search committee for a new N.L. head. "It's his [White's] if he wants it," said an owner. Ultimately, he did, becoming the majors' first black president (1989–94). "It's time to move on after 18 years of saying, 'Ground ball to shortstop.' If I didn't think I could do it, I would have been foolish to take it for social significance."

White's significance is more than 50 minority big-league Voices. An outsider might not share his wounds. You might, however, feel the pride.

BILL WHITE

LONGEVITY:	7	19 years.
CONTINUITY:	9	New York A.L. 1971–88; ABC TV "Monday Night Baseball" 1976–79; CBS Radio "Game of the Week" 1985–89.
NETWORK:	8	"Monday" 1976–79 (ABC TV). L.C.S. 1976–79, 1984–85, and 1987–88; World Series 1976–78; and "Game" 1985–89 (CBS Radio).
KUDOS:	5	One of 88 bigs to homer in first at-bat.
LANGUAGE:	6	No-nonsense.
POPULARITY:	7	Tied in part to Scooter's.
PERSONA:	10	Pathfinder.
VOICE:	8	Bass.
KNOWLEDGE:	10	Detailed.
MISCELLANY:	4	Spurned post of Yankees' skipper and G.M. "Anyone can manage. A kid can tell you when to bunt or hit away."
TOTAL:	74	(80th place).

DEWAYNE STAATS

Dub Allen Citation; Caray, War Admiral; Scully, Kelso. DeWayne Staats was more an up-to-snuff mare. "I give you meat and potatoes," he laughed, having grown up thinking baseball light and airy, like chiffon.

Staats consumed it in the Bermuda Triangle of central (Wood River) Illinois. "You've got Cubs, White Sox, Cardinal fans. At night, you'd pull them in." Strangely, another team wooed over WWL New Orleans. To the fourth-grader, Houston might have been the moon.

"I'd tune in Gene Elston," he said, sending a note. Answering, Staats's hero became a pal. DeWayne graduated from Southern Illinois University, joined KPLR TV St. Louis, and did Triple-A Oklahoma City. Small world: in 1976, he auditioned with Elston's Astros (nee Colt .45s).

"Bob Prince had come from Pittsburgh that season and didn't like it," said Staats. Gunner, spying him, hugged his might-be successor. "Don't worry, kid, we'll fuck it up together." DeWayne replaced him next year.

Ninety percent of baseball, Elston told the rookie, is preparation. Staats, then 23, had been preparing since age nine.

"I'd grown up with Jack Buck," DeWayne would say. "Now I see him when the Cards are in town. Lou Boudreau and Milo Hamilton were icons of my youth. Now I'm eating dinner with them." He relished another hero's *bonhomie.* "Harry wakes up and says it's August 7. That day, like every day, meant something."

Caray: "Today's the anniversary of a day I wrote an alimony check for my first wife. I compose, '____, How long must this go on?'" Her reply read: "Dear Harry. Till death do us part."

Harry dueled Hamilton at Wrigley. In late 1984, Milo and Staats swapped jobs. "The quintessential baseball experience," DeWayne called the Confines. In 1987, MVP Andre Dawson's 49 dingers bound Wrigleyville. Change split it. "Activists had kept lights out." Finally, "Baseball [*sic,* network TV] ordered the Cubs to play postseason at night, or move the games to St. Louis." Prime time crashed August 9, 1988. Arcs bred revenue, not the elu-sive-since-'08 world title.

The '89ers slumped in June. A patron mailed a parody of *Macbeth,* which Staats one day read: "Anson, Chance, and Wilson, Hartnett, Hornsby, Brown, and Grimm / hex the Mets, the Birds, and Expos / stand behind the Cubs and Zim. Double, double, toil, and trouble / fire burn and Cubbies bubble. Eye of newt and raven beak / presto, it's a winning streak. So heed this curse from Bill Veeck's vines. Our Cubs are the champs of '89."

Rallying, Cubs win! The ballad works!—till the L.C.S. Next year Staats joined the Yankees' MSG TV. In 1995, he left the Bronx—"the Yanks reneged on salary," said a friend, "as they [MSG parent Viacom] cut costs"—did ESPN "Wednesday Night Baseball," and helped wife Dee endure brain tumor sur-gery. "ESPN was a blessing," DeWayne mused. "Unlike, say, a team, I was home on weekends and with my wife when she went through it all."

In 1998, it all led to Tropicana Field. The name implied sun, fun, and breeze. Actually, "the sterile park," wrote *Sports Illustrated,* "has the ambiance of a warehouse." The Trop did afford a great view of Tampa-St. Petersburg's Sunshine Skyway Bridge. Sadly, it required that you sit on the roof.

What he wanted, Staats would say, is to "help the community, take care of my family, and live on the beach." His Devil Rays commenced March 31, 1998. "His pacing is great for 162 games," said partner Joe Magrane. "He's not going to wear you out with adrenaline in the first game where you go, 'I gotta listen to this guy all year.'"

As the Rays dimmed, attendance missed a million, and Commissioner Bud Selig scurried to Florida to ask what gave, DeWayne tried to "look at life as a positive." It wasn't easy in their "Ballpark of the 21st Century." A writer said, "We need some old-fashioned baseball." They got it, temporarily, August 7, 1999.

Needing three hits for 3,000, "All I could think of was Little League," mused Tampa-reared Wade Boggs. Getting two, the five-time batting champion faced Cleveland's Chris Haney. "Swung on and a long drive! Hit deep to

DEWAYNE STAATS

LONGEVITY:	9	28 years.
CONTINUITY:	7	Houston N.L. 1977–84; Chicago N.L. 1985–89; New York A.L. 1990–94; ABC/NBC TV The Baseball Network 1994; ESPN TV "Wednesday Night Baseball" 1995–97; Tampa Bay A.L. 1998– .
NETWORK:	3	TBN 1994 (ABC/NBC TV). "Wednesday" 1995–97 (ESPN TV).
KUDOS:	6	Southern Illinois Distinguished Alumnus of the Year 1987. Host, St. Louis Emmy Award-winning "Weekend In St. Louis" show. Emmy Award, Devils Rays coverage.
LANGUAGE:	9	Spartan.
POPULARITY:	8	Staying in one place the test: Tampa, so far a hit.
PERSONA:	9	Professional announcer.
VOICE:	9	Low, resonant.
KNOWLEDGE:	10	In-depth.
MISCELLANY:	7	"Each of my teams had a guy embodying the work ethic": Nolan Ryan, Houston; Dawson, Chicago; Don Mattingly, New York.
TOTAL:	77	(67th place).

left! That baby's going to go!" said DeWayne. "Number 3,000—it's a home run for Wade Boggs! On a 2–2 pitch! Simply unbelievable!"

Near second base, Boggs pointed upward and blew his late mother, killed in a 1986 car accident, a kiss. Then he kissed home plate. "Something ran through my mind to say, 'You stepped on it enough, you might as well kiss it.'"

Generations hugged: Wade, mates, father, wife, and 12-year-old son Brett, the Rays batboy. "His godfather is [fellow 3,000er] George Brett," said Staats. "Sometimes the magic overcomes the park." At that moment, even inside baseball tasted like chiffon.

BOB MURPHY

The Greek poet Sophocles wrote, "One must wait until the evening to see how splendid the day has been." Bob Murphy's included four World Series, grand use of "marvelous," and "the happy recap" upon a Mets victory in the ephemera capital of the world.

The last four digits of his phone number—6-3-8-7—spelled Mets. Once, drained by a long trip, he signed into a hotel, "Robert E. Mets." Murphy's Law was simple: "I tried to bring friendliness to the game."

In 1962, Bob, Lindsey Nelson, and Ralph Kiner began airing the Amazin's. Murphy joined them at Cooperstown in 1994. "Can you believe it?" he said. The early Mets had trouble turning two. Their Voices went three-for-three.

In 1942, the Okie entered the Marines, became master technical sergeant, and graduated from the University of Tulsa. He returned from war adrift. "You like sports," said brother Jack, later San Diego *Union* sports editor. "Why don't you try radio?"

Bob soon did Oklahoma football, Oklahoma A&M hoops, and hockey, having never seen a game. "Those days made you use your imagination and form an ad-lib ability." Each grew at Class C Muskogee and Texas League Oklahoma City. "In the minors, you sell ads, do play-by-play, set equipment up."

In 1954, a break set up his life: Curt Gowdy's aide left Boston. "I replace him, still trying to lose my accent," said Bob. "Curt said, 'You're wearing a cardigan sweater, cowboy boots, and a cowboy hat. We got work to do.'" Three years earlier, Allen had made Gowdy join the Sox. The 1960 Orioles offered the Cowboy's sidekick No. 1. "You can't not go," Curt said, recalling. The Birds came out of nowhere to finish second.

A year later Jack Fisher faced Roger Maris. "It's number 60!" Murphy said on WBAL Radio. "He's tied the Babe!" Next month the O's dumped sponsor Theo. Hamm Brewery. Bob "got lost in the shuffle," approaching the newly born Mets. G.M. George Weiss "wanted a household name": Nelson was a network paladin. Ex-jock Kiner would have cachet. The third man should leaven them, he explained: "be a steady professional."

Bob submitted his Maris tape. Listening, George found his man. "Bob had a distinctive voice that filled the air," Nelson later said. "Calling baseball, guys now sound the same." In 1962, New York hadn't been the same since the Dodgers and Giants skipped town.

Some fans went underground. Others forswore baseball for a time, or life. "Coming in against [the champion Yankees]," said Murphy, "I thought we would have to struggle." For a while he did. "Curt taught a conversational style and Lindsey didn't like it. He was a straight-ahead announcer, eyes on baseball."

The 1962–78 Mets' became its longest-ever triad. After Nelson's next-year exit, Bob increasingly seemed "the first sign of spring," Jay Greenberg wrote. Marty Noble called his "the voice of all things Met"—at the beach, aboard the Staten Island Ferry, in the back yard, rabbit ears ferrying Channel 9 —summer's soundtrack, dog-eared and beloved.

Murph's baritone could still rise an octave. "Heee struck heeem out!" Another batter flew to left. "Deep . . . it may go . . . let's watch." Then: "Here's the throw. *Out* at the plate!" Finally: "Fasten your seat belt—we're on to the ninth." In 1969, Jerry Koosman was "wonderful"; 1973, Tug McGraw "unbelievable"; 1985, Darryl Strawberry's "the most amazing homer I've ever seen," striking the clock at Busch Stadium. Baseball was always "a game of redeeming features."

In 1986, Game Six redeemed the L.C.S.: 7–6, vs. Houston, in 16 innings. "Swing and a miss! Swing and a miss! [Jesse Orosco] Struck him [Kevin Bass] out! Struck him out! The Mets win it!" cried Bob, calling "of the more than 6,000 games I've broadcast, easily the best."

Or was that the 1986 World Series'? Pick 'em, still.

Game Six began commonly, as epic theater can. Up, 3 games to 2, Boston fronts, 2–0. Mets tie. Red Sox retake the lead. Mets retie: 3-all. At 11:59

P.M., Dave Henderson's 10th-inning belt gave the Sox a 4–3 lead. "I remember," said Murphy, "how he reached the dugout as Shea's scoreboard hit midnight." Boston added another run. The first two Mets flew out in the bottom of the inning. The board blazed, "Congratulations Boston Red Sox." The Series trophy entered their clubhouse. One out would win.

Gary Carter got a hit to left. Kevin Mitchell and Ray Knight singled, Carter scoring: Sox, 5–4. Bob Stanley's fifth pitch to Mookie Wilson eluded Rich Gedman's glove to score Mitchell: 5-all. The din aped a 747 over Shea. "Three–two the count," said Murphy. "And the pitch by Stanley. . . . And a ground ball trickling . . . it's a fair ball . . . it gets by Buckner! Rounding third is Knight! The Mets will win the ballgame! They win! They win!"

In Game Seven, Knight's homer put New York ahead, 4–3. Before midnight, the day turned splendid: Metsies, 8–5, an unforgettable, unanswerable second world title.

Afterword. The '88ers won the East, beat the Dodgers 10 of 11 games, but swallowed an antigen of an L.C.S.: Los Angeles, in seven. Having aired "Bowling for Dollars," the Gator Bowl, and AFL New York Titans, Bob added a third and final year of CBS Radio's "Game of the Week." In July 1990, Philadelphia scored six ninth-inning runs and put the tying run on base. "Line drive! It's caught! It's over! The Mets win the ballgame!" cried Murphy, who seldom swore. "They win the damn thing by a score of 10 to 9!"

He entered Cooperstown, voice thicker, gait slower. Trimming workload bought another decade: "The happy recap" became a life, not game. "I can't remember first saying it. I do remember thinking it was corny, dropping it, then mail on its behalf." Meeting him, pitcher Al Leiter retrieved youth on the Jersey shore. "Then and now, Bob is the Mets."

The Mets' radio booth was named for Murphy. He retired in 2003, musing, "It was a lot easier to say hello 42 years ago than it is saying good-bye."

The Shea crowd cheered, "Mur-phy! Mur-phy!" Former infielder Ed Charles wrote a poem, "Ode to Murphy." A giant card read: "Dear Bob. Wishing you all the best in your retirement. The Mets family." Signing: thousands of friends, who cried a year later on his death, at 79.

Byron wrote in "The Prisoner of Chillon": "My hair is gray, but not with years, / Nor grew it white / In a single night, / As men's have grown from sudden years."

Give Sophocles a season pass.

BOB MURPHY

LONGEVITY:	10	50 years.
CONTINUITY:	8	Boston A.L. 1954–59; Baltimore A.L. 1960–61; New York N.L. 1962–2003; CBS Radio "Game of the Week" 1985–86 and 1988; ABC/NBC TV The Baseball Network 1994–95.
NETWORK:	3	"Game" 1985–86 and 1988 (CBS Radio). TBN 1994–95 (ABC/NBC TV).
KUDOS:	10	Cooperstown 1994. Mets Hall of Fame 1984. William Slocum Award 2000. NSSA and North Carolina State Broadcasters Association Halls of Fame 2002. Mets radio booth named in honor 2002.
LANGUAGE:	10	Faster than Elio Chacon.
POPULARITY:	10	Metsies' public patriarch.
PERSONA:	10	Set tone, daubed drama, and outlasted 112 Mets third basemen.
VOICE:	10	Crackling.
KNOWLEDGE:	10	From Roger Craig to Roger Cedeno, saw it all.
MISCELLANY:	8	Turning 79, received U.S. flag that flew over Iwo Jima memorial on birthday.
TOTAL:	89	(20th place).

RALPH KINER

"I speak Spanish to God, Italian to women, French to men, and German to my horse," said Charles V, Holy Roman Emperor. English is reserved for baseball's men of letters.

"Today is father's Day," Ralph Kiner begins. "So to all you fathers in the audience, happy birthday."

The American Cynamid Co. becomes a Mets TV sponsor. Kiner goes to break. "We'll be right back, after this word from American Cyanide."

Again he nears commercial: "We'll be back after this word for Manufacturers Hangover."

Once Ralph said of Marvelous Marv Throneberry, "Marv never made the same mistake twice. He always made different ones." Ibid, the Mets' comic, cosmic, and ultimately beloved Voice.

"Home run hitters drive Cadillacs. Singles hitters drive Fords," Kiner is alleged to have said. At four, his father died. Soon mom and son left Santa Rita, New Mexico, for Alhambra, California, where a neighbor and semipro baseball manager "let me tag along and shag." Ironically, softball fueled the Cadillac. "There wasn't the high arc on the ball that we see now. So I started to swing upstairs, and it stuck."

To mom, upstairs meant becoming "a lawyer or doctor. She accepted baseball only when I paid off her mortgage." The Yankees scouted Kiner, who instead signed with Pittsburgh, got a $3,000 bonus, and bought a 1937 Ford-V roadster. In 1941, Ralph twice went deep in his first exhibition: "I [then] got a little fat-headed." Pirates skipper Frank Frisch aimed to shrink.

"Kiner, why aren't you running laps?"

"Mr. Frisch, I have only one pair of baseball shoes, and if I wear them out running, I won't have any for the games."

"Well, that's fine," he reddened. "You can take those shoes to Barnwell [South Carolina, Bucs minor-league camp], because that's where you'll be playing your next game."

After the Eastern League, International League, and Pacific Theater, Ralph went to Pittsburgh in 1946. Next season it added Hank Greenberg: neither laid down a squeeze. Forbes Field was a pitcher's park. The Bucs put pens in left field, strung an inner fence, and cut the line by 30 feet. A year later Hank retired. Greenberg's Garden became Kiner's Korner.

"Hank got me to stand near the plate. It was my difference," he said, leading the N.L. in dingers every year from 1946 through 1952. 1948: Ralph reached 100 in the bigs' least-ever career at-bats (1,351). 1949: "Baseball's Amiable Killer," said *The Saturday Evening Post,* had 54 with just 61 Ks. 1950: *TSN* Player of the Year got a league-high $65,000. 1952: The Bucs finished 42–112. "How bad were we?" Kiner said. "Joe Garagiola was our catcher."

That fall he asked Branch Rickey for a raise. "I know you hit all those homers," said the Pirates general manager, "but we could have finished last without you." Joining the Cubs and Indians, Ralph retired with 369 homers: only Ruth had more per at-bat.

"He's the only reason people came to the park," laughed Greenberg. "Pittsburgh roared, 'Thank God for Ralph Kiner!'" How to top the topper? It took until 1969, but Ralph found a way.

In 1956, the P.C.L. Padres named Kiner G.M. He put on a microphone in 1961. "I'd played mostly in the National League, and here I am doing the White Sox," re-creating the A.L. by day if Chicago played at night. The Hose was a first-division team. The '62 Mets formed a league of their own. "I don't ask how we lost 120," Stengel said later. "I wonder how we won 40."

Casey often specked WOR TV's post-game "Kiner's Korner." Ralph tossed an early guest a lob. "Choo Choo, how did you get that nickname?"

Clarence Coleman: "I don't know."

"What's your wife's name and what's she like?"

"Her name is Mrs. Coleman, and she likes *me,* bub."

In hindsight, "Korner" seems a period piece: black and white, host and star, "the best bad show," Mushnick said, "in TV history." Then it seemed revolutionary: "anecdotes, interviews with big shots—few of whom were Mets." Once Pittsburgh's Jim Pagliaroni and Don Schwall appeared eating grapes in togas and Roman gladiator helmets. To Kiner, it felt like '52 again. The Amazin's could have finished last without him.

Yearly the team beamed from 100 to 137 games. The idea of anyone else calling it never crossed your mind. "That's why Lindsey's leaving was a shock. It broke us up," said Ralph. Like Murphy's, his badinage, voice, and vernacular denoted The Metropolitan Baseball Club of New York.

Many *mots* bared a baseball life. Terry Forster lost 15 pounds because "his wife slept in front of the refrigerator. *She* gained 15 pounds." Another pitcher, Rick Sutcliffe, "does interior designing on the side." Partner Fran Healy was puzzled. Breaking chairs, "He redesigned Tommy Lasorda's office." Lines were planned: "Statistics are like bikinis. They show a lot but not everything." Some, uh, were not. "The Mets didn't do well in the month of Atlanta." In Montreal, "the Phillies again beat the Mets."

Howard Johnson became Walter Johnson; Darryl Strawberry, Darryl Throneberry; Gary Carter, Gary Cooper; and Milt May, Mel Ott. In 1983, Tim McCarver joined Ralph on cable TV's SportsChannel. Kiner renamed him Tim MacArthur.

"Ralph, you're probably thinking of General MacArthur," Tim said.

"What did I say?"

"'Tim MacArthur.' It's McCarver."

Ralph: "Well, close enough."

Mets lose, 9–1. "Earlier in the broadcast we talked about General MacArthur," Tim said. "One of his favorite lines was 'Chance favors a prepared man.' Obviously the Mets weren't prepared tonight."

Kiner eyed the screen: "MacArthur also said, 'I shall return,' and we'll be right back after this."

In 1960, Soviet premier Nikita Khrushchev banged a lectern with his shoe at the United Nations. Often the Mets' Mr. K put a shoe in his mouth. Once reliever Brent Gaff entered a game. Kiner couldn't see the number. Trying to help, Tim put Gaff's name on paper.

Ralph said, "I beg your pardon, Frank Gaff is in the game."

Alarmed, Tim wrote "Brent." Kiner amended that "Frank Brent" was pitching.

McCarver shook his head. "Check that," Ralph told his audience, "it's Brent Frank."

In 1995, WOR canceled "Kiner's Korner," arguably the Apple's longest-running TV show. "They could make more money going to news," Ralph explained. 'Ninety-seven was worse: he suffered Bell's Palsy, temporary slurred speech and facial paralysis. Three weeks later, wife DiAnn learned she had cancer. "He started sobbing. He's such a tender-hearted man."

Ralph left the air, returning in late 1998 physically challenged, in the argot of the time. Next year "he was fine," said his wife, "like he'd never been away."

Kiner seemed a post-9/11 piece of New York's DNA—"as decent a man as you'll meet in your life," mused Murphy, softly, thoughtfully. "And a survivor."

Courage shouts in any tongue.

RALPH KINER

LONGEVITY:	10	44 years.
CONTINUITY:	9	Chicago A.L. 1961; New York N.L. 1962– .
NETWORK:	2	L.C.S. 1973 (Robert Wold Radio) and 1976–78 (CBS Radio).
KUDOS:	9	Cooperstown 1975, as player. Babe Ruth Crown 1974. Mets Hall of Fame 1984. No. 4 retired by Pirates 1987. William Slocum Award 1990. Three-time Emmy Award. Mets TV booth named in honor 2000.
LANGUAGE:	6	Kinerisms eclipse fine home run call, "Going, going, going, gone, good-bye!"
POPULARITY:	10	Mets' quasi-timeline.
PERSONA:	10	King Ralph. "Man, I made it," pitcher and Brooklyn native John Candelaria said. "I'm on 'Kiner's Korner.'"
VOICE:	7	Homey.
KNOWLEDGE:	10	Story for every eventuality.
MISCELLANY:	10	Dated Elizabeth Taylor and Janet Leigh. Only Scully leads consecutive years with a club.
TOTAL:	83	(42nd place).

7

WHERE YOU LEAD (BASEBALL NOW, 1990–)

Bob Costas

Joe Morgan

Jon Miller

Tim McCarver

Jaime Jarrin

BOB COSTAS

The Smithsonian Institution, June 1993: "I thought Howard Cosell was history's most successful sportscaster," Jack Buck said, "but Bob Costas has surpassed them all." Many in the crowd nodded. "And at his age [41], brother. I've got older neckties." Growing up, Bob lived for baseball. "It's not a laser show, not a spectacle. It's just tonight's game." Today he does not announce his once-Arcadia.

"I'd have given anything to do the Cardinals," Costas said in the 1980s. Instead, he settled for being among the USA's top—what?—25 celebrities. Life turned when, in late 1988, NBC TV lost baseball. "Whatever else I did, I'd never have left 'Game of the Week.'" On the night of its demise Bob seemed 36, nearing 63.

His postlogue shows the law of unintended consequences. "Game"'s end crushed, then freed, him. "Dateline," "Later With Bob Costas," and the Olympics: what might Bob have missed? Once pining to be Mel Allen, he may retire owning NBC.

In 1957, John Costas, a Greek electrical engineer, fan, and gambler, took his five-year-old son to Ebbets Field and the Polo Grounds. Baseball had meant radio, or black and white TV. "I walk in," said Bob, "and see this green diamond, like the Emerald City." Two years later, the Long Islander sat with a cousin at Yankee Stadium. Each inning they crept closer, like Dorothy spying Oz. "Soon we're in left-center's front row and sure a ball'd be hit there: 500 feet, no chance, but 457 a cinch."

The Stadium was renovated in 1974–75. Until then, you could leave via bullpens on the field. At seven, Costas flanked right field's 344-foot sign. "I pretend I'm Hank Bauer, jumping up to steal a homer." Next: right-center's 407, glowing on TV. Up-close "Sam Loves Sally" marred the sheen. "I didn't care what Sam and Sally did on their own time," Bob fumed, "but I couldn't grasp why they'd desecrate a shrine."

Finally, the Costases stopped at center-field monuments of Babe Ruth, Lou Gehrig, and Miller Huggins. "[Pre-'74] they were in play [461 feet]. With the pitcher's mound rising, a kid couldn't see the plate." He could, however, fear.

Bob started crying. Pop asked why.

"Whaddaya mean? The Bambino, Iron Horse, and Little Skipper are here!" Surely, DiMag and Mick would follow.

Junior heard dad explain being laid to rest. He wasn't buying it: solemnity overwhelmed. "Then he put me on his shoulders for the rest of the walk around the track. Dad wore a yellow shirt, and smelled like Old Spice. I liked him a lot that day."

In 1960, the clan left for California. Radio baseball made it bearable. "In Ohio, we'd pick up Waite Hoyt, later the Braves' Earl Gillespie, Buck and Caray." Nevada spawned Vin Scully. "Dad said, 'That's the Dodgers. We're almost there.'" A Yanks Series made L.A. seem like home. *At* home, Bob said he planned to watch each game. "You can send me to school, but you'll never see me again because I'll run away."

New York trailed, 4–0, led, 7–4, fell, 9–7, and tied Game Seven, 9-all. Bill Mazeroski retired Costas to his room. "I'm sitting there, eyes welling, as I take a vow of silence. My initial vow was not to speak until opening day 1961. That impracticality dawned on me quickly. But I kept mute for 24 hours—protesting this injustice."

A greater bug was dad, betting up to $10,000 daily: "a terrific storyteller, would meet his bookie on a street, under a lamp," a Philip Marlowe figure returning East in 1961. Bob got nightly scores in pop's car by turning the dial: "calibrating it like a safecracker." Phils–Braves could lose their house: Cubs–Cards, reclaim it. "If his teams were losing, I'd stay outside. Winning, I'd race inside to tell Dad what was happening." Happening, was love.

"Listening to these announcers, they became the game," he mused. "Its mythology drew me in. I fell asleep with a transistor under the pillow." Scully enticed. Saam and Prince seemed voice pals. Allen spellbound: "So much warmth that a fan relates to readily." His colleague seemed interior: "By now Barber was bitter, dry, not nearly as good as in Brooklyn." Like Red or Mel, Bob could have given an hour lecture on each member of the Stripes.

His idol, of course, was No. 7. His company was the world.

Teresa Brewer's "I Love Mickey" spoke to Costas and other Boomers. If you couldn't fantasize about being Mantle, you were out of it, a nerd. He was three-time MVP, made 20 All-Star teams, and won the 1956 Triple Crown. The Switcher could reach first base in 3.1 seconds, but swung to go yard. For a long time, Bob carried a dog-eared 1958 Mantle All-Star card in his wallet. "I believe you should carry a religious artifact with you at all times."

On May 22, 1963, Mick's drive hit "[The Stadium facade] like a plane taking off," said Costas. "Nobody else could do that [literally], or two-strike drag bunt with the infield back." In 1991, he entered a restaurant to find

Mantle and Billy Crystal. For four hours they rehashed his career. "Billy had grown up on Long Island, idolized Mantle. The whole time Mickey's saying, 'I don't remember that, damn, did that happen, holy sh . . . , 'ya know. He *did* it. Billy and I *remembered* it. Tells you something there."

Costas played infield for the Little League Farmington, Connecticut, Giants, near Hartford. A photo at 10 tells why he chose television. Bob eyes the lens—eager, intense, and small. "I was good-field, no-hit, and you know about guys who can't even hit their weight. That was true of me, and I weighed 118 pounds."

At Syracuse University, Bob began working on the campus FM station and shedding his New York accent. In 1973, he moonlit as WSYR TV fill-in sports anchor, weatherman, and "Bowling for Dollars" host. Next year the journalism major trekked to KMOX St. Louis. "You could see," said sports director Buck, "Bob had the assets"—except for on occasion working on Costas Standard Time.

Bob's first gig was the ABA Spirits of St. Louis. Buck found him in the office one afternoon. "What are *you* doing? You've got a game in Providence tonight." He shrugged. "I got a late-afternoon flight." Delayed, he arrived near halftime. Next day Jack huffed, "This will *not* happen again." What did: the rookie's ability to "talk about anything without a script."

Costas did Missouri and Chicago Bulls basketball and CBS bits and pieces. In 1979, joining NBC, he swapped barbs with analyst Bob Trumpy. One week the Jets' Richard Todd grabbed a *New York Post* writer. "You can only take so much criticism," Trumpy warned. "After that a reaction is justifiable."

Horsefeathers, said Costas.

"You don't understand the pressures of playing in the NFL," said Trumpy.

"Disproportionate pressures, disproportionate rewards."

Another Sunday Trumpy called Todd's delivery "tragic."

Costas balked: "Ah, Bob, maybe tragic overstates it."

"It *is* tragic."

"Does that leave any room for a famine, air crash, earthquake, or tornado?"

Trumpy sulked: "I don't care what you say—it's tragic."

A Todd incompletion bared Costas's lance. "And now, tragically, the Jets must punt."

Pundits glowed: What style! What economy of language! Bob's then-spouse was football; his mistress, an old flame. "Baseball's the best sport for an announcer because of the history and context and it allows for storytelling and exchange of opinion." Baseball was made for talking: the bar, hotel, or cage.

In 1982, the wonder child turned 30. The Peacocks kindly gave him "Game." Costas's partner was his childhood shortstop: "I'd grown up watching Kubek." Looking in a rear-view mirror, he saw the future in its face.

"'Game' was a clearing house. Didn't matter where you were, tune in to share a baseball *feel*." Wrigley Field: June 23, 1984. Chicago cabbies still lower a window: "'Hey, Bob, the [Ryne] Sandberg Game.' That's what they call it—and it's two decades ago."

At one point St. Louis led, 9–3. Bruce Sutter hurls the ninth. Sandberg dings to left-center: 9-all. Next inning the Cards refront, 11–9. Chicago's Bob Dernier walks with two out. Ryne again goes deep—"identical spot, his fifth hit. The same fan could have caught it." Thousands of Redbirders gasped. "Game" and Wrigley shook.

"That's the real Roy Hobbs because this can't be happening!" Bob cried. "We're sitting here, and it doesn't make any difference if it's 1984 or '54— just freeze this and don't change a thing!" It became "a telephone game [Cubs, 12–11] where you say, 'Who likes baseball as much as me?' and call around the country. 'Are you watching? Channel 4, quick.' Absent 'Game,' that can't happen outside post-season. You don't have the stage."

Costas's favorite stage was County Stadium, tending pizza, Polish sausage, and "secret stadium" bratwurst sauce. "The formula's in a vault. It tastes like another planet." Brats's arrival signaled an official game. "Tony and I had to alternate talking because one of us always had a mouthful. This became [so] legendary" that the Brewers sent him industrial-size brat vats.

"I'd get jars of secret sauce and letters from Cub fans saying Wrigley had better hot dogs." One Brewman, Ma Pesh, of Stevens Point, Wisconsin, demanded a brat-eating duel. "In his picture, Ma wears bib overalls, looks 430 pounds, and claims he holds the record for County bratwurst consumption" —O's–Brewers, August 1972—shocking, Pesh said, since he had never eaten well vs. Baltimore. "I wrote back, he wrote back, and now we're pals."

County's feel denoted 1956, like Bob's favorite photo from Don Larsen's perfect game. "Mantle's catching a fly. You've got the bleachers, auxiliary scoreboard, and shadows—October in the Bronx. Could this be any place but Yankee Stadium? Could Fenway Park be anything but itself?" Another soulmate: Tiger Stadium: "It's like when I grew up. You couldn't confuse one park with another."

One "Game," Reggie Jackson cleared the roof. Next up, whistling to Costas, he pantomimed tying a shoe. "Reggie says that when we're back on the air, he'll enter the box, call time to pretend to tie his shoe, and let us discuss the homer and show his replay."

Jackson singled, touched his helmet, and pointed to the booth. "'Hey,' as if to say, 'it's all a great show.'"

All in the family. In the mid-eighties, Bob lost his Mantle card. Tony issued an SOS. "Game"ers sent fifty Micks. Another week Costas, expecting a child, lunched with Kirby Puckett, who asked about its sex. Daddy didn't know.

"How about Kirby?" Puckett said. "That works either way."

"Tell you what," Bob posed. "If you're at .350 when he's born, we'll name him after you." Having never hit .300, Puckett "was above .360" the day Keith Michael Kirby Costas was born.

At 33, the youngest-ever National Sportscaster of the Year hosted radio's "Costas Coast to Coast," NBC's Summer Olympiad XXIV, NBA, Super Bowl XX, XXIII, and XXVII, and pre-game "NFL Live." In 1987, he introduced Dick Enberg at Cleveland Stadium. "Who needs domes? Who needs artificial turf? It's cold. It's dark. It feels right. And it's for the championship of the AFC. Next."

Next fall felt even better: Series opener, ninth inning, two out, A's, 4–3. "Kirk [Gibson] is hurt, supposedly unable to pinch-hit," said Bob, charting post-game. From a runway he sees Kirk enter the trainer's room. A shadow shows Gibson hitting a ball off a tee. Coach Ben Hines nods: one swing left. "If we get to the ninth spot, we'll go," agrees Tom Lasorda. Dennis Eckersley walks Mike Davis. Gibson jaw-drops into the seats: L.A., 5–4.

NBC's next-day pre-game likened Gibson to *The Natural*. Producers Mike Weisman and David Neal got the film, "stayed up all night at Paramount Studios, then took the piece by police escort to Dodger Stadium," said Costas, completing it at air-time. "Look at that and tell me what's wrong with baseball on TV when it's done by people who care"—the problem being, he found, that not enough did.

In December, CBS TV paid $1.04 billion for 1990–93 bigs exclusivity. Robert Redford as Hobbs: "I hadn't seen it [a shooting] coming." Costas, neither: NBC had done the sport since 1947.

"Who thought baseball'd kill its best way to reach the public? It coulda kept us and CBS—we'd have kept 'Game'—but it only cared about cash." CBS only cared about October, airing 16-game regular-season coverage. "You wouldn't see a game for a month," said Marv Albert. "Then you didn't know when CBS came back on." For Bob, ready to "do baseball on a full-time basis anywhere, even if I have to give up everything else," the black hole meant deliverance, though he did not see that then.

"I'd rather do a 'Game of the Week' getting a 5 rating than host a Super Bowl." Instead, leapfrogging sport as 1989 "Today" host, he found the water fine. In 1992, Costas did Barcelona's Olympiad (four more through 2004). "I almost didn't recognize you without Bob Costas on a voice-over," said President Bush, welcoming the U.S. team. Soon, Bob was recognized as the lineal descendant of Jim McKay.

On "Later," he interviewed Ted Koppel, Chevy Chase, Bob Hope, and Aaron Spelling. Bob graced "Nightline" and "Meet the Press," quizzed Ray Charles and Woody Allen on prime-time "Now" and "Dateline," appeared on "Frasier," "Cheers," and "NewsRadio," and virtually retired the Emmy and NSSA Sportscaster of the Year award.

Be careful what you ask for. Beware of what you don't. "Nothing could be worse than CBS until [1994–95's ABC/NBC 12-game/invisible till July/no national or day coverage] The Baseball Network." Its Division Series and L.C.S. created areas of "natural" interest. The N.L. went dark in Boston. In St. Louis, the A.L. never made a peep. Neutral markets summarily fell to one or the other league. What you saw depended on where you lived.

"Yes, sir, that's baseball: America's regional pastime," *Sports Illustrated* wrote. "Such an abomination is The Baseball Network that in Seattle, where people don't cross against a red light on the emptiest of streets, fans booed whenever the Kingdome P.A. announcer made mention." Wising up in 1996, baseball went back to the future: Fox, resuming "Game"; NBC, dividing postseason and All-Star Game. The future, as usual, seemed to settle in the Bronx.

A.L. 1996 L.C.S. opener: eighth inning, Baltimore, 4–3. The Yanks' Derek Jeter's fly to right was thought by Tony Tarasco a can of corn. "Suddenly," Costas said, "this kid [Jeffrey Maier, 12] puts his glove over the [Stadium] fence and steals it." Umpire Richie Garcia ruled dinger. "Merlin must be in this house," said Tarasco. Why didn't Bob feel the spell?

"It's what happened in the nineties," he said in 2001: the strike, realignment, wild card, expanded playoff, and "Game." "I still love the game. I just felt a certain alienation from the institution. NBC only did a few games each year. I also lacked the forum I have today [HBO's "On the Record"] to express my views, so to some extent I started editorializing in games." A scold, some said: the Commissioner! jibed others. The fact is that Bob had much to editorialize about.

Gallup Poll, 2002: 14 percent name baseball their favorite sport (vs. 1985's 25). Barely one in eight homes watch the World Series (vs. 1952's one in two). "Give me afternoon Series, regular-season network continuity, batters who don't step out, pitchers who throw the ball, and fine announcers," Bob said, "and I'll get you a renaissance." Inevitably he rued the bigs' high command. The late Edward Bennett Williams owned the Orioles and Washington Redskins. "What's dumber than the dumbest football owner?" he said. "The smartest baseball owner."

For a long time Mick was dumb, by No. 7's own reckoning. His father had osteomyelitis, a degenerative bone disease. Boozing and chasing, he expected to die by 40.

"When we called him a hero, he wasn't," Costas said. "Later Mick became one when he thought he wasn't." Mantle went dry, slowed a fast-lane life, and did TV spots that said, "Kids, don't be like me." Bob interviewed him on "Dateline." He was warm, shy, and penitent. The hour pealed respect and love.

"As he's talking," said Costas, "I'm thinking of standing holding my father's hand in deepest center field at Yankee Stadium—the whole dimension of the place is so overwhelming for a child—and saying to my father [who died at 42], 'Is this where Mickey Mantle plays? Is this where he stands? Can Mickey Mantle throw a ball from here all the way to home plate? Can Mickey Mantle hit a ball here?'"

The Switcher died, at 63, in 1995. Costas gave the eulogy at a Dallas memorial. "We wanted to crease our caps like him," he said, "kneel in an imaginary on-deck circle like him, run like him, heads down, elbows up." Not knowing it would be televised, "All I wanted was to be worthy of the family."

Returning to New York, Bob was mobbed by passersby. "'Hey, nice job,' they'd say. You don't feel boastful at a time like that," he stopped, "just gratified, that it was something that Mick hopefully would have liked."

It was no secret that Costas disliked our cesspool age. In his youth, "You didn't measure someone by how profane they were, or crass and mean. I'm stunned by how rapidly the culture has been coarsened by vulgarity, tastelessness, and mean-spiritedness."

Baseball could be an oasis—kinder, gentler. "So accentuate the differences between it and other sports."

To many, Costas did between himself and other Voices. *Fair Ball: A Fan's*

Case for Baseball became the *Times* 2001 No. 1 bestseller. HBO's "Record" and "Inside the NFL" reflected the host's depth, brass, and smarts. In 2000, Fox bought exclusivity. Bob will air the Triple Crown, Breeder's Cup, U.S. Open, Ryder Cup, and Olympics—but not the bigs again till at least 2007.

"It's nowhere near as devastating as a decade ago," he said of the baseball blackout. "Different circumstances, different time." Perhaps someday Costas will again date his childhood love. By then, he might be older than the late Jack Buck's ties.

BOB COSTAS

LONGEVITY:	5	14 years.
CONTINUITY:	9	NBC TV "Game of the Week" 1983–89; ABC/NBC TV The Baseball Network 1994–95.
NETWORK:	10	"Game" 1983–89; L.C.S. 1983, 1985, 1987, 1989, and 1995–2000; All-Star Game 1994, 1996, 1998, and 2000; Division Series, 1995–97 and 1999; World Series 1995, 1997, and 1999 (NBC TV).
KUDOS:	10	16-time Emmy Award: 12 play-by-play; two writing; two hosting. Nominated in five different categories: play-by-play, hosting, writing, interviewing, and journalism. Eight-time NSSA Sportscaster of the Year: 1985, 1987–88, 1991–92, 1995, 1997, and 2000. ASA Sportscaster of the Year 1989 and 1991–93. "Favorite Sportscaster," TV Guide Awards, based on voting by readers of *TV Guide.* St. Louis Walk of Fame 1995.
LANGUAGE:	10	Precise.
POPULARITY:	10	"There may be nobody better at walking the line between whimsy and journalism," read *SI.*
PERSONA:	10	Ultimate reporter-fan.
VOICE:	10	Crystalline.
KNOWLEDGE:	10	Moves effortlessly between then and now.
MISCELLANY:	6	Appeared in such films as *BASEketball, The Paper, The Scout,* and *There's Something About Mary.*
TOTAL:	90	(18th place). *Scores based on 1–10 point scale.*

JON MILLER

In 1983, Larry King called him "among baseball's best young broadcasters." Two decades later, a writer hailed his "works of baroque genius," the "voice as smooth as caramel"—an outside-of-Vin-Scully Eden.

Some announcers make you want to throw up. Miller is a throw*back*. "Many now are automatons," Jack Buck observed. "Same voice and style." Like Mel, Diz, and Gunner, Jon was a personality and a hoot. "Baseball entertains you and you care about it. What I like is the company of baseball." The listener enjoys *his* company—in English, Spanish, or Japanese.

Circa 1961: Hayward, a small town east of San Francisco. Broadway, like baseball a peculiarly American institution, fills Jon's home. "My mom kept playing *Camelot*. I got hooked." Pals ride the surf. In his bedroom, Miller plays the baseball board game Baseball Strat-O-Matic. It suggests the future in a way that seems ordained.

Already Jon, 9, loves the art of rhetoric. For hours he mimes the public address Voice, organist ("dum-dum-dum," in key), crowd (blowing, like wind), and home team's Russ Hodges or Scully from Chavez Ravine. "Friends'd say, 'Let's hit the wave.' I'd say, 'I got a big series coming up—first place up for grabs.'"

Mom wanted to grab Jon around the neck. Friends of hers heard sonny through the door. "Mrs. Miller, who *is* this?" She denied even knowing him. "It sounds, though, like he has a little bronchial condition."

Miller saw his first bigs game in 1962 at Candlestick Park. Los Angeles outhit Frisco, 15–12, but lost, 19–8! Billy O'Dell threw a complete game. Three Giants homered. Attendance was 32,189. "Other than that, I don't remember a thing." Jon, dad, and their transistor sat in Section 19, upper deck, behind first base. "I looked down at the booth with binoculars, like being backstage. I was hearing and watching what Russ and Lon [Simmons] were saying."

To Miller, the year became "my coming of age as a fan." Its Khyber Pass was the final week. San Francisco played at day. "I'd hear Russ, then he'd re-create the [leading] Dodgers at night," Scully coursing over distant KFI. Pardon the peroration: "Giants keep winning, Dodgers losing. I'm sitting in a car, on a hill to help reception, switching back and forth!"

On September 30, the 49ers played at Kezar Stadium. "The crowd's going nuts hearing baseball. The football guys wonder what's going on." Giants win, 2–1, at the Stick. Russ then re-creates on P.A. L.A.'s 1–0 playoff-forcing loss. The Jints make the Series. In Game Seven, Miller is in a dentist's chair as Bobby Richardson snares Willie McCovey's drive. "Given the pain, how appropriate I almost bit my dentist's finger."

At 15, Jon fingered his first play-by-play in high school basketball. Next morning the voice—"highlights, from reel-to-reel recorder"—filled the intercom. The whiz broadcast from the bleachers at Candlestick and the Oakland Coliseum. Ambition, meet adolescence. He loved every word.

In 1972, the College of San Mateo graduate, becoming Santa Rosa TV sports director, noted the NHL California Golden Seals being treated like castor oil. Owner Charlie Finley OK'd his offer to televise odd games. "You sound like you've done this for years," a producer said until Miller accidentally began *puck* with *f.* "In baseball, you call a ball 'fall' and nobody notices," Jon said, thereafter calling the puck *it.*

The Seals ended up moving to Cleveland in 1976. In 1973, Miller targeted Finley's A's. "He owned them for 13 years and had more broadcasters than managers—and more managers than any team." Voice Monte Moore hired Jon, 21, by tape. Balding, he looked 31. His resume read 26. "What's truth in advertising when you have baseball on your mind?"

In April 1974, Jon visited Baltimore. "I'd grown up on Chuck Thompson doing CBS football. Now I'm amazed: He's doing the O's." That fall, another hero did the Series. "I say, 'A curve, 2–1.' Vinnie's much more elegant. 'It's on the way, currrve loow.'" Laughing, he mimicked Scully. "'Two-and-one, and it's interesting to note that as Moliere said in 17th-century Paris.' Whoever heard of baseball in the 17th century? Yet people go bonkers about Vinnie quoting Moliere!"

That fall, Finley fired him. "Charlie had axed guys like Harry Caray, Bob Elson. My stock went up in the business." By 1980, Jon trekked to Boston via Texas. Quickly its literati embraced the muse. "He'd done imitations since childhood," said Ken Coleman, "and I pushed him to do Scully, Chuck, Caray." Thompson left O's radio in 1982. Next Opening Day, his successor hosted a rally at Inner Harbor. Fifty thousand cheered O-R-I-O-L-E-S. "People ask, 'How do Oriole fans compare to the Red Sox'? I ask, 'How do Boston fans compare to the Orioles'?'"

Miller inherited a seven-state network. 'Eighty-three enlarged it. The L.C.S. swung on Game Three. "There's a high fly ball to deep right-center field! And, baby, way back! It's long gone!" said Jon. "Upper deck! Right-center field! Kiss it good-bye! Three–nothing, Orioles! And Eddie Murray's first hit is a monster shot at Comiskey Park!"

Baltimore's first post-1970 title completed a monster year. "The [World Series Game Five] cheering you hear is from Orioles fans," Miller said in Philadelphia. "Everybody else is in muted silence. The pitch! Line drive! Ripken catches it at shortstop! And the Orioles are champions of the world!"

Strat-O-Matic. Mimicry. A rookie crown. Everything came early for Mrs. Miller's son. Baseball on TV, he said, was film: "You see what the producer shows you." Radio was a novel, absorbed and transformed. "He is [now] The Franchise, with great broadcast instincts and sensibilities," wrote *The National.* Jon's company warmed Camp David through Little Italy to Maryland's Eastern Shore.

"Before ESPN Television, you never knew anything until the radio announcer said it," said Bob Costas. "This romantic figure sitting in a booth, very personal, mostly gone except for Jon as the Thompsons and Harwells disappear and Bob Princes and Jack Bucks and Mel Allens die." The dinosaur tethered the banquet circuit, NBC's backup "Game," and ESPN "Sports-Look." Following his own drummer, Miller built a cult to beat the band.

Each March, wife Janine said, "Have a good day, honey. Listen, any time you're in town, stop by."

He nodded. "I'm Jon Miller, your husband. See you in October."

In 1989, ESPN inked a four-year, $400 million, six-day-a-week pact. "Coverage went to cable," said Costas, "because CBS [replacing NBC] didn't want a 'Game.'" The network forecast a 5.0 Nielsen rating (7 million of 140 million homes). "The weekend's over," Jon, hopeful, said, "you come back from the beach, and there it is."

"Sunday Night Baseball" began April 15, 1990. Sow's ear: a final 3.0 average. Silk's purse: It doubled ESPN's other bigs programming (1.5). "It's an exciting opportunity if you consider standing on the edge of a cliff exciting," said Miller, winning the 1991 play-by-play cable ACE Award.

"I am incredibly honored to win this award with this room full of talented people," he said at the Beverly Wilshire Hotel. "What am *I?* I go to games and my best lines are, 'low, ball one,' or probably the line I'm most proud of—'line drive, foul.'"

Baseball already burlesqued a Hessian chorus line. "Don't talk money," Jon advised: "I'm an *artiste,* you know."

A year later, the Orioles began milking a cash cow. "They tried to make Camden Yards like Fenway. Now new parks want to be like the Yards." In 1992, a record 3,567,819 paid. Baseball repaid them with The Strike.

On September 6, 1995, a game became official after 4 1/2 innings.

"History!" said Miller over ESPN. "For baseball, what great news"—Cal Ripken, Jr.'s record 2,131st straight game.

The warehouse banner shed "2-1-3-0." Tipping his cap, Cal began a hand-shaking/high-fiving voyage around the Yards.

Jon was happy, in his adopted burg, barbing and critiquing. "Bud Selig's name is a code word for everything wrong with baseball." Replacement strike games "would be a joke." Players "sign for the most money—which is out-and-out greed." Leave the place where he cried, "Thirty-six thousand people are jumping up and down and saying, 'We believe! We believe!'"? What happened next was more unbelievable than redubbing *puck*.

In 1996, new O's owner Peter Angelos complained, "Jon's not much of an advocate. He should bleed orange-and-black once in a while." Miller's contract expired that year. Phoned by agent Ron Shapiro, Angelos declined to phone back. Shapiro kept calling. Peter was busy. Ron set a deadline. Angelos phoned the *Baltimore Sun:* "This is an employee, mind you, issuing an ultimatum, to the owner."

Baseball watched, wide-mouthed. Peter was a trial lawyer, explained a friend. "He's not used to sharing the attention." Axing Miller, he should have sued himself.

1997: Washington's National Press Club. A guest asks if the Voice should be a fan or a reporter. "I think the announcer should be an advocate for the team," Jon twinkled. "I think the announcer should bleed the colors of the team. I have seen the light. Hallelujah!" The crowd roared. That year, CBS Radio lost baseball. ESPN gave Miller the All-Star Game, L.C.S., and Series. A season later its largest-ever bigs TV audience (9.5 Nielsen rating) watched Mark McGwire's homer 61. "In Bristol [Connecticut's ESPN]," said a friend, "Jon means the game."

In 1965, his dad, returning from a business trip to Minnesota, yawped, "The Twins got *nothing* on Russ and Lon. The *voices* of the Giants' two!" Jon joined their booth in 1997. "It's all a little much. I grew up with these guys." Pacific Bell Park ultimately replaced the Stick, selling out before Opening Day. "All those years when the Giants didn't draw. Now it's like the early sixties."

Jon built a Moss Beach house, could see his boyhood home across the bay, and studied ships in McCovey's Cove. "I love boats. Once I saw FDR's [the *Potomac*] there. Wish I could go everywhere by ship." Instead, he flew 100,000 miles a year. One day: ESPN's Toronto–Texas, Puerto Rico. Next: Jints opener, emceeing pre-game. "For a baseball fan, it's the best of all worlds."

On October 4, 2001, Barry Bonds whacked McGwire-tying 70. A day later he faced Chan Ho Park. "There's a high drive deep into right-center field! To the big part of the ballpark! Number 71! And what a shot! Over the 421-foot marker! . . . And Barry Bonds is now the home run king! Number 71! And it was impressive!"

Less impressive was O's interest. "God gave him the sublimest vocal chords," said the *Washington Post*. Jon's were missed in Birdland. "Sometimes it's good to make a change," Miller said, discreetly. As good would have been a happier 2002 Series.

Ahead, 3 games to 2, Frisco led Anaheim, 5–0, in the seventh inning. "Deep to right! Going back, Sanders! . . . It's gone! A home run! Scott Spiezio has made it a two-run game! The Angels are breathing!" he brayed on ESPN. Next inning Troy Glaus hit: "Swing and a shot! Left-center! . . . It's over Bonds! It goes to the wall! Figgins scores the tying run! Anderson scores the go-ahead run! A double! . . . The Angels have come all the way back from a five-run deficit, and they lead the game!"

JON MILLER

LONGEVITY:	9	28 years.
CONTINUITY:	6	Oakland A.L. 1974; Texas A.L. 1978–79; Boston A.L. 1980–82; Baltimore A.L. 1983–96; NBC TV "Game of the Week" 1986–89; ESPN TV "Sunday Night Baseball" 1990– ; ABC/NBC TV The Baseball Network 1994–95; San Francisco N.L. 1997– .
NETWORK:	10	"Game" 1986–89 (NBC TV). "Sunday" 1990– (ESPN TV). TBN 1994–95 (ABC/NBC TV). Division Series 1996–2000 and 2003– (ESPN TV) and 2002 (ABC Family TV). All-Star Game, L.C.S., and World Series 1998– (ESPN Radio).
KUDOS:	9	"Best Play-by-play Broadcaster" 1986 *Washingtonian* magazine. Cable ACE award 1991 and 1996. NSSA Hall of Fame 2001. ASA Sportscaster of the Year 1999.
LANGUAGE:	10	Lyric, with vast lexicon.
POPULARITY:	10	*Is* ESPN bigs.
PERSONA:	10	Well-read, -fed, and -spoken.
VOICE:	10	Rich, baritone.
KNOWLEDGE:	10	Evinced by 1998 memoir, *Confessions of a Baseball Purist*, with Mark Hyman.
MISCELLANY:	7	Host, 1994–95 ESPN "Voices of The Game." In 2004, rode maiden launch of ocean liner *Queen Mary II*.
TOTAL:	91	(14th place).

The final was academic: Halos, 4–1. Miller then took a cruise. "Forget spring training. I'm ready for ball by New Year's." Ronald Reagan told how a young boy found a room of horse manure Christmas morning. "Yes," said the optimist, "but there must be a pony in here someplace." Deem baseball a room. Miller is broadcasting's pony.

JOE MORGAN

Joe Garagiola couldn't wait to retire. In the bullpen, Bob Uecker announced a game. Bud Blattner was a singles-hitting journeyman. Many jocks-turned-talkers began as Duke Carmel, not Snider.

Other Voices peaked earlier. Sandy Koufax's speeding bullet slowed on NBC. Bob Gibson's cosmic fastball fell to earth. "Genes aren't transferrable," said Tim McCarver. "Knowing the game doesn't mean you can express it."

A 1963–71 and 1980 Houston, 1972–79 Cincinnati, 1981–82 San Francisco, 1983 Philadelphia, and 1984 Oakland dynamo did, succinctly and subtly.

"He'll get the job done," he predicted of Javy Lopez, who homers.

David Cone failed to waste a pitch. "He's tired," says the analyst. Cone is shortly shelled.

A ball eluded Roberto Alomar. "He didn't try to catch it in front of him, but underneath where you lose sight of it."

Joe Morgan has seldom lost sight of baseball, or TV baseball of him.

Born September 19, 1943, in Bonham, Texas, he grew up in Oakland, attended Oakland City College and California State-Hayward, and resented scouts who deemed Joe small. By contrast, Houston's Bill Wight found the 5-foot-7, 170-pounder "self-assured without being cocky." The 1964 Texas League MVP briefly played at Houston's anile Colt Stadium. A year later the renamed Astros moved inside. Joe led the league in walks, replaced idol Nellie Fox at second base, and became *TSN* Rookie of the Year.

His likeness lingers: Joe, off first, the scoreboard urging steal. "Some image," he said. "Go-go dancers!" The 'Stros tap-danced near the cellar. Houston 1968–72 manager Harry Walker knew hitting—but not how to gain respect. The 1947 N.L. batting champion sat on the bus with a hat over his head. To the rear players sang.

"Now Harry Walker is the one that manages this crew. He doesn't like it when we drink and fight and smoke and screw. But when we win our game each day, then what the hell can Harry say?" Kicker: "It makes a fellow proud to be an Astro." Joe couldn't wait to put "ex-" before his team.

Walker called him a troublemaker. "Anyone was a troublemaker who was smarter than Harry Walker," Joe replied, "and that didn't take much." In late 1971, he went to Cincinnati. "I told [then-Reds G.M. Bob] Howsam," said Sparky Anderson, "you have just won the pennant"—actually, a Big Red Machine 1972–73, 1975–76, or 1979 division, league, and/or world title.

Pressure greased its ignition. In the 1975 World Series, Morgan pulled to right—a triple or tater—till Dwight Evans turned, caught the ball, and began a Game Six double play. "I thought I'd done it," Joe said. Next night he did, plating the winning 4–3 run. The '76ers became first not to lose a playoff or Classic game. Daily he worked out, punched a speed bag, used hand grips—and played dominoes.

"You look at him wave that bat, arms swinging like a chicken wing," said Sparky, never giving Joe a take sign, "or the glove," as small as a bambino's. In 1980, released, he helped win Houston's first division. Morgan, Pete Rose, and Tony Perez reunited in 1983: The Wheez Kids (starting lineup age 301) made the Series. "Gotta be coincidence," joked Rose. "Where Joe plays, you win."

Next year he retired with a then-record 266 dingers as a second baseman—first man at that position with 200, 2,000 games, and 2,000 hits—1975–76 Most Valuable Player, three Gold Gloves, 10 All-Star teams, and leading the league three and four times in fielding and on-base percentage, respectively.

"My career is a salute to the little guy," he said. What peak remained to climb?

For a time Joe imagined managing. Taking one job, he reconsidered in the morning. "I woke up thinking, 'You're hired to be fired.'" Morgan started a beer company, opened three fast-food restaurants, and aired 1985 Reds and 1985–88 ESPN college baseball. The player was a chatterbox. Could the analyst parse? "What I'll try to do is act like I'm on the bench and you're sitting with me. Hopefully, I'll think of the questions before you ask."

In 1986, tweaking MTV, Morgan began Giants play-by-play. "Ours is a quick-gratification society. I like deferred": Cooperstown 1990 and B.A. from Hayward. "I told mom if she let me enter baseball, I'd get my degree." That year, ESPN began "Sunday Night Baseball." Morgan hoped to educate. "I'm in the business to help the viewer." Risk loomed: strategy can bore.

"Chemistry takes a while," said Miller. At first Joe mused, "What you see is the end of something. When we first started, we didn't always see eye-to-eye. Jon came from radio, me TV. He adjusted, and lightened me up," each side-saddle in a chair, almost facing the other. In time, M dialed meshing: Miller's lore and Morgan's game within the game.

Joe began an ESPN.com column, wrote *Baseball for Dummies,* and went "where the game takes me." By 1995, joining NBC's two Bobs, Costas and Uecker, it took him to post-season double duty. One week he traveled 12,000 miles: "every night, different airport, different motel." George Steinbrenner took pity: "Please contact me," he wrote, tongue-in-cheek, "regarding a comeback as a second baseman."

Morgan passed.

His mother had not raised a fool.

Instead, he called a 1999 O's–Cuba exhibition in Havana. "I am relearning Spanish. The usual stuff. Where's the bathroom. I'm hungry." Tossing the

JOE MORGAN

LONGEVITY:	7	20 years.
CONTINUITY:	6	Cincinnati N.L. 1985; San Francisco N.L. 1986–94; NBC TV "Game of the Week" 1986–87; ABC TV "Monday Night Baseball" 1988–89; ESPN TV "Sunday Night Baseball" 1990– ; ABC/NBC TV The Baseball Network 1994–95; Oakland A.L. 1995.
NETWORK:	10	College Baseball 1985–88, "Sunday" 1990– , co-host "Players Choice Awards" 1997–99, and "Home Run Derby" 1998– (ESPN TV). "Game" 1986–87; L.C.S. 1995–2000; World Series 1995, 1997, and 1999; All-Star Game 1994, 1996, 1998, and 2000 (NBC TV). "Monday" 1988–89 (ABC TV). TBN 1994–95 (ABC/NBC TV). Division Series 1996–2000 and 2003– (ESPN TV), 1998– (ESPN Radio), and 2002 (ABC Family TV).
KUDOS:	10	Cooperstown 1990, as player. Cable ACE award 1990. Emmy Award 1997. Number 8 retired by Reds 1998. ASA Award 1999. Vice chairman, Baseball Hall of Fame 2000– .
LANGUAGE:	6	Intense.
POPULARITY:	9	Residue of '70s Reds.
PERSONA:	10	Little Joe.
VOICE:	7	Pleasant.
KNOWLEDGE:	10	Maddeningly inside.
MISCELLANY:	4	Once Wade Boggs went 0-for-22. "I was up to 12," Joe said, "but never made it to 22."
TOTAL:	79	(60th place).

usual first ball, ex-Senator Connie Marrero continued to pitch; whereupon Brady Anderson bunted toward third; at which point Joe shrieked, "Bunting on an 84-year-old pitcher!"

A gentleman would never do that—rather, watch and muse. "There's more of a flow and pace to National League baseball," Morgan said. The A.L. was "disjointed." Home Run Derby belonged in softball. "That's not the way our game should be." Managers "do more off the cuff than they ever did before." Money has "changed everything. Players should cater more to the fans."

Give baseball that old-time religion.

It's good enough for Joe.

DAVE CAMPBELL

In 1995, Connie Chung interviewed Newt Gingrich's mother on CBS TV. "This is just between us," she whispered, ignoring 40 million viewers. Forget age, lines, and cancer. Just between us, our age loves a tan.

Dave Campbell is baseball's bronze warrior. His skin accentuates eyes, hair, and teeth. It conjures George Hamilton, Jennifer Lopez, yea, *Playboy*'s Girls of Kokomo. "Dave met the tan," said a friend, "and the tan won."

For a decade, it colored ESPN's 10 P.M. and 12 A.M. "Baseball Tonight." Campbell cajoled, inveigled, but never overwhelmed, the viewer—candor, as vital as the corner salon.

Born in March 1990, "Baseball Tonight" brewed highlight, lowlight, feature, and minutiae—before long, George W. Bush's favorite show. Broadcasting, like infra-red light, had already settled in Dave's bones.

"I always wanted to play baseball," said the 6-foot-0, 185-pound righty, growing up in Michigan. He heard Heilmann and Patrick, haunted Briggs Stadium, and craved second base. "Charlie Gehringer's old position. I couldn't wait to play there."

In 1962, his Michigan team won the NCAA title. Class of '64 made the Tigers, hitting .102 from 1967 to 1969. In 1970, Campbell soared to .219 in San Diego. "Just call me Babe. Things fell from bad to worse." One year he managed 12 home runs and 40 RBI; another, went 2 for 23. "I made $7,000 my first year, and $26,000 tops. Part was the time, part my skill."

Dave played six positions, twice had achilles tendon surgery, and joined the Cards and Astros. By 1974, a Splengarian descent ended his career. "Here

I am, 32, what do I try?" he said, retiring with a .213 average. First, San Diego TV. Then, Texas League Amarillo, managing. In 1978–79, Giants and Padres radio, respectively.

In 1984, Tony Gwynn won his first batting title, San Diego took the pennant, and Dave aired the Series on flagship KFMB. "My tan loses a little on radio. Maybe I should stick to television."

Instead, he began a post-game and baseball history show, created the board game "Extra Bases," and added San Diego State hoops and football. Gehringer's nickname was "The Mechanical Man." Campbell became a juggernaut—until the Padres junked him in late 1988.

"My career here is a closed book," he said, perplexed by the firing. Pages of local-paper letters wanted it reopened. Owner Joan Kroc refused: in 1990, Dave joined ESPN's six-game-a-week schedule. "I liked it, but we had too much time." CEO Roger Werner called baseball "a substantial loss leader." Coverage waned to "Sunday Night Baseball" and a Wednesday doubleheader.

Many Voices vanished. Campbell ballooned: "Baseball Tonight"; "Sports Center" pre/post-season analysis; Wednesday, playoff, and Triple-A World Series color. He also called the 1994–97 Colorado Rockies. "Every home game was a sellout"—and potential conflict with ESPN.

DAVE CAMPBELL

LONGEVITY:	9	27 years.
CONTINUITY:	7	San Francisco N.L. 1978; San Diego N.L. 1979–89; ESPN TV "Major League Baseball" 1990– ; Colorado N.L. 1994–97.
NETWORK:	7	"Baseball Tonight" and "Baseball" 1990– (ESPN TV). L.C.S. 1998– (ESPN Radio).
KUDOS:	4	1980s San Diego awards included 1988 *San Diego Tribune* "Best [Local] Play-by-Play Man."
LANGUAGE:	9	Incisive.
POPULARITY:	10	ESPN's long-time bigs hub.
PERSONA:	9	Tall and tan and young and lively.
VOICE:	9	Mellow.
KNOWLEDGE:	10	Wired into every team. "He doesn't bull," said Al Michaels.
MISCELLANY:	4	In 1964–70 minors, moved 42 times.
TOTAL:	78	(64th place).

In 1998, Dave repaired solely to Bristol. "Only so much time in a day for the important things"—like rays. Just between us: "Baseball Tonight" bound coverage. "I can't imagine being a fan," said Bush, soon taping it at the White House, "and not seeing this every day."

Today Karl Ravech anchors. Peter Gammons, John Kruk, and Harold Reynolds add tale and view. A constant is Campbell, still heard irregularly. He and the tan endure.

SKIP CARAY

Early Wynn knocked his grandmother down to win, making hitters cry uncle. Depending on your view, he was a son of a bitch, the mother of competitors, or no kissin' cousin. Nepotism is a way of baseball life.

Jack Buck begot Joe. Marty Brennaman helped son Thom. In 1991, three generations of Carays called a game. Making history, Harry kicked himself. "If I'd had sense enough before I was born to nickname myself Flip, we'd'a had Flip, [grandson] Chip, and [son] Skip"—the Singing Carays, for your watching and listening pleasure.

"Having a father in the business was a help and curse. Some people didn't like dad. Others opened doors," Skip said. At first it bothered him—coasting on pop's cocktails. He even thought of changing the last name. "Chances are, I wouldn't have gotten a job if I weren't Harry's son. I also knew, because of that, I'd have to be even better."

It was a trade Skip had not considered as a child.

"I didn't want to call sports," growing up in and around St. Louis. "I wanted to play 'em," and did, as an all-city high school linebacker. Caray then hurt his knee. Suddenly, the booth beguiled. The "soprano, back then" began a radio show. At the University of Missouri, he worked each summer as a KMOX writer, director, and producer.

In 1963, Skip joined Texas League Tulsa, then Triple-A Atlanta Crackers. As we have seen, WSB Atlanta beamed the not-yet-marching-to Georgia 1965 Braves. That May, Voice Mel Allen's mother died. "Given my Atlanta experience," Caray said, WSB asked him to sub. A cup of coffee denotes a brief bigs stay. Sipping, Skip then cracked the NBA St. Louis Hawks.

In 1968, both moved to Atlanta: "Best thing that ever happened. I got my own identity. Finally I stopped being Harry's kid." Soon Skip occupied a world of hoops, hockey, and football, chucking raw kid for stardom. The star he wished upon was baseball. Irony reached it.

In 1954, Jack Buck joined the Cards. Boss Harry sent Milo Hamilton packing. From 1966 to 1975, the Braves' Voice was too busy to settle scores. Milo was then axed again. Caray *fils* replaced him! "I'm not good-looking or a threat to Twiggy," he said. Added Ernie Johnson: "It was interesting how fans reacted. People expected Skip to be Harry." They were soon disabused.

Harry roared. Skip intoned. Senior could drink dry a saloon. Junior gently mused about "cocktail hour" in Atlanta. In one way, they knit. "The worst call by a major league umpire in fifty years," Skip raged. "[Ed] Vargo should be fired because he made all umpires look bad." You could see pop beaming.

"I didn't set out to be different," said the son, more reflexively than defensively. "My dad was an orphan, a self-made man, more elemental as a broadcaster. We're just not the same human being." A larger concern was that his Braves and aptitude seemed strangers in the night.

In 1977, Caray added WSB Radio to WTCG TV. Celebrating, the Braves lost 17 straight games. Once San Diego's Gene Richards broke for second base. The catcher's throw hit Buzz Capra in the head, bounced high, and knocked the pitcher to the ground. "Capra was a friend and I was afraid he might be dead," said Skip, "but it was so typical of our team that I started laughing."

Later, Atlanta hosted Philly—and All-Star Mike Schmidt. "Here's the pitch," said Caray. "Bouncing ball to third. Schitz is up with it, and throws to first. In time." Red-faced, he went to break. "Skip, *who* plays third for Philadelphia?" Ernie began next inning. Laughter got them through a lot.

Phil Niekro won 318 games. Said brother Joe: "That knuckler got anybody out"—except Dave Parker. At dinner, Phil asked, "How do I get Parker out? My knuckler's not working."

"Forget the knuckler," Skip said. "Throw your blooper and see what happens."

Twice Niekro knuckled: Parker lined out and singled. Next up, Phil threw a blooper after waving to the booth. Dave hit it 400 feet. His final at-bat went 390.

"Phil takes my advice, Parker bombs two balls 800 feet, and both are caught!" said Caray. "I still say, 'I told you so.'" For too long, Georgia said that about its team.

Niekro became a Yankee, then Indian. The Braves could have used him July 4, 1985: Mets, 16–13, ending at 3:55 A.M. Fireworks began at 4:01—"so late," laughed Skip, "many thought the city was under attack." The 1987–90 Braves dredged last. "Loosen up," he told partner Billy Sample. "We might be the only team in history not to win a game all season." Caray recalled '82: Where had the dream gone wrong?

"That year I got cheered in a restaurant or grocery store. Now if I put on shades, I can slink into Kroger's unnoticed." *TSN,* among others, noticed: "He is perhaps America's most prominent baseball announcer," available on WTBS TV in 63 million homes 130 times a year. "The Braves [even losing] have developed a loyalty among many fans regions distant from a major-league team."

They heard: "Guys ask how to crash broadcasting. 'Hit .350 or win the Heisman'"; in "attendance, Sam Scoresby and Linda Yavnov," the brand of scotch and vodka, respectively, in the Braves lounge bar; about a standing O for Skip at a college basketball game. In San Francisco, he lunched with a friend of his wife's. "'That's not your wife,' a stranger told me. 'I caught you. I hear you talking about her on TV.' That was the first time I realized cable's impact."

In 1991, son Chip joined Atlanta—the first bigs Voice's radio or TV grandson. "How overprotective is telling your kid to be quiet?" said pop. More history: the troika's game. "They had a news conference at Dad's restaurant. We went to Wrigley Field in a limo. For the first time I felt like a rock 'n' roll star—mikes in your face, dumb questions" except for one: Were the Braves the Decade's Team?

The '91ers met Minnesota in a worst-to-first World Series. In Game Seven, Lonnie Smith's single began Atlanta's eighth inning. Terry Pendleton then found an alley. Decoyed by infielders Greg Gagne and Chuck Knoblauch, Smith slowed, stopped at third, and died: Twins, 1–0, in 10. Even the "Tomahawk Chop" chant seemed weary. Sadly, it revived.

Yin: team's past. (K-ing batter 1,000, Charlie Leibrandt forgot to call time, rolled the ball to the dugout, and let a runner take second.) Yang: 1992 L.C.S. Game Seven's ninth inning, three on, two out, 2–1, Pittsburgh. "My biggest thrills have been my kids' successes in Little League or school events," said Skip. "Professionally, it's easy. Frank Cabrera," singling to plate David Justice and Sid Bream: Braves, 3–2.

As Bream slid, people in the booth began pounding Skip on the back. He never knew it. "I didn't feel it, my concentration calling the play was total. All I knew was Frank's hit meant the pennant." Stick a fork in him. He's numb.

The Braves lost the Classic, 4 games to 2. The finale again drained. "Eleventh inning, we're behind [4–3, Toronto]," Caray looked back. "Otis Nixon makes out bunting—the tying run's on *third!*" Yin and yang: Atlanta dropped the 1993 L.C.S.; in 1995, it finally took a Series. "Fly ball, deep left-center!" Skip roared on radio. "Grissom on the run! Yes! Yes! Yes! The Atlanta Braves have given you a championship!"

TV as connecting tissue: the Chip off Skip's block—"He got the looks in the family"—left Seattle for Fox's "Game of the Week." Turner Field replaced Atlanta-Fulton County Stadium. The nineties Yanks took three Series to the Braves' one. Harry died in February 1998. That May, Skip visited Wrigley. "I think about Dad all the time. Within five minutes of waking up each day and before I close my eyes at night."

By then, Chip had become WGN's window on the Cubs. "I talked to granddad in January. We were going to do fifty TV games," one of Harry's two wishes before dying (the other, two martinis). "To come so close to fulfilling that dream and have it taken away seems unbelievably cruel." His son, said pop, "came from a broken home, like I did, and was starting to get to know his grandfather. They were just starting to bond."

Holy cow! Try following Harry Caray. "Give [Chip] a chance to be heard," pled the *Chicago Tribune*. Dad did an NBC Division Series, had an angioplasty, and got a pacemaker that "triggers airports' metal detecting device."

In 2003, WTBS busted him to wireless and Turner South regional TV: "He's identified with the Braves. We want a national feel." Skip shrugged. "I said, 'Run that by me again.'" Life, however, was relative. Just keep the moolah coming.

Ratings dropped. Having missed the light, WTBS felt viewers' heat. "It's nice to be back," smiled Skip, reinstated. "The fans made it happen." Perry Como sang, "Oh, My Papa." In 2005, Chip joined his in Atlanta. The Carays are enough to give nepotism a good name.

SKIP CARAY

LONGEVITY:	10	29 years.
CONTINUITY:	10	Atlanta N.L. 1976– ; ABC/NBC TV The Baseball Network 1994–95.
NETWORK:	4	WTBS 1976– (SuperStation TV). TBN 1994–95 (ABC/NBC TV). 2000 Division Series (NBC TV).
KUDOS:	6	Seven- and one-time Georgia Sportscaster of the Year and Emmy Award, respectively. Honored by Atlanta for quarter-century of broadcasting 2000. Braves Hall of Fame 2004.
LANGUAGE:	8	Saucy.
POPULARITY:	10	Like Tanqueray, wears well.
PERSONA:	10	Like Braves', nice and easy (till October).
VOICE:	9	Medicinal.
KNOWLEDGE:	9	Doesn't force-feed.
MISCELLANY:	6	Growing up, Skip heard Dad say nightly at 8:30, "Let's pause for station identification. Good night, Skip. This is the Cardinals Baseball Network."
TOTAL:	82	(45th place).

PETE VAN WIEREN

In 2003, like Caray, Pete Van Wieren was briefly dropped by WTBS. "Not seeing and hearing them," wrote Jim Tucker, "is going to be as weird as not seeing Ted Turner in the owner's box." The victim shrugged. "You broadcast when they tell you. And you'd better be ready when they do."

Casey Stengel was a.k.a. The Perfessor. "The Professor" educed spectacles, brains, and work. "We're on the air so long and talk about a player four or five times a game and a pitcher all game long. If you don't constantly prepare, you run out of things to say."

Van Wieren forged an Upstate New York frame of reference: born, Rochester; liked, Allen and Barber; English degree, Cornell University. One day, covering campus baseball, he got hooked replacing an injured announcer. "Writing or talking, I'd consume papers and magazines—the best possible training for baseball radio."

Pete joined the *Washington Post,* a 500-watt Warrenton, Virginia, station—"I did news, sports, football on tape-delay"—and outlets in Manassas, Binghamton, and Toledo. In 1974, school took him to Mets' Triple-A Tidewater. Ted Turner bought the Braves in January 1976. Two weeks later, the Professor made the untenured bigs: "a double whammy in two ways."

He and Caray were both freshmen. Van Wieren also handled Braves travel. "Planes, buses, equipment, trucks, hotels, meals, tickets—you name it, I did it." Next year he moved solely to radio/TV.

By then, Turner could *literally* count a typical Atlanta crowd. Curiosa starred camel relays, bathtubs on wheels, and an ostrich race. Once Ted and Tug McGraw rolled baseballs from home to first and third base, respectively—with their nose. "Look at yours," said a friend. Turner: "Yeah, but I won."

Pete's bulging satchel helped avoid the field. "Those were the years," he said, "we would have killed to be .500 in June." Van Wieren lived on Flames hockey, Falcons/Big Ten football, and TBS/TNT's NBA. In 1991, the Braves finally contended. Daily he circled Fulton's club level. "I arrived early, not wanting to miss a thing, because it might not happen again."

October 1: Atlanta led the Dodgers by a game. "Stretch by Smoltz," Pete said on WTBS. "The pitch to Cedeno. A high fly ball to right field! It's fairly deep! Back goes Justice! He's got it! And the magic number for Atlanta is down to one! The Braves have clinched a tie for [N.L. West] first!" The Giants then beat L.A.

In 1995, Van Wieren co-wrote the book *America's Team*. That fall, the Braves became the first team to win the Series in three different cities.

"I keep thinking of '91. Little did we know that we'd be going back and back"—13 straight playoffs over three presidencies, two recessions, and two Gulf Wars. Empty post-season seats mirrored a growing yawn. "We've gotten spoiled," said Pete, who hadn't, prepping as if calling the '62 Mets.

In 2002, he attended the Society of Baseball Research convention. At the time, many feared another strike. "It wouldn't hurt," Van Wieren told a panel, "if the Commissioner would say something positive about the game once in a while." Unlike Pete, Bud Selig had run out of things to say.

Woody Allen said that 90 percent of success is showing up.

The Braves show up each October.

TBSers again smile that Van Wieren shows up each night.

PETE VAN WIEREN

LONGEVITY:	10	29 years.
CONTINUITY:	10	Atlanta N.L. 1976– ; ABC/NBC TV The Baseball Network 1994–95.
NETWORK:	3	WTBS 1976– (SuperStation TV). TBN 1994–95 (ABC/NBC TV).
KUDOS:	6	Nine-time Georgia Sportscaster of the Year. Ivan Allen, Jr. "Mr. Baseball Award" 1998. Honored by Atlanta for quarter-century of broadcasting 2000. Braves Hall of Fame 2004.
LANGUAGE:	9	Scholarly.
POPULARITY:	9	Low-key.
PERSONA:	8	Professor.
VOICE:	9	Brisk.
KNOWLEDGE:	10	*Summa cum laude.* Rereads rule book cover-to-cover several times a year.
MISCELLANY:	5	Often writes column for Internet CNNSI.com.
TOTAL:	79	(59th place).

TIM MCCARVER

"I am always ready to learn, though I do not always enjoy being taught," Churchill said. Hoping to learn, a bigs junkie can despair of being taught. "Baseball fans best know their game," Jack Buck felt. "Because of that, you can't teach 'em much that's new."

Two corollaries boost angst: ex-jock-turned-analyst and strategy gone mad. "In football, you have to explain 18 pass routes!" Harry Caray rasped. "Baseball's in the open. Who cares about whether the pitch is a knuckler or curve? Boring! Tell stories!" Analysts miss because they misread the game.

Tim McCarver can explain the Uncle Charlie—also why Omaha Beach was gorier than Gold. The 1959–80 catcher is said to talk a lot. Smoking a cigar, turning notes in a loose-leaf pad, and citing Lady MacBeth's "What's done cannot be undone," he likely has a lot to say.

Shakespeare's quote, says Tim, applies to baseball. "You prepare, you relax, then you let 'er rip." Teach, and learn.

McCarver was born ten days after the 1941 World Series. "A great event," said the son of a police officer, "but the real pressure is the playoffs. Lose it, and you're forgotten by Thanksgiving." He could not forget how fastballs and sliders left the left thumb torn and twisted. "On cold days it hurts—a *USS Arizona* memorial to the craft. Baseball did *to* me physically, and *for* me cerebrally."

Football was Tim's first love at Memphis's Christian Brothers High School. Baseball became "my final love" after his 1959 signing. The Cardinals owned the mid-South, including McCarver's Shelby County, Tennessee. "I'd hear Harry Caray say certain names: *Rip Repulski. Jocko Jablonski.* Marvelous." Gradually, he marveled at how "baseball was central to my life."

In 1963, St. Louis named Tim, 21, catcher. Next year, the Classic began there. In New York, Mickey Mantle won Game Three. Next day the Yanks led, 3–0, until Ken Boyer's slam. "Ken neared third as brother Clete got in the baseline, making him run behind him as Kenny whacked him on the ass." Blood was even thicker than a winning Series share.

McCarver's tenth-inning whippet carved a Game Five victory. "Those three games in New York are as good as baseball gets." It got better in Game Seven: St. Louis's first title since 1946. Tim hit a Series-high .478. Two years later, his 13 triples led the league. 'Sixty-seven soldered 14 homers, 69 RBI, and career-high .295.

Orlando Cepeda—Cha Cha—named his team "El Birdos." Once they boarded the bus.

"Everybody on? We're ready," manager Red Schoendienst said.

"No!" shouted Bob Gibson, pitching. "[1967 N.L. MVP Orlando] Cepeda isn't on, and we're not leaving till he gets here."

Thrice Gibbie beat Boston to take the Series. In 1968, he lost Game Seven: McCarver made the final out. Otherwise, Bob beat the world.

Tim met him in spring 1960. "He was black, I was from the South, segregation ruled, and it was a terribly hot day." McCarver gave Bob a sip of orange drink, later terming him "the luckiest pitcher I knew. He pitches when the other team gets shut out." In Gibbie's 34 games, 1968 Nationals scored 49 runs.

Bob worked like an eggtimer, mocking Tim's plea to slow down. "Go back behind the plate. Only thing you know about pitching is that it's hard to hit." The mound became a sanctuary. "What can *you* teach *me*?" Gibson bullied pitching coach Barney Schultz. "You were a knuckleballer. I throw *fast*-balls!" Ultimately, McCarver and another pitcher were traded to Philadelphia. They would anchor the same cemetery, he laughed, sixty feet and six inches apart.

"Before a game, Steve'd be in a trance-like state," Tim said of Carlton.

Once he apologized for knocking Lefty's motion. "That's okay," Steve shrugged. "I didn't pay attention, anyway." The 1972 Cy Younger led the N.L. in complete games, Ks, innings, ERA, and victories—27 of Philly's 59! "Greatest season I ever saw," said McCarver, peddled that June. In 1975, the sphinx regained his guru. "I spent the next few years catching Steve, pinch-hitting," and becoming one of seven modern four-decade players.

Spring 1980: the new Phils Voice cuts the cord. "When you retire, you're an outsider, not player. Broadcast like one," Tim said. Mike Schmidt got a double after prematurely strutting his home-run trot. Next day McCarver bearded him in the clubhouse. "I hear you ripped me for not hustling," Mike snapped. Tim asked if he was.

"No," said Schmidt.

"Did I tell the truth?"

"Yes," Mike confessed.

By 1983, McCarver had hustled to Flushing Meadows.

In baseball, like real estate, location matters. "He has received much praise for his work as a broadcaster for the [then-WOR and SportsChannel] Mets," *TSN* soon noted. "This is much better than being lauded in Kansas City or Houston because the networks are in New York, and so are their decision-makers."

Tim analyzed several 1980 NBC "Game[s] of the Week." By 1984, he aired the syndicated "Greats of the Game" and ABC's All-Star Game and L.C.S. A year later, McCarver did the Series. John Tudor was "a surgeon. The only difference is that when he takes the heart out of the team, he doesn't replace it." Mused *SI*: "Nobody explicates the game with as much patience and . . . good humor."

In Chicago, spotting a rooftop wedding, Tim began a game-long divertissement.

"If the game gets rained out, does the wedding count?"

Said Ralph Kiner: "Only if it goes five innings."

One inning, Tim praised Stan Musial. The next Man, Harry Truman, "threw pitches left- and right-handed." The Broadway junkie referenced Stephen Sondheim's "The Little Things You Do Together." Tonight, he said, "It was the little things the *Mets* did together." How could he *know* so much? Curiosity: the "first, not second, guess."

Dub baseball a narcotic. "You ask, 'When do I walk away? *Do* I?'" He couldn't, vacationing at year's end. "Otherwise I spend too much time thinking about the game."

The kicker *was* the end.

McCarver's got later every year.

Tim called 1986's N.L. L.C.S. Game Six: "the most tiring thing [Mets vs. Astros] I have been part of as a spectator or player." 1987: hosted HBO's "Greatest Sports Upsets" and an ABC children's show. 1989: toppled to the TV booth floor on the Earthquake Series. 1990: joined CBS's Jack Buck. "The network has exclusivity," said *Broadcasting* magazine. "Much rides on them." Buck rode out to pasture in 1991. Next fall, Deion Sanders doused McCarver with three buckets of ice water for scoring football "moon-lighting." Nothing changed "the great impression," wrote *USA Today,* "that the network doesn't care."

McCarver did, musing, "You take what they give you." A viewer took his insight straight. Many players have "invisible injuries. They're ducking responsibility." Bobby Valentine had Mel Rojas face Paul O'Neill. "A mistake," said Tim. O'Neill went deep. Behind, 4–3, a Reds runner clung to third on a fly. "This game should be tied, and it's not." He tied MSG's "The Tim McCarver Show," four books including *Oh, Baby, I Love It!,* and revived the 1996– "Game of the Week." Increasingly, the term *analyst* brought Fox's new color man to mind.

In 1999, the Mets axed his $500,000 salary for Tom Seaver: "a decision so small," wrote Mike Lupica, "it could fit inside a batting glove." His fit pleased the Yanks. "Tim's been critical of me," said George Steinbrenner, "but that makes no difference." In 2000, New York's twin tiaras staged the first Subway Series since 1956. Roger Clemens threw a bat barrel at Mike Piazza. Instantly, McCarver recalled Atlanta, 1962. "I was in Triple-A, slammed my bat, and it bounced up into the lap of a 13-year-old." The father said, kindly and simply, "We understand."

Tim won his first Emmy as top sports analyst. Stripes coverage then turned cable. Leaving, he spliced the new (Giants TV) and old (ultimately, record 21st straight post-season). Don't know much about history? Barry Bonds's bases-full intentional walk evoked Leo Durocher passing Willie McCovey. "Baseball was shocked. But everybody does that with Bonds." Don't know much biology? Triples fell due to "guys not running hard out of the box."

"The most credible man in baseball broadcasting," said columnist Tim

Kawakami. Not all agreed: A *San Francisco Chronicle* poll overwhelmingly named him TV's "most annoying sportscaster." One e-mailer wrote: "The biggest braying blowhard in baseball blathers on. The baboon is just such a stultifying simpleton, so mindnumbingly awful, so wretchedly moronic, so incredibly incompetent, such a complete and utter abomination in the eyes of man and God."

Dead-pan, Tim paused: "Guess he's not a fan."

McCarver left the Jints in December 2002. "I'm not here to please people. I'm here to report and have a good time doing it." Next year, he telecast his record 78th Series game, passing Curt Gowdy's 77. On occasion, even an old-guarder sees a gosh, I've never seen that play. We *hear* it from McCarver.

Teach, and learn.

TIM McCARVER

LONGEVITY:	*8*	25 years.
CONTINUITY:	*5*	NBC TV "Game of the Week" 1980; Philadelphia N.L. 1980–82; New York N.L. 1983–98; ABC TV "Monday Night Baseball" 1984–89; CBS TV "Game of the Week" 1990–93; ABC/NBC TV The Baseball Network 1994–95; Fox TV "Game of the Week" 1996– ; New York A.L. 1999–2001; San Francisco N.L. 2002.
NETWORK:	*10*	"Monday" 1984–89 (ABC TV). L.C.S. 1984 and 1986 (ABC TV), 1990–93 (CBS TV), and 1996– (Fox TV). World Series 1985, 1987, 1989, and 1995 (ABC TV), 1990–93 (CBS TV), and 1996, 1998, and 2000– (Fox TV). All-Star Game 1986 and 1988 (ABC TV), 1990–93 (CBS TV), and 1995, 1997, 1999, and 2001– (Fox TV). "Game" 1990–93 (CBS TV) and 1996– (Fox TV). TBN 1994–95 (ABC/NBC TV).
KUDOS:	*9*	Emmy Award 2000–02, outstanding sports analyst. Missouri Sports Hall of Fame 2004. Stadium named in honor in Memphis.
LANGUAGE:	*10*	Punful. David Cone twice K'd Casey Candaele: "Cone burned the Candaele at both ends."
POPULARITY:	*10*	Talks well, with will.
PERSONA:	*10*	Analyst of his age.
VOICE:	*8*	Effusive.
KNOWLEDGE:	*10*	Encyclopedic.
MISCELLANY:	*10*	Co-hosted CBS 1992 Winter Olympics. Only Voice to call each post-1983 regular- and post-season.
TOTAL:	*90*	(17th place).

JOE BUCK

"You may solve the Berlin Crisis, or not," Joseph P. Kennedy told son Robert, then Attorney General, in 1961, "but nothing is as important as how you raise your family." Jack Buck raised eight children to think independently—yet it was important to his second-youngest to enter broadcasting. "Baseball," said Joe, "is that which binded me to the man I most admire."

In 1989, Buck *fils* joined Triple-A Louisville. In 1991, he joined *pere* at KMOX St. Louis. Before long, Joe aired Fox TV baseball and football: the youngest to regularly do either. "When Jack heard something by him," said mother Carole, a former actress, "he'd say, 'God, he's good.'"

Seeing dad, Joe plunked a hug and kiss. "Take it easy, kid," Jack cautioned. "Not everybody knows we're father and son."

Like pop, Joe felt baseball "the last thing I think about before I fall asleep—and the first thing I think about when I wake up in the morning."

They differed in time and place.

Pop's youth and game were umbilically attached. A generation learned that Lincoln, on his deathbed, told Abner Doubleday, "General, preserve baseball for the future." Many Generation Xers felt it an anachronism. A sport without *attitude*? Sooner grunge shirts with starch. Joe grew up as trash became king; deviance, first minister. The culture affected. It did not overwhelm.

Mojo, rising. Joe was born in St. Petersburg on April 25, 1969. "If the Cardinals'd trained in Oklahoma," he said, "I'd have come out crying there." Hannibal lay 118 miles from St. Louis. Like Tom Sawyer, Joe soon began missing school. "I'd do homework on road trips." Grandma ghost-wrote papers. Mom signed absences. "She knew how important it was to me to be with my dad."

Buck never took geometry, diagrammed a sentence, or read *An American Tragedy*. "I'd follow Dad into the clubhouse, the parking lot, and hold his beer while he signed autographs." Joe copied him on a tape recorder. In Las Vegas, he watched the old man play craps. "On those trips the broadcasting was about the 10th most important thing."

In 1987, the Bucks and colleague Mike Shannon man the booth. Suddenly, pa says, "The birthday boy [18] will take us through the fifth inning." He and Shannon leave. Like Jack a half-century earlier, Joe was on his own. Entering Indiana University, he called ESPN's 1989 Triple-A All-Star Game.

"Keep your volume low, repeat the score, don't treat it like *War and Peace*," Jack said.

Joe smiled at the memory. "Where could you get better advice?" Soon junior joined senior's firm. "Even then, I had to remind myself that it wouldn't be like this forever."

Nightly Carole heard their father-and-son reunion. "You were never aware that they were related on the air," she said. "But if I had a choice of listening to one or the other, it was Joe. But that's a mother talking."

In 1993, Buck began talking on CBS Radio's "Game of the Week." Listening, I had no idea that, spoiled by the calendar, he was all of 24.

Until 1987, network TV owned an NFL monopoly. Cable ESPN and TNT then joined the clan. In 1993, Godfather CBS lost rights to Fox. "I was working at KMOX when I heard the story. My first thought was all the days I spent at the stadium seeing my father do football [CBS TV, then Radio]. Never did I think of whom Fox might hire."

Mom did.

In 1994, Carole collared Fox Sports head Ed Goren at the Super Bowl: "If you're putting together football, you can't do it without Joe!" Nodding, president David Hill added baseball, yelping, "No more dead guys!" Babe Ruth flunked the test. Nepotism passed. Buck, 26, became lead "Game of the Week"man. Other Voices were Chip Caray, Thom Brennaman, and John Rooney. Mickey Rooney denied DNA.

Ironically, Brat Pack leavening sprung from Jack's ex-CBS analyst. Unlike dad, Joe and Tim McCarver fused. "The play-by-play man [should] explain what and where and analyst answer why and how," Tim said. "He does both." In 1996, Buck became youngest Series Voice since 1953's Vin Scully, 25. "When I think of announcers who went before, it sends chills up your spine."

The Classic opened in the Bronx. Afterward Joe called home. "What time is the game on?" Jack asked: no swelled head for sonny. Interrupting, mom assured that pop heard each word. A week later, Fox announced a 17.4 Nielsen rating. "Three times our nightly norm," said Hill. "That's why we got into baseball [for $120 million a year]."

Joe grasped the bottom line. "I refuse to fill a page about what baseball means to me with the typical syrup," he mocked, adding, "Oh, God, pass the syrup." Its symbol: a red-haired titan who seemed cleaner than a Gillette Blue Blades shave.

"Not even Hemingway," Buck said, "could explain what Mr. McGwire meant."

In 1997, McGwire left Oakland for St. Louis a slugger but not a hero—"not especially known around the country," Joe mused. He ended the year with 58 homers, tying Jimmie Foxx for most by a righty. The '98ers drew a franchise high 3,195,021. "McGwire is almost solely responsible," wrote *Sports Illustrated,* "for this era of unprecedented interest in the Cardinals."

On September 7, Mac's No. 61 tied Roger Maris. Next night Fox showed Cards–Cubs. Buck had scripted No. 62. "There it goes," he planned to say. "Here it is. A new single-season home run champion, Mark McGwire, as he floats around the bases and into the history books." Instead, Mac hit a text-busting blast vs. Steve Trachsel. "Down the left-field line, is it enough?" Joe said, no time to amplify. "Gone! There it is, 62. Touch first, Mark [he missed, then tagged, it], you are the new single-season home run king!"

I was flying to New York. The pilot announced Mac's blast. Passengers began applauding. At Busch Stadium, history, fireworks, and 43,688 fused. "Everybody in the park was a fan," said Buck. "I broadcast like a fan. I'm not so sure that on a night like that it's wrong to act like a fan." McGwire embraced members of the Maris family. Blacked out in Chicago, Fox still got a 14.5 rating. "I'm worn out. How much can we take?" Mark took it to the limit: 5 homers in his last 11 ups.

Signs dappled Closing Day: "McGwire, You Are the Man." Buck was doing football. Mac faced Carl Pavano. "Swing! And it, get up, baby, get up, get up, get up!" caroled Mike Shannon. "He's done it again! Seventy home runs! Take a ride on that for history! How can you end a season better than Big Mac has just done?"

In 2001, Fox began six-year "Game," All-Star, and postseason exclusivity. Joe became its one size fits all. By 2006, his ninth TV Series would trail Gowdy (12) and Allen and Scully (11). Only Curt topped Buck's seven, including 2000, in a row. On one hand, cable cut the audience. On the other, Fox's quick cuts, miked managers, and FoxBox, a diamond graphic with updated score, inning, count, out, and base runner, wowed.

Buck won a 1999, 2001–02, and 2004 Emmy. "Baseball is my stock market, my assembly line, my court case, my operating table." Stock rose in 2002: the busy camper, 33, replaced lead NFL Voice Pat Summerall, 70. Said *SI*: "Curt Gowdy and Al Michaels are the only other broadcasters ever to have been their networks' No. 1 Voice for baseball and football simultaneously."

Joe aired four NFL and Division Series games in a week—"juggling them, marriage, kids, and my side job as a clown"—eager to seem cutting-edge. *SI* asked if he preferred nepotism or birthright. "Nepotism. It pisses people off a lot more." Gowdy grew up with Tyrone Power. Buck kept a life-sized cutout of Mike Myers as Austin Powers. Curt's weekly "Game" was national. Fox's 16-game menu was regional, began late May or early June, and, like Joe, vanished at season's peak.

"That last month, they stick him on the NFL," barbed an ex-Fox Voice. "Its baseball guy, on *sabbatical,* missing the most crucial time!" In 2004, "Game" appeared only thrice after August 28. "Fox is MIA on the pennant race, and Joe doesn't even do [September 18's] Red Sox–Yankees," said the broadcaster. "What kind of sport would tolerate that?"

Plainly, baseball. "I don't think I'm destined for more than 10 more years in baseball. I'm enjoying football," Buck told *The New York Times.* "The 'Game of the Week' isn't what it was. I put a lot of work into those games, but you don't get the same payoff as you get from a great football game."

Fox was not your father's baseball network. As clear: Joe's grieving, over dad.

By 2002, Buck had cut his local schedule to 25 games. "I don't want to be gone all the time. I was a part of this on the other end, with my dad gone a lot and trying to spend more time with his kids." Jack entered the hospital in January. Unable to speak, he heard Joe whisper, "You have to get out of here and help me through the season."

On June 18, doctors removed the respirator. Doing a game—"Dad woulda given me hell if I'd missed it"—Joe arrived at Barnes-Jewish Hospital near 11 P.M. "Go ahead and go," he said, unsure if Jack was breathing. "I have everybody covered back here. I know what you did in your lifetime and we all respect it. I've been given more than any son." He would admit to hero worship. There are worse ways to regard your father.

The son left without looking back. "I knew what he was thinking. 'Get out of here, kid.'" Jack died minutes later. That week, Cardinals pitcher Darryl Kile also died. Buck, on "Game," didn't miss a beat. "Dad would have wanted me to go get back to work. I just wish I could call him after a game to talk about it now."

On occasion, Joe will call dad's cellphone to hear his best friend's voice. Jack's signet was "That's a winner!" Perhaps he was speaking about his son.

JOE BUCK

LONGEVITY:	5	14 years.
CONTINUITY:	9	St. Louis N.L. 1991–92 and 1995– ; CBS Radio "Game of the Week" 1993–95; Fox TV "Game of the Week" 1996– .
NETWORK:	10	"Game" 1993–95 (CBS Radio). "Game" and L.C.S. 1996– ; World Series 1996, 1998, and 2000– ; All-Star Game 1997, 1999, and 2001– (Fox TV).
KUDOS:	10	2002-04 NSSA Sportscaster of the Year. Four-time Emmy award, outstanding play-by-play.
LANGUAGE:	6	From group Spinal Tap through movie *The Karate Kid*, heavy on pop culture.
POPULARITY:	10	Soared after calling football's Randy Moss "disgusting" for 2005 TV incident.
PERSONA:	9	Depending on slant, hipster or wiseguy.
VOICE:	10	Authoritative.
KNOWLEDGE:	10	Thorough.
MISCELLANY:	5	In 2004, President Bush opened the Cardinals season. "Hey, Joe, how do you like my guys?" he said of sharpshooters on the roof.
TOTAL:	84	(39th place).

PAT HUGHES

"Some guys are lucky," said Pat Hughes. "They get that once-in-a-lifetime year." Russ Hodges got 1951. The '69 Amazin's amazed Lindsey Nelson. Baseball swung to 1998's McGwire–Sammy Sosa homerthon. "Baseball's been very, very good to me," said Senor Sammy. He and Mac were very good to Hughes.

As a teenager, Pat already liked the Cubs. "I'd hang around Candlestick Park to see the players. One day I snuck into their clubhouse. Williams. Santo. Ernie Banks was a friendly guy. He had such big hands. I remember him shaking my hand and squeezing it." Hughes left squeezing for the bigs.

He began at San Jose and Columbus. In 1983, Clippers boss George Sisler got the A.L.'s Lee MacPhail to send a letter asking "if [teams] were interested in checking me out." The Twins were. After a year, Pat left them for Milwaukee. "Mr. Baseball! Try inventing Bob Uecker's wheel." A decade later, the sport's needed it more.

A 1994 CBS poll showed the percentage of Americans liking baseball down to 39 from 1990's 61. The strike evinced a game not content to leave bad enough alone. "Some timing," said Pat, joining WGN Radio in 1996. "Baseball had become the Flying Dutchman." Needed: Port Reborn.

"What a record-assaulting, home run–blasting summer," *SI* wrote of 1998. Bars, stores, and water coolers mixed echo chamber and rumor factory. "You couldn't go anywhere, and not be affected," Bud Selig added. Sammy had never had forty dingers: on June 20, he hit No. 20 of the month.

Sosa and Mac dueled Ruth and Maris. Their Great Race fueled a feud. Even in bad years each team filled the other's park. "Forget Red Sox–Yankees," said Hughes. "Baseball's greatest rivalry is Cardinals–Cubs."

In 1998, adherents howled like reprobates. "In St. Louis, Cubs fans would cheer Sosa. In Chicago, it got bananas when McGwire launched one onto Waveland." The Race would have stirred, at any rate. Cubs–Cardinals made it sing.

"Daily the pressure rose," said Hughes, "the crowds, reporters, history, the drama." Daily he fretted about No. 62. "It's okay to plan a few words," warned Milo Hamilton, calling Hank Aaron's 715, "but you have to sound extemporaneous." On September 8, Mac "drives one to deep left—this could be!—it's a home run!" Pat bayed. "Number 62 for Mark McGwire!" Pause. "A slice of history and a magical moment in St. Louis! A line drive home run to left for Mark McGwire of the St. Louis Cardinals!"

Mark hugged his mates and 10-year-old son at the plate. Sosa clasped him near the first-base line. "Incredible. I had tears in my eyes," said Hughes. Joe Buck and Mike Shannon also aired the Maris-breaker. Tense and vivid, Pat's call is most replayed, even now.

On September 11, Sosa's 61 and 62 left Wrigley. Of 65, Hughes cried "'Holy cow!' and 'Hey-hey!' for Harry [Caray] and Jack [Brickhouse]!" Sammy's 66th/last briefly took the lead. He finished first in runs, total bases, and RBI, was second in homers and slugging, and hit at least 50 dingers a year through 2001.

In 2003, Sosa braved a corked-bat suspension. Hughes's partner bore bladder surgery, had a leg amputated, and missed post-season. For Ron Santo, the Cubs' collapse rivaled '69's. They led the L.C.S., 3 games to 1. In Game Six, Chicago, up, 3–0, was five outs from a Series.

"Our closest chance since '45," said Hughes. "It's gonna happen, we can feel it"—until Florida's Luis Castillo sliced to left. "Toward the line. Alou over. Does he have room? And leaping up, Alou cannot make the play!" Pat said. Steve Stone: "And Moises is unhappy with the fan [Steve Bartman]! A fan interfered with him! . . . If a fan just gets his hand out of the way, Moises makes the catch! . . . I can't believe that a fan would do that!"

We know the script: Marlins, 8–3. On cue, the Cubs died next night. "Lifted to left. Playable for Conine. And the Marlins are going to the World Series," Pat rued. "The Florida Marlins have stunned the Chicago Cubs, winning the last three in a row." There you go again: next year's team blew a last-week wild card.

"I remember joining the Cubs," said the San Jose University alumnus. "I was uprooting one daughter from first grade. I'm not a gypsy. I felt I'd be content to stay here the rest of my life."

Feeling had become fidelity. "Oh-three's collapse was indelible, Sammy, incredible. I think of Earl Gillespie [1957 Braves], or Ken Coleman with the Impossible Dream. One year, one guy."

In *Casablanca,* Bogart tells Bergman, "We'll always have Paris." Like Wrigleyville, Hughes will always have The Race.

PAT HUGHES

LONGEVITY:	8	22 years.
CONTINUITY:	9	Minnesota A.L. 1983; Milwaukee A.L. 1984–95; Chicago N.L. 1996– .
NETWORK:	1	WGN Radio network of its own.
KUDOS:	5	Three- and two-time Wisconsin and Illinois Sportscaster of the Year, respectively.
LANGUAGE:	9	Versatile: Hits to all fields.
POPULARITY:	9	Like ivy, bloomed on North Side.
PERSONA:	9	America's Station, America's Cubs.
VOICE:	10	Vigorous.
KNOWLEDGE:	10	Prepared.
MISCELLANY:	6	Airs each Cubs inning: counting exhibition, more than 1,600 yearly. Spends off-season doing hoops: at one time or another, Marquette, Northwestern, Wisconsin, and ESPN.
TOTAL:	76	(75th place).

KEN HARRELSON

The Cubs' Vince Lloyd would say, "Come on, let's score a run." Pittsburgh's Bob Prince often chimed as in a seance, "We had 'em! We had 'em! We had 'em!" Many mikemen use "our side," "home team," and "us." The Hawk is their kind of guy.

Mel Allen balked at being called a homer: "I'm partisan, not prejudiced." Since 1989, Ken Harrelson has colored White Sox for Chicago. Partisan or prejudiced: the Hawk is a hoot to hear.

At Comiskey Park, the Pale Hose may be albino. The Hawk still owns his nest. The Sox are "black shirts." "Yes!" affirms a knockout play. The "good guys" may smack a homer. "Put it on the board!" he says.

My fondness is heretical: elites dislike Harrelson's beating his own drum. I like how Ken follows his own drummer. Ibid, most viewers, craving personality and opinion. Fun is not a four-letter word.

Born in Woodruff, South Carolina, Harrelson, 10, moved to Savannah in 1951. Mother Jesse loved baseball. Sonny fancied "a [hoops] scholarship with Kentucky," played four sports at Benedictine College, and signed with Kansas City in 1959.

Charles O. Finley soon bought the Athletics. "Cheap! Italicize it!" said Ken, joining them in 1963. On August 3, 1967, he flew from Boston to Missouri. "Other teams took charters. We took a regularly scheduled plane."

Somewhere over Pennsylvania, pitcher Lew Krausse allegedly harassed a flight attendant. Charlie dunned him $500. Ken stormed, "Finley is a menace." The A's could deal him, or claim a $50,000 waiver. Instead, Finley released Hawk unconditionally: "a rare case," said the first baseman/outfielder, "where temper overrode his wallet."

Baseball's first free agent signed with Boston, which "won the pennant in *spite* of me!" said Ken, hitting .200. Mate Carl Yastrzemski won the 1967 Triple Crown. "That winter I worked my butt off to beat him," forging a 1968 35 homers and A.L.-high 109 RBI. "Better, fans wanted a character, so I gave 'em flair, bigger than life, the clothes"—love beads, bellbottoms, and cowboy hat.

"This was my Utopia," Hawk said. "You know how it is. A gentleman meets a lady. They've never seen each other before. Suddenly, sparks fly. It just happens. That's how it was here." At one point, he had 150 pairs of pants. A cedar chest housed seventy sweaters. "Remember the Nehru suit?" Harrelson bought thirty. "Before I wore five, they were out of style."

De trop: "Hawk," Duke Sims's name for Ken's aquiline nose. "I'd get mail addressed to 'Hawk,'" becoming his *alter ego*. "In the on-deck circle I'd say, 'Get out of Hawk's way and let him go.'" Later, announcing, "I'd let my partner call a good game. But in a rout, you need entertainment. I'd tell myself, 'Enter Hawk.'"

Enter Cleveland in 1969.

"Where else in the A.L. is the lake brown and the river a fire hazard?" Ken said. "I couldn't believe [nor the Hub] where I'd been traded." Fans picketed. Switchboards jammed. Vowing to quit, he cried "like a baby. Baseball was never fun again."

A year later, Harrelson broke a leg, took up golf, and found it a handicap. November 1974: "I decided to give it up. Golf ain't cuttin' it." At 3 A.M., clammy, he awoke. That morning the Red Sox called. "A year before, G.M. Dick O'Connell'd offered TV color. Now to renew it when he didn't know I was shucking golf—unbelievable."

The first exhibition ensued, Ken surviving till Tim Foli hit. "He's a feisty little guy," ad-libbed the Hawk. "Lot of balls." WSBK TV Voice Dick Stockton's jaw dropped. Even golf looked good. Quickly, he learned that Red Sox Nation is a forgiving, if not forgetting, lot. Hawk learned not to refer on-air to gonads. He also learned what worked.

"Some guys, especially ex-jocks, coast on their name. Others numb you with statistics. I try to avoid each." He did up to 97 games yearly, called (1975) and blew (1978) a pennant, and chased a Series like Ahab, Moby Dick.

"Lots of New England is remote. Radio matters," said Ned Martin, spreading with Jim Woods a portable seventies feast. "TV was second banana," Hawk rued. Working, learning, he hoped to climb the tree.

In early 1981, Boston mailed Carlton Fisk's contract after the deadline. "The Red Sox," Ken said, are "in disarray, confused, and chaotic." The free agent bolted to Comiskey Park. Next year Harrelson, joining him, replaced Cubs-bound Holy cow! "Yes! He's Harry Caray," Hawk bayed of kitsch, heart, and camp. "And these were the Cubs"—America's teddy bear of a team. "All we could do was have fun, not number you to death." Harry could not have said it better.

The 1983 White Sox won the A.L. West. Tom Seaver won game 300 in August 1985. "Two outs! Fans come to their feet. . . . The biggest media representation in Yankee Stadium in years!" said Harrelson. "So it'll be two veterans—Seaver and Don Baylor, who represents the tying run. Baylor hitting at .240, 18 homers, 67 RBIs. High to left, playable! Reid Nichols camps underneath it! History!"

Ken *became* history after the next year as Sox G.M. "Why'd I try it? My mama said, 'Son, you're a good kid and I love you, but you ain't the smartest thing I ever saw.'" Hawk flapped to Yanks' 1987–88 SportsChannel TV. Axed again—"overwhelming negative reaction from viewers and executives," cited the *New York Post*—he refetched the white-cubed rectangle on Chicago's South Side.

Comiskey turned 80 July 1, 1990: New York's Andy Hawkins lost a 4–0 no-hitter. On September 30, the once-Baseball Palace closed: Sox 2, Seattle 1, before 42,849. "THANKS for the Memories, 1910–90," read the board.

In 1991, its namesake copied the original's grass, exploding scoreboard, and rose exterior. Missing: charm, caprice, and the old park's open arches. New Comiskey solidified the Cubs' prepotency. "They have atmosphere and location," said pitcher Bill Simas. The Sox had Harrelson: reading notes, citing birthdays, and wooing viewers one by one.

The 1993 and 2002ers won their division. "Good guy" Frank Thomas was named back-to-back MVP in 1993–94. Sadly, disdain for Comiskey grew. Owner Eddie Einhorn began a facelift. The Big Guy didn't need one. "Let the home team win!" boomed Ken, or was it Bert Wilson, Brickhouse, or Lloyd? Maybe Hawk belonged at Wrigley Field.

Advice, and dissent. "[He grows] on you as little as the taste of lima

KEN HARRELSON

LONGEVITY:	10	29 years.
CONTINUITY:	6	Boston A.L. 1975–81; Chicago A.L. 1982–85 and 1989– ; New York A.L. 1987–88; ABC/NBC TV The Baseball Network 1994–95.
NETWORK:	3	TBN 1994–95 (ABC/NBC TV). WGN TV, like WTBS, a quasi-network.
KUDOS:	4	2000 Illinois Sportscaster of the Year.
LANGUAGE:	10	Hawkspeak unique.
POPULARITY:	10	"Still talks with a charm," said a writer, "that could have swept Scarlett O'Hara off her feet."
PERSONA:	10	Fuses instinct, empathy, and jazz.
VOICE:	10	Dixie, distinctive.
KNOWLEDGE:	10	Can discuss 3-2 curve or *Three Faces of Eve*.
MISCELLANY:	8	Introduced batting glove to baseball. Made one-handed catch. "With bad hands like mine, one hand is better than two."
TOTAL:	81	(50th place).

beans," wrote *USA Today*'s Stephen Borrelli. What seems vanilla to you may taste like chocolate to me.

Hawk's eight-year contract runs through 2008. Thankfully, you can put *that* one on the board.

JOHN ROONEY

Remember a time before elbow-in-rib scatology? When cool and mean were contrary? When the wiseacre deserved contempt, not praise? Boy, those were the days.

"That quaint period," Tennessee Williams described the 1930s, "when the huge middle class of America was matriculating in a school for the blind." For a son of Richmond, Missouri, the scales fell in the middle-class and -brow 1950s. Pudgy and bespectacled, John Rooney wanted to call ball.

He did at Oklahoma City, then Cardinals' Triple-A Louisville. In 1984, the Swifties' Dan Kelly aired preseason hockey. "They asked me to sub for him in a game against Cincinnati," Rooney noted, falling silent. The game wrung a date with his past.

"My father'd sit in the car, get the only bigs station he could," and hear KMOX's Buck and Caray cut the air like Zeus. A quarter-century later, Jack and John man the booth. A bunter struck by the throw is ruled out by the umpire. Buck says the ball hit him leaving the batter's box. John corrects him—"He's out for running in fair territory"—on the air.

Cincy's Dick Wagner nods. Jack splashes egg from his face. In a tizzy—"My career's going up in smoke"—Rooney resumes play-by-play. Soon Buck hits the mute button. "Son, slow down," he says, gently. "You'll be on 190 games a year if you do a team full-time. You'll wear the guy out by the end of the inning."

The rookie was already worn.

The guest spot caromed Rooney to CBS Radio's 1985 "Game of the Week." Lions in winter included Jerry Coleman, Gene Elston, Curt Gowdy, and Lindsey Nelson. John and Ted Robinson allayed age.

Nelson did a game from Minnesota. "He'd been known for those wild sport coats," said Rooney, "and I couldn't wait to see what he had on."

He wore a pale blue jacket. "The first time we meet," John moaned, "and you're wearing this conservative outfit."

Lindsey smiled. "Young fellow, it's a perfect choice for radio."

Coleman was even better. "It's so beautiful here in Kansas City that you can see Missouri." Rooney paused, unsure what to say. Finally: "Jerry, we're *in* Missouri. You used to play down the road five miles west of here [Triple-A Blues]."

"Well, John, it's a beautiful day, anyway."

Later Jerry was reading notes when the batter fouled a pitch. "Grounded on the right," he told his audience. At that moment the ball struck the booth.

In 1938, Edward R. Murrow and William S. Shirer sired CBS's "World News Roundup." Rooney's network roundup added the 1987–93 and 1995–97 L.C.S. and Series and 1990–97 All-Star Game to "Game"'s 6 million listeners.

A 1990 Reds throw swung the N.L. playoff. "A drive into center field! Back to the wall. [Billy Hatcher] leaps! The ball goes over his glove and off the wall! [Pittsburgh's Bobby] Bonilla had a double—he's going for third! Here comes the throw into third—and he's out!" Next year a Game Six hit waved Georgia's first pennant. "Olson swings and rips it down the left-field line! The ball goes to the corner—Ronnie Gant scores! . . . One–nothing, Atlanta!"

Still, memory scent of dad, tuned to KMOX, in love with local radio. John's first team was 1987 Minnesota. Next year he joined the White Sox. An old friend brooked broken doors, chipped asphalt, and paint on a weary face. "I saw Comiskey as a kid. It was strange seeing it like this." One night a stranger body reached first, forgot mind and place, and began pulling down his pants. Steve Lyons flushed. "Psycho" rose. "It may be an overcast night," said John, "but the moon's shining brightly inside Tiger Stadium."

In 1997, the sun set on CBS Radio. Rooney was concerned, not crushed. A year earlier, Fox began "Same game, new attitude" coverage. Ignoring John's, it hired a man who, though not naive or sentimental, was neither snide or mean.

"Not hip or edgy enough," a producer said after Fox canned him. Locally Rooney returned to his famously unedgy sport. "I just tell the story," John said, letting others coarsen it. For Soxaphiles, it seems quite enough.

JOHN ROONEY

LONGEVITY:	7	20 years.
CONTINUITY:	8	CBS Radio "Game of the Week" 1985–97; Minnesota A.L. 1987; Chicago A.L. 1988– ; ABC/NBC TV The Baseball Network 1994–95; Fox TV "Game of the Week" 1996–98.
NETWORK:	10	"Game" 1985–97 (CBS Radio) and 1996–98 (Fox TV). L.C.S. and World Series 1987–93 and 1995–97 and All-Star Game 1990–97 (CBS Radio). TBN 1994–95 (ABC/NBC TV). Division Series 1995–97 (CBS Radio) and 2002– (ESPN Radio).
KUDOS:	5	Missouri Sports Hall of Fame 2004. Bill Teegins Award.
LANGUAGE:	7	Straightforward.
POPULARITY:	8	Steady.
PERSONA:	7	Trusty.
VOICE:	10	Broadcasting 101.
KNOWLEDGE:	10	Attentive.
MISCELLANY:	6	CBS Radio includes Cotton, Fiesta, Las Vegas, and Orange Bowl, NCAA hoops title game, and NFL "Game of the Week."
TOTAL:	78	(66th place).

JIM KAAT

Let us not bury but praise baseball lifers. Jimmie Reese bridged John McGraw and John McNamara. Cal Ripken, Jr. was born into and breathes the game. Envision Tom Lasorda without a Dodgers uni. You can't.

"You love baseball more than me," says Mrs. Lasorda.

"Yes," Tom replies, "but I love you more than basketball or football."

Voices can be lifers, too. Joe Garagiola spanned Yogi Berra to Yogi Berra. Boys Club catcher Bob Uecker's .200 average made Cooperstown. Jim Kaat absorbed the Cubs growing up in Zeeland, Michigan, 150 miles northeast of Wrigley Field.

"I'd follow Bert Wilson and Jack Brickhouse," Kaat said, "the Tigers' Harry Heilmann, later Earl Gillespie." Each Sunday he tuned the family Zenith to WCFL Chicago. "The Old Commander [Bob Elson] would do a doubleheader, and I'd be eating popcorn." TOC transfixed—the name, and sound.

Ultimately, Jim became a pitcher, pitching coach, and broadcaster, saying, "I don't think I've ever cashed a non-baseball check." Kitty was born in 1938. In 1956, signed by Washington, he began using nine lives.

Kaat made the major leagues at 21. In 1961, the Senators of the Nation's Capital since 1892 became the Minnesota Twins. Jim pitched through 1983—the last Nat to dot the majors. "I'll never be considered one of the all-time greats, maybe not even one of the all-time goods. But I'm one of the all-time survivors."

Jim won 283 games. "Great control and curve," said mate Harmon Kille-brew. "Knew how to play the game." He hit 16 dingers, had a pitching high 134 sacrifice hits, and was a palatine on the mound. "No one noticed my fielding until a bouncer knocked out six of my teeth." Kaat smothered bunts, covered first like jam, and wore 14 straight Gold Gloves.

He pitched like being double-parked: to Killebrew, "always kept you on your toes." In September 1965, Kitty clinched the Twins' first flag, beat Sandy Koufax in the Series, but lost twice to Mr. K, including Game Seven. "Next time," Kaat laughed, "I think I'll pitch against a mortal."

In 1966, Koufax had 27 victories, 317 Ks, and a 1.73 ERA. Baseball then awarded one Cy Young award. "Maybe my best year," said Sandy, "and it had to be, to beat Kaat [A.L.-high 25 victories and career-low 2.75 ERA]." In 1972, Jim started 10–2 but broke a wrist sliding. Next year he slid to Comiskey Park.

Mate Dick Allen loved taters, horse racing, and Kitty's two-hour games. "You pitching, old-timer? Good. I'll be early at the track." Once, blowing a double play, Dick allowed three runs. "Old-timer, I'll get those back for you," he said, and did: two two-run homers.

In 1974, Elliot Gould visited Comiskey Park to hype his movie *M*A*S*H*. Allen asked, "Who is that?"

Kaat explained. "Yeah," Dick shrugged, "but can he hit a slider?"

"No, but he probably can hit my Peggy Lee fastball: You know, 'Is that all there is?'"

Kitty joined the Phillies, Yanks, and Cardinals, then, retiring, became Reds pitching coach: "I liked it, but hoped that my talent wasn't limited to my arm."

In 1984, ESPN TV named the lifer to minor-league and college base-ball. Ex-CBSer Gene Kirby warned of tilt. "If you say, 'Trouble. There's a ball in the corner,' ask yourself, 'Trouble for *whom*?' Don't be a homer." Dick Enberg noted the baseball nut, no-nothing, and tepid fan "listening at the same time," Kaat said. "Not the easiest job to ever come down the pike."

It got harder in 1986. The rookie Stripes colorman was stranded by Phil

Rizzuto: "Kaat, I got to go to the men's room." Producer Don Carney burned. "I know he went back to the hotel room. Phil does that all the time." The freshman soloed. Dicier: enduring George Steinbrenner. "He'll send notes telling you what to say," Bill White said. "You have to take a stand."

Kaat did and was sacked, the truth having set him free. "George's a good-luck charm. After my release, the Cards sign me and win the '82 Series. In '86, George fires me and my career takes off." 1987: Jim joins Atlanta. 1988: Minnesota rehires him. 1990: Columbia's new backup analyst flashes a good-guy air. "This was a [L.C.S.] night for pitchers to excel," wrote Ron Bergman. "Dave Stewart. Roger Clemens. Jim Kaat [on commentary]." Kitty wanted coverage to "go on forever." Instead, it went belly-up.

In 1994, Jim manned ESPN and The Baseball Network. A year later, succeeding Tony Kubek, he revisited Camp George's giants, ghosts, and ghouls. "It's the Yanks," Kitty said, calling MSG TV color. "What more can you ask for?" Four world titles from 1996 to 2000.

On August 7, 1995, dysfunctional Darryl Strawberry joined the Bombers. Said Kaat: "If [replaced Luis] Polonia was a tax evader, alcoholic, cocaine

---

JIM KAAT

LONGEVITY:	7	19 years.
CONTINUITY:	5	New York A.L. 1986 and 1995– ; Atlanta N.L. 1987; Minnesota A.L. 1988–93; CBS TV "Game of the Week" 1990–93; ESPN TV "Major League Baseball" 1994; ABC/NBC TV The Baseball Network 1994–95.
NETWORK:	8	"Game" and L.C.S. 1990–93 (CBS TV). "Baseball" 1994 (ESPN TV). TBN 1994–95, including L.C.S. 1995 (ABC/NBC TV).
KUDOS:	6	Nominated, local Emmy Award. MSG Network three-time Emmy Award, Yanks coverage. Past President, Major League Baseball Players Alumni Association.
LANGUAGE:	9	Tells what's happening.
POPULARITY:	8	"At first seemed mild for New York. He grows on you," said sidekick.
PERSONA:	8	Credible.
VOICE:	8	High, plain.
KNOWLEDGE:	10	Swedes like core, not glitz.
MISCELLANY:	9	Pitched more years (25) than anyone else in bigs history.
TOTAL:	78	(65th place).

abuser, wife abuser, he'd probably still be on the team." In 2002, having pitched or announced for 14 teams or networks, Kitty, settling down, made Steinbrenner's new regional cable-TV network. *Un*settling to hacks and flacks was his Upper Midwest nothing-but-the-whole-truth hub.

As Commissioner, Bud Selig barely foiled a 2002 work stoppage. "Baseball people will tell you if they left it to [ex-CEO Paul] Beeston, not Selig," Jim said, "they would have had an agreement a year ago."

In 2003, manager Joe Torre ordered Jose Contreras to Triple-A. Overruling him, Steinbrenner sent the pitcher to instruction. "It undermines his [Torre's] credibility, and makes him look like he lied."

Like Selig, Boss George fumed. Insiders nodded. For one lifer, baseball means looking in the mirror—and being able to look back.

JOHN STERLING

"It is impossible to think of any other franchise like the Yankees," wrote *The New York Times.* Several Voices ape their glow. Barber was a diva. Allen made cricket riveting. Jim Woods crackled like kept wood. Rizzuto was Rizzuto. "Inimitable announcers," said Lindsey Nelson, "but they haven't had as many as you'd think."

Frank Messer made vanilla racy. The comic Bob Gamere chanted *ad nauseam,* "Here it comes, there it goes." Thirty-eight striped players, coaches, skippers, or execs people Cooperstown. Of Hall mikemen, only Mel, Red, Arch McDonald, Joe Garagiola, Curt Gowdy, and Buck Canel, several briefly, nested in the Bronx.

In 1989, John Sterling, born in New York July 4, 1948, joined his childhood club. Is he Allen's heir, Gamere *redux,* or somewhere in between?

Spotting him, a driver screams, "Bern, Baby, Bern! [John's panegyric to Bernie Williams] You're the reason the Yankees are great!"

Phil Mushnick counters: "Condescending, self-centered. Thoroughly absorbed. A lost cause."

Are we discussing the same *homo sapien*?

Sterling Time, and the quarreling is easy.

"Give us the tools and we shall finish the job," said Churchill. John's blazed zest, brass, and a silken voice. Early jobs included WMCA talk radio, Morgan State football, hockey Islanders, and basketball Nets. "Give it to Julius

[Erving]!" he shouted in a playoff game. In 1983, Sterling left Bullets hoops for Braves radio/TV. Five years later "it was time to move on," but where?

The 1961 Cubs' College of Coaches rotated skippers. By late 1988, the Yanks suffered a rotating door. Sterling became their 17th Voice hired in a decade. Soon he, Joe Angel, Tony Kubek, Rizzuto, Tom Seaver, DeWayne Staats, and Al Trautwig shared color/play-by-play. "Splitting radio and free and cable TV, we had separate teams," said Kubek. "The result was that no one guy really dominated the rest."

The '93ers placed second. A .619 percentage led the 1994 league. "Holy cow!" rasped Rizzuto. "The strike cost us the Series." Scooter fled in fits and starts. Kubek left the game. Staats moved to ESPN. Enduring, Sterling boarded baseball's most successful wagon train since Mel (14 1949–64 flags) and Skip Caray and Pete Van Wieren (1991–93 and 1995–2004 first place). It began in 1996.

Atlanta took a 2-0 game Series edge. In Georgia, New York won thrice. For months, "[new manager Joe] Torre's brother had been trying for a heart donor," wrote Phil Pepe. "The day before [Game Six] Frank got a heart." The Yanks got their first title since 1978. Next year, the Madison Square Garden Network bought its radio. "MSG To Sterling": said Mushnick. "Clean Up Your ['smug and self-smitten'] Act."

New York lost the 1997 Division Series to Cleveland. "The bear bit us," said Torre. Actually, the Yanks were hibernating, awaking next year.

In 1998, New York won a league-record 114 games, swept the Series, and finished an otherworldly 125–50. A year later, it drew 3 million for the first time. In 1985, Steinbrenner had axed Yogi Berra, who snubbed the Bronx for 14 years. "He had somebody else tell me," said No. 8. "That's what I didn't like." Finally the Boss apologized, his clan communing July 18, 1999. "It's the history," said Torre, giving Berra a 1998 Series ring. Rizzuto, Whitey Ford, Gil McDougald, and Bobby Richardson stood nearby. Yogi snagged Don Larsen's pregame pitch, then gave his mitt to Joe Girardi, who used it vs. Montreal.

Inning after inning sealed a laying-on of hands. "He popped him up! He's going to get it! Brosius down from third!" Sterling said. Pointing skyward, David Cone grabbed his head in disbelief. "Ballgame over! A perfect game! . . . A perfect game for David Cone! Twenty-seven up! Twenty-seven down! David Cone has attained baseball immortality!" At that moment, John seemed a successor to Woodsie, Red, and Mel.

That fall, New York again met the "Team of the Decade." The "Team of the Century" swept. The usual suspects took the usual parade down Manhattan. Said Torre: "This stuff never gets old." New: the 2000 Subway Series. "Bernie back! Away back! He's there! He makes the catch! Ballgame over! World Series over!" John puffed: third straight world title, four in five years, and 26th overall.

Sterling and 1992–2001 partner Michael Kay emceed the title party, "The-eh-eh-eh-eh Yankees win!" ferried through City Hall. The cry became John's logotype: also, "The-eh pitch," French lilt ("De-TWAH," for Detroit), and exchange with the ex-*Daily News* reporter. It included Sterling's triplets (Veronica, Bradford, and Derek, born October 11, 2000), Kay on fashion ("interlocking NY"), and sidekick's distaste of today's slow-mo game ("length: an unmanageable three hours and thirty minutes").

"See-ya!" Kay cried of a homer.

"It is high! It is far! It is gone!" John replied, filing with the U.S. Patent and Trademark Office—officially, SN 75-205, 213—to put the call on T-shirts and sweatshirts.

"[Their] image," wrote a columnist, "[is] two friends who . . . happen to be spending the day at the park." Some thought baseball prop for ego. Said Bob Raissman: "He's doing a talk show disguised as . . . baseball." Harry Caray's "Cubs win!" seemed a kettle of Americana. "Stop being a copycat," said a friend, "give 'Yankees win!' a rest, and John's a great announcer."

In 2001, Arizona's Luis Gonzalez's Game Seven ninth-inning World Series bloop put the lid on "TYW!" Next year, Kay launched play-by-play, the "Center Stage" talk show, and other programming on TV's new Yankees Entertainment and Sports (YES) network.

Replacing him on radio: a Brooklynite who heaped new connotation on coming home.

"I found out my future in the game wasn't as a player the first time I played a fungo softball game around the block from my home," allowed Charley Steiner. "Donnie Sorensen, an experienced veteran of eight or nine," said to hit the ball, then run to first base (elm tree), second (towel), third (another elm), and home (cardboard). Charley was nothing if not literal, racing for the tree, towel, tree, and "home. I mean *home*. All the way to my *house*. I couldn't figure why everyone was chasing after me, laughing, screaming, and telling me I was running the wrong way."

Steiner took his last piano lesson in October 1960. "My teacher wouldn't let me out, despite it being Game Seven. She looked me and, in broken English, asked, 'What's the World Series?'" Bill Mazeroski cost him a $1 bet. "Not only was that a monthly allowance, but my piano career came to at end. Maz swings, and I'm playing 'On Top of Old Smokey.'"

In 1967, Charley entered Bradley University, later sold an underground paper in Haight-Ashbury, kibitzed with Abbie Hoffman and Bobby Seale, and at Woodstock mixed mud and drugs. "We were right about the war in Viet Nam, and how wrong it was. We were right about civil rights, right about women's rights, right about questioning authority."

Graduating, he rightly trekked to Iowa, Connecticut, Ohio, and WXLO New York's Jets and USFL New Jersey Generals. In 1988, Steiner added ESPN TV boxing and "Sports Center." A decade later he began its radio network's "Sunday Night Baseball." Looking at the bases, "I knew I'd arrived." They did not include a cardboard, towel, or tree.

Charley spent 2002–04 in New York, then joined the Dodgers as Vin Scully's second. "How's this for karma?" he said. "I knew I wanted to be a broadcaster the first time I heard Vin's voice doing a Brooklyn Dodger game on the radio. Had to be '55 or '56. I was six or seven."

Like Steiner, Sterling loved the field, friends, and radio of his youth. "Listening to Mel Allen, I knew this was my life."

JOHN STERLING

LONGEVITY:	8	22 years.
CONTINUITY:	9	Atlanta N.L. 1982–87; New York A.L. 1989– .
NETWORK:	1	WTBS 1982–87 (SuperStation TV).
KUDOS:	4	Spokesman, Leukemia Society of America.
LANGUAGE:	9	Take pick: affected or "highly stylized," said John.
POPULARITY:	10	Big Apple's biggest baseball Voice.
PERSONA:	10	Over the top, or rainbow. Said the *Daily News*: "The Voice some love, and some love to hate."
VOICE:	10	Among bigs' finest: classic, elegant.
KNOWLEDGE:	10	Can discuss food, fiction, Bo Derek, or Derek Jeter.
MISCELLANY:	8	Has never missed a Braves or Yankees game. Hosts Emmy-Award winning YES series "Yankeeography."
TOTAL:	79	(58th place).

By 2003, it infused New York. Sport's Athens and Sparta staged a scorched-earth L.C.S. Game Seven passed midnight at The Stadium. In the 10th, Aaron Boone arced Boston's Tim Wakefield's 5-all pitch.

"There's a fly ball deep to left! It's on its way! There it goes!" howled Steiner on flagship WCBS. "And the Yankees are going to the World Series for the 39th time in their remarkable history!"

Unable to desist, John bellowed "The-eh-eh-eh-eh-eh Yankees win!" A city caroled every sound. "I'd rather do my own thing," he said, "than be a straight-laced, homogeneous, play-by-play drone."

An Ohio writer said: "In a perfect world we'd all be Yankees." Our world is not perfect. Neither is Sterling.

He is, however, perfect for New York.

GARY COHEN

Ebbets Field was flattened in 1960. At Coogan's Bluff, "you could see soccer, hoops, midget auto racing, and boxing [after 1957]," wrote Dick Young. "Even football. Just no baseball." Ultimately, New York Mayor Robert Wagner formed a five-man committee chaired by lawyer William A. Shea to regain a team.

In 1959, Shea named the eight cities of a proposed new major—Continental—League. The threat made the National League expand. An N.L. owner told New York its club pivoted on the site. "Send a telegram to each owner promising that the city will build a new ball park," Shea phoned Wagner, who did.

By 1961, the New York State Senate OK'd $55 million. Meanwhile, the city spent $250,000 to clean up the Polo Grounds. "Not much has changed since the Giants," Young recalled, except, of course, the team.

Growing up in Queens, Gary Cohen inherited Metsomania from his dad, visiting Shea Stadium, christened with Holy Water from Brooklyn's Gowanus Canal and the Harlem River at the point it passed the Polo Grounds. "Lots of folks found it cold and barren. This is not a politically correct thing to say, but to me it seemed very warm."

As a child, Cohen learned to see with his ears. "Lindsey and company, with those great word-pictures," he said. "[Today] I scream when I *can't* see what's happening. The one thing I knew I wanted in radio was not to have preconceived phrases." Plot decided script.

In 1969, Gary, nine, watched the Mets' otherworldly L.C.S. sweep from Section 48, Row R, "in left field, five rows from the top." After Game Three, he "got my little piece of turf from the field." Later Cohen studied political science at Columbia, worked for athletic teams there and at Penn and Old Dominion, and called Spartanbug, Durham, and Triple-A Pawtucket.

In 1988, airing a test game at Shea, he froze. Reaching over, Bob Murphy patted Gary's hand. "He started talking, reassured me. It was my greatest memory." Next season Cohen made the Mecca of his youth. "One New York club always leads in popularity," wrote Mike Lupica. "Now it's the Mets." A decade later, The House that Ruth Built lodged The Team the Apple Loved.

Yankee Stadium boomed, "New York, New York." Queens' din sprang from nearby LaGuardia Airport. Bobby Bonilla wore earplugs to blot noise— and boos. Cohen survived by height of skill, not sleight of hand. Locally: Brown football, Providence hockey, and Friars, St. John's, and Seton Hall basketball. CBS Radio: NCAA hoops, baseball "Game," and Olympics hockey. After the 1998 Winter Games, a letter tanned his hide.

Gary likened Nagano, Japan, to Newark with mountains. Newark Mayor Sharpe James soon sent "the only hate mail," he laughed, "I ever got." In 1997, ESPN Radio bought bigs rights, and Cohen. By then, New York's Nationals had forged a push-pull polarity. Anthony Young lost a record 27 straight games. John Franco got his lefty-high 253rd save. Mets 6, Yanks 0, in their intra-city bow: fair and studied, Gary was, said a writer, the best broadcaster in the park.

The television job-seeker is told he has the perfect face for radio. By contrast, TV-handsome Cohen "exists," wrote the *Post,* "almost exclusively [on radio] as a voice without a face." Once in a while he was recognized from his year-book picture. "Otherwise, no," said Gary. "It's what happens when you don't do TV." In 10 years, the newspaper didn't get a single anti-Cohen letter. "I do not aspire to TV. If I'm offered $10 million, okay, I'd reconsider. But I love what I do."

On April 15, 1998, a beam falling in the Bronx made the A.L.ers play at Shea. "For the first time this century," said Gary, "one park hosted two games in one day for four different teams": Yanks 6, Anaheim 3; Mets 2, Cubs 1. Next year, Mike Piazza had 40 homers, the Amazin's won a wild card, and their infield made the fewest-ever muffs. "That, and how our league doesn't have the designated hitter, meant a lot of quick games."

New York won the Division Series. Polarity swung its L.C.S. Behind, 3 games to 0, the Mets parried, 3–2. In Game Five, "The Mets trying [in the 15th] to send it to Atlanta! A drive in the air to deep right field! . . . That ball is outta here!" said Cohen. "A game-winning grand-slam home run off the bat of Robin Ventura! They're mobbing him before he can get to second base! I don't know if they'll let Ventura circle the bases [they didn't: thus, a grand-slam single] but it doesn't matter! The Mets have won . . . the ballgame!"

In Game Six, New York trailed, 5–0, tied at 7, led, 8–7 and 9–8, and lost, 10–9. "Theater doesn't get better than this mad week of games," wrote the *Journal*'s Dorothy Rabinowitz. The 2000 season's wasn't bad. Three Series games were one-run; the losing Mets seemed as warm as a housebroken pup.

Soon they again slumped. In 1962, Casey Stengel had spied the future: "Can't anybody *play* this here game?" No one asks if Gary Cohen can call it.

GARY COHEN

LONGEVITY:	6	17 years.
CONTINUITY:	8	CBS Radio "Game of the Week" 1986 and 1994–97; New York N.L. 1989– ; ABC/NBC TV The Baseball Network 1994–95.
NETWORK:	7	"Game" 1986 and 1994–97 and L.C.S. 1988–1991 and 1995–97 (CBS Radio). TBN 1994–95 (ABC/NBC TV). Division Series and L.C.S. 1998 and 2001– (ESPN Radio).
KUDOS:	4	1992, 1994, and 1998 Winter Olympics.
LANGUAGE:	10	Fluent, apolitical.
POPULARITY:	10	Is highest among radio-literate.
PERSONA:	9	Shea-Hey Kid.
VOICE:	10	Glossy.
KNOWLEDGE:	10	In sports-drenched market, not obsessed with flaunting it.
MISCELLANY:	5	In 2006, Mets begin regional cable network. Will Cohen star?
TOTAL:	79	(57th place).

GARY THORNE

"A man and his work," said Earl Weaver. "That's the way it's gotta be." As a boy, Gary Thorne liked baseball and hockey. The workaholic adult calls each.

By 1976, Thorne graduated from the University of Maine and Georgetown Law School, paying tuition as a sportscaster/disc jockey. The sundowner became Bangor district assistant attorney, joined the bar of the U.S. Supreme Court, and turned from law to love.

"The court's dull compared to broadcasting," Gary said, starting hockey in 1977 on Augusta radio/TV. By 1984, he had leverage with baseball's Triple-A Maine Guides: co-owner, Thorne named himself.

"My family thinks I'm out of my mind [leaving law], but here I am," said the Red Sox and Bruins fan, "calling my two girls." Take two, and hit to right. He shoots—he scores! Thorne's goal was the bigs, reached in 1985. Presently the *real* work began.

Joining Murphy on Mets radio, Gary loved "big games and buzz." His 1987–93 NHL New Jersey Devils oozed anonymity. "Worse were my neutral games [SportsChannel America]—hockey's sick idea of a network." In 1988, he launched ESPN's still-running "The Sports Reporters." That winter, a hockey conflict gave the Mets the boot. Thorne covered the 1989 White Sox and ABC TV, including the Series as on-field reporter. Timing was the rub.

"Great reviews," he laughed, "just as ABC baseball ends." In 1990, Gary and Norm Hitzges, the pastime's would-be Dick Vitale, began twice-weekly coverage. "They threaten the very core of the game," barbed *The National*'s Norman Chad, "if not the nation at large." I agreed, calling Thorne "banal and humorless." The last laugh was his.

October 3, 1990. A.L. Boston leads second-place Toronto: one game up, and left. At Fenway, the Red Sox front, 3–1, ninth inning, on ESPN: like 1986, one strike to go. Two White Sox reach base. Ozzie Guillen then lined to right, Tom Brunansky vanishing in the corner. "No camera showed whether he caught the ball," said *The New York Times*, "not even a slow-motion version of the original view."

Thorne wavered. "Brunansky dives!" he said. "Did he get it? Yes, the Red Sox win! No, he dropped the ball! He dropped the ball!" amending, "Wait! He got it! Believe it, New England!" ESPN head Steve Bornstein disbelieved the play. "Murphy's Law struck. What used to happen to the Red Sox happened to us."

Bearing blame, Gary hiked appeal. He began: 1989 ESPN Big East hoops. 1992: "National Hockey Night." 1994: Mets and The Baseball Network TV. Jim Leyritz's 1995 playoff poke drowned the Mariners. "It took five hours and 13 minutes . . . but he gets [a] two-run homer in the 15th inning!" Post-'97: ABC hockey, CBS hoops and Olympics, ESPN home run derby and "Big League Challenge," and Major League Baseball International.

In 2000, Thorne called his fourth Series on Armed Forces Radio in England, Israel, Saudi Arabia, and the Netherlands, among others. On one hand, you "have to explain the hit-and-run." The other: People say "hello from Bangladesh."

Of Roger Clemens's Mike Piazza–zinging, Gary pronounced, "Unacceptable." Unimaginable: his schedule. "I'm not sure I'd recommend it to others, or to myself."

If it is Tuesday, says the traveler, this must be Belgium. Thursday: in Denver, Thorne does ESPN hockey. Friday, Miami: Mets. Saturday, Detroit: NHL, ESPN2. Sunday: God rests; Metsies don't. Gary, with John Davidson, did three of NBC's four Olympic hockey games February 20, 2002.

"He has been filled with bionic devices affording his body more powers than an average human," wrote Ron Digby. The unfilled '02 Mets placed last. Only the Amazin's would blame one of their scant assets. Said Gary, laughing: "The firing just gives me more time with [daughter] Kelly."

Lindsey Nelson was asked about his fast-forward life. "I'm glad I lived it. I'd just hate to live it again." Voyeurs of Thorne's "two girls" keep hoping that the Downeaster does.

GARY THORNE

LONGEVITY:	7	20 years.
CONTINUITY:	7	New York N.L. 1985–88 and 1994–2002; Chicago A.L. 1989; ABC TV "Thursday Night Baseball" 1989; ESPN TV "Major League Baseball" 1990–93, 1996–2000, and 2003– .
NETWORK:	9	"Thursday" 1989 (ABC TV). "Baseball" 1990–93, 1996–2000, and 2003– ; L.C.S. 1996 and 2000– ; and "Big League Challenge" 2003– (ESPN TV). TBN 1994–95, including Division Series 1995 (ABC/NBC TV). World Series 1997– (Major League Baseball International).
KUDOS:	4	Unlike most Voices', some global.
LANGUAGE:	9	Breezy.
POPULARITY:	9	Greater than Mets grasped.
PERSONA:	9	Yokes two small-town sports.
VOICE:	9	Plays in Portland.
KNOWLEDGE:	7	Once predicted two-out suicide squeeze.
MISCELLANY:	7	At Shea, worked with great battery: Tim McCarver (WOR), then Tom Seaver (WPIX).
TOTAL:	77	(70th place).

SEAN MCDONOUGH

Milo Hamilton followed Bob Prince. Better root canal. Someone will air the post-Kalas Phillies. Send a sympathy card. The Bible deems it easier for a camel to fit through a needle than to enter the Kingdom of Heaven. In baseball, it is easier than to replace a beloved announcer.

Ken Coleman did the 1966–74 and 1979–89 Red Sox. Ned Martin etched the 1961–92 Olde Towne Team. Both fought in World War II. Each was bright, diffident, had a novel voice, and recoiled at splitting verbs.

"Following them was like topping Paul Revere," said Sean McDonough. One if by Ned. Two if by Ken.

McDonough's ride began among liniment, jocks, and sun. Each spring, dad Will, a *Boston Globe* reporter, took his 1960s family to Florida. "I'd be out of school a month," Sean said. "Teachers gave my mother lesson plans." Martin and Coleman taught him to keep score.

Muting TV audio, McDonough practiced at age five on a tape recorder. In 1985, the Syracuse University graduate began recording the Triple-A Chiefs. Soon the part-time official scorer gave an E to Marty Castillo, dumped recently by Seattle.

"I'll hit ten out there and see how many *you* stop!" steamed Marty.

"I'm not a Triple-A third baseman and you are," snapped McDonough. "You should have stopped it."

In 1988, Martin left free TV for cable. Replacing him, the balding Sean, like Jon Miller, looked a decade older than his age (26). On a flight to Cleveland, players drank and quarreled. Only McDonough—the team *Voice*! aging further—reported it on the air.

"I'm embarrassed to be part of the traveling party," he explained. "I mentioned it because it hurt the Sox."

"Next plane, Sean," said right fielder Dwight Evans, "skip a parachute."

The rookie feared a pink slip. Instead, team owner Jean Yawkey said, "Keep up the good work"—more than McDonough wished for umpire Dale Ford or second baseman Marty Barrett.

In June 1989, Wade Boggs was sued for $6 million. Among other things, ex-girlfriend Margo Adams said, the hit machine covertly photographed mates with other women. A "Mar-go!" road chant rose. Evans and the married Boggs fought on the Sox bus.

One night, Dale Scott blew a call. Immediately Boston began needling another Dale. "Ford [had] ejected a couple of players several weeks ago," Sean said, "and it's obvious the Sox have bad feelings."

Ford, blaming him for a feud, refused to review the tape. "If this is you how handle disputes on the field," McDonough jibed, "no wonder you have problems."

A year later, dad Will ripped Barrett. "Sean, he can kiss my ass," Marty said, visiting father's sins upon the son. "I laugh when I read comparisons about you and Bob Costas. You're about as close to him as I am to Ryne Sandberg."

McDonough flushed: "If that's supposed to be an insult, at least you know how far away you are from Sandberg."

That week, he urged that Barrett be pinch-hit for. Next day, Marty's wife phoned in a hissy-fit: "Why do you *say* these things?"

Imagine: a Voice knowing his team, game, and mind. Sean was uncontrite. "You stand by your word."

A word soon turned on ESPN TV. McDonough began innocently: "Here's Dwight Evans, one shit high of 2,300 hits."

Partner Ray Knight broke up. "I did say he was one hit shy of 2,300, didn't I?" Sean hoped.

A man greeted him in Texas: "Do me a favor. Just call 'one hit shy.'"

In 1992, McDonough, replacing Jack Buck, got CBS TV baseball. "[Executive producer] Ted Shaker called about my interest." Hanging up, "I didn't want to act like a 10-year-old. But I jumped up so high I . . . put a hole in the ceiling." Next-year Series scoring was higher. In Game Four, "The Phillies have taken the lead by a field goal, 10-7," Sean said. Game Six: Canada takes the Series. "Well-hit down the left-field line! Way back! And gone! Joe Carter with a three-run homer! The winners and still world champions! The Toronto Blue Jays!"

Losing baseball, CBS gave McDonough the Olympics, Masters, U.S. Open, college hoops, and pro/NCAA football. In 1999, he returned to ABC. Sean also darned the Sox on local TV outlets 68, 56, 25, and twice 38 and 4. "They keep changing flagships." Changeless: "It's the only thing I do where I care who wins and loses."

The Sox made the 1995, 1998–99, and 2003 A.L. playoff. In 2004, they proved that pigs fly, the earth is flat, and the cow jumps over the moon. "No one expected it," McDonough said of Boston's first world title since 1918— or his firing six weeks later.

SEAN MCDONOUGH

LONGEVITY:	6	17 years.
CONTINUITY:	9	Boston A.L. 1988–2004; ESPN TV "Major League Baseball" 1990 and 1994–96; CBS TV "Game of the Week" 1992–93; ABC/NBC TV The Baseball Network 1994–95.
NETWORK:	8	"Baseball" 1990 and 1994–96 (ESPN TV). "Game," All-Star Game, L.C.S., and World Series 1992–93 (CBS TV). TBN 1994–95 (ABC/NBC TV).
KUDOS:	7	Five-time New England Sports Emmy Award, outstanding play-by-play. Syracuse University Sports Wall of Fame. *TV Guide* named among three best TV sportscasters 2003.
LANGUAGE:	9	Tongue-in-cheek.
POPULARITY:	9	Unshill, pleasingly unhip, and never unprepared.
PERSONA:	8	"People tune in for the game. I'm not a TV star."
VOICE:	9	Cutting.
KNOWLEDGE:	10	Still has scorebook from sixties spring training.
MISCELLANY:	6	For a time daily talk show, "The McDonough Group," topped Boston radio market.
TOTAL:	81	(52nd place).

JOE CASTIGLIONE

"People say, 'You have the job I'd love to have,'" McDonough said in early 2004. Joe Castiglione does, succeeding Jon Miller and Ken Coleman on Sox radio in 1983 and 1990, respectively. He takes defeat hard. "My partner is sitting here," said Bob Starr, "looking like he's just been harpooned."

As a Connecticut Yankee, the oldest of eight children revered Mel Allen, then attended Colgate, did Raiders football, and made his first trip to Fenway. "A good year to change your loyalty," he said of 1967. No Evil Empire could match The Impossible Dream.

Castiglione got an M.A. at Syracuse, spent a decade in Cleveland news/sports, covered the *Edmund Fitzgerald*'s sinking, and aired another wreck, the Indians. He joined Milwaukee in 1981. "The Brewers win the second half! The Brewers win the second half!" Joe said, like Russ Hodges. Cheeseheads still chant it between bowling, brats, and beer.

In 1983, WPLM bought Sox radio. The sixties Colgate disc jockey— "Give me the Rolling Stones, the Kinks, the Animals, and my favorite, Motown Sounds"—found Coleman caught between Perry Como and Patti Page. "Sort of like the Red Sox fan, likes things as they were."

On April 29, 1986, Roger Clemens Ks a bigs-record 20 Mariners. In the second inning, Ken begins reading the Boston yearbook.

"How about this! Roger's favorite singer is Steve Nicks."

"Ken, I believe that's Stevie Nicks," said Castiglione.

"Well, I know him well. I call him Steve."

"Uh, Ken, Stevie is a girl."

That October, Joe was in the clubhouse, eying the Series trophy, when Bill Buckner missed The Ball. Three days later, entering the manager's office, he found a broken man. "Why me, Joe? I go to church," said John McNamara. "I don't understand why this had to happen."

Castiglione outlived Game Six, Ken's exit, and a "feeling by some that Ned Martin should still be on radio." Son Duke became a New York sportscaster. Clemens, Mo Vaughn, Alex Rodriguez, and Pedro Martinez came or almost did, and went. Joe became the Jimmy Fund's liaison between the charity and Sox players and staff.

Offseason, he teaches broadcasting at Northeastern University and Franklin Pierce College, quoting a retired Jesuit priest, Boston College historian John Day, about bigs radio being an apostolate to shut-ins, the disabled, and elderly. "When he said that," mused Castiglione, "I knew I was freeloading for life."

In 2004, Joe wrote *Broadcast Rites and Sites,* a travelogue of park, town, and craft. It is not required course reading. The season of its publication is.

First, Boston swept the Division Series against Anaheim. New York then took a 3-0 game L.C.S. lead. As usual, the tide was out. The stars were misaligned. The Almighty was a Yankees fan. Amazingly, the Sox revived. David Ortiz evoked Yaz in '67. "And a little flare, center field! . . . Here comes Johnny Damon with the winning [5–4 14th inning] run!" partner Jerry Trupiano bayed in Game Five. "And . . . Ortiz has done it again! . . . Another wild celebration at Fenway Park!" Next game, Curt Schilling tugged at Superman's cape. A day later, the Townies completed "the greatest victory in team history!" whooped Castiglione. "Move over, Babe, the Red Sox are American League Champions!"

The Sox swept St. Louis in the Series, stunning a diaspora of the devoted and the crazed. "One–oh pitch," Joe said as a lunar eclipse veiled Busch Stadium. "Swing and a ground ball! Stabbed by [reliever Keith] Foulke! He has it! He underhands to first! And the Boston Red Sox are the world champions! For the first time in 86 years the Red Sox have won baseball's world championship. Can you believe it?"

No, even now. "This is the biggest story in New England," said owner John Henry, "since the Revolutionary War." MTV becomes PBS. Teresa Heinz Kerry takes a vow of silence. Dick Cheney grows hair.

"Read, work, build a reputation," Professor Joe told students that off-season. "Then don't mislead."

Don't slight your predecessor. "You're inheriting a bequest."

Don't copy, either. "To thine own self be true," said Hamlet, who would have prized the '04ers knowing how "the play's the thing."

JOE CASTIGLIONE

LONGEVITY:	8	25 years.
CONTINUITY:	9	Cleveland A.L. 1979 and 1982; Milwaukee A.L. 1981; Boston A.L. 1983– .
NETWORK:	1	In effect, Red Sox are.
KUDOS:	5	Dick Young Award 2002. New England chapter, Italian-American Sports Hall of Fame 2003. Franklin Pierce College ballpark entrance named in honor.
LANGUAGE:	9	Conversational.
POPULARITY:	10	Italian ikon on Boston's North Side.
PERSONA:	10	Uncle Joe.
VOICE:	7	Like Bob Murphy's, can rise an octave.
KNOWLEDGE:	10	Lives Protestant—here, Catholic—Work Ethic.
MISCELLANY:	7	Has done New England College, Northeastern, NESN, and pro hoops. Walking encyclopedia of what to visit on the road.
TOTAL:	76	(74th place).

JAIME JARRIN

Desi Arnaz vowed to 'splain a thin' or two. Carmen Miranda's come-on was a befruited head. "The Cisco Kid" made English elementary. Pancho: "Oh, Cisco." Cisco: "Oh, Pancho." Broadcast Latinos were once prop, joke, or foil.

In baseball, Hispanics were rarer than teetotalers at 21. "Mostly we didn't exist," said Jaime Jarrin, joining the Dodgers in 1959, his voice still chilly, its edge unreceding. "Those who did were thought unAmerican. It's a time you don't forget."

Buck Canel was unforgettable. The bigs' first Spanish-speaking Voice began at the Staten Island *Advance* and French wire service Havas and News

Agency France-Press. Later: NBC Radio "Gillette Cavalcade of Sports," 1937–78 World Series throughout the Hemisphere, and 1942–78 Yanks home games to and for Latins in New York.

"Buck was our Cortez," said Jarrin. Rafael "Felo" Ramirez followed on Havana's Radio Salas, Puerto Rico, and Venezuela, and Caguas Natives, Santurce Crabs, San Juan Senators, and Magallanges Navigators. Gillette's co-host aired 31 Series, 43 All-Star Games, and 1993– N.L. expansion Florida. "Estaaaaaan ganado los Maaaaaarlins!" Felo roars. "The Marlins are winning!"

Rene Cardenas launched bigs (L.A. 1958–61 and 1982–98), Lone Star (Houston 1962–77), and A.L. (Texas 1981) Spanish coverage, reaching as many as 82 million people. Voices now list Julio Gonzalez, Hector Martinez, Gustavo Moreno, Eduardo Ortega, and Ulpiano Villa—not mainstream, but no longer another orb's. Said Jaime: "It took [post-seventies] immigration for baseball to wake up."

Almost every club struts a Spanish-speaking network. Hispanics forge the U.S.'s fastest-growing minority, swelling *beisbol*'s public between and beyond the lines. "Without a doubt," said ESPN's Peter Gammons, "tomorrow lies as much with Hispanics in the cities as with white suburbs of Ozzie and Harriet." In Los Angeles, that meant going back to a future, say, of 1725.

L.A. was an 18th-century Spanish colony. It again became one after Jaime, born in Cayambe, Ecuador, attended Central University of Quito, studied engineering, philosophy, letters, journalism, and broadcasting, and migrated in 1955. "Southern California was mostly white and middle-class," said Jarrin, becoming Pasadena Spanish KWKW sports and news director. The ex-Bums arrived three years later. "Scully did English. I got Spanish." Vin still introduces him on TV.

Scully made Cooperstown. At first, Jaime—to many, *"La Voz de Oro,"* the Golden Voice—couldn't make the booth. Wearing headphones, he translated in-studio. "I was in awe," Vin said. "He'd immediately interpret me." Arriving from Colombia, journalist Sandra Hernandez "listened to two things on the radio": Spanish soaps and Jaime. "He was our evangelist," ferrying the Dodgers—*"Esquivadores"*—to barrio, tract, and farm.

"I learned baseball slowly," he said, watching Cardenas in the Coliseum press box. "To be honest, at first I was a more of a newsman": John F. Kennedy's 1963 funeral, Winston Churchill's 1965 memorial service, and Pope John Paul II's 1979 U.S. visit. Once a gunman held a plane and

56 hostages on an airport tarmac until Jarrin arrived to negotiate his surrender.

In 1973, L.A.'s Spanish *Network* began. Leaving studio, Jarrin went *live*. "Better than four walls," he said of Dodger Stadium's five tiers, flowing lawn, and palm trees. "Finally! First class," moving uptown, if not upstairs.

"La pelota viene como una mariposa": The ball moved like a butterfly.

"Es el momento del matador, el momento de la verdad" preceded a 3–2 sacks-full pitch: to Jaime, the bullfighter's moment of birth, in a game of life or death.

Ultimately, Hispanics totaled 35 percent of team attendance. The demographic ground was shifting under baseball's feet, though the sport seemed oblivious at the time.

In 1981, rookie Fernando Valenzuela's debut blanked Houston. Soon the San Fernando Valley seemed to signify his name.

By May 20, No. 34 had four shutouts, 0.20 ERA, and .348 batting average. Hispanics jammed the Ravine. "The [legal and illegal] flood had begun. Our network was growing. The kicker was Fernandomania," said Jaime, doubling as translator.

On June 4, 1990, Ramon Martinez K'd 18 Braves to tie Sandy Koufax. Later, Dennis Martinez hurled Dodger Stadium's first rival perfect game. "On the field, you saw Hispanic names." When would you, above?

In 1997, Colombian Edgar Renteria's Game Seven hit won the Series. "An Hispanic hits it," said Jaime. "Another calls it. Our [Latina Broadasting Company] audience of 35 million heard it." Next year, 35 Hispanics did the majors: eight had, a decade earlier. Jarrin entered Cooperstown—"the third Hispanic [Canel '85 and Ramirez '01] and maybe the greatest in exposure to U.S. Latins," said then-official Bruce Markusen, himself Puerto Rican.

"Finally, I am getting the impact of what this means," Jaime said Induction Week. Son Jorge—"The Captain"—began covering traffic for English and Spanish radio.

A baseball in his office bore Dad's and Scully's name: L.A. "[becoming] the only team with two active Hall of Famers." Added ex-owner Peter O'Malley: "If Jaime'd wore a uniform, we'd retire the number."

The Cuban patriot Jose Marta said, "I am America's son. To her I belong." For decades Jaime belonged to baseball. Finally it belongs to him. The Spanish *"Mi casa es su casa"* means "My house is your house." No longer must Hispanics enter through the bigs' back door.

JAIME JARRIN

LONGEVITY:	10	46 years.
CONTINUITY:	10	Los Angeles N.L. 1959– .
NETWORK:	10	16-time Fall Classic on CBS Radio, Latina Broadcasting Company, Cadena Latina, and Cadena Caracol.
KUDOS:	10	Cooperstown 1998. Southern California Radio and Television News Association Golden Mike 1970–71. *Hispanic Business Magazine*'s Top 100 American Hispanics. Ecuador's highest non-military prize: *La Gran Cruz al Merito en El Grado de Comendado*. Star, Hollywood Walk of Fame 1998. California Broadcasters Association Hall of Fame 2002. Hispanic Heritage Baseball Museum 2003. Southern California Sports Broadcasters Hall of Fame and Foreign Language Sports Broadcaster Award 2004.
LANGUAGE:	7	Theatral.
POPULARITY:	10	"Ambassador might be a fitting title," a writer said.
PERSONA:	10	To Scully: "Numero Uno." Led Hispanic radio/TV rise.
VOICE:	9	Less Ricky Martin than Ricardo Montalban.
KNOWLEDGE:	8	Included more than 30 boxing title bouts.
MISCELLANY:	3	Directed 1984 Summer Olympics radio coverage.
TOTAL:	87	(28th place).

8

Billy Gomez, who played bass with pianist Billy Evans, termed the jazzman's aim "to make music that balanced passion and intellect." Dizzy Dean's sired idiom. Joe Buck's reflects a hipper, rougher time. Vin Scully's changes tunes within a batter. One pitch recalls a Dodgers stopper: the next, hit to shortstop, the Ancient Mariner— he stoppeth one in three.

Voices can be beach bud, mountain messenger, summer music, nighttime light, and pillow pal. "They don't just broadcast baseball. They are baseball," wrote Jayson Stark. When Ernie Harwell did football, neighbors asked what he did each winter. "They didn't know. In baseball, you're on so much, people appreciate you more."

Byrum Saam painted like a minimalist. Ned Martin fused irony and melody. Whatever the play or game, Ernie Johnson plucked a story from the shelf.

"Two little ladies entered the park about the fifth inning and sat down behind a priest," he said. "'What's the score, Father?' they said.

"The priest said, 'Nothing-nothing.'

"One lady told the other, 'Oh, good, we haven't missed anything.'

"In the eighth inning a pinch-hitter batted for the local team. He makes the sign of the cross before stepping into the box. The little old lady leaned over and said, 'Father, Father, will that help?' The priest turned around and said, 'Not if he can't hit.'"

Voices of Summer ranks baseball's all-time greatest 101 announcers by criteria detailed in Chapter One: longevity, continuity, network coverage, kudos, language, popularity, persona, voice, knowledge, and miscellany. Each criterion is rated from 1 (try another job) to 10 points (*creme d' la creme*). A perfect score is 100. As the reader has seen, some Voices have the same point total. "Prologue" describes how longevity, continuity, network, and kudos break the tie. If still deadlocked, the tie-breaker is the average fan's view as perceived by the author. The scorecard:

1. Vin Scully (100 points). **2.** Mel Allen (99). **3.** Ernie Harwell (97). **4.** Jack Buck (96) **5.** Red Barber (95). **6.** Harry Caray (94). **7.** Bob Prince (94). **8.** Jack Brickhouse (93). **9.** Dizzy Dean (92). **10.** Lindsey Nelson (92). **11.** Curt Gowdy (91). **12.** Bob Uecker (91). **13.** Chuck Thompson (91). **14.** Jon Miller (91). **15.** Joe Garagiola (90). **16.** Bob Elson (90). **17.** Tim McCarver (90). **18.** Bob Costas (90). **19.** Jerry Coleman (89). **20.** Bob Murphy (89). **21.** Ned Martin (89). **22.** Al Michaels (89). **23.** Bob Wolff (89). **24.** Milo Hamilton (87). **25.** Harry Kalas (87). **26.** Dave Niehaus (87). **27.** Phil Rizzuto (87). **28.** Jaime Jarrin (87). **29.** Lon Simmons (86). **30.** Byrum Saam (86). **31.** Marty Brennaman (86). **32.** Merle Harmon (85). **33.** Graham McNamee (85). **34.** Herb Carneal (84). **35.** Ken Coleman (84). **36.** Tony Kubek (84). **37.** Gene Elston (84). **38.** Dick Enberg (84). **39.** Joe Buck (84). **40.** Jim Woods (83). **41.** Jimmy Dudley (83). **42.** Ralph Kiner (83). **43.** Ernie Johnson (83). **44.** Dave Van Horne (82). **45.** Skip Caray (82). **46.** Tom Cheek (82). **47.** Denny Matthews (81). **48.** Bud Blattner (81). **49.** Vince Lloyd (81). **50.** Ken Harrelson (81). **51.** Russ Hodges (81). **52.** Sean McDonough (81). **53.** Richie Ashburn (80). **54.** Monte Moore (80). **55.** George Kell (80). **56.** Bill O'Donnell (80). **57.** Gary Cohen (79). **58.** John Sterling (79). **59.** Pete Van Wieren (79). **60.** Joe Morgan (79). **61.** Ross Porter (79). **62.** Waite Hoyt (78). **63.** Don Drysdale (78). **64.** Dave Campbell (78). **65.** Jim Kaat (78). **66.** John Rooney (78). **67.** DeWayne Staats (77). **68.** Hal Totten (77). **69.** Al Helfer (77). **70.** Gary Thorne (77). **71.** Lanny Frattare (76). **72.** Bill King (76). **73.** Hank Greenwald (76). **74.** Joe Castiglione (76). **75.** Pat Hughes (76). **76.** Ray Scott (75). **77.** Bob Starr (75). **78.** Jim Britt (75). **79.** Joe Angel (75). **80.** Bill White (74). **81.** Earl Gillespie (74). **82.** Mark Holtz (74). **83.** Gordon McLendon (74). **84.** Tom Manning (73). **85.** Arch McDonald (73). **86.** Pee Wee Reese (73). **87.** Jack Graney (72). **88.** Jerry Doggett (71). **89.** Gene Kelly (71). **90.** Connie Desmond (70). **91.** Rosey Rowswell (70). **92.** Van Patrick (69). **93.** Bert Wilson (69). **94.** France Laux (68). **95.** Joe Nuxhall (67). **96.** Mel Proctor (67). **97.** Ty Tyson (65). **98.** Pat Flanagan (65). **99.** Fred Hoey (62). **100.** Johnny O'Hara (61). **101.** Harold Arlin (60).

In *September Song,* "the days dwindle down to a precious few." Some feel that baseball's radio/TV artisans dwindle down each year.

"When I started, we didn't have models," said Harwell. "Now guys are trained at radio school and college," sounding dull, programmed, and alike. "Bad game, you need to *leave* the game," boomed Jim Woods. Alas, as Red Barber said, "Radio and television have forgotten about the most beautiful thing I know next to human love, and that's the English language."

Except for Lindsey Nelson, the top 16 *Voices of Summer* began on radio. On TV, they merely eased the tempo: 78 turned 45 RPM. Many now start on video, deem radio shabby-genteel, and use "TV's sparse approach on radio, which doesn't work," Bob Wolff observed. Worse, some prefer other sports, thinking baseball nothing special.

You don't awake at age 35 and suddenly become, say, a Pirates fan. Said Jon Miller: "You have to follow it from childhood"—a small boy's link to the outside. Baseball's rhythm exposes a Voice's ignorance: a fraud, a *poseur*! A lifetime of study lets you chat around a fire. A listener can tell.

"It's conversation. It's quirky. Tell us what you did today," said Bob Costas. "Tell me about the guy sitting down at the end of the dugout. Is he a character? Does he come from some tiny little town in Arkansas somewhere? Did he always dream of being a big-leaguer? How did he get here? It's a story-teller's game."

Quoting Eugene O'Neill, Scully often says of a weak infield hit, "A humble thing, but thine own." On May 3, 1959, he spun poetry alien to another sport. Roy Campanella, crippled a year earlier, was wheeled near the pitcher's mound. Lights dimmed, like the catcher's broken body. Each guest lit a match, like Campy's vaulting heart.

"The lights are now starting to come out, like thousands and thousands of fireflies, starting deep in center field, glittering around to left, and slowly the entire ballpark . . . a sea of lights at the Coliseum. Let there be a prayer for every light," said Vin, speaking beautifully, magically. At such a time, the announcer seems connecting tissue between the public and the game.

SOURCES

Brief portions of this book have appeared in slightly different form in *Voices of The Game* and *Storied Stadiums*.

Grateful acknowledgment is made for permission to reprint excerpts from the following.

FDR: A Centenary Remembrance, by Joseph Alsop, copyright the Viking Press, 1982. Reprinted by permission of Thames and Hudson Limited.

North Toward Home, by Willie Morris, reprinted by permission of Houghton Mifflin, 1967.

Rhubarb in the Catbird Seat, by Red Barber with Robert Creamer, reprinted by permission of Doubleday and Company, 1968.

Sports Illustrated, reprinted by permission the issues of April 15, 1957; April 13, 1959; April 11, 1960; and April 10, 1961.

The Gas House Gang, by J. Roy Stockton, reprinted by permission of A.S. Barnes and Company, 1945.

When It Was a Game, reprinted by permission of Home Box Office, 1991.

Grateful acknowledgment is also made to: ABC Television, CBS Radio, Fleetwood Recording Co., Major League Baseball and its thirty teams, Mutual Radio, National Baseball Hall of Fame and Museum, and NBC Radio and Television.

BIBLIOGRAPHY

Allen, Mel, *It Takes Heart,* with Frank Graham, Jr. New York: Harper and Brothers, 1959.

————, *You Can't Beat the Hours,* with Ed Fitzgerald. New York: Harper and Row, 1965.

Alsop, Joseph, *FDR: A Centenary Remembrance.* New York: The Viking Press, 1982.

Barber, Walter (Red), *The Broadcasters.* New York: Dial Press, 1970.

————, *Rhubarb In the Catbird Seat,* with Robert Creamer. Garden City, New York: Doubleday, 1968.

Buck, Jack, *That's a Winner!,* with Bob Rains and Bob Broeg. Champaign, Illinois: Sagamore Publishing, 1997.

Castiglione, Joe, *Broadcast Rites and Sites,* with Douglas B. Lyons. Lanham, Maryland: Taylor Trade Publishing, 2004.

Costas, Bob, *Fair Ball: A Fan's Case for Baseball.* New York: Random House, 2000.

Gowdy, Curt, *Cowboy at the Mike,* with Al Hirshberg. Garden City, New York: Doubleday, 1966.

Greenwald, Hank, *This Copyrighted Broadcast.* San Francisco: Woodford Press, 1997.

Halberstam, David, *Summer of '49.* New York: William Morrow, 1989.

Harmon, Merle, *Merle Harmon Stories,* with Sam Blair. Arlington, Texas: Reid Publishing, 1998.

Harris, Jay S., *TV Guide: The First 25 Years.* New York: Simon and Schuster, 1978.

Hodges, Russ, *Baseball Complete.* New York: Grosset and Dunlop, 1952.

————, *My Giants.* Garden City, New York: Doubleday, 1963.

Kahn, Roger, *The Boys of Summer.* New York: Harper and Row, 1971.

Keegan, Tom, *Ernie Harwell.* Chicago: Triumph Books, 2002.

Lewine, Harris, and Okrent, Daniel, *The Ultimate Baseball Book.* Boston: Houghton Mifflin, 1979.

McNeil, Alex, *Total Television.* New York: Penguin Books, 1980.

Manchester, William, *One Brief Shining Moment.* Boston: Little, Brown and Company, 1983.

Miller, Jon, *Confessions of a Baseball Purist,* with Mark Hyman. Simon and Schuster: New York, 1998.

Morris, Willie, *North Toward Home.* Boston: Houghton Mifflin, 1967.

Powers, Ron, *SuperTube.* New York: Coward-McCann, 1980.

Stockton, J. Roy, *The Gas House Gang.* New York: A.S. Barnes and Company, 1945.

Thompson, Chuck, *Ain't the Beer Cold!* with Gordon Beard. South Bend, Indiana: Diamond Communications, 1996.

Vecsey, George (edited by), *The Way It Was.* Mobil Oil and McGraw-Hill Book Company, 1974.

Vincent, Fay, *The Last Commissioner.* Simon and Schuster: New York, 2002.

White, Theodore H., *The Making of the President 1960.* New York: Atheneum, 1961.

————, *The Making of the President 1964.* New York: Atheneum, 1965.

Wolff, Bob, *It's Not Who Won or Lost the Game.* South Bend, Indiana: Diamond Communications, 1996.

PHOTOGRAPHIC CREDITS

Photography courtesy of:

Page 5:   Harold Arlin, Bob Elson, Arch McDonald, and Graham McNamee, *National Baseball Hall of Fame and Museum Library;* Tom Manning, *The Sporting News.*

Page 37:   Red Barber, *Rochester Democrat & Chronicle;* Jack Brickhouse, *WGN Television;* Ernie Harwell; Byrum Saam, *National Baseball Hall of Fame and Museum Library;* Bob Wolff.

Page 95:   Mel Allen, Jack Buck, and Vin Scully, *National Baseball Hall of Fame and Museum Library;* Harry Caray, *Smithsonian Institution;* Dizzy Dean, *CBS Television.*

Page 183:   Joe Garagiola, Curt Gowdy, and Ned Martin, *The Sporting News;* Harry Kalas, *Philadelphia Phillies;* Chuck Thompson, *National Baseball Hall of Fame and Museum Library.*

Page 261:   Jerry Coleman, Al Michaels, Bob Murphy, Phil Rizzuto, and Bob Uecker, *National Baseball Hall of Fame and Museum Library.*

Page 329:   Bob Costas, *NBC Television;* Jaime Jarrin, *National Baseball Hall of Fame and Museum Library;* Tim McCarver, *The Sporting News;* Jon Miller and Joe Morgan, *ESPN Television.*

ABOUT THE AUTHOR

Curt Smith is an author, award-winning radio/television commentator, and former presidential speechwriter. He is generally considered America's leading baseball radio/television historian.

Smith's ten books are *What Baseball Means To Me, Storied Stadiums, Our House, Windows on the White House, Of Mikes and Men, The Storytellers, A Fine Sense of the Ridiculous, Voices of The Game, Long Time Gone,* and *America's Dizzy Dean.* Says Bob Costas: "Curt Smith stands up for the beauty of words."

Smith hosts the syndicated series "Perspectives" on Rochester, New York's National Public Radio outlet WXXI. He is Senior Lecturer in English at the University of Rochester, an Upstate New York Messenger Post Newspapers columnist, and regular contributor to Rochester's CBS TV affiliate WROC.

Raised in Caledonia, New York, Smith was a Gannett Company reporter, *The Saturday Evening Post* senior editor, and speechwriter to George H. W. Bush. He wrote more speeches than anyone else for the 41st president, including the State of the Union, "Just War" Persian Gulf address, speech on the 50th anniversary of Pearl Harbor, and Bush's emotional 2004 eulogy to Ronald Reagan at Washington's National Cathedral.

Leaving the White House in 1993, Smith hosted Smithsonian Institution series before turning to radio/TV. His radio commentary has been voted "Best in New York State" by Associated Press. He hosted the Fox Empire Sports Network "Fan TV" series, wrote ESPN TV documentaries based on his *Voices of The Game,* and helped write ESPN's *SportsCentury* series.

Smith has written for, among others, *Newsweek, The New York Times, Reader's Digest,* and *Sports Illustrated.* He has appeared on numerous network programs, including ABC's "Nightline," Armed Forces Radio, BBC, "CBS This Morning," CNN, CNBC, ESPN, Fox News Channel, MSNBC, Mutual Radio, Radio America, and The History Channel.

The 1973 SUNY at Geneseo graduate has been named among the "100 Outstanding Alumni" of New York's State University System, is a member of the Judson Welliver Society of former presidential speechwriters, and lives with wife Sarah and children Olivia, 5, and Travis, 4, in Rochester.

Acknowledgments

In 1961, Theodore H. White received a Pulitzer Prize for his book *The Making of the President 1960*. John F. Kennedy sent a note: "It pleases me that I could provide some of the plot."

This book's plot is peculiar to baseball's *Voices of Summer*. I wish to thank the many broadcasters who provided fact and recollection. Numerous writers were also helpful: Bob Broeg, Jack Craig, Joseph Durso, Joe Falls, Peter Gammons, Leonard Koppett, Phil Mushnick, Marty Nolan, Rob Rains, Bob Raissman, Harold Rosenthal, Richard Sandomir, Russell Schneider, Bill Schulz, Morris Siegel, Jayson Stark, John Steadman, Larry Stewart, George Vescey, Paul White, and George Will.

Broadcast officials, some now deceased, were generous as well: Geoff Belinfante, Dan Bell, Bryan Burns, Scotty Connal, Harry Coyle, John Lazarus, Carl Lindemann, Bill MacPhail, Dan Quinn, Joe Reichler, Jack Rosenberg, Larry Shenk, and Tom Villante.

I am grateful to major- and minor-league officials: Mary Appel, Joe L. Brown, Chris Eno, Glenn Geffner, Jim Healy, Larry Lucchino, Laurel Prieb, Brent Shyer, Stu Smith, and Bill Veeck. Veeck entered Cooperstown in 1991. Its great Hall of Fame staff is still there: Jeff Idelson, Vice-President, Communications; Bill Francis, Senior Researcher; and Jeremy Jones, Manager of Recorded Media.

Bobbe Siegel helped me create this book. My wife, Sarah, nursed it to completion. Our children, Olivia and Travis, supplied love and support. Philip Turner and Ken Samelson edited the manuscript with care and insight. I also wish to thank audio/video archivist John Miley and attorney Phil Hochberg. The facts and opinions herein, of course, are mine.

Finally, let me acknowledge the reader. The poetess Marianne Moore observed, "Baseball is like writing. You can never tell with either how it will go or what you will do." Thank you for caring about each.

—Curt Smith, Rochester, New York
February 4, 2005

INDEX